PUBLIC FORGIVENESS IN POST-CONFLICT CONTEXTS

SERIES ON TRANSITIONAL JUSTICE

The Series on *Transitional Justice* offers a platform for high-quality research within the rapidly growing field of transitional justice. The research is, of necessity inter-disciplinary in nature, drawing from disciplines such as law, political science, history, sociology, criminology, anthropology and psychology, as well as from various specialised fields of study such as human rights, victimology and peace studies. Furthermore, the research is international in outlook, drawing on the knowledge and experience of academics and other specialists in many different regions of the world.

The series is aimed at a variety of audiences who are either working or interested in fields such as crime and justice; human rights; humanitarian law and human security; conflict resolution and peace building. These audiences include academics, researchers, students, policy makers, practitioners, non-governmental organisations and the media.

All books published within the series are subject to a double-blind peer review by recognised authorities in the field.

Published titles within the series:

1. Stephen Peté & Max Du Plessis, *Repairing the Past? International Perspectives on Reparations for Gross Human Rights Abuses* (2007), 978-90-5095-492-1
2. Laura Stovel, *Long Road Home, Building Reconciliation and Trust in Post-War Sierra Leone* (2010), 978-94-000-0028-5
3. Andy Aitchison, *Making the Transition. International Intervention, State-Building and Criminal Justice Reform in Bosnia and Herzegovina* (2011), 978-94-000-0140-4
4. Stef Vandeginste, *Stones left unturned. Law and Transitional Justice in Burundi* (2010), 978-94-000-0115-2
5. Antoine Buyse (ed.), *Margins of Conflict. The ECHR and Transitions to and from Armed Conflict* (2011), 978-94-000-0157-2
6. Gaby Oré Aguilar and Felipe Gómez Isa (eds.), *Rethinking Transitions. Equality and Social Justice in Societies Emerging from Conflict* (2011), 978-1-78068-003-3
7. Richard Zajac Sannerholm, *Rule of Law after War. Ideologies, Norms and Methods* (2012), 978-1-78068-008-8
8. Nicola Palmer, Phil Clark and Danielle Granville (chief editors), *Critical Perspectives in Transitional Justice* (2011), 978-1-78068-035-4
9. Edda Kristjánsdóttir, André Nollkaemper and Cedric Ryngaert (eds.), *International Law in Domestic Courts: Rule of Law Reform in Post-conflict States* (2012), 978-1-78068-041-5

SERIES ON TRANSITIONAL JUSTICE, Volume 10

PUBLIC FORGIVENESS IN POST-CONFLICT CONTEXTS

Edited by

Bas van Stokkom
Neelke Doorn
Paul van Tongeren

intersentia
Cambridge – Antwerp – Portland

Intersentia Publishing Ltd.
Trinity House | Cambridge Business Park | Cowley Road
Cambridge | CB4 0WZ | United Kingdom
Tel.: +44 1223 393 753 | Email: mail@intersentia.co.uk

Distribution for the UK:
Hart Publishing Ltd.
16C Worcester Place
Oxford OX1 2JW
UK
Tel.: +44 1865 517 530
Email: mail@hartpub.co.uk

Distribution for the USA and Canada:
International Specialized Book Services
920 NE 58th Ave. Suite 300
Portland, OR 97213
USA
Tel.: +1 800 944 6190 (toll free)
Email: info@isbs.com

Distribution for Austria:
Neuer Wissenschaftlicher Verlag
Argentinierstraße 42/6
1040 Wien
Austria
Tel.: +43 1 535 61 03 24
Email: office@nwv.at

Distribution for other countries:
Intersentia Publishing nv
Groenstraat 31
2640 Mortsel
Belgium
Tel.: +32 3 680 15 50
Email: mail@intersentia.be

Public Forgiveness in Post-Conflict Contexts
Edited by Bas van Stokkom, Neelke Doorn and Paul van Tongeren

Intersentia
Cambridge – Antwerp – Portland
www.intersentia.com | www.intersentia.co.uk

Artwork on cover: Author Jan Jordaan, title 'Hurt', medium Linocut, 1999. From the *Universal Declaration of Human Rights – International Print Portfolio, Article 5*, published by Art for Humanity, South Africa, 1999

ISBN 978-1-78068-044-6
NUR 828

GPRC
Guaranteed
Peer Reviewed
Content

British Library Cataloguing in Publication Data. A catalogue record for this book is available from the British Library.

ACKNOWLEDGEMENTS

The papers presented in this volume were first published in a conference at the Radboud University in Nijmegen, the Netherlands (March 2010). The conference was organised by the Centre for Ethics, Radboud University and Cordaid, an international development organisation. The conference was supported by ICCO, interchurch organisation for development cooperation, Sormani Fonds, and Radboud University Nijmegen.

The editors wish to express their gratitude to these institutions for their generous support. Thanks is also due to Professor Stephan Parmentier, who kindly chaired the afternoon session in Nijmegen, and pointed our attention to the Transitional Justice Series of Intersentia Publishers. Thanks also to the other editors of the Series and two anonymous reviewers for their fruitful comments on earlier versions of the chapters.

Those who wish to watch and listen to some conference presentations, please see the website www.publicforgiveness.com. This site includes presenters whose speeches are not incorporated in this book (Johan Du Toit, Alistair Little, Stephan Parmentier, Daniel Philpott, Marlies Stappers, Wilhelm Verwoerd and George Wachira). Thanks to all contributors for their hard work and cooperation, and especially their sound grasp of many particular aspects of transitional justice processes.

CONTENTS

PART 2
PUBLIC FORGIVENESS IN POLITICAL AND RELIGIOUS CONTEXTS

LIST OF CONTRIBUTORS

Sanderijn Cels is currently senior fellow at the Consensus Building Institute and research associate at the MIT-Harvard Public Disputes Program (both located in Cambridge, US). She is a scholar and writer in the field of political communication and public sector innovation, and she is specialized in case teaching and writing. She has (co) authored six books, including *Becoming an Agent of Change: Strategy and Tactics of Social Innovation* (Brookings Institution, 2012). Cels is also a PhD candidate at Loughborough University (UK). Her thesis focuses on political apologies and aims to conceptualize those as public performances in multi-actor environments.

Neelke Doorn is assistant professor of Ethics of Water Governance at the Department of Philosophy of Delft University of Technology. She recently finished her work on the project Moral Responsibility in R&D networks (PhD thesis). Neelke has a master degree in Civil Engineering (Delft 1997, MSc) and Philosophy (Leiden 2005, MA). Between 2006 and 2010, she was affiliated to the Radboud University in Nijmegen, where she held a part-time research position at the Centre of Ethics focusing on justice issues in post-conflict situations.

Nir Eisikovits is Assistant Professor of Philosophy, Department of Philosophy, Suffolk University Boston (USA). He teaches legal and political philosophy and directs the Graduate Program in Ethics and Public Policy. His publications focus on how countries emerge from war and how they come to terms with their past. His book *Sympathizing with the Enemy: Reconciliation, Negotiation and Transitional Justice* (2010) was published by Brill and Republic of Letters.

Erik Doxtader is a Professor of Rhetoric at the University of South Carolina and a Senior Research Fellow at the Institute for Justice and Reconciliation in Cape Town. A past recipient of a MacArthur Foundation-Social Science Research Council Fellowship, he has authored, edited, and co-edited a number of books and essays on transitional justice and the dynamics of reconciliation in South Africa, including *Truth and Reconciliation in South Africa – The Fundamental Documents* (2008), *With Faith in the Works of Words: The Beginnings of Reconciliation in South Africa, 1985–1995* (2009) and *In the Balance: South Africans Debate Reconciliation* (2010).

Trudy Govier is a philosopher and the author of many articles and books, including *Forgiveness and Revenge* (Routledge 2002), *Taking Wrongs Seriously* (Humanity Books, Prometheus 2006), and *A Practical Study of Argument* (Wadsworth/Cengage, Seventh Edition 2010). In addition to academic work, she has been a key participant in peace education and advocacy groups. Trudy Govier is presently Professor of Philosophy at the University of Lethbridge in Alberta, Canada.

Catherine Guisan is Visiting Assistant Professor in the Department of Political Science, University of Minnesota, Twin Cities, and teaches in European universities also. She is the author of *Un sens à l'Europe: Gagner la paix 1950–2003* (Paris: Odile Jacob, 2003) and *A Political Theory of Identity in European Integration: Memory and Policies* (Oxford and New York: Routledge, 2011).

Alice MacLachlan is an Assistant Professor of Philosophy at York University (Toronto, Canada). She has written articles and book chapters on forgiveness, reconciliation, and apology in personal and political contexts; her recent publications include "The State of Sorry: Official Apologies and their Absence" in the *Journal of Human Rights* (2010), "Unreasonable Resentments" in the *Journal of Social Philosophy* (2009), and "Practicing Imperfect Forgiveness" in *Feminist Ethics and Social Philosophy: Theorizing the Non-Ideal* (ed. Lisa Tessman, Springer 2009). She is currently completing a manuscript on forgiveness and co-editing a volume of essays on moral issues in the wake of violent conflict.

Stephen J. Pope is Professor of Theological Ethics in the Theology Department at Boston College in Chestnut Hill, Massachusetts. He is the author of *Human Evolution and Christian Ethics* (Cambridge, 2007) and "Restorative Justice as a Prophetic Path to Peace", *Catholic Theological Society of America Proceedings* 65 (2010): 19–34. He is the editor of *The Ethics of Aquinas* (Georgetown, 2002).

Robert Schreiter is professor of theology at the Catholic Theological Union in Chicago. He has been involved with peace/building on all six continents, especially around the healing of societies in post-conflict reconstruction, and the building of resilience for local peace-builders. For twelve years he was the theological consultant to *Caritas Internationalis*, the umbrella organization for 165 relief and development agencies in the Roman Catholic Church, for its programs in peace-building. Among his works are: *Reconciliation: Mission and Ministry in a Changing Social Order* and *Reconciliation: Spirituality and Strategies.* With Scott Appleby and Gerard Powers he edited *Peacebuilding: Catholic Theology, Ethics, and Praxis.*

Margaret E. Smith is a Scholar in Residence in the Division of International Peace and Conflict Resolution at the School of International Service, American University. Her areas of specialization include nationalist and ethnic conflict, uses of memory in politics, and post conflict reconstruction in deeply divided societies. She has studied the revision of the teaching of history as a tool of post-conflict reconstruction, and is the author of *Reckoning with the Past: Teaching History in Northern Ireland* (Lexington Books, 2005).

Bert van Roermund is Professor of Philosophy, Tilburg University in The Netherlands. He has published extensively on various fundamental legal concepts and contemporary legal problems (constitutional review, democracy, punishment, contract law). His monograph *Law, Narrative and Reality* (1997; also in Spanish) concluded a period of research on law and language. Since 1997, he has focused on problems of authority and representation (sovereignty, identity, normativity) in supra-national contexts (in particular the EU), as well as transitional justice and reconciliation. Currently, his main topic is the first-person perspective in law, with special emphasis on human rights and democratic law making.

Bas van Stokkom is lecturer and research fellow at the Criminological Institute, Radboud University Nijmegen, The Netherlands. His research concentrates on the fields of citizenship, deliberative democracy, restorative justice, and legal / punishment ethics. He is secretary of the Dutch-Flemish journal *Tijdschrift voor Herstelrecht* (Journal of Restorative Justice) and co-editor of the studies *Images of Restorative Justice Theory* (2008) and *Reflections on Reassurance Policing in the Low Countries* (2008).

Paul J.M. van Tongeren studied theology in Utrecht (The Netherlands) and philosophy in Louvain (Belgium). He is professor for moral philosophy at Radboud University Nijmegen and special professor for ethics at the Catholic University of Leuven. He published widely on Nietzsche as well as on moral philosophy. Further info and list of publications can be found at: www.paulvantongeren.nl

Wouter Veraart is professor of legal philosophy at the Department Legal Theory and Legal History of the Faculty of Law, VU University Amsterdam. His research is focussed on redress and restitution after periods of injustice, and the tension between remembering and forgetting (which was also the main subject of his inaugural lecture in 2009). In 2011 he published together with Laurens Winkel, *The Post-War Restitution of Property Rights in Europe, Comparative Perspectives*, Scientia Verlag, Amsterdam & Aalen.

Annelies Verdoolaege obtained Ma degrees in Germanic Languages and in African Languages and Cultures from Ghent University and an Ma degree in Africana Studies from the State University of New York at Albany. Her PhD dissertation (June 2005) involved a discursive analysis of the victim hearings of the South African Truth and Reconciliation Commission (TRC). From May 2006 onwards she works as a postdoctoral researcher at the department of African Languages and Cultures at Ghent University. She has published in the fields of discourse analysis, political sciences and cultural studies, and on various aspects of the TRC (see http://cas1.elis.rug.ac.be/avrug/trc/cv.htm).

PUBLIC FORGIVENESS: THEORETICAL AND PRACTICAL PERSPECTIVES

Bas VAN STOKKOM
Neelke DOORN
Paul VAN TONGEREN

1. INTRODUCTION

Over the last decades the notions of forgiveness and reconciliation have increasingly been expressed in the public sphere in many countries. There is a pervasive trend towards public apologies, forms of national introspection and public appeals to grant forgiveness.

Archbishop Tutu's motto that "there is no future without forgiveness" is well known. He has argued that forgiveness is the only way to liberate oneself from the prison of past animosity and rancour.[1] Partly due to Tutu's efforts, the South African Truth and Reconciliation Commission (TRC) has become an important model and source of inspiration for many other countries that want to deal with their past grievances and internal conflicts. For others, however, to speak of forgiveness in politics is inappropriate and risky. What is more unforgivable than the atrocities of the powerful? Forgiveness is seldom a servant of justice, some claim.[2]

The opposition between proponents and opponents of public forgiveness raises conceptual, philosophical, empirical and practical questions: What does 'forgiveness' mean, how does speaking in terms of 'forgiveness' function, and under what conditions can it foster transitional justice processes?

Section 2 will start with some philosophical questions regarding the meaning of 'public forgiveness' and we will relate these to questions about the conditions under which the oratory of public forgiveness does occur. We will elaborate two positions, one labelled 'minimalist', in section 3, and the other 'maximalist', in section 4. In section 5 we will discuss the notion of 'invitational forgiveness' and the question whether a forgiving attitude is a necessary aspect of mitigating a confrontational social climate. In section 6 we will pay attention to some cultural

---

1 Tutu 1999.
2 Shriver 1995.

and religious contexts in which public forgiveness may occur. Which conditions do promote or impede that process?

2. WHAT IS PUBLIC FORGIVENESS?

Philosopher Trudy Govier stated: "Some find the notion of forgiveness in politics naïve to the point of absurdity."[3] An extension of the use of forgiveness to the public realm does indeed evoke many questions. What exactly is "forgiveness"? Do we have to distinguish between different kinds of forgiveness? To what extent is it bound to "face-to-face" relationship between individuals? Under what conditions can people grant forgiveness or ask for it? Is vicarious or representative forgiveness possible? Can collectives ever be entitled to grant forgiveness (or even act morally at all)? What are the conceptual implications and what are the empirical consequences of extending the use of forgiveness to the public realm?

Certainly, forgiveness is a daunting notion for a post-conflict society. Many deem public calls to forgive to be offensive, in the sense that the personal nature of the act of forgiveness should remain private and separate from the collective reconciliation process. Philosophers have often stressed how extremely difficult forgiveness is and suggested that public forgiveness is even completely "impossible."[4]

However, even within Christian circles, the view that forgiveness is a private virtue is often challenged. For instance, Pope John Paul II repeatedly stressed that forgiveness is not inimical to justice but rather an essential component of stable, peaceful and just societies.[5]

According to Amstutz, legal and political philosophers have ignored the political dimensions of forgiveness. They have done so in the belief that the major moral purpose of the state is to enact justice, conceived in terms of the protection of individual rights. They tend to view forgiveness as a private, spiritual ethic. Forgiveness is assumed to be an aspect of personal morality that is to be applied among individuals in their private relationships, and thus not part of political morality. Accordingly, although individual victims can forgive, institutions cannot. Instead, their chief task would be the pursuit of justice.

One of the first philosophers to explore the political aspects of forgiveness was Hannah Arendt. She identified forgiveness as one of the two human capacities that allow for genuine political action (the other being our capacity to make promises or covenants). Forgiveness has the power to "undo the deeds of the past", that is, "the possible redemption from the predicament of

3 Govier 2002: 78.
4 See, for example, Derrida 2000; 2001; Van Tongeren 2008.
5 Amstutz 2005.

irreversibility".[6] It enables human beings to liberate themselves from the prison of the past, to be born anew in politics. For Arendt, forgiveness is not moral sentiment, but part of politics, in which love and authentic, personal feelings should not play a role.[7]

Ever since Arendt's claims, public forgiveness has evoked lively philosophical discussions. Many authors object to Arendt's argument and stress that forgiveness is an individual act directed toward a perpetrator, meaning that groups or states cannot forgive. However, as Govier argues, groups can be regarded as moral agents and seem to display attitudes and feelings (for example, they may feel harm, respond with hatred, or show solidarity). At the very least, collectives behave *as if* they have feelings and it is possible to attribute feelings to them. If we can grant them actual feelings, then we should also grant them the ability to forgive.[8]

Daku argues that although the state cannot bestow personal forgiveness or offer forgiveness on behalf of persons, it can offer forgiveness to citizens' groups as a political unit.[9] Thus a perpetrator may be granted forgiveness as a citizen of the state. This would imply that one can be forgiven politically while not being forgiven personally, and vice versa. Perhaps it is in this way that churches and religious organizations are able to grant perpetrators forgiveness, not on behalf of victims, but as citizens of God's kingdom.

These perspectives do not imply that perpetrators might escape punishment, nor does it mean that forgiveness would not demand remorse, repentance and reparation.[10] Some authors define political forgiveness as the relinquishment of a right to retributive justice.[11] However, this view does not seem convincing because it obscures the differences between pardon and forgiveness. When state officials express forgiveness in public, all they say is that the state will no longer resent the actions of those political actors to whom forgiveness is granted.[12]

Daku also argues that while the state cannot determine personal forgiveness, state actions can clearly contribute to its emergence. Political and religious leaders are 'forerunners' – they hope that their appeal to the people will bring about change and contribute to political order and stability. Although political and religious calls to forgive may be premature, they may change attitudes and

6 Arendt 1958: 236.

7 In a similar vein Elshtain (2003) contends that we have to reverse the order of our thinking in order to understand political forgiveness: in some circumstances it may be that forgiveness makes politics itself possible. Wanting to forgive creates space for truth-telling and opens up the possibility of an interpretative struggle over the significance of past wrongs. In this view forgiveness is not so much oriented to restoring wrongdoers to a moral community, but to open the way to the realization of a world held in common (see also Van Roermund 2001; Schaap 2006).

8 Govier 2004.

9 Daku 2008.

10 See Soyinka 1999.

11 Diseger 2001.

12 Daku 2008.

bring about the trust that is needed for long-term reconciliation.[13] In particular, by implementing truth commissions the state is able to create 'truth-value' and foster the appropriate conditions for personal forgiveness to emerge. In Daku's view, the TRC did a good job because it made the complete disclosure of incriminating facts a prerequisite to amnesty: "In doing so they managed to construct a much denser account of the atrocities of Apartheid than would have been possible in a traditional trial. This creation of truth-value – of facts and accounts – can be a direct contribution to personal-forgiveness."[14] Since the accounts of events may disclose who is responsible, victims may change their understanding of the accused persons.[15]

Political and religious leaders may grant forgiveness in the name of peace and stability. They assume that the quest for an absolute 'human right' based on justice generally cannot be met.[16] In other words, 'civil peace' is deemed more important than the 'high' morality of retributive justice. Many church leaders support the case of unconditional forgiveness through religious language. Generally liberal authors have no a priori objection against church-leaders including forgiveness in their agenda. But in a liberal culture introducing religious notions into public life is a contested issue, all the more when religious oratory is used.

Religious leaders like archbishop Tutu challenged the dominant discourse of individual human rights and offered an altogether different set of concepts as a new basis for unity.[17] Religious metaphors and gestures may inspire innovative political practices. According to Hatch, religious language tends to express rhetorical coherence better than the secular, democratic politics of debate and dissent. It provides a horizon or prophetic vision of the ultimate good. Hatch states that: "The spirit of reconciliation displayed by leaders and citizens of faith can reanimate a disenchanted public with fresh visions of human potential for creating a common good."[18] Where social agents have lost faith in the workings

---

13 Govier 2004.

14 Daku 2008: 18.

15 Daye (2004) also argues that the greatest success of the TRC has been this truth-telling aspect, rather than its assumption of responsibility and the facilitation of healing. Surveys have shown that South Africans have internalized the details of Apartheid atrocities. Nonetheless, there is much disagreement concerning whether the TRC helped the process of forgiveness. According to Daye, on the level of public opinion, the answer appears to be yes. However, some reports in South Africa suggest there is a risk of retraumatization for victims giving testimony to the TRC (Chapman 2007). There are many reasons to distrust the saying that 'truth necessarily heals'. In Rwanda, female victims testifying in the *gacaca* courts (in which witnesses are surrounded by an audience consisting of former *génocidaires* or their families) were subjected to threats, harassment and violence (Brouneus 2007). For some groups of victims truth may be a release, but for others it is a source of new pain. Past sensibilities may be too strong, and for many victims self-respect is still lacking (see Doorn 2008).

16 Levy and Sznaider 2006.

17 Doxtader 2009.

18 Hatch 2006: 19. In the U.S.A, Hatch adds, the reconciling spirit of civil rights leaders (such as Martin Luther King) is still able to energize national initiatives to restore moral coherence to race relations.

of present power structures to bring about good, reconciliation as religious metaphor may frame political discourse about violence and its end in a way that restores "working faith in the works of words".[19]

But Hatch also argues that Tutu's rhetorical strength was at the same time a political weakness. "His reconciling ethos and faith were of a fundamentally Christian character; yet he called a nation of deep racial, cultural, economic, and religious disparities to enter into the thick of reconciliation so conceived, laden with the weight of divine grace, messianic promise, redemptive sacrifice, and unconditional forgiveness. It is one thing to call a church congregation, or even a village or clan with a shared religious tradition, to live into the drama of divine history and destiny. To expect the same of a pluralistic, secular state is another matter. To some extent Tutu's presence conflated the two: it appeared to go beyond *informing* transitional politics with a sacred understanding of reconciliation to *pressing* a model of confession, forgiveness, and transcendence on a watching nation."[20]

According to Brudholm, Tutu's "boosterism" of forgiveness seems on a par with irresponsible 'marketing'. The invocation of Jesus on the cross and the attitude of God to his creation may put improper pressure on the believer to comply. The glorification of forgiveness, often enacted with charisma, assumes and imposes a deep moral and religious consensus and silences or makes inappropriate the voicing of dissent and resistance.[21]

In summary, "public forgiveness" has generated many discussions and reactions, ranging from severe criticism to approval. Two fundamental perspectives can be distinguished. On the one hand, we find authors who assume that forgiveness in the public sphere is often difficult if not impossible to achieve, and that the search for justice will be obstructed when participants are encouraged or 'forced' to offer forgiveness. Such authors call for "reconciliation without forgiveness." On the other hand, authors claim that public calls for forgiveness may contribute to the peace process. Political statements in which the wrongdoer is granted forgiveness may relieve the burdens of the past, bring about hope, and stimulate cross-community contacts and the development of an out-group perspective. In these two divergent perspectives, the relationship between justice and forgiveness is reflected in fundamentally different ways. These two positions – which we have called minimalist and maximalist respectively – have to be related to empirical data and historical experiences. We will briefly elaborate each position below.

19 See Doxtader 2009.

20 Hatch 2006: 19.

21 See Brudholm 2009: 145. Moon (2004) argues that Christian narratives of forgiveness and reconciliation work to produce the effect of 'recovering' a 'lost harmony' between victim and perpetrator. Tutu's words call upon a prelapsarian human condition, a return to unity that preceded "The Fall" (also Moon 2008).

3. THE MINIMALIST ACCOUNT: 'RECONCILIATION WITHOUT FORGIVENESS'

Generally liberals are skeptical that healing and forgiveness belong in politics. Gutmann and Thompson criticize the overt religiosity with which reconciliation was represented in South Africa.[22] They see in Tutu's theological vision of reconciliation a danger of a "deeply illiberal idea", an idea that involves the expectation that all groups would "subscribe to a single comprehensive moral perspective. … The difficulty is that many victims do not share Tutu's Christian faith, and even those who do may hold a different view about the appropriateness of forgiveness in such situations." In the context of a truth commission – a public, state sponsored institution – the official invocation of forgiveness represents an unwelcome intrusion of religious discourse into the public, political sphere.[23]

Liberals argue that expressing forgiveness in the public domain is not a straightforward matter, and that we need a more pragmatic or "minimalist" approach to transitional justice processes. According to this view, forgiveness may be too high a demand for reconciliation and the processing and recognition of wrongdoing must occur before forgiveness can be considered.[24] In Northern Ireland, many deemed public forgiveness to be offensive, in the sense that the personal nature of the act of forgiveness should remain private and separate from the collective reconciliation process.[25]

Many authors assume that victims might feel the granting of forgiveness by the government as a lack of acknowledgment of their suffering. They indicate that justice must first be done through punishing the guilty, especially in more extreme cases of violence. Doing justice affirms the moral order, thereby increasing the feeling of security. It is considered that the failure to respond to injustice can actually harm victims once more, and that it supports impunity by offering to accept the past without requiring changes to the perpetrator's behaviour. If political leaders do not refer appropriately to brutalities and offences suffered by many citizens, they may further damage those concerned.[26] Some research findings on the TRC have shown that the emphasis on forgiveness sometimes hampers rather than promotes the rapprochement of formerly hostile groups. Many victims who testified felt forced into reconciliation and perhaps it is not always appropriate to seek forgiveness in the first instance but to aim

22 Gutmann and Thompson 2000.

23 Brudholm (2008; 2009) has criticized the Christian advocacy of forgiveness after mass atrocity for being hasty and uncritical. He calls into question the practice of forgiveness by leaders as Tutu who would often pressure victims to forgive, deny the positive value of anger and resentment, ignore the fact that victims might not share his Christian faith, and generally flout victims' autonomy.

24 Hamber 2007.

25 Collins 2008.

26 See Doorn 2008.

instead for an enlarged sense of human connectedness, responsibility and cooperation.[27] According to this view, the central notion is not forgiveness but the engagement required to restore trust.[28] In public contexts, a weak or limited form of reconciliation might therefore be more promising than the view according to which forgiveness is the *sine qua non* for reconciliation.[29]

An important question in this regard is whether citizens really feel free not to offer their forgiveness when it is promoted on a large scale. The experience in Rwanda is important in this respect as it was found that when asked to forgive, many people believed they were obliged to by religion, the authorities or cultural custom, and so seemed simply to obey these authorities.[30] Forgiveness might therefore be considered to imprison the past narrative within certain circumstances rather than setting it free. It is possible as a result that forgiveness-related programmes could be used by paramilitaries and state bodies to curtail the desire for an exploration of the truth and its maintenance in the public eye.

Smith adds that a weaker party may forgive a stronger party because the weaker party feels it has no alternative.[31] Collectives may place pressure upon minorities who have suffered harm to make a gesture of forgiveness in order to provide reassurance that the bonds of society are still intact. In such circumstances, showing too much forgiveness may be instrumental in a group's return to the abusive relationship that existed previously. Thus, public calls to forgive might be a tool for silencing the oppressed, with the implicit message transmitted being "ignore how you feel" and "let go of your anger". The result may be that survivors are not given the chance to confirm their self-worth and, as Smith also argues, public forgiveness may suggest a trivializing of the injuries and a disinclination to hold perpetrators accountable. In this sense, public calls for forgiveness can seem condescending and might be considered disempowering.[32]

These observations suggest that the notion of "forgiveness" might in many respects be ill-suited to function as a principle of peace building.[33] Would the process of moral learning within peace-building processes be better conceived of in terms of opening up, truth telling and developing understanding, rather than being presented in terms of forgiveness?

---

27 Chapman 2007.
28 The role of trust is discussed in Govier and Verwoerd 2002; Verwoerd 2007.
29 See Chapman 2007.
30 Staub 2005.
31 Smith 2008.
32 Smith 2008.
33 Van Stokkom 2008.

4. THE MAXIMALIST ACCOUNT: 'NO FUTURE WITHOUT FORGIVENESS'

It is questionable whether this minimalist approach is satisfactory. It seems to have its own problems, such as underestimating the significance of symbolic public messages. Moreover, minimalist perceptions seem to have implicit Western biases, such as individualism and competitiveness.

A key element of many African approaches is the centrality of the collective responsibility of the community when it comes to resolving disputes. This sense of interdependence is referred to, for example, as *karakor* in Sudan and *ubuntu* in South Africa. In this context, it is interesting that the Maasai (Kenyan) word for "peace" means "relationship."[34] African mediators (elders or religious leaders) often move away from an adversarial approach (win-lose) and adopt a longer-term perspective in which both parties feel understood and respected.

In Africa, many reconciliation processes are initiated at the religious leadership level. In times of insecurity and conflict, ordinary people look to religious organizations for security and guidance, with religious leaders providing moral leadership and often being involved in encompassing ordinary people to become involved in the peace process. For example, in the Nigerian region of Kaduna, the coordination of the Muslim-Christian Dialogue Forum is carried out by two men: a pastor and an imam. The two clergymen stress that forgiveness gives strength and leads people away from paralyzing feelings of fear. It is suggested that forgiveness sets society as a whole free from the burden of past grievances, divisions and hatred.[35]

The spirit of Ubuntu has been at the heart of the decision to take the path of the TRC in South Africa. Archbishop Desmond Tutu claims that Ubuntu is characteristic of traditional African jurisprudence insofar as its "central concern is not retribution or punishment but, the healing of breaches, the redressing of balances, the restoration of broken relationships".[36] Tutu rejects all the arguments against the role of forgiveness. He argues that forgiveness does not mean condoning what has been done and that it is important to keep remembering.[37]

Journalist Helena Cobban points out that many Westerners prescribe criminal prosecutions as the best policy response to the atrocities of the past, and she adds that Western-based rights movements consider the juridical process to be the best way of holding perpetrators accountable. However, in taking this position, other aims, such as trying to comfort the bereaved, succour the injured or repair broken relationships, are deemed less relevant. The following words of

---

34 Naber 2006: 87.

35 Wuye and Ashafa 1999; see also the documentary titled "The Imam and the Pastor", directed by Alan Channer.

36 Cited by Roche 2003: 27.

37 Tutu 2000.

South African minister Rejoice Mabudhafasi may illustrate African thoughts on the potential punishment of the Apartheid system's abusers and torturers: "We can never do anything to them as bad as what they did to us. It's not in our nature. God will deal with them. We leave that to Him."[38]

Moreover, the consequences of prosecutions might be counterproductive. ANC leader Alex Boraine pleaded against the notion of obligatory prosecution, because such circumstances could lead to new bloody confrontations and thus cause new harm. The pursuit of justice through prosecution may encourage powerful factions to resist the peace process.

Rather than, or at least alongside, these legal measures, a moral appeal might have its own and stronger results. The symbolism of a "new beginning" and the striving towards a "shared future" is sometimes deemed to be a way out of the burdened past and as articulating expectations and hopes. In South Africa, many peace-promoting gatherings have tried to achieve a future-oriented solution to conflict, arguing that such measures will "make for a better tomorrow". For example, in the Zwelethemba model, the matters under dispute are not addressed through a backward-looking process that seeks to balance wrongs with the burden of punishment, but through a forward-looking view that seeks to guarantee that the disputants' moral worth will be respected in the future. Contrary to what one might expect from deontological approaches, the parties involved experience this peace making as both just and effective.[39]

Although a "maximalist" account may overstate the possibilities of forgiving, healing and restoration, its future-oriented aspects are appealing. It meets the wish of the population to look towards a positive future, free from fear and from the threat of repeated victimization. Can the wish to realize peace and the readiness to forgive be so strong that they can override the dominant language of "offender" and "victim", often trapping the parties in the events of the past?

5. CONTEXTS OF PUBLIC FORGIVENESS

The preceding reflections show that forgiveness must be studied in relation to the cultural contexts in which an appeal to it is being made. In some contexts, inciting the public to forgive may promote a willingness to look ahead and develop broader cross-community perspectives without relapsing into conflicting views on the poisonous past – public statements of forgiveness may function as a "leap forwards". In other contexts, making appeals to forgive may have counterproductive results. In these contexts, understanding each other's perspectives and developing empathy may be enough.

38 Cited by Cobban 2006.
39 Froestad and Shearing 2007.

It is important to come to grips with factors that affect citizens' willingness to forgive and apologize. Every country with a troubled and discordant history has its own difficulties in bringing about reconciliation. Amongst the social and cultural factors that might inhibit the willingness to forgive are the power imbalances between former or present adversaries, cultural differences and differences between religions, and a lack of trustworthy political and religious leaders.[40]

Religious leaders and their organizations have in fact played remarkably varied roles in transitional justice.[41] In many locales, they have encouraged and even conducted truth commissions. In other instances they have exercised little influence at all due to a legacy of complicity in authoritarianism or even mass atrocity. The Catholic Church in Chile and Catholic and Protestant leaders in Brazil investigated the human rights violations of their countries' dictators. The Catholic Church of Guatemala, led by archbishop Juan Gerardi, launched its own Recovery of Historical Memory Project (REMHI). In East Timor, Peru, Sierra Leone, religious leaders have lobbied their governments for truth commissions. In those countries, religious communities contributed logistical support, assisting in organizing and carrying out hearings, finding and encouraging victims and witnesses, and providing counseling once hearings were over.[42] In other countries, by contrast, religious communities played little or no role at all. The established churches in Rwanda, Argentina, El Salvador and former Yugoslavia did little to bring about trials or truth commissions. The Catholic Church in Argentina or catholic and protestant hierarchies in Rwanda exercised not much distance from their regimes and thus had hardly influence on transitions.

Philpott concludes that thus far the vast majority of national efforts at transitional justice have occurred in majority-Christian countries, but there is some evidence of support for truth commissions among Muslims as well. "In South Africa as well as Sierra Leone, whose population is 60% Muslim, prominent Muslim leaders have promoted truth and reconciliation efforts. Morocco is the

---

40 For an overview see Kriesberg 2003 and Auerbach 2003. Furthermore, factors that stem from the specific aspects of the conflict may inhibit the reconciliation process and the willingness to forgive, for example, if all parties claim to be victims or if a clear consensus about the perpetrator's actions is lacking. In some countries and regions, the sources of violence and the attribution of blame might be very complex, while in others it is more or less clear which persons, factions and subgroups are responsible for the violence (Celik and Kantowitz 2008). Of course, the severity of past conflicts and oppression also plays a role.

41 Philpott 2009.

42 Regarding the South-African TRC Van der Merwe (2003) concludes: 'The TRC made extensive use of church networks when setting up Human Rights Violations Hearings in local communities. Through the Council of Churches and other religious networks, local ministers were drawn into the process of coordinating meetings, arranging publicity, statement taking and other crucial functions to ensure effective community engagement in the hearings.' The most profound impact of religion was however through the implementation of the TRC's mandate by particular religious leaders who functioned as commissioners and key staff.

first country with an almost solely Muslim population to carry out a truth commission."[43]

Many truth commissions did not succeed to bring former enemies together and involve the population. May be South Africa is an exceptional case, since the stigmatization of the Apartheid-regime was broadly endorsed. Many white perpetrators rejected the former regime. The elites of both parts of the population wanted to encourage reconciliation. On both sides leaders stressed inclusiveness and the acknowledgement of victims. In particular the following conditions seem to have stimulated the forthcoming of the South-African TRC:[44]

- The importance of attractive leadership: Mandela was able to convince not only the black population but also most whites. He also enjoyed great fame and respect internationally.
- In South Africa there was an absolute rupture with the past: the Apartheid regime was condemned by all (international) parties.
- Both parties, including the ANC, were pleading for truth finding, to clear up violations in their own group.
- All parts of the population were involved in the transition; the conflict was clear (no in between positions).

These conditions seem very difficult to replicate elsewhere. In many countries the notion of public forgiveness does not seem to be very relevant or is plainly dismissed. The case of Northern-Ireland may illustrate this. Research findings in Northern Ireland show that both Catholics and Protestants are generally not willing to forgive.[45] Victims often reject the option of forgiveness because they equate it with pardoning or forgetting.[46] The concepts of reconciliation and forgiveness are scarcely used in everyday language. For many, these terms generate negative and cynical reactions, and are dismissed as being theological and therefore irrelevant. Citizens prefer terms such as 'good relations', and they emphasize acknowledgment of the past. Reconciliation is also seen as a threatening process in which 'coming together' is promoted – it is often associated with some compromise, at least the re-humanization of old enemies. Amongst politicians, researchers have found nervousness about promoting reconciliation, with many continuing to engage in sectarian and polarizing politics.[47]

In other countries the spokespersons of reconciliation and forgiveness seem to be more successful. According to Philpott, in Sierra Leone, East Timor and Peru the churches contributed to strong truth recovery, in part because their

43 Philpott 2007: 42.
44 Ellian 2003.
45 Cairns et al. 2005.
46 Hamber 2007.
47 Hamber and Kelly 2005. See also Smith in this volume.

architects sought to improve upon South Africa's experience.[48] In all three countries, transitional justice emerged from a peace agreement that did not involve the total defeat of one side.

6. AIMS AND OVERVIEW

The main questions that will be dealt with in this book are related to the sketched divergent scenarios: 'reconciliation without forgiveness' over against 'no future without forgiveness'. These scenarios reflect specific cultural and religious backgrounds in which forgiveness may be stimulated or discouraged.

The focus of the book is twofold: (1) We want to explore the concept of 'public forgiveness'. Does the concept of 'forgiveness' enable a public or political use of the term? Is it possible to forgive on behalf of others, and if so, under what conditions? May political and religious leaders stimulate forgiving attitudes? What is the role of religious oratory in public appeals? (2) At the same time, we want to relate these conceptual questions to a reflection on the empirical data regarding the cultural and religious contexts of reconciliation and peace building, and the way the oratory on public forgiveness has occurred. In what contexts did the incitement to forgive promote a willingness to look ahead, develop broader cross-community perspectives and prevent a relapse into conflicting views on the poisonous past? In what contexts did political appeals to forgive have counterproductive results? In which contexts is the 'push' towards forgiveness experienced as a highly unfair process? What is the role of religion in this respect?

By focusing on these two sets of problems the book also aims to find answers to practical questions such as: Under what conditions does it make sense to use the concept 'forgiveness' in processes of transitional justice? In which cultural contexts does inter-group forgiveness make sense? What are the factors that stimulate such a process?

The chapters in this volume are divided into two parts. In the first part, we seek to explore philosophical accounts of public forgiveness. In the first contribution Trudy Govier meets the skeptical arguments about the notion of public forgiveness and counters major logical objections ("groups cannot have attitudes") and ethical objections. These ethical objections include themes as "only the direct victim is entitled to forgive" (The Victim Prerogative Principle), and "public forgiveness facilitates a culture of impunity and is incompatible with justice". She argues that a viable concept of public forgiveness is conceivable, one that is defensible in the context of philosophical criticisms. She also criticizes arguments which claim that public forgiveness is not practically achievable.

---

48 Philpott 2009.

In line with Govier, Alice MacLachlan tries to keep up the possibility of forgiveness in the public sphere, although she concentrates on the notion of "political forgiveness". Likewise she responds to the major objections to extending forgiveness to political contexts. The main question she presents is the following: "Are philosophical fears about the dangers of thinking about forgiveness in political terms warranted – or do they perhaps depend in part on conceptual conservatism regarding what exactly political forgiveness might be?" If we want to adapt the concept of forgiveness to a political account, MacLachlan argues, we need to surpass the Emotional Model (genuine forgiveness involves an individual "change of heart") and make conceptual space for descriptions of forgiveness in performative and social terms. The author examines some political grounds for forgiveness and concludes by reflecting on some of the forms that political forgiveness might take. She concludes that acts of forgiveness release us "just enough" to be able to move forward; they function as renewals of trust required to sustain a political space of verbal disputes.

After these chapters on the specified meanings of public forgiveness, two contributions will examine some issues of philosophy of law. Wouter Veraart contends that there are three principal ways in which we can respond to a period of severe injustice and violence. These periods are followed by an urge to forget what has happened, to remember it, or to seek forgiveness. The author frames these responses to historical injustice as 'collective duties'. The concept of forgetting symbolizes the letting go of the past. The present is temporarily disconnected from its relationship with the past. The concept of remembrance on the other hand enables society to arrive at a point where it can establish the truth, come to terms with what has happened, and provide compensation and satisfaction. When forgiveness is the principal response, the relationship with the past is released while the future is anticipated. The author argues that blocking each of the three routes should be prevented. According to Veraart, conceptually, forgiveness is much closer to memory than to forgetting: in order to be able to forgive, one need to know what has happened and who is morally accountable for it. Therefore, it is much closer to the delivery of justice than to amnesty (akin to legal forgetting). Although a duty to forgive is even harder to imagine than a duty to forget or to remember, a humane and mundane legal order should maintain conditions in which forgiving may become a meaningful human practice.

In the next contribution, Bert van Roermund is building upon Ricoeur's philosophy in which reconciliation and forgiveness can only be understood within a conceptual framework that goes 'beyond the legal and the political'. From Ricoeur's analysis of 'difficult forgiveness' both a negative and a positive consequence follow. The negative thesis says that there is no public dimension in forgiveness. The "people" cannot be the agent of forgiving and there cannot be political institutions of reconciliation and forgiveness. The positive thesis says that forgiveness can only be thought in a "time beyond time", in the optative mode of wish and hope, what Ricoeur calls "eschatology", or "time beyond time". Van Roermund tries to formulate a protology of "time before time", i.e., a "proto-politics" as the vestigial memory of a polity about its origin. With Ricoeur, he agrees that forgiveness and reconciliation can be conceived of as conceptually prior to political institutions. But he maintains – contra Ricoeur – that the collective vow of the "we" is a genuinely political "we", expressing a self-enclosure that follows the logic of representation. Addressing the representatives of the former oppressor invokes a more embracing "we" of a "polity-yet-to-be-established", reminiscent of a "polity-once-established" that would have included, rather than excluded, the former perpetrators qua fellow-citizens. This act, van Roermund argues, has to be regarded as proto-political, in the sense of being not framed by political institutions. It is "prior" to politics as well as "posterior" to politics.

Erik Doxtader's essay is an inquiry into the conditions, dynamics, and value of speech. He discusses the question whether forgiveness is (un)speakable. The public call for forgiveness arises at moments in which the capacity to ask and the capacity to answer are not given. According to the author, public forgiveness abides as a rhetorical question which communicates the power to make a new start, "a question in which the question-ability of language is an inextricable if not irresolvable part of the problem". To examine this problem, Doxtader turns back to the accounts of forgiveness offered by Arendt and Derrida. Although they diverge in important ways, they take pains to consider precisely how speaking marks a central occasion for human beings to utter the question whether they might be forgiven. The aim of Doxtader is to grasp how forgiveness begins with a question of language that may well be inexpressible. The question that inaugurates forgiveness is looking perhaps less for a reply than a 'movement toward' that opens an inquiry into the experience of "suffering (of) language", words that possibly provoke and disrupt or sound baseless. This experience to "giving over to language as such" does have several dimensions: (a) the vulnerability of the speaking subjects, (b) interruption of the given ends and means of interpretation and (c) opening space "in which to invent the constitutive grounds of interaction and argumentation".

Nir Eisikovits criticizes the notion of public forgiveness and maintains that we can steer clear of revenge and the never-ending circle of violence without relapsing into the language of forgiving. One does not have to advocate forgiveness in order to avoid vengeance. Political reconciliation might better be conceived in terms of what Adam Smith called "sympathy" – the ability to imaginatively enter the minds of others. Sympathy makes our enemies more concrete and more 'real', "human beings with complicated wants, loves, hates, priorities, desires". Sympathy might be effective in offsetting moral blindness, which is often the result of campaigns of de-individuation, perceiving victims as faceless stand-ins for an entire group. Eisikovits argues that sympathy is particularly important in the case of physically inseparable enemies, when relationships are explosive and arguments about resources tend to turn into statements about one's identity. He makes his case by looking at two examples: the relationship between Israeli Jews and Israeli Arabs and the enmity between Israelis and Palestinians. Despite horrific starting conditions, Israeli Jews and Israeli Arabs coexist quite peacefully and have similarities in life style. People killed are not faceless. The existence of de facto sympathies can avert disaster. The Israeli Palestinian conflict offers a different picture: both parties refuse to be sensible to other's needs and refuse to acknowledge the impact of their actions on specific, flesh and blood human beings.

In the second part of the book, the notion of public forgiveness is related to political and religious developments in (post)conflict regions. In her essay on Arendt's concept of political forgiveness, Catherine Guisan argues in line with MacLachlan: this concept is too often conflated with quasi-religious understanding of the term, referring to a "change of heart" and giving up resentment. Guisan offers other counterpoints to the usual interpretations of Arendtian forgiveness: first, the connection between forgiveness and promising is what endows forgiveness with its political character and secures justice. These two faculties "belong together" and have world-changing potentialities. And secondly: Arendt theorized reconciliation as the attempt to understand one's place in the world, a kind of pondering that admits self-reflection. Thus, forgiving, promising, and understanding belong together. Only together can they deploy their full effects in the public realm. In the second part of the essay, Guisan discusses three real life examples to illustrate that this perspective matters for politics. First, she presents the role of promising and forgiveness in the launching of the 1952 European Coal and Steel Community and the deficit of understanding. Subsequently, the South African Truth and Reconciliation Commission is sketched, including the deficit of promising. Finally, Guisan portrays the deficit of forgiving and understanding in some of the current Iraq and US reconciliatory attempts.

In her contribution, Margaret Smith presents an interdisciplinary reflection of the forgiveness process, if any, in Northern Ireland. She explores the question what to expect from reconciliation and forgiveness initiatives. The new government, in which the former warring parties share power, has had limited success in delivering a polity with a new sense of goodwill between the two communities. Neither community accepts culpability or adopts a spirit of contrition with regard to the conflict. Smith explains how the deeply divided nature of Northern Ireland society does not permit amnesty, reduces the likelihood of a truth commission, and prevents leaders from making reconciliatory gestures. For these reasons, the British government focuses mainly on the needs of 'innocent victims', although the two victim-camps are the least likely to be forgiving. On the basis of an in-depth analysis of the conflict, Smith concludes that the victims' ability to come up with a societal process of healing is likely to be limited. This is rooted in the historical nature of the conflict, the strong in-group identification, and the sense of severe victimhood that both communities have developed. She argues that public forgiveness, if it is possible at all in Northern Ireland, has to emerge from non-official quarters and grass-roots initiatives.

In *Forums of Apology and Forgiveness*, Sanderijn Cels attempts to answer two questions: (1) under which conditions are official apologies acts of public forgiveness; and (2) what are the possible consequences for the meaning and reception of official apologies, if these conditions are not met? On the basis of the official apology issued by then Prime Minister Blair to the Irishmen who were wrongly jailed for the Guildford and Woolwich bombings, she analyzes the practice of public and official apologies. Many formal apologies are prefabricated ("a one man show") and do not allow a public response by the victims. Cels argues that the scholarly literature on public apologies often fails to take the performative features of official apologies into account. Cels pleads for a practice of apology as a mutual process of transformation in which both offender and victim take part. Thus victims have the possibility to speak up and may refuse the gestures. This means that the forum of apology should allow for a full rehabilitation of the victim as moral interlocutor and that the offender – or his spokesperson – will find himself in a vulnerable position. Cels concludes that only if a forum openly reflects the morality of both offender and victim, it can deliver on this moral promise.

The Truth and Reconciliation Commission (TRC) in South Africa is the direct outcome of Mandela's gestures of forgiveness. The 'wrong' in the South African situation is relatively undisputed compared to other countries. Few people would insist that the system of Apartheid was morally acceptable. Annelies Verdoolaege presents a discursive analysis of the language created at the Human Rights Violations hearings – the victim hearings – of the TRC. Her central argument is that the TRC reconciliation discourse strengthened the willingness to reconcile among South African citizens. On the basis of a number of testifying victims, Verdoolaege demonstrates that the testifiers were allowed to frame reconciliation in different ways, be it religious, political, cultural, or by referring to national unity. Additionally, victims were also allowed to be highly critical about reconciliation or to only conditionally accept the notion of reconciliation. Verdoolaege argues that this inclusive nature of the "reconciliation discourse" urged South Africans to accept reconciliation, to relate to the term reconciliation, and to identify with this concept in many divergent ways. As a result of the discourse taking shape at the victim hearings, reconciliation became a central feature in post-TRC South Africa.

Stephen J. Pope addresses the question whether Christian contributions to transitional justice should focus on reconciliation, herewith directly focusing on the dilemma between peace and justice in El Salvador. Pope stresses that the language of reconciliation was employed in El Salvador, as well as in Chile and Argentina, well before the South African experiment was conceived. Yet human rights activists in Latin American countries often suspect appeals to reconciliation as attempts to evade accountability. Pope's main argument is that the promotion of forgiveness may easily slide, affirming that justice is unnecessary and even irrelevant to Christian concern. He stresses that justice is a critically necessary component of the path to reconciliation. Following the Catholic Christian faith, enlivened by the Second Vatican Council, he argues that the church has a special role in not allowing society at large – and political elites in particular – to forget about victims or unfairly to subordinate their well-being to others. Negatively, this means that the Church ought to resist "cheap forgiveness" or any initiative that ignores justice and seeks to protect perpetrators. Phrased positively, this commitment to justice means that the Church can embrace a mission as being a "voice for the voiceless".

Robert Schreiter offers a concluding essay in which he reflects on some of the core concepts and questions that are dealt with in this book. But he also explores the Christian meanings of reconciliation and forgiveness and compares this religious discourse with a more secular discourse to show both their potential contributions and their limits. The author argues that reconciliation and forgiveness in the Christian sense exhibit exocentric (or ec-centric) dimensions. These terms are never just about the actions between discrete human beings or communities; they have ontological or cosmic dimensions as well. God is perceived as an intrinsic actor in the repair of every form of human breach. In so doing, Schreiter says, the importance of human agency is not played down, but the frailty and finitude of human life are rather recognized. Thus, whereas Christianity opens up an exocentric view, a secular reading might start by positing human rights as the point upon which all else stands. Both views have strengths and limitations. Too much emphasis on the exocentric quality of forgiveness and reconciliation can lead to a passive stance against injustice. Too much emphasis on 'the bounded character' of secular peacemaking can lead to situations where nothing can change.

Nearly all contributions in this volume deal with Arendt's perspective on forgiveness and approve her interpretation that political forgiveness should not be grasped in "private" emotional terms of "love" and "compassion". Expressing forgiveness in the political sphere has not much to do with overcoming vengeance, nor with exoneration or relieving offenders of moral obligations. Many endorse the view that the quasi-religious language of "change of heart" would be unfit in the political sphere. Expressing forgiving words in public is a performative act, to be sure a hazardous undertaking that may confuse, dazzle or wound – and thus a manifestation of "suffering language" – but still this act may open up a dialogue between former enemies and fill up a discursive vacuum in a troublesome transitional period. The foundation or survival of a political community is at stake, not the needs of actual victims. To put it in Arendtian words: public forgiveness allows for a new beginning of a state or nation and finds its appropriate place in a proto-political setting. Expressing forgiving words offers the possibility to reactivate the political space of verbal disputes, or to use Govier's terms, to "invite" former oppressors to make shifts in their views, in the hope of establishing improved relationships and to defuse the confrontational emotions that are often so prevalent after serious wrongs are inflicted. For these reasons, many standard-objections against public forgiveness as affronting victims, excusing misdeeds or impeding justice, do not seem to strike the right note.

Of course many aspects of public forgiveness need wider discussions. On the practical level, the authors in this volume seem to diverge when it comes to the question which settings might be best qualified to express gestures of forgiveness. Some opt for the peacemaking activities of grassroots movements, others stick to the idea that politicians and church leaders could take the initiative. Another issue is that many post-conflict regions or countries – like Northern Ireland or El Salvador – do not have a "proto-political setting". In many – if not most – of those territories old (oppressive) institutions survive, the combatant parties stick to their positions and privileges, and perpetrators remain unknown. In other countries, the power differential is too big, so there is little or no acknowledgement of the severity of the wrong. Still another question is which role public forgiveness could play during victim hearings and truth commission gatherings. Forgiveness as "inviting strategy" to engage (former) leaders and partisans into political discourse might be justified for good reasons (in the name of a common polity that needs to be established; developing a new narrative of "we"), but confronting victims with forgiveness-talk could impede their interests and overwhelm them. Finally, a theme that is not worked out well in this volume is the relationship between economic development, social security, and distributive justice on the one hand and peacemaking – including public calls to overcome former animosities – on the other hand. It would be great when future research projects would take on these daring themes.

REFERENCES

Amstutz, M. (2005). *The Healing of Nations: The Promise and Limits of Political Forgiveness*, Lanham, MD: Rowman & Littlefield Publishers.

Arendt, H. (1958). Irreversibility and the Power to Forgive, in *The Human Condition*, Chicago: Chicago University Press, 236–243.

Auerbach, Y. (2004). The Role of Forgiveness in Reconciliation, in: Y. Bar-Siman-Tov (ed.), *From Conflict Resolution to Reconciliation*, Oxford: Oxford University Press, 149–176.

Boraine, A. (2000). *A Country Unmasked: The Story of South Africa's Truth and Reconciliation Commission*, Cape Town: Oxford University Press.

Brouneus, K. (2008). Truth Telling as Talking Cure? Insecurity and Retraumatization in the Rwandan Gacaca Courts, *Security Dialogue*, 39(1), 55–76.

Brudholm, T. (2009). On the Advocacy of Forgiveness after Mass Atrocities, in: T. Brudholm & T. Cushman (eds.) 2009, *The Religious in Responses to Mass Atrocity, Interdisciplinary Perspectives*, Cambridge University Press, 124–156.

Brudholm, T. (2008). *Resentment's Virtue: Jean Amery and the Refusal to Forgive*, Philadelphia: Temple University Press.

Cairns E. et al. (2005). Intergroup Forgiveness and Intergroup Conflict: Northern Ireland. A Case Study, in E.L. Worthington Jr. (ed.), *Handbook of Forgiveness*, New York: Routledge, 461–476.

Celik, B. and R. Kantowitz (2008). Trauma and Forgiveness. Comparing Experiences from Turkey and Guatamala, paper presented at the Inter-disciplinary.net Conference Forgiveness: Probing the Boundaries, Salzburg.

Chapman, A.R. (2007). Truth Commissions and Intergroup Forgiveness: The Case of the South African Truth and Reconciliation Commissions, *Peace and Conflict*, 13(1), 51–69.

Cobban, H. (2006). *Amnesty After Atrocity?* Boulder: Paradigm Publishers.

Collins, M. (2008). Forgiveness in the Post-Conflict Environment: Liberation or Imprisonment?, paper presented at the Inter-disciplinary.net Conference Forgiveness: Probing the Boundaries, Salzburg.

Daye, R. (2004). *Political Forgiveness. Lessons from South Africa*, Maryknoll NY: Orbis Books.

Daku, M. (2008). Forgiveness and the State: Re-imagining the Role of Forgiveness in Politics, paper presented at Princeton Graduate Conference in Political Theory, April 11–12, 2008, <https://politicaltheory.princeton.edu/daku.pdf>.

Derrida, J. (2000). On Forgiveness, *Studies in Practical Philosophy*, 2(2), 81–102.

Derrida, J. (2001). *On Cosmopolitism and Forgiveness*, London: Routledge.

Digeser, P. (2001). *Political Forgiveness*, Ithaca, NY: Cornell University Press.

Doorn, N. (2008). Forgiveness and Reconciliation in Transitional Justice Practices, in *Ethical Perspectives* 15(3), 381–398.

Doxtader, E. (2009). *With Faith in the Works of Words. The Beginnings of Reconciliation in South-Africa, 1985–1995*, East Lansing: Michigan State University Press.

Ellian, A. (2003). *Een onderzoek naar de Waarheids- en Verzoeningscommissie in Zuid-Afrika*, Nijmegen: Wolf Legal Productions.

Elshtain, J.B. (2003). Politics and Forgiveness, in: N. Biggar (ed.), *Burying the Past: Making Peace and Doing Justice after Civil Conflict*, Washington: Georgetown University Press. 45–64.

Froestad, J. and C. Shearing (2007). Conflict Resolution in South Africa: a Case Study, in G. Johnstone and D.W. Van Ness (eds.), *Handbook of Restorative Justice*, Cullompton: Willan Publishing, 534–555.

Govier, T. (2007). *Taking Wrongs Seriously*, Amherst: Prometheus Books.

Govier, T. (2004). Political Forgiveness, *Dialogue – Canadian Philosophical Review*, 43 (2), 380–86.

Govier, T. (2002), *Forgiveness and Revenge*, London & New York: Routledge.

Govier, T. & Colin Hirano (2008). A Conception of Invitational Forgiveness, *Journal of Social Philosophy*, 39 (3), 429–444.

Govier, T. and W. Verwoerd (2002). Trust and the Problem of National Reconciliation, *Philosophy of the Social Sciences*, 32 (2), 178–205.

Gutmann, A. & D. Thompson (2000). The Moral Foundations of Truth Commissions, in: R.I. Rotberg & D. Thompson (eds.), *Truth v. Justice. The Morality of Truth Commissions*, Princeton: Princeton University Press, 22–44.

Hatch, J. (2006). *Between Religious Visions and Secular Realities: (Dia)logology and the Rhetoric of Reconciliation*, http://global.wisc.edu/reconciliation/library/papers_open.

Hamber, B. (2007). Forgiveness and Reconciliation: Paradise Lost or Pragmatism?, *Peace and Conflict*, 13 (1), 115–125.

Hamber, B. and G. Kelly (2005). *A Place for Reconciliation? Conflict and Locality in Northern Ireland*, Belfast: Democratic Dialogue.

Johnston, D. (2005), Faith-Based organizations: The Religious Dimensions of Peace-Building, in P. van Tongeren et al. (eds.), *People Building Peace II; Successful Stories of Civil Society*, London: Rienner, 206–218.

Kriesberg, L. (2004). Comparing Reconciliation Actions within and between Countries, in Y. Bar-Siman-Tov (ed.), *From Conflict Resolution to Reconciliation*, Oxford: Oxford University Press, 81–110.

Lederach, J. (1997). *Building Peace: Sustainable Reconciliation in Divided Societies*, Washington DC: United States Institute of Peace Press.

Levy, D. & N. Sznaider (2006). Forgive and Not Forget: Reconciliation Between Forgiveness and Resentment, in E. Barkan and A. Karn (eds.), *Taking Wrongs Seriously: Apologies and Reconciliation*, Stanford: Stanford University Press.

Louw, D.J. (2006). The African concept of *ubuntu* and restorative justice, in D. Sullivan and L. Taft (eds.), *Handbook of Restorative Justice. A Global Perspective*, London and New York: Routledge, 161–173.

Minow, M. (1998). *Between Vengeance and Forgiveness: Facing History after Genocide and Mass Violence*, Boston: Beacon Press.

Moon, C. (2004). Prelapsarian State: Forgiveness and Reconciliation in Transitional Justice, *International Journal for the Semiotics of Law*, 17, 185–197.

Moon, C. (2008). *Narrating Political Reconciliation: South Africa's Truth and Reconciliation Commission*, Plymouth: Lexington Books.

Naber, J. et al. (eds.) (2006). *African Faith-based Communities. Advancing Justice & Reconciliation in Relation to the ICC*, Faith and Ethics Network ICC & Centre for Justice and Reconciliation.

Pettigrove, G. (2006). Hannah Arendt and Collective Forgiving. *Journal of Social Philosophy*, 37(4), Winter 2006, pp. 483–500.

Philpott, D. (2007). *Religion, Reconciliation, and Transitional Justice: The State of the Field*, SSRC Working Papers.

Philpott, D. (2009). When Faith meets History: The Influence of Religion on Transitional Justice, in: T. Brudholm & T. Cushman (eds.), *The Religious in Responses to Mass Atrocity, Interdisciplinary Perspectives*, Cambridge University Press, 174–212.

Philpott, D. (ed.) (2006). *The Politics of Past Evil: Religion, Reconciliation, and the Dilemmas of Transitional Justice*, Notre Dame: University of Notre Dame Press.

Roche, D. (2003). *Accountability in Restorative Justice*, Oxford: Oxford University Press.

Shriver, D.W. (1995). *An Ethic for Enemies*, New York / Oxford: Oxford University Press.

Smith, M.E. (2008). An Exploration of Forgiveness, Empowerment and the Journey of Healing, paper presented at the Inter-disciplinary.net Conference Forgiveness: Probing the Boundaries, Salzburg.

Soyinka, W. (1999). *The Burden of Memory, the Muse of Forgiveness*, New York/Oxford: Oxford University Press.

Staub, E. (2005). Constructive rather than Harmful Forgiveness, Reconciliation, and Ways to Promote them after Genocide and Mass Killing, in E.L. Worthington Jr. (ed.), *Handbook of Forgiveness*, New York: Routledge, 443–460.

Tavuchis, N. (1991). *Mea Culpa: A Sociology of Apology and Reconciliation*, Stanford: Stanford University Press.

Tutu, D.M. (1999). *No Future Without Forgiveness*, New York: Random.

Van der Merwe, Hugo (2003). The Role of the Church in Promoting Reconciliation in Post-TRC South Africa, in: A. Chapman & B. Spong (eds.), *Religion and Reconciliation in South Africa*, Philadelphia: Templeton Foundation Press, 269–281.

Van Stokkom, B. (2008). Forgiveness and reconciliation in restorative justice conferences, *Ethical Perspectives* 15 (3), 399–418.

Van Tongeren, P. (2008). Impossible forgiveness, in *Ethical Perspectives* 15 (3), 369–379.

Verwoerd, W. (2007). *Equity, Mercy, Forgiveness: Interpreting Amnesty within the South African Truth and Reconciliation Commission*, Leuven/Dudley: Peeters.

Wolterstorff, N. (2006). The Place of Forgiveness in the Actions of the State, In: J.M. Wuye and M.N. Ashafa (1999), *The Pastor and the Imam: Responding to Conflict*, Lagos: Ibrash Publications.

PART 1

PHILOSOPHICAL ACCOUNTS OF PUBLIC FORGIVENESS

PUBLIC FORGIVENESS: A MODEST DEFENCE

Trudy Govier

In the wake of initiatives by Nelson Mandela and Archbishop Desmond Tutu, there was a surge of interest in the idea that forgiveness could play a constructive role in political life and help to prevent cycles of violence. Of late, there has been considerable skepticism about that notion, with some even suspecting Tutu of boosterism about the notion of forgiveness. The grounds for that skepticism are important to consider and set the theme for this book. I do not claim to address all relevant arguments against the notion of public forgiveness; rather, I will attempt here to counter major logical and ethical objections. I argue that there is a viable concept of public forgiveness, one that is defensible in the context of fundamental philosophical criticisms. Although public forgiveness may be difficult to achieve, I believe that it is worth seeking and should not be dismissed as theoretically ill-founded or practically impossible.

The topic of public forgiveness has been of interest mainly due to its connection with another topic, that of *reconciliation* between groups and individuals alienated in the aftermath of bitter conflict or repression.[1] Reconciliation requires the establishment of social trust between previously opposed factions – enough social trust so that they can cooperate as needed to coexist in a decent society. This account of reconciliation in terms of trust is not a minimalist account, based simply on coexistence without violence. Rather, it requires the development of attitudes facilitating cooperation between former enemies. Nor is it a maximalist account: it does not require warm emotion, apologies and tears of remorse – but instead enough social trust and good will for formerly alienated people to function together within social institutions. Wilhelm Verwoerd and I argued for such an account in a 2002 paper on trust and national reconciliation[2] and I developed it further in my book, *Taking Wrong Seriously*, published in 2006.

---

1 Although some use the terms "forgiveness" and "reconciliation" almost interchangeably in contexts of transitions toward peaceful relations, I distinguish them and would argue that it is, strictly speaking, possible to have either without the other. I have discussed this matter in *Forgiveness and Revenge* (Govier 2002) and *Taking Wrongs Seriously* (Govier 2006).

2 Govier & Verwoerd 2002a.

For the purposes of this discussion, I define forgiveness as follows:

Forgiveness requires:

a. The overcoming of resentment and bad feelings towards a person or persons believed to have accountably committed serious wrongs in the past;
b. The re-framing or shift in attitude toward such persons so as to regard them as capable of engaging in decent relationships in the present and future;
c. The setting of the wrongful deeds in the past.

As the grammatical form here will suggest, I am envisaging forgiveness not as an act or single event, but rather as a process. If we say that there is public forgiveness in a given society, we are saying that its attitudes to wrongdoers have changed, or are changing, in the directions indicated here. To the extent that there is public forgiveness, attitudes in society will have shifted away from resentment and bad feelings in the direction of acceptance and an anticipation of constructing decent relationships. The past will not be forgotten, but it will be regarded as past; this important theme I owe to Margaret Walker.[3] The past and its wrongs will not dominate present discussion; they will not persistently be called up in attempts to define the future. Those who were, or were deemed to be, perpetrators of wrongdoing are not reduced only to the status of perpetrators. They are, rather, regarded as human beings who are potentially equal members of a decent society. In other words, they will be allowed a fresh start. (The notion of a fresh start, in this sense, was introduced by Jean Harvey.)[4]

We may distinguish various forms of forgiveness. In *bilateral forgiveness*, two parties are involved. The wrongdoer acknowledges that he or she committed wrongs and expresses remorse in some form; the victim responds to that acknowledgment and forgives the wrongdoer. In *unilateral forgiveness* (sometimes called unconditional forgiveness), there is no acknowledgement or remorse and victims forgive nevertheless. Unilateral forgiveness has been defended on Kantian grounds by Margaret Holmgren and is often urged by therapists as a central aspect of the healing of victims.[5] An intermediate form of forgiveness – articulated by myself and Colin Hirano in a 2008 paper – is also of interest in contexts of reconciliation. This is *invitational forgiveness*.[6] Invitational forgiveness may be understood as a unilateral initiative toward bilateral forgiveness. To forgive invitationally is to forgive in the absence of perpetrator acknowledgment and moral change, but to do so in the hope of eliciting such shifts. Invitational forgiveness is like unilateral forgiveness in that it is offered in

3 Walker 2006.
4 Harvey 1995.
5 Holmgren 1998.
6 Govier and Hirano 2008.

the absence of acknowledgement from perpetrators. It is like bilateral forgiveness to the extent that the expectation is of establishing an improved relationship between victim and wrongdoer; the idea is that ultimately two parties will be involved. Mandela's forgiveness of white South Africans is best described as invitational forgiveness in this sense. It was clearly not bilateral, given the absence of general acknowledgement of the wrongs of apartheid South Africa. Nor was it unconditional forgiveness in any straightforward sense; it was a unilateral initiative made in anticipation of a bilateral relationship based on acknowledgment. I believe that Mandela's announcements of forgiveness can best be understood as invitations to white South Africans to recognize the past for what it was, acknowledge their wrongdoing and resolve to move forward to develop and support new non-racist institutions. Invitational forgiveness is not an invitation *to forgive*; it is already forgiveness. Rather, invitational forgiveness is an invitation *to acknowledge and reform*.[7] It is one way of urging moral change in those responsible for past wrongs.

Usually, the topic of public forgiveness arises as it did in the South African case, in the aftermath of serious and widespread wrongdoing, where state and society seek a nonviolent transition to a society of sustainable peace. Reconciliation requires the cultivation of social trust and for this, attitudes and relationships are centrally important. If individuals and groups have wronged each other, especially if they have done so in the context of sustained struggles over a long period of time, they are likely to remain resentful, angry, and suspicious in the aftermath. Such attitudes will stand as major obstacles to reconciliation and to the building of functional institutions and the cooperation needed to make those institutions work. Public forgiveness would mean overcoming these attitudes; suspicion, fear, and animosity towards persons blamed for wrongdoing in a past conflict would dissipate so that their reintegration into an improved society would become possible. Though public forgiveness in this sense is not strictly necessary for reconciliation in a minimal sense, it would obviously constitute a major step forward.

Many will be tempted to say at this point, 'sure, public forgiveness would be wonderful if you could get it, but realistically, can there be any such thing?' I shall respond to several sorts of arguments disputing public forgiveness – first logical, then normative, and finally practical. The logical argument is that it makes no sense to attribute attitudes and beliefs to collectives in the first place, so questions about changes in group attitudes do not arise. The normative arguments are several and purport to show that even if we could make logical sense of public forgiveness, there would be powerful ethical and political reasons against it. The practical arguments are more empirical and, though based on

7 The word "repent" comes naturally in this context, but is not used here, since some associate it strongly with religious contexts.

cases, may purport to show that even if public forgiveness makes logical and ethical sense, it is not practically achievable, given the realities of political life.

When we speak of public forgiveness, our discourse concerns groups, or collectives. We may be referring to the *state* as a collective, and ask whether a state could forgive and what it would mean for it to do so. One suggestion is that a state could *forgive a debt* through an authorized spokesperson issuing a statement to the effect that the debtor was released from any obligation to repay the amount owed. In most such circumstances, the debtor would be another state. An authorized spokesperson might announce the forgiveness of a debt and thereby forgive it. In this context, we have what is called performative forgiveness, issued in a speech act. (To say that one forgives, presuming the right authorization and circumstances, just is to forgive.) Other state acts relevant to forgiveness are amnesties and pardons. Through authorized spokespersons, states can issue *amnesties*, which are immunities from criminal and civil prosecution. Authorized officials (typically leaders) can also issue *pardons*, releasing convicted persons from penalties.[8] Like forgiveness of debts, amnesties and pardons are performatively issued. They may result from beliefs and attitudes similar to those of forgiveness, but they not necessarily do so.

For some it has been tempting to construe public forgiveness in terms of verifiable speech *acts* issued by authorized agents of the state. Tying public forgiveness to *acts*, such conceptions may be tempting since they avoid referring to hard-to-measure attitudes, feelings, and values. However this approach, taken by Peter Digeser in his 2001 book, leaves out a crucial dimension at the very core of forgiveness, namely *attitudes* to those persons who have been perpetrators in the past, and *beliefs* about how such persons should be treated.[9]

What I am considering here to be the subject of public forgiveness is not only or even primarily the state, but rather the broader society – civil society and sub-groups within it. Attitudes to former enemies will be apparent through the actions, policies, and statements of many individuals and groups in a society and will affect social trust, the capacity to cooperate, and the ability to move forward without renewed violence.

1. THE LOGICAL OBJECTION

The negative argument here is simple and straightforward. Just say this: Public forgiveness requires that groups change their attitudes; changing attitudes in

[8] On my view, pardons and amnesties are acts undertaken by authorized officials and should be distinguished from forgiveness.

[9] Digeser 2001. I reviewed this book in *Dialogue* (Canada) 2004, arguing that it is not feasible to construe forgiveness in terms of acts and then try to link it significantly with reconciliation, as the latter involves attitudinal shifts in directions that will better relationships between previously opposed groups.

turn requires having attitudes; but groups cannot have attitudes because they are not persons and are not capable of consciousness. Therefore public forgiveness is impossible. The crucial sub-argument here is that *groups cannot have attitudes because groups are not capable of consciousness.* In other words, the problem is that groups have no minds. I submit, to the contrary, that we can make sense of groups having attitudes despite the fact that there is no such thing as group consciousness.[10]

It should be noted here that skepticism about group attitudes is far more often expressed with regard to *positive* attitudes such as generosity, compassion and forgiveness than with reference to *negative* attitudes such as resentment, vindictiveness and hatred. After all, even hard-headed social scientists feel comfortable asserting such claims as that there exist attitudes of resentment and grievance among Serbs. From a logical point of view, if we can make sense of groups having negative attitudes, we must also make sense of groups having positive attitudes. And if that is the case, we should also be able to make sense of attributing to groups various changes in their attitudes.

Groups can *act*. In fact, there are many human actions – performing a choral work, mounting a public vaccination campaign, fighting a war, or running an election – that cannot be performed by individuals. These are acts are carried out by human beings who stand in relationships to each other and work together. Clearly they are the actions of groups. They require cooperation, organization, and coordination.[11] Furthermore, groups can be *harmed*, as when public infrastructure or cultural resources are destroyed, or a generation of people is exposed to disease or to denigration and abuse, resulting in a diminished capacity for effective parenting of the next generation. Now I will argue, as I have previously in my 2002 book on forgiveness, that groups can have *attitudes* – including attitudinal responses to harms wrongfully inflicted on them.

In fact, ordinary language and plain old inductive reasoning allow us to attribute attitudes to groups. People as individuals are said to have this or that attitude toward various issues of the day including climate change, social justice, war, immigration policy, and the like. Typically attitudes are attributed based on survey data about individuals. Consider this example. Suppose that the government of country A, in response to a public campaign, sends a billion dollars worth of aid to country B in the aftermath of an earthquake. Suppose further that media coverage of this action in country A is generally positive and that reliable opinion polls indicate that most people in A approve of the aid being sent being sent from A to B. Then say that, on the basis of this evidence, we attribute *compassion* to A. It is largely from surveying individuals that we get our evidence, but those individuals express attitudes in collective institutions (media

10 I have discussed related logical points in detail Govier 2009.

11 Larry May defended the idea of group action quite effectively in his 1987 book on the morality of groups (May 1987).

in this case) in which people are responding to a state (collective) initiative. In this case, I presume an interpretation of discourse about social attitudes that is *distributive:* a group is said to have an attitude on the grounds that most of its (surveyed) members do. On a distributive interpretation, 'Society A has attitude X' *just means* 'Most individuals in A have attitude X'. Contrary to what some have alleged, the Fallacy of Composition is not involved in such reasoning. If we adopt a distributive interpretation of the attitudinal claim about the group, we are not jumping levels from individual to group. Rather, we are reasoning through inductive generalization from a sample to a population.

Now obviously many mistakes can be made when people speak of social attitudes. One can find in such contexts insufficient or biased samples, hasty generalizations, flawed questions, faulty interviewing practices, and unclear conclusions. Social scientists, media commentators, and ordinary people can make certainly mistakes when reasoning about social attitudes, and often they do. But to allow that such mistakes occur is not to say that they are inevitable.

Sometimes, however, our attribution of attitudes to collectives is not simply distributive in this way. We may wish to characterize a collective *as such*. For instance attitudes may be attributed to a group or institution to help in explaining its actions – to render them intelligible. We explain why an individual agent does something by attributing to him or her various values and beliefs. When those actions are the actions of some collective – and we have seen that collectives can act – attitudes may similarly be attributed to it. Suppose, for example, that the chief officers of a corporation decide on a policy of seeking out female executives. If, as the operating board, they adopt and implement such a policy, people may ask why, and the answer will include reference to the beliefs, values, and decisions *of that board* – meaning the board as such, not just the individuals on it. Now there is, of course a *logical gap* between a premise to the effect that certain *individuals* have a given attitude and a conclusion to the effect that a *collective* such as a corporate board has it. If we cannot bridge the gap, an argument from premises concerning individuals to a conclusion about the group would commit the Fallacy of Composition. To avoid that fallacy while finding legitimate support for collective attribution, we need to bridge the gap. One way to do it is through the recognition of group process. Suppose that persons A, B, C, D, and E enter into a discussion at the board meeting. These people likely begin with various individual attitudes and beliefs. Decisions about action emerge from their communications and deliberations. If the group decides to seek more female members, that decision has emerged from its discussions and may be attributed to the *board as such*. Individuals participated in a group process, arriving at a decision to act, and attitudes can be attributed to the group as such when we seek to explain that decision.

In civil society more broadly, discussion happens through the media and within many institutions and sub-groups.

There is much to be learned from skeptically probing claims about groups and societies such as 'Danes,' 'the West,' 'Muslims,' 'Serbs,' and so on. Hasty reasoning and unclear language often support simplistic stereotypes, at considerable cost to both accurate understanding and decent relationships. As noted, significant errors can be made. Clearly it is important to avoid such errors – not least when reasoning about forgiveness and reconciliation. What I am arguing here is not that there are never problems of logic when we reason about the attitudes and values of groups, but rather that such problems of logic can be avoided: we can sometimes get it right.

2. NORMATIVE OBJECTIONS

I now wish to consider normative considerations, discussing three major themes. These are (a) the victims' prerogative to forgive; (b) considerations of justice; and (c) the roles of church and state.

(a) **Victims.** The objection here is that public forgiveness presumes an ethical mistake, because it removes the right to forgive from victims and thus amounts to disrespect.

This objection assumes a principle of strict victim prerogative, namely that only the direct victim of a wrong is entitled to forgive its perpetrator. For anyone else to do so is wrong and expressive of disrespect for the victim. I will for convenience refer to this Victim Prerogative Principle as the VPP. We can begin by noting that even if we accept a strict version of the VPP, there remains some space for public forgiveness, because a collective as such may itself be the victim of a wrong – as, for instance, when its hospitals are destroyed or when widespread crime necessitates prolonged and expensive legal procedures to be administered and funded by the state. If a collective were the direct victim of a wrong, it would entitled to grant or withhold forgiveness to the perpetrators of that wrong, according to a unqualified version of the VPP.

However, the VPP principle appears to need qualification, as indicated in recent discussions by Alice MacLachlan and Kathryn Norlock.[12] Verwoerd and I earlier argued that primary victims are not the only victims of wrongdoing: secondary victims (family, friends and colleagues) may be seriously harmed as a result of the harm done to primary victims. On these grounds one could say (as we did) that VPP will tell us that each person is entitled to forgive the harm done to him or her – nothing more, nothing less. But this response leads in the end to a somewhat inelegant result. It is, after all, *persons* – not harms or acts – that are the objects of forgiveness. Applying an unqualified VPP, these various victims

12 Alice MacLachlan argues from solidarity (MacLachlan 2009). In the same volume, Kathryn Norlock points out the issue with regard to self-forgiveness (Norlock 2009).

each have the moral authority to forgive the wrong doer or not.[13] We arrive at a situation where a perpetrator is forgiven by and not forgiven by others and all of these people are authoritative. The result is highly awkward when the question is one of social attitudes in a political context. Further reasons to qualify VPP lie elsewhere. As put forward by MacLachlan and Norlock (separately), they include moral solidarity, victim unreasonableness, and the phenomenon of self-forgiveness. There are, then, larger issues concerning the moral authority often presumed for victims in contexts of reconciliation: an unqualified VPP should not be taken for granted.

To be sure, victims should not be ignored. To be sure, victims need sympathy, understanding, and in many contexts, reparations. To be sure, they should not be manipulated or exploited or made to feel they have to forgive out of religious obligation or in loyalty to the state and its leader. Victims' personal responses to injuries and trauma are for them to work out. But having said all this, we must remember that *victims are not moral authorities*. They can be unreasonable, belaboring their grievances, refusing to move forward, and handicapping processes of political reconciliation and social reconstruction. I would urge accordingly that the VPP be interpreted as a rule of thumb and not as an absolute immune from qualifications. Understood in this way, the VPP does not support a negative general verdict on the morality of public forgiveness.

(b) **Considerations of justice**. Does justice argue against forgiveness? If one urges public forgiveness, as a means to reconciliation and peace, will that mean condoning serious acts of brutality and violence, thereby facilitating a continuing culture of impunity? Some have urged that the answers to these questions are affirmative and argue on those grounds that public forgiveness is incompatible with justice.

To what extent trials and punishment are desirable in the aftermath of serious political conflict will vary depending on the context. Reflecting on this matter, it is important to remember that public forgiveness is a matter of attitudinal shifts and is not to be identified with the offering of amnesties and pardons. In fact, it is possible for public forgiveness to come in the wake of criminal trials and punishment. It is also possible to combine a truth commission approach for some sorts of agents with criminal trials for others.

If persons imprisoned are not executed, issues of the attitude to be taken toward them will remain. There will be choices to be made concerning the reintegration into society of those labeled as perpetrators. The only way to avoid having some attitude toward these people would be to isolate them indefinitely, purge them from the society, or eliminate them altogether. Needless to say, such strategies are not conducive to building a sustainable peace in the wake of widespread oppression or conflict. Along a spectrum of possible responses, one

---

13 Wilhelm Verwoerd and I discuss this problem in Govier & Verwoerd 2002b.

can envisage accepting that persons identified as perpetrators are capable of moral change and may, under some circumstances, be given a fresh start. One can envisage accepting a conception of human nature and human potential according to which human agents are not reducible to their past deeds and character. Such a response will be more conducive to reconciliation and sustainable peace than killing or isolating all former perpetrators, or seriously restricting their activities in a transitional society on the grounds that they acted badly in a previous society. Execution, prolonged incarceration, and lustration are policies sometimes adopted to avoid having to deal with former perpetrators. Unlike public forgiveness, these responses do not aim at perpetrator reintegration; their pragmatic potential presupposes that numbers are comparatively small. Like public forgiveness, these responses presuppose attitudes with regard to former perpetrators. Keeping these things in mind, let us return to the question: does public forgiveness amount to injustice?

Suppose you believe that justice is penal justice, that penal justice is retributive penal justice, and that retributive penal justice is a higher value than peace. You are likely, then, to oppose public forgiveness, reasoning that it is incompatible with justice.[14] But note now just how many suppositions you are urged to make, to arrive at this conclusion. There are three and each is highly controversial. I would go further: I think each of the three suppositions is false. I urge that it is not the case justice is only penal justice (there is, for instance, social justice), that penal justice need not be understood as retributive (it may be rationalized as deterrence, or moral education) and finally that retributive penal justice should not be deemed a higher value than peace. Furthermore, in many contexts there is no dilemma of 'peace versus justice' because we are not forced to make a choice. The either/or construction here is distorting. One important way to appreciate that fact is to understand that the absence of peace will mean the absence of rule of law and nonviolent means of settling conflicts; these gaps in turn will lead to breakdowns in penal justice, social justice, and, indeed, minimal personal security. Accordingly, the absence of peace in a society will mean more violence, more harms, and more victims – and less justice.[15] Thus urging policies on the grounds that they will positively contribute to peace does not amount to sacrificing justice in the interest of peace – even though it might sometimes mean sacrificing retributive penal justice.

(c) **Church and state.** The objection here is that forgiveness is a religious notion, urged for religious reasons, and as such has no proper role to play in matters of state.

---

14 This argument is developed at greater length in Govier 2006.

15 The point that without peace, there will be further victims of violence and, hence, further injustice, comes from Wilhelm Verwoerd.

There is a short answer to this problem, and then a longer one. The short answer is that forgiveness is not an exclusively theological notion; forgiveness need not be urged or pursued for religious reasons. Questions about how individuals and groups should respond to wrongdoing and wrongdoers are perfectly general in nature and arise whether we take a theological perspective or not. Public forgiveness may be urged for secular reasons and need not involve an intrusion of religious faiths and leaders into the affairs of state.

For the longer answer, we need to consider what is involved in the separation of church and state. Many societies in transition will be characterized by a plurality of religious faiths. In contexts of reconciliation, there is a desire to make a transition to a *peaceful society* in which persons from diverse traditions can participate and enjoy respect and full citizenship. In these situations, there is clearly much to be said in favour of a separation of church and state. Let me just say that I endorse some such principle and anticipate that most of my audience would do so as well.

But what is meant by the separation of church and state? Narrowly, it would mean that the state should not endorse or favour any particular religion and should make illegal various types of discrimination based on religious affiliation, with regard to education, housing, employment, and political life. If there is a separation of church and state, the state will not, for instance, be a Christian state, a Hindu state, a Jewish state, or an Islamic state. The separation of church and state will also entail that public officials should not urge persons to adopt attitudes or endorse actions on the grounds that they are in accord with the teachings of some particular religion. I submit that these restrictions, due to separation of church and state, are fully compatible with public forgiveness.

Accordingly a person holding a state office should not, with the authority of his or her office, direct people that it is their *religious duty as Christians* to forgive. I have discussed this phenomenon in my book *Taking Wrongs Seriously*, calling it Directed Forgiveness. I argue against it.[16]

Now some have interpreted the separation of church and state more broadly so as to imply that individuals exploring and debating policy, concerning public issues, in public contexts should never advance arguments based on religious premises. I would urge that this restriction goes too far because it would so considerably restrict public speech by persons of faith. In public deliberations in a free society, persons with religious convictions should be able to express those convictions publicly, inviting others to consider their application to questions of the day. This point has been argued from a secular point of view by Austin Dacey in a 2009 book, *The Secular Conscience*.[17] Some such questions may concern past conflict and responses to it. There is space for public reasoning about issues of forgiveness, and even for forgiveness as understood within various religious

16 Govier 2006.

17 Dacey 2009.

traditions. Those who dissent from a religious foundation may nevertheless find elements in these arguments that push forward their own thinking, or they may gain insights from resisting them. The views resulting from inclusive public deliberations may or may not favour forgiving attitudes toward those regarded as perpetrators.

3. PRACTICAL CONSIDERATIONS

So far I have offered a philosophical defence of the concept of public forgiveness. None of the considerations I have put forward address the very many practical problems that are likely to arise in societies in transition. Such problems are obviously of the utmost importance. I cannot prejudge them and they lie outside the contexts of philosophy and theory. But I will try to make a few preliminary comments.

One might very well judge that public forgiveness would be impossible or unsuitable in some context, for a variety of reasons. Circumstances might be so dire that public deliberations are impossible. There might be too many angry victims with solid platforms for advertising and cultivating their grievances. Politicians might be highly influential as 'ethnic entrepreneurs' successfully exploiting the divisions of the past.[18] Particular circumstances require particular consideration and a response to logical and ethical objections cannot by itself provide an algorithm for achieving public forgiveness, reconciliation, and sustainable peace. I am of course read to grant that there will be contexts in which urging public forgiveness would be an unpromising approach in the quest for reconciliation. What I am not ready to grant is that public forgiveness is impossible for logical reasons or inappropriate for general normative reasons.

It will often be over-bold – in fact, falsely optimistic – to presume that a society can overcome its problems by seeking public forgiveness. In some contexts, appeals to forgive may be unrealistic; in others, they may be based on facile and manipulative readings of one religious tradition or another. It is an understatement to say that there are many things that can go wrong in the quest for reconciliation. But to acknowledge these difficulties is not to rule out public forgiveness as a viable concept and, in some circumstances, a worthy goal. Reconciliation will require enough social trust to make possible the cooperation needed for the rule of law and functioning social institutions. The needed shifts in attitude may be difficult to achieve; they may come slowly; they are more likely to appear in some contexts than in others. But none of this is to say that they are impossible.

---

18 I owe the suggestive term "ethnic entrepreneur" to Kirsten Juhl, who employed it in discussions of the Balkan wars of the 1990s.

REFERENCES

Dacey, Austin (2008). *The Secular Conscience: Why Belief Belongs in Public Life*. Amherst, NY: Prometheus.

Digeser, P.E. (2001). *Political Forgiveness*. Ithaca, NY: Cornell University Press.

Gamlund, E. (2009). A Change of Heart: Essays in the Moral Philosophy of Forgiveness, doctoral dissertation in philosophy, University of Oslo.

Garrard, E. and D. McNaughton (2004). In Defence of Unconditional Forgiveness, *Proceedings of the Aristotelian Society* 103 (1), 39–60.

Govier, T. (2002). *Forgiveness and Revenge*. London and New York: Routledge.

Govier, T. (2006). *Taking Wrongs Seriously: Acknowledgment, Reconciliation, and the Politics of Sustainable Peace*. Amherst, New York: Humanity Books.

Govier, T. (2009). Duets, Cartoons, and Tragedies: Struggles with the Fallacy of Composition, in *Pondering on Problems of Argumentation*, edited by F. van Eemeren and B. Garssen. Dordrecht: Springer.

Govier, T. & Colin Hirano (2008). A Conception of Invitational Forgiveness, *Journal of Social Philosophy*, 39 (3), 429–444.

Govier, T., and W. Verwoerd. (2002a). Trust and the Problem of National Reconciliation. *Philosophy of the Social Sciences*, 32 (2), 178–205.

Govier, T., and W. Verwoerd. (2002b). Forgiveness: The Victim's Prerogative. *South African Journal of Philosophy*, 21 (2), 97–111.

Griswold, Ch. (2007). *Forgiveness: a Philosophical Exploration*. New York: Cambridge University Press.

Harvey, J. (1995). The Emerging Practice of Institutional Apologies, *International Journal of Applied Philosophy* Winter/Spring, 9 (2).

Holmgren, M.R. (1993). Forgiveness and the Intrinsic Value of Persons, *American Philosophical Quarterly*, 30 (4), 341–352.

Holmgren, M. R. (1998). Self-Forgiveness and Responsible Moral Agency. *Journal of Value Inquiry* 32 (1), 75–91.

MacLachlan, A. (2009). Forgiveness and Moral Solidarity. In *Forgiveness: Probing the Boundaries, E-Book [978-1-904710-62-2]*, edited by D. White and S. Bloch-Schulman. Oxford: Inter-Disciplinary Press.

Maclachlan, A. (2007). *The Nature and Limits of Forgiveness*, Doctoral dissertation, Boston University.

May, L. (1987). *The Morality of Groups: Collective Responsibility, Group-Based Harm, and Corporate Rights*. Notre Dame, Ind.: University of Notre Dame Press.

Norlock, Kathryn J. (2009). Why Self-Forgiveness Needs Third-Party Forgiveness. In: *Forgiveness: Probing the Boundaries, E-Book [978-1-904710-62-2]*, edited by D. White and S. Bloch-Schulman. Oxford: Inter-Disciplinary Press.

Tutu, D. (1999). *No Future without Forgiveness*. New York: Doubleday.

Verwoerd, W. (2007). *Equity, Mercy and Forgiveness: Interpreting Amnesty within the South African Truth and Reconciliation Commission*. Leuven: Peeters Publishing.

Walker, M. (2006). *Moral Repair*. Cambridge: Cambridge University Press.

THE PHILOSOPHICAL CONTROVERSY OVER POLITICAL FORGIVENESS

Alice MacLachlan

1. INTRODUCTION

The question of forgiveness in politics has attained a certain cachet. Indeed, in the fifty years since Hannah Arendt commented on the notable absence of forgiveness in the political tradition, a vast and multidisciplinary literature on the politics of apology, forgiveness, and reconciliation has emerged. A number of historical events can account for this sudden turn: the efforts of former Soviet Bloc countries to acknowledge state spying and other infractions on the rights of their citizens; the establishment of truth commissions in Argentina, Uruguay, Chile (among others) to investigate state-sanctioned disappearances, kidnappings and tortures; and, perhaps most famously, the work of the Truth and Reconciliation Commission (TRC) in South Africa. At the same time, there have been gestures by parties to World War II on both sides of the conflict to apologize and repair for various war crimes and infractions, and settler societies like Canada, the USA, and Australia have been called to task for past injustices by various members of their own citizenry: indigenous peoples, the descendants of former slaves, linguistic and ethnic minorities, and immigrant groups who have suffered from discrimination and exploitation.

Analyses of these new politics typically touch on the potential role for a *political* notion of forgiveness, although few have provided a detailed or consistent theoretical explanation of what would make an act of forgiveness political, and what distinguishes political forgiveness from its more familiar counterparts in everyday life.[1] Instead, this task has fallen to philosophers, and they have embraced it with no small degree of cynicism. To a novice scouring the relevant literatures, it might appear that the only discordant note in this new veritable symphony of writings on political forgiveness has been sounded by

1 Peter Digeser (2001) is a notable exception to this; I discuss his account of political forgiveness below. Trudy Govier also offers a detailed analysis of forgiveness between groups, and in political contexts – most specifically the South African Truth and Reconciliation Commission – although she does so by extending the Emotional Model to account for group resentment. See Govier 2002: 90–92.

philosophers writing on the topic. Where others see new hope for politics, philosophers fear an uncritical promotion of forgiveness, which risks distorting and cheapening forgiveness as a moral ideal, on the one hand, and ignoring justice, accountability, and the need to end harmful relationships, on the other.[2] After all, when philosophers take up the question of forgiveness, it is usually in order to shape it into something resembling a rationally defensible moral ideal.[3] This ideal, many argue, depends on the rich nature of our private interpersonal relationships, and the space for trust, empathy, and emotional expression afforded by them. Once transported to the political realm, forgiveness is subject to inevitable distortion and decay.

Are philosophical fears about the dangers of thinking about forgiveness in political terms warranted – or do they perhaps depend in part on conceptual conservatism regarding what exactly political forgiveness might be? In this paper, I will make the case that most – if not all – objections to political forgiveness emerge from theoretical reliance on a picture of forgiveness I will call the Emotional Model. Once we make conceptual space for descriptions of forgiveness in performative and social terms, the concept is more easily adapted to a political account without the risks feared by philosophers.

My argument takes the following form. First, I present and briefly defend a multidimensional account of forgiveness. Next, I consider how best to understand forgiveness as political. Third, I respond to the major objections to extending forgiveness to political contexts, in turn:

1. Political actors have no right to forgive on behalf of individual victims;
2. Forgiveness imports inappropriate and illiberal notions of deep, psychological change into politics.
3. Only persons, not collectivities, can forgive.

My answer to each of these draws partly on the account of multidimensional account of forgiveness I advocate. Finally, I consider a slightly different sort of objection to political forgiveness. Given that, as I have argued, forgiveness is a personal reaction to wrongful harm, forgiveness cannot be a political matter because:

4. Acts of political forgiveness cannot be grounded in the appropriate kinds of reasons.

---

2 The work of Jeffrie Murphy (1988) and, more recently, Thomas Brudholm (2008) represent excellent examples of this cynicism.

3 I discuss the philosophical interest in forgiveness *qua* ideal, and some its shortcomings, in another paper. I argue that the mainstream philosophical approach to forgiveness results in a narrow and unhelpful set of dichotomies: we either resent or forgive; either forgiveness is deserved or it is unwarranted; either forgiveness is conditional on repentance or it is unconditional. See MacLachlan 2009.

I counter this claim by examining some political grounds for forgiveness. Having argued that there are no unanswerable philosophical objections to forgiveness as a political concept, I conclude by reflecting on some of the forms that political forgiveness might take. Obviously the politics and particularities of reconciliation are enormous: the main purpose of this discussion is to remove some of the most salient philosophical objections to political policies that employ the language of forgiveness. While the language of forgiveness may be more or less appropriately applied (depending on the context of the political dispute) to policies of amnesty, pardon, or apology, as gestures of reconciliation or restoration, certain examples of each are capable of performing the work of forgiveness.

2. A WORKING THEORY OF FORGIVENESS

Since forgiveness is very much a part of the everyday moral of the contemporary western world, it makes sense for a theory of forgiveness to take, as its starting point, 'average' or 'everyday' understandings – insofar as these can be extracted.[4] In philosophy, forgiveness is typically understood as a personal reaction to wrongful harm, which both confronts the wrongdoing qua wrongdoing and is characterized by either a shift from a negative to a positive stance toward the wrongdoer, or the adoption of a positive stance when a negative one is expected. Philosophers have also argued that the change of stance in forgiveness is essentially – or ideally – characterized in cognitive-affective terms: that is, as the effort to overcome or reduce resentment, undertaken for moral reasons. I call this the Emotional Model of forgiveness, since it characterizes forgiveness essentially as a change in emotion.[5] Outside of philosophy, on the other hand, social practices of forgiveness are varied. Acts of forgiveness can manifest

4 Here, any philosophical author confronts the danger of speaking in the voice of an authoritative "we", presuming social and cultural homogeneity where there is little or none. Contemporary notions of forgiveness in English-speaking philosophy draw heavily on the cultural inheritance of the Judaic, Christian and Islamic religious traditions, as well as cultural norms that have developed in European cultures. Jacques Derrida (2001) has written about how this "Abrahamic" tradition of forgiveness is now writ global. I am not convinced that this is a fait accompli and suspect that social practices of forgiveness, like social practices of apology, admit of significant cultural variation. For a discussion of cultural variation in practices of apology, see Renteln (2008).

5 Trudy Govier has rightly noted that the term "Emotional Model" suggests that she and others reduce forgiveness to a matter of mere feelings when in fact she understands it primarily as a change in reactive attitudes, which have cognitive and volitional content not reducible to feelings. Let me be clear, therefore, that I understand emotions to be complex adaptive responses to certain situational factors, often socially experienced and understood, an episode of which may or may not include physiological changes, ways of feeling, motivations and dispositions to act in certain ways and – importantly – particular thoughts, perceptions and evaluations of this situation. In other words, rich emotional experiences like resentment include but are not reducible to evaluative construal of the agent's environment that is open to rational assessment. Thus, in overcoming resentment, the forgiver – on the Emotional

themselves as primarily affective (a change in feelings), cognitive (a change in judgments and attitudes) and/or socially performative (participation in some established action or ritual – perhaps the simple acts of saying "I'm sorry" and "I forgive you"). While many typical cases of forgiveness will have elements of all three, no one dimension – affective, cognitive or performative – is essential to 'real' or 'genuine' forgiveness. In other words, I advocate a multidimensional account of forgiveness. In long-standing and complex relationships marked by distrust and resentment on both sides, words of forgiveness alone may be deeply unsatisfying – and somewhat suspicious. In a more casual, distant or formal relationship, talk of deep emotional change or moralized judgments might actually exaggerate and sustain what would otherwise have been minor, even fleeting hostilities. What 'counts' as an act of forgiveness, will depend in part on whether those involved see it as such.

How then do we determine when someone has forgiven? Since practices of forgiveness vary in their expression, we can better understand what constitutes an act of forgiveness by examining its function or meaning to those involved rather than looking for a singular phenomenology of emotion, gesture, or performance. An act of forgiveness can have three functions: it can release the wrongdoer from emotional remainders like subjective guilt, it can offer relief to the wrongdoer (or indeed, the victim), and it can assist in the repair of right relationships, trust and the re-establishment of moral values.[6] The nature of a particular act of forgiveness will depend very much on the context in which it arises: the characters of forgiver and forgiven, the relationship between them, and the extent of the original harm. Finally, we forgive for a multiplicity of reasons; these reasons are typically drawn from the context of the harm, the wrongdoer's subsequent behavior, and the forgiver's anticipation of future states of affairs. The forgiver's reasons may also appeal to broader norms and values she takes to be important (e.g. the importance of interpersonal harmony). In many situations, our reasons to forgive are compelling but not conclusive; thus, potential forgivers have a certain amount of discretion regarding when it is appropriate to forgive. When we forgive for good reasons, however, our actions respond appropriately to the moral needs of the victim and wrongdoer, contribute to morally valuable states of affairs, and are capable of expressing moral values of trust, compassion and sensitivity.

Model – experiences a change in attitude, perception and evaluation of the wrongdoer, which takes place for moral reasons.

6 The three functions of forgiveness can be seen in the multiple metaphors used to describe it we talk about forgiveness as a change of heart, or the decision to turn the other cheek, but equally, forgiving can wipe clean the slate, release the wrongdoer (and victim) from the burden of the harm, remit the wrongdoer's moral debt, or function as a gift.

3. MAKING FORGIVENESS POLITICAL

When theorists take up the question of 'political' forgiveness, they often have in mind large-scale cases of wrongdoing between social and political groups on a national, or even international, scale.[7] Yet there are plausible counterexamples to the claim that all political forgiveness is collective forgiveness, and vice versa. Equating the two would exclude those cases where individual political actors (state representatives) seek or offer forgiveness, except insofar as they represented a larger collectivity, and there are plausibly cases of political forgiveness where those individuals involved (as victim and wrongdoer, in any case) speak for themselves alone.[8] For example, many of the cases heard by South Africa's Truth and Reconciliation Commission involved atrocities committed by a single individual against another, within the context of systemic political oppression and struggle. In those cases, politics entered the equation as the motivation for the wrong, the context that made such occurrences possible, and in the scene of (possible) forgiveness: a public, state-mandated tribunal with the power to grant amnesty. Furthermore, we can imagine situations of collective forgiveness that are not especially political in nature: for example, collective forgiveness among members of an extended family or between factions of friends, fans of two rival sports teams, or colleagues in a workplace dispute.

Instead, we might recognize that much of the philosophical work on interpersonal forgiveness takes as its starting point, a very particular (if familiar) kind of interpersonal relationship: most typically, a casual friendship or acquaintance between agents who are relatively equal, and fairly independent from one another – friends, neighbours, or colleagues. But a philosophical theory of forgiveness that aimed to be comprehensive would need to apply to a wide variety of interpersonal relationships (partners, family, friends – ranging to complete strangers or new introductions), while acknowledging that these relationships vary in importance to the agents involved, as well as in closeness,

---

7 Trudy Govier moves quickly from discussing skepticism over forgiveness in politics to asking, "can *groups* forgive?" Donald Shriver also speaks of political forgiveness as a "*collective* turning from the past," and Mark Amstutz claims: "political forgiveness represents an extension of interpersonal forgiveness to the actions of *collectives*." See Govier 2002: ix, Shriver 1995: 9 (italics added); Amstutz 2005.

8 Nicholas Tavuchis' (1988: 48) taxonomy of "structural configurations of apology and forgiveness" is helpful here. Tavuchis divides apologies (and gestures of forgiveness) into four categories:

One to One
One to Many
Many to One
Many to Many

Tavuchis assumes that the first is interpersonal, and the other three importantly different from the first. He is right to acknowledge the implications of a *public* apology, but in dismissing the first, perhaps fails to consider the role of the public as witness (or relevantly located third party) in politically charged acts of One-to-One (interpersonal) forgiveness.

affection, knowledge of the other, and in power. Rather than treating political forgiveness as a *sui generis* phenomenon, to be contrasted with interpersonal forgiveness understood as a singular paradigm, we might recognize how forgiveness potentially emerges from within a host of different types of relation – with political relationships being one type among these (admittedly, one with its own unique complications).

Thus, I propose the following definition of political forgiveness. An instance of forgiveness is political, when it takes place in one of the following three types of circumstances:

1. Forgiveness between collectivities that are clearly recognizable as politically constituted or organized, or between their mandated representatives (e.g. states, political organizations, ethnic groups or other national minorities, or between groups of marginalized and disadvantaged individuals and the larger political society).
2. Forgiveness between individuals or groups whose primary relationship, or the relationship in question (i.e. that relationship implicated in the wrongdoing), is political, for e.g. forgiveness for politically motivated or politically charged wrongdoings: hate crimes, for example, or the torture of political prisoners and hostages, as well as individual acts that are part of – and made possible by – wider systemic state policy (e.g. atrocities committed under apartheid policies).[9]
3. Forgiveness enacted as part of – or in service to – the ongoing process of making the conditions for political society possible (that is to say, a broader political effort to establish lasting peace, build democratic institutions, and take responsibility for past political wrongdoing).[10]

While the first set of circumstances will entail collective forgiveness, if any, both the second and the third set can produce political forgiveness without it necessarily being collective. Yet insofar as they concern the structure and arrangements determining a political society and arise in the aftermath of political conflict, instances of forgiveness in (2) and in (3), whether individual or collective, are reasonably described as political.

---

9 I realize, of course, that (2) could include any act of crime between two citizens, provided they did not have a prior personal relationship. I do not intend to discuss forgiveness in judicial systems – at least not in those of a functioning democracy – at this point. I focus on political wrongdoing rather than purely criminal wrongdoing. However, I am open to the possibility that much of my analysis could be applied to discussions of restorative justice in the ordinary functioning of a criminal justice system, as well as situations of political upheaval and change.

10 This last set of circumstances is very much in keeping with a claim by Hannah Arendt (1958: 198) that forgiveness is fundamentally a political faculty, since she claims that political activity always concerns itself with the conditions of its own possibility; that is, we are political when we act in order to create or sustain conditions of public plurality and debate.

In fact, philosophical discussions of political forgiveness suffer from a failure to recognize how many different events and processes are already referred to under the rubric of political forgiveness (whether or not those writing subscribe to a broad account of forgiveness, as I do). Those arguing for or against the possibility of political forgiveness describe it, in turn, as a collective effort to engage in "knowing forgetting,"[11] a collective "process of overcoming resentment and anger,"[12] "the decision to relieve individuals and groups from their moral debts or deserved punishments,"[13] specific decisions to pardon or offer debt relief,[14] a value that must be present for any successful political policy of reconciliation,[15] or the authoritative academic discourse governing contemporary political transition.[16] While I do not necessarily object to any one of these qualifying as an act of political forgiveness, this kind of equivocation can confuse the question of whether *political* forgiveness is a good idea. It is not always easy to know what collective, knowing, forgetting might entail, or how the specific decisions to pardon, relieve punishment or release moral debts might contribute to the collective process of overcoming resentment. Those who endorse and those who criticize political instances of forgiveness are often talking past one another.

This is exactly why the multidimensional account of forgiveness is helpful for its political application. Perhaps even more than in the case of interpersonal forgiveness, there are clearly multiple, competing, and sometimes conflicting intuitions about the character of political forgiveness. Those writing on the topic struggle to combine acts, policies, and the occasionally intangible effects of broader social change into a single philosophical concept. Thus, treatments of political forgiveness in the literature will refer to the following distinct phenomena almost interchangeably, without acknowledging a shift in reference:

i) A specific act or government policy of reconciliation or peace-making: for example, the decision to implement truth commissions, to grant collective amnesty to perpetrators, to offer an individual political pardon, to issue a public apology or to make (or accept) an offer of reparation following harm.
ii) Individual acts or events that take place within the context of such policies: for example, the actual ceremony of apology between two heads of state, or the 'scenes' of forgiveness between individual victims and wrongdoers that Desmond Tutu describes as taking place in the context of the South African Truth and Reconciliation Commission.
iii) The goal or end result of such policies; this third category treats political forgiveness as a synonym for a rich notion of political reconciliation. Thus,

---

11 Elshtain 2001: 42–56.
12 Govier 2002: viii.
13 Amstutz 2005: 77.
14 Digeser 2001: 7.
15 Rigby 2001: 184.
16 Moon 2004: 185.

political forgiveness – in this sense – is achieved when such acts or policies are concluded with some standard of success, or to the satisfaction of those involved.

iv) A side effect of these policies, such as a widespread shift in general social attitudes and behaviors between former victims and perpetrators. This could be measured by a number of indicators, including media reports, polling, records of inter-community incidents and police reports, success of integrated schooling, and through cultural artifacts like novels, films, plays, and songs.

v) A value governing policies and process of social reconciliation, a value usually listed alongside truth telling, justice and peace. Such values function as reference points for the mandates and commitments of specific committees, task forces, commissions, and so on.

One might endorse policies described in i) without insisting on a rich notion of reconciliation, like iii) – or equally, promote the kind of broader social change described in iv) without believing that specific government policies or actions are the best way to achieve it. Finally a government or set of governments could demonstrate commitment to forgiveness as a value (as in v) without implementing any of the specific policies in i) or ii).

Which one of these is 'real' political forgiveness? First, I see good reason not to condemn any of these scenarios as necessarily incomplete – or to view them necessarily as partial fragments of a larger, unified *real* 'political forgiveness'. In the first place, it is unclear what (or how desirable) that larger, unified phenomenon is: that is, how i) through v) are all necessarily required for any particular process of political transition (or reconciliation with history) to meet relevant moral and political standards.[17] Second, there may be times when items on the list actually conflict or are in tension with one another, as when policies listed in i) and ii) detract from the broad social change described in iii) and iv) or do not represent the best strategy for striving to meet and respect the values described in v). And finally, even if all five were potentially compatible, in a given case, I see reason to resist treating their combination as 'real' forgiveness: such a phenomenon would represent a difficult, almost impossible ideal, for those struggling through the messy, difficult and heart-wrenching business of reconciliation; impossible ideals can discourage and undermine moderate successes in peacemaking.[18]

Should the length and complexity of the list above lead us to dismiss the question of political forgiveness as incoherent or ill-formed? I think not, for the

17 For an excellent discussion of the appropriate moral and political standards, please see Murphy 2010.

18 I am grateful to Nir Eisikovits, another contributor to this volume, who brought this point home to me in his talk entitled "Truce!" at a focal conference on reconciliation, held at the Boston University Institute for Philosophy and Religion in March 2009.

following reason: there is power in the language of forgiveness, accrued from its legacy in many of the religious, cultural and literary discourses of the western world.[19] This power is potentially valuable and the functions I attributed to forgiveness – relief, release, and repair – are very much needed in the aftermath of political conflict. We have at least a prima facie reason to keep looking for a workable definition of political forgiveness, even if that definition turns out to be more pluralistic and particularistic than some would like. Once we accept that forgiveness is already a multidimensional set of overlapping acts and practices, the appropriate questions shift from "whether political forgiveness?" to "which act of political forgiveness, if any, is appropriate here and now?" We can focus on how these different acts and occasions of political forgiveness intersect, cause and react with one another, which (if any) are most politically valuable in a particular situation, and how we can best understand the political grounds for these acts of forgiveness and the conditions under which they are morally, as well as politically, appropriate.

I return to the potential moral and political values grounding political forgiveness in my conclusion. First, however, I take up the major objections to political forgiveness, and demonstrate how they can be answered.

4. FIRST OBJECTION: POLITICAL ACTORS CANNOT FORGIVE FOR VICTIMS

"No government can forgive... No commission can forgive... Only I can forgive. And I am not ready to forgive." – a South African woman reacting to the testimony of her husband's killer at a TRC hearing.[20]

This woman's testimony encapsulates much of what people find disquieting, even distasteful, about political applications of forgiveness. There is something alarming in imagining a situation where the choice to forgive is taken from victims, or they are unduly influenced. Such a situation offends against the elective character of forgiveness, the particularistic nature of the reasons we have to forgive or not forgive, and also, belies the respect we rightly assume is due to those who have suffered wrongful injury. Victims' forgiveness should not be politically mandated.

---

19 Of course, this legacy is sometimes as problematic as it is powerful. As I note elsewhere, the Christian overtones of forgiveness, in particular, and the association between Christianity and European global colonialism may give reason to avoid discourses of forgiveness in some post-colonial situations of reconciliation. Also, conflicting religious understandings of forgiveness may render it a contested topic in conflicts inflected by religious difference, such as Northern Ireland or the Middle East.

20 As recounted by Desmond Tutu and by Alex Boraine, Deputy Chair of the TRC. Cited in Ash, 1997: 36. Also cited in Gutmann and Thompson, 2000: 31 and Derrida, 2001: 43.

But acts and policies of political forgiveness, even as enacted by a government or political body, need not be mandated victims' forgiveness. In cases of serious, political wrongdoing, it is unlikely that the primary victim of wrongdoing was the only person harmed.[21] Furthermore, not all acts of forgiveness are victims' forgiveness, primary or other. As several philosophers have argued, not only are there plausible instances of secondary and tertiary victims' forgiveness, but under certain conditions the so-called victim's prerogative can legitimately be extended to relevantly connected third parties: those who have a prior relationship to the wrongdoing, and who are prepared to engage appropriately with the victim's experience.[22] These are not equivalent to the primary victim's forgiveness, but they may also play an important role in the aftermath of wrongdoing. In a society torn about by civil war, for example, it is likely that very many people will find themselves in at least a position of a secondary or tertiary victim, as well as of a relevantly connected third-party; sadly, there is no shortage of relevant connections to harm.

Nevertheless, the argument that forgiveness by a government or state falls neatly into third-party forgiveness is perhaps a little too quick. While third-party forgiveness does not, in theory, replace victim's forgiveness, there is a danger that the initiative to forgive, if taken by others, may feel like pre-emption to the victim. This danger is magnified exponentially when the others whose initiative it is to forgive act from positions of institutional authority and political power. Proponents of the South African TRC, for example, note that the commission's mandate was truth for amnesty on behalf of society, not forgiveness on behalf of victims; it offered the occasion for individual acts of victim's forgiveness, but did not compel or command them. However, in early hearings, Archbishop Desmond Tutu would sometimes ask victims if they were ready to forgive and reconcile after they had recounted their stories. A request from such a charismatic, morally authoritative figure, made in a public forum, may well have felt like pressure to conform to the wider political culture of forgiveness and reconciliation.[23] Similarly, the leaders of a particular group may accept the official apology of another group before all their constituents are prepared to put the wrongdoing in the past. In doing so, they may have the power, effectively, to put the question to rest before victims would like.

An institutional expression of forgiveness carries authority that other acts of third-party forgiveness may not. Not only is its voice more powerful than those of individual victims but also, in some cases, it has been elected to speak on their behalf. And it is simply true that sometimes the political leadership of a

21 For a discussion of primary, secondary and tertiary victims of wrong, see Govier and Verwoerd, 2002.

22 For discussions of third-party forgiveness, see MacLachlan 2008, Norlock 2009, Pettigrove 2009 and Radzick 2009.

23 See Haynor 2001: 156, Brudholm 2008: 30–31, and – especially – see Verdoolaege's discussion in this volume of the reconciliation discourse at the TRC.

particular group is prepared to forgive before all members of the group are prepared to do so – or to endorse the equivalent public action.[24] But of course this is not always a bad thing. Cultures of enmity and resentment can become so deeply entrenched that it appears impossible to imagine a resolution to longstanding social and political conflict. Political decisions to forgive – manifested as the cessation of hostility, promotion of better relations, or agreements to power-share, to hold truth hearings instead of trials, or to grant amnesty for moral-political reasons – may play an important role in shifting the broader culture. External researchers investigating the long-term effects of the TRC on particular South African townships noted, "it appears that for the most part the Commission has contributed to a greater commitment to the process of reconciliation."[25] Sometimes policies of forgiveness may be an extremely effective part of wider political peace making. While respect and reparation will always be important ways of honoring victims' experiences, assuming that in all cases policies of forgiveness must be postponed until each individual victim has done the same risks over-sanctifying the victims' position, at tremendous cost.

Finally, not all acts of political forgiveness are acts of third-party forgiveness. Gutmann and Thompson suggest: "crimes like those committed against apartheid are acts not only against particular victims but also against society and state. In addition to the victims of crimes having something to forgive, so do society and state."[26] Insofar as entire groups can be harmed by violence, injustice, and discrimination, their political leadership may have the appropriate standing to forgive as secondary or tertiary victims of wrong.

The relationship between government acts of forgiveness and individual victims' forgiveness is variable, and must be negotiated carefully. While the quotation with which I began this section expresses one victim's frustration at a politically negotiated process of forgiveness, a second quotation is cited nearly as often, expressing the need for exactly this process: "I am ready to forgive, but I need to know whom I have to forgive. If they would just speak up and acknowledge what they have done, they would be giving us the opportunity to forgive."[27] Insofar as some acts of forgiveness incorporate profoundly personal

---

24 Indeed, a political leader may be prepared to enact political forgiveness before he or she has *personally* met the criteria articulated by the Emotional Account (i.e. overcoming his or her own, individual resentment). I am indebted to Mathias Thaler for directing me to consider how public acts of apology or forgiveness, when given by figures who are privately ambivalent or resentful, may be instances of hypocrisy with 'civilizing force' described by Judith Shklar. For more discussion, see Shklar 1984, 45–86.

25 Taken from a report by Hugo van der Merwe, *The South African Truth and Reconciliation Commission and Community Reconciliation*, Johannesburg: Centre for the Study of Violence and Reconciliation, 1998. Cited in Haynor, 2001: 157.

26 Gutmann and Thompson, 2000: 30.

27 Cited in *The Report of the Chilean National Commission on Truth and Reconciliation*, Part Three, Chapter Four. Accessed Online at the United States Institute of Peace (www.usip.org/library/tc/doc/reports/chile/chile_1993_pt3_ch4.html).

changes of attitude and beliefs, it seems that these cannot be politically commanded, nor can a commission or a government perform them on behalf of an individual victim. Yet a political body can set the scene for individual acts of deeply emotional forgiveness, and can even promote it as part of a wider culture.

The extent to which such political efforts will be interpreted as forceful or coercive will depend on the sensitivity and wisdom of the policy in place. Furthermore, there are other plausible practices of forgiveness in which a government or political body appears perfectly able to participate on behalf of its constituents: issuing and accepting official apologies, making other public gestures of conciliation and contrition, welcoming estranged perpetrators back into civil society by re-establishing certain civil rights, for example, or waiving penalties for the appropriate reasons. Indeed, individual victims will never have the power to perform these acts. One final note regarding political forgiveness and victims' forgiveness: I have spoken of a political relationship between a powerful political body and its (presumably) less powerful citizens. The dangers of authority and coercion reduce when the parties in question are two groups of roughly equal power or two political actors; forgiveness could end a political feud, for example, or hostilities between two heads of state.

5. SECOND OBJECTION: POLITICAL FORGIVENESS IS ILLIBERAL

There is a second source of discomfort with political forgiveness, which once again arises from the intuition that forgiveness is personal and thus private, best kept between individuals.[28] Politics should not concern itself with the deep-seated sentiments and attitudes motivating the behavior of political actors; forgiveness involves a 'change of heart', and the state has no place in the hearts of its citizens. In other words, the second objection begins from the premise that forgiveness is always a matter of deep psychological attitudes, namely, the effort to overcome resentment and restore goodwill. In a liberal society, we cannot demand that citizens feel a certain way towards one another, so forgiveness is ruled out from the start.

28 Timothy Garton Ash warns that political forgiveness, as "reconciliation of all with all" is a deeply illiberal idea while Amy Gutmann and Dennis Thompson note that a certain degree of moral disagreement, and even animosity, is important to a flourishing democracy See Ash 1997: 37 and Gutmann and Thompson, 2000. Rich notions of forgiveness and reconciliation, they argue, deny the space for debate and accountability that is required for a healthy political society. Peter Digeser, 2001: 17, describes a fear of 'politics as soul-craft' as generating much of the skepticism surrounding political forgiveness.

Not surprisingly, this objection is very much geared toward the Emotional Model of forgiveness.[29] If one accepts the premise of the Emotional Model, then there are two possible responses to the claim that emotional work has no place in politics. The first is to bite the bullet, and reject the liberal premise of a political sphere free from thick moral and emotional demands. Mark Amstutz takes this approach, arguing for an explicitly communitarian account of political reconciliation.[30] Political forgiveness, as Amstutz sees it, resembles the change in attitudes and rich reconciliation described in iii) and iv) listed above.

The other possible response from within the framework of the Emotional Model, is to accept that standard notions of forgiveness cannot be applied politically, but to argue for a secondary, related account of specifically political forgiveness.[31] Peter Digeser does this, focusing only on the image of debt relief; in politics "to forgive means to release what is owed, either financially or morally" and so an act of political forgiveness "relieves what is due and is done for reasons".[32] In focusing on public commitments to release debt (moral or political), Digeser argues for what he calls an action-based rather than sentiment-based theory of political forgiveness. Yet Digeser discounts the role of attitudes and sentiments in the political realm perhaps a little too quickly; it is not clear that political acts of forgiveness always take place according to the model of debt relief. For example, sincere gestures of respect, contrition and acceptance can play an important 'face-saving' role, particularly in international relations. Here, the scene of forgiveness resembles a collective change of attitude or a symbolic effort to 'turn the other cheek' more than it does the release of what is due.

Viewing forgiveness according to the Emotional Model demands either that we choose between all or nothing: either we always appeal rich emotional attitudes and personal responses to explain an act of political forgiveness or we create a separate, restricted notion of political forgiveness that merely resembles its interpersonal cousin, excluding affective dimensions altogether. The former sits uneasily with liberals, and while the latter could account for policies of pardon, collective amnesty and – arguably – decisions not to retaliate violently against aggression, it cannot explain many political practices of truth-telling and reconciliation, institutional apologies and their acceptances, or more general political exhortations to forgive collectively. Thus, neither response is ultimately

29 Implicated are those theorists who argue, like Charles Griswold, that "forgiveness is necessarily connected to the sentiments" or who, like Murphy, comment that forgiveness is "a matter of how I *feel* about you, (not how I treat you)..." See Griswold 2007: 268 and Murphy 1988: 21. This is not to suggest that Griswold would disagree with the limit placed on political forgiveness. In fact, for this reason among others, Griswold argues that what he calls the scene of forgiveness does not have a place in political life.

30 Amstutz 2005: 225–227.

31 Griswold cites the political acts of pardon and debt relief as cases of non-paradigmatic or "imperfect" forgiveness: see Griswold 2008.

32 Digeser 2001: 4–20. The concept of remitting a debt is only one of six possible metaphors for forgiving: for a complete list, see footnote 9.

satisfying. Attitudes and subjective responses are a larger part of political life than Digeser gives them credit, but not all acts of political forgiveness require deep emotional change.

The core of the second objection – that, no matter what the potential benefit to social stability, compelling citizens to experience a change of heart is illiberal – is true. Governments or other political bodies may enact policies of forgiveness, but they cannot legislate the inner life of their citizens. Furthermore, given that even the promotion of certain attitudes and relationships (without sanctions or legal enforcement) may require a thick understanding of the common good, communitarians like Amstutz are far more likely to be comfortable with primarily affective accounts of political forgiveness than those with liberal leanings. But once forgiveness is conceived as a multidimensional set of practices rather than a unitary phenomenon, this is not a damning conclusion even for committed political liberals. While government policies may not be able to legislate anything resembling a collective 'change of heart', they can certainly wipe the slate clean so that wrongs are no longer held against the wrongdoers, either in public record or in terms of their legal standing as citizens. Government policies can also promote wider forgiveness without thereby demanding it as an obligation. Government policies of forgiveness might resemble mildly paternalistic safety or literacy initiatives, or educational efforts to change a broader social culture of discrimination; there need not always be legal coercion or political sanctions involved. Political forgiveness need not entail the harmonizing of all interests, attitudes and beliefs, but can merely serve to "[bring] matters into a framework within which conflicts can be adjudicated short of bloodshed."[33]

This second objection shares a moral intuition with the first: any effort to institutionalize forgiveness, in a particular body or through the political representatives of larger collectivities, ends up either taking something from individual victims (their prerogative to forgive) if they are not involved in the process of forgiveness, or demanding too much of them (their emotional commitments, for example), if they are. In both cases, the danger is that individual victims are not given due respect; that is, the state infringes on a properly personal matter. This issue is pragmatic as well as principled; if the percentage of the population victimized by past wrongdoings is resentful of a particular policy of forgiveness, larger efforts to promote social reconciliation may fail. Thus, peace advocates suggest that the distinction between constructive and destructive post-conflict forgiveness lies in negotiating some congruence between "sociopolitical public statements" and "psychological private readiness" to forgive. Public policies and statements of political forgiveness must remain

33 Elshtain, 2001: 41. So, for instance, it seems that Ash moves too quickly from a specific policy of forgiveness to the assumption that what is entailed, as an end result, is "harmony of all with all."

sensitive to the conditions of other members of the offended social or political group; political forgiveness can happen too soon or too late, and risk further conflict and casualties as a result.[34] In general, a successful (constructive) policy of forgiveness must be combined with more general policies of social justice and reparations to victims.[35]

6. THIRD OBJECTION: GROUPS CANNOT FORGIVE

The third objection to political forgiveness arises from its close association with collective forgiveness. Persons can forgive, but groups cannot; to argue otherwise, the claim goes, is to attribute too rich a notion of moral agency to political collectives. Govier deals with this claim at great length, noting that we have no trouble ascribing negative moral agency to groups: "many who speak without hesitation of groups hating each other, resenting each other, or seeking revenge against each other tend to become skeptical when they are told that groups might be characterized by more positive attitudes such as compassion, understanding, trust or forgiveness."[36] Since we regularly attribute many kinds of activity to groups qua agents, including rational deliberation, policy-making, decision, and even the ascription of certain attitudes, just how rich a notion of moral agency is necessary to forgive? To be forgiven?[37]

Certainly, groups of people can suffer from harm; wrongs done to groups of people can be collective or distributive. And while we may take pains to identify individual perpetrators and hold them accountable, there are some situations in which it is simply the case that entire groups have either participated in wrongdoing or passively acquiesced, while benefitting from the results. If groups can act to harm one another wrongfully, what is the resistance to groups forgiving? Once again, the answer can be found in part within the Emotional Model of forgiveness. We have less trouble imagining a large group electing to have their representatives waive certain claims or penalties, or even perform certain gestures or utterances, than we do imagining a group granting their representatives the power to overcome resentment, or to have a similar change of heart.

But this does not yet explain the asymmetry that Govier describes; why do we attribute negative and not positive attitudes to groups? In the case of forgiveness, the answer seems to lie in its elective nature, discussed above – the extent to which many decisions to forgive will be underdetermined by reasons.

34 Montiel 2000: 95.

35 Orr 2000: 239–249; Montiel 2000: 201.

36 Govier 2002: ix. See also her contribution to this volume.

37 Indeed, because Govier covers this issue so thoroughly – albeit from a slightly different understanding of forgiveness than the one I espouse – I do not go into substantial detail here. See Govier, in this volume.

The phenomenology of forgiveness is highly particularistic; insofar as reasons to forgive depend on particular, contextual, perceptions of the wrongdoer, the wrong, the wider situation and the potential moral value in any future relationship between victim and wrongdoer, the extent to which different individuals forgive – and the time in which they do it – will vary tremendously. Our hesitation over ascribing collective forgiveness is, I suspect, not so much a matter of rejecting collective attitudes in general, but difficulties imagining a collective readiness to forgive. More than with many attitudes, forgiving seems to be something that people (rightly) do at very different paces and for different reasons, and about which they have very different attitudes. But such variation, combined with a general reluctance to disrupt the victim's prerogative, makes it difficult to imagine how, in a large group, all the affected individuals could come to the decision to forgive without some level of coercion.

The intransigence of groups would be an insurmountable barrier to forgiveness, if all acts of forgiveness required a spontaneous, unanimous, and whole-hearted group decision. And given that such a happy event is unlikely, there are certainly limits to the kind of forgiveness we can ascribe to groups. Elshtain notes that political forgiveness always involves "the painful recognition of the limits to forgiveness, if what one seeks is full expiation, a full accounting, total justice, or a kind of annihilation of the past…this recognition is itself a central feature of an overall structure of political forgiveness."[38] Dissent and reluctance are often intractable features of group experience, even at the best of times; resentment, recalcitrance, and unwillingness to cease bearing grudges will often be a significant feature of any collective effort to put wrongdoing in the past. For this reason, I identified potential acts of political forgiveness not only in terms of individual policies or events, but also in longer processes of social change and struggle. The multidimensional account is a broad, 'lowest common denominator' approach to forgiveness; not only the best, most whole-hearted acts of forgiveness are counted as such, but also painful, reluctant, and resistant efforts to do the same.[39] It is an unfortunate truth that political forgiveness may see more examples of the latter than the former.

7. FOURTH OBJECTION: ACTS OF POLITICAL FORGIVENESS LACK APPROPRIATE REASONS

I have described forgiveness as a *personal* reaction to wrongful harm, described the reasons we have to forgive as particularistic, contextual and even relational, and argued that the prerogative to forgive is ultimately grounded in our ability

38 Elshtain 2001: 44.

39 I borrow the term 'lowest common denominator' forgiveness from Glen Pettigrove, 2004, who cites Iris Murdoch.

to take the wrongdoing personally. While I argued above that all interpersonal relationships should neither be seen as identical to one another nor necessarily apolitical, it seems intuitively true that our political relationships are more formalized and distant (both affectively and physically) than most interpersonal relationships. We see family, friends, colleagues – and even the stranger who confronts us – face to face, while many political relationships are conducted through representatives and media. Given this rather sustained emphasis on the personal qualities of forgiveness, can political forgiveness ever get off the ground? Perhaps politics and political relationships alone cannot generate sufficient reasons to forgive. Political policies may resemble acts of forgiveness in all other ways, but if they lack this necessary property then they ought not to be described as such.

In part, any answer to this objection will depend on how we understand political relationships. In the section following this one, I consider a theory of political relations that might generate acceptable grounds for political forgiveness: Hannah Arendt's account of political action.[40] I turn to Arendt for several reasons. First, she is among the first political philosophers to take seriously the idea that forgiveness is a legitimate part of the political sphere, and thus the conception of politics she envisions is of particular interest to those of us who want to defend her claim. Second, Arendt writes during the period when responsibility for political crimes and repair of historically damaged political relationships was beginning to the forefront of international relations, from the Nuremburg trials to transitions away from former colonial rule. Arendt is unstinting in her concern for those without political rights or their precondition – what she calls "the right to have rights" – and for victims of political violence. Thus, she concerns herself with exactly the kinds of political relationships in which forgiveness comes into question. Furthermore, her normative account of political speech and action resonates with much of what I have described as the *work* of forgiveness. For Arendt, action and speech become political when they reveal the agent who speaks or acts (and thus, represent a risk to that agent), when they create or contribute to a new political narrative (i.e. an authoritative public record) and when they forge some new political relationship. Finally, Arendt represents a kind of puzzle for philosophers of forgiveness: she advocates its application to politics even as she resists any effort to import moral norms or affective, emotional standards into the political sphere. Given the difficulties inherent in applying a primarily Emotional Model of forgiveness to political situations, it is hardly surprising that Arendt has become an appealing authority for those considering forgiveness in political life.

---

40 For a far more detailed and thoughtful discussion of Arendt on forgiveness, please see Guisan in this volume. I am convinced by Guisan's argument that Arendtian forgiveness, in itself, is insufficient for political reconciliation: understanding and promises are also required. However I do not have space to consider that relationship here.

But before turning to Arendt and her account of political action, I first consider the objection itself. I have argued that we are able to forgive insofar as we have good reason to take the wrongdoing personally, and furthermore, we forgive *well* if we forgive when we have good reasons to do so. There is no reason to think either of these conditions is impossible in a political context. The frequency of ethnic and political conflict suggests that many people take the wrongs associated with their collective identities and political affiliations very personally indeed. In situations of political occupation, civil war or ideological conflict, individuals will commit themselves to a political cause with a fervor and determination that they reserve for little else, even sacrificing their lives. Moreover, the stories that emerge in the aftermath of political oppression or violence are often very personal. Molly Andrews recounts how in the weeks following the release of the "Stasi" files and under the auspices of the East German Truth Commission, opponents of the regime were horrified to learn how their colleagues, neighbors and friends had spied on them.[41] We have no trouble recognizing ways in which these *conflicts* can be personal; it seems strange to insist that their resolution cannot be equally personal.

Indeed, this final claim resembles the claim that collectivities cannot experience positive attitudes of trust and compassion. Our skepticism is skewed toward constructive, positive gestures; we tend not to doubt the reality or the sincerity of their negative, destructive counterparts. But political actors, public figures, and spokespeople for institutions of authority can have reason to take wrongs personally (and thus, a prerogative to forgive) from a number of different positions: as secondary or tertiary victims, as relevantly connected third parties, as the sincere, committed, elected representatives of the same, or – in some cases – as these and *also* as primary victims of wrongdoing.[42]

Of course, it could be argued that while political figures can take things personally, they cannot do so in their roles as political figures. In the latter role, they are not acting as individual persons, but on behalf of institutions, collectives, states etc. Attempts to personalize these roles risk distorting and corrupting their proper, impersonal function. One critique, lodged at acts of public apology as well as public acts of forgiveness, is that when political actors make public displays that are meant to be personal, they engage in an insincere display of 'crocodile tears' or 'trembling lips' that imports inappropriate tropes from personal life. We can trust interpersonal displays of emotion – in seeking or granting forgiveness, for example – because they are a reliable gauge for

41 Andrews 1999, 110.

42 For example, Nelson Mandela suffered personally under the apartheid regime and, following his release, he was able to forgive his jailors as a primary victim, then speak on behalf of South African black communities who suffered under apartheid, etc. Mandela is perhaps a rare example, as his multiple prerogatives to forgive are almost overwhelming, but many political leaders will stand in at least some personal relationship to the political harms that have faced their people.

determining an individual's commitment to change her behavior, alter her attitudes, and otherwise shift her stance. But inasmuch as political decision-making is not an individual affair, whatever attitudes and feelings a political figure has regarding a particular political decision or policy do not play the same determining role as they would in her personal life.[43] Instead, public 'personal' displays are, at best, a distraction from the real political work to be done and, at worst, a strategic ploy for 'cheap grace' or an easy exit strategy.

This would perhaps be a troublesome consideration, if it were the case that public acts of forgiveness always amounted to public displays of emotion, that is, if political forgiveness is conceived along the lines of the Emotional Model. But while ceremonies and gestures of remembrance and reconciliation may play a role in a larger process of political forgiveness, and while these may include tearful gestures and utterances by the parties involved, political forgiveness usually goes beyond public ceremony – and we can account for this within the terms of the multidimensional account.

Moreover, it is perhaps a mistake to dismiss the potential sincerity of such ceremonies, simply because the close causal connection between emotion and motivation we rely on in our interpersonal relationships is not available. Public gestures of forgiveness can mark measurable commitments to future behavior (providing *release* or *release* from past injustices), can initiate just and compassionate decisions of policy, and, especially, can represent an authoritative change to the public record. Truth Commissions find their primary purpose in the need to uncover atrocities of the past; the earliest truth commissions in Chile and Argentina had a specific mandate to investigate the disappearance of political activists and opponents of previous regimes. Donald Shriver comments, "to have your story of unjust suffering entered into a public record and thence into future history-writing is to experience an increment of justice."[44] In other words, personal acts and statements in the public realm are not without reliable standards altogether, but their evaluation will be slightly different from that of private utterances: we assess them as acts of disclosure, as efforts to take risks on behalf of a potential greater good (peace-making), their contributions to public record, and their ability to issue new commitments and – in particular – to initiate new and just political relationships (*repair*).[45]

---

43 Other reasons cited for distrusting expressions of sorrow and remorse include the ability of political figures to compartmentalize between their own lives and their political work. Robert McNamara spoke of this ability at great length in the documentary about his role in the Vietnam War, *The Fog of War*, describing the need to leave decisions of state behind when returning home. Moreover, decisions made in the context of a particular role may affect our self-understanding less than decisions we make in our personal life – it is easier to blame the burdens of office, or the constraints of an institution, and we may be less willing to incorporate them into a robust sense of our own agency.

44 Shriver 2001, 37.

45 Interestingly, these standards of evaluation conform to what Arendt describes as properly political action: an act is political insofar as it reveals something about the doer (self-

Are there *reasons* to forgive available to political figures that are at once politically appropriate and appropriate to forgiveness? The kinds of reasons to which a potential forgiver might appeal include the nature/extent of the harm and the wrongdoer's intentions, the victim's suffering and ongoing vulnerability, the wrongdoer's subsequent behavior and the victim's assessment of how forgiveness might affect it, their pre-existing relationship and the victim's desire for future reconciliation or closure. I see no good reason why political analogues of these reasons cannot manifest themselves in public life: the desire for future reconciliation or closure seems particularly compelling reasons in political cases, when the costs of wrongdoing are so high, as does the victim's assessment of her (or their) vulnerability and the wrongdoer's likely reactions.

Yet, an opponent of political forgiveness might argue, the point is not that we lack *good* reasons to forgive in political life, but that our good reasons to forgive are somehow fatally compromised by the other kind of reasoning that takes place in politics; after all, political decisions are almost always strategic. They appeal to necessity, advantage, negotiation, power and control. Even the decision to release (moral or legal) power over the wrongdoer, in the form of a release from retaliation of penalty, is always – ultimately – a calculation of interests and agendas. Indeed, the desire for political reconciliation is also a kind of calculation. Nelson Mandela admitted that "without these enemies of ours, we can never bring about a peaceful transformation to this country."[46] This was not a vague or metaphorical realization: the former apartheid regime had only agreed to hand over power on the condition of some kind of amnesty. Political reconciliations thus lack the voluntary, unconstrained quality of interpersonal reunions – or at least, interpersonal reunions at their best.[47] Or so, the final case presented against political forgiveness might go.

8. POLITICAL GROUNDS FOR FORGIVENESS: AN ARENDTIAN ACCOUNT

In fact, the fourth objection reveals yet another danger inherent in sharply dividing forgiveness into mutually exclusive categories of 'interpersonal' and 'political:' our notions of interpersonal forgiveness are all too easily idealized, and treated with undue reverence. Here, the multidimensional account – focusing as it does on actual, everyday practices of forgiveness – is particularly

disclosure), is courageous (self-risk), produces meaningful narrative (contributes to public record) and initiates new relationships (1958, 236–244).

46 Cited in Shriver 2001, 33.

47 Here, again, I see evidence of a tendency to idealize the interpersonal at the expense of the political. Many interpersonal reconciliations take place because of the need to co-exist in shared households, neighbourhoods, or workplaces – or because the animosity is too costly for third parties, or because of other interests and commitments.

helpful. In all walks of life and in any type of relationship we forgive for a multiplicity of reasons, and these reasons include assessments of our own needs, our expectations of remorse and reform by the wrongdoer – or the overriding desire for harmony or peace of mind. We can forgive for self-pertaining reasons, we can forgive reluctantly and over a long period of time, and we can forgive in better or worse ways. While individual practices of forgiveness may not include formal calculations of public relations, material reparations and strategic security initiatives, we are capable of taking into account our vulnerability, safety and our various needs, in deciding whether to forgive, without hopelessly 'tainting' the act itself so that its characteristic 'work' of relief, release or repair is no longer recognizable. Praiseworthy acts of forgiveness express important social values of trust and compassion, may alleviate the suffering of all concerned, and may produce better states of affairs, but none of these consequences relies on a pure, disinterested act of spontaneous generosity, without reason. In other words, the idealized contrast used to ignite skepticism about political forgiveness is itself a misrepresentation of actual interpersonal forgiving practices.

Perhaps the skepticism surrounding political forgiveness simply reflects deeper skepticism about the moral possibilities of the political sphere: somehow, forgiveness is always necessarily too much to expect from politics and, if astonishing acts of political forgiveness appear too good to be true, then they probably are. Certainly, the first wave of enthusiasm over the groundbreaking approach of the South African Truth and Reconciliation Commission was followed quickly by a barrage of criticism, much of which rightly noted the South African government's failure to compensate and acknowledge victims appropriately, the remaining civil tensions and social violence across the country, and so on. While our personal relationships may involve conflicts of interest, selfishness and other calculation, these are balanced by richer relationships of concern and mutual goodwill. In politics, one might argue, the relevant political relationship is not substantial enough to generate the kind of thoughtful, contextual reasoning necessary to identify truly compelling reasons to forgive.[48] The quotation from Arendt at the beginning of the chapter goes on to cite as the reason for forgiveness' absence from the public realm, that is its close connection with the intimate and what she calls apolitical relation of love.[49] Forgiveness cannot be political because our political relationships cannot sustain it.

Is there a political analogue for the kind of love that Arendt believes grounds interpersonal acts of forgiveness? Arendt characterizes forgiveness as one of two essentially *political* faculties; along with our ability to make and keep promises to others, our ability to forgive and be forgiven grounds our political will to "live

48 Recall, for instance, that the second scenario in which forgiveness might properly be called *political* is when the wrongdoer and victim have no relationship beyond a minimal, political one. Scenes of political forgiveness can be identified by the *lack* of prior relationship between those involved.

49 Arendt 1958, 243.

together with others in the mode of acting and speaking."[50] That is, forgiveness grounds the ability to enter into and sustain political societies.[51] For Arendt, forgiveness is not only possible in the political realm; it is actually essential. Given a plurality of free but mutually dependent individuals, conflicts, competitions and confusions – what Arendt calls 'trespassing' – are inevitable. Thus, Arendt acknowledges that relationships conducted politically will occasionally fall short of what we might want and expect from other people, morally speaking. But, she argues, efforts to import private morality into the political realm will either fail, or distort the importantly free and plural nature of political action and will, in the worst instances, lead to political tyranny and violence. For the most part, politics and morality cannot be reconciled in Arendt's eyes.[52] In other words, Arendt is sympathetic to the skepticism about political morality I described above. But – significantly – she sees forgiveness as an exception to this general injunction against political morality: "[morality] has, at least politically speaking, no more to support itself than the good will to counter the enormous risks of action by readiness to forgive and to be forgiven, to make promises and to keep them."[53] Unlike most ethical mandates, Arendt claims, forgiveness actually depends on plurality: that is, on a multiplicity of agents with conflicting interests and wills, all sharing a public space.

What exactly does Arendt mean by forgiveness? Her account differs from more recent philosophical discussions in that she pays little, if any, attention to the emotional dimension of forgiving. Indeed, her very willingness to acknowledge forgiveness as political indicates her resistance to anything resembling the Emotional Model. Arendt has little time for moral sentiments in politics; she claims that sentiments like pity – while virtuous in the private sphere – become vices in politics.[54] Rather than a matter of emotional change, therefore, Arendt describes the act of forgiveness as a 'release' or a 'dismissal,' noting that "without being forgiven, released from the consequences of what we have done, our capacity to act would, as it were, be confined to one single deed from which we could never recover."[55] Forgiveness 'undoes' those acts whose consequences have bound us – either as the doer or as the sufferer of the deed – and from which we wish to escape. Indeed, Arendt suggests that forgiveness bears the same relation to action as destruction does to creation.[56] In other words, Arendt's conception of forgiveness resembles the metaphors of relief from burden and

---

50 Guisan discusses these two political faculties alongside our capacity for *understanding*. See Guisan, in this volume.

51 Ibid, 246.

52 For a longer discussion of the relationship between politics and morality in Arendt, please see Williams 1998; MacLachlan 2006.

53 Arendt 1958, 243.

54 Arendt 1963, 84.

55 Arendt 1958, 237–8.

56 Ibid, 238.

remission from debt; forgiveness frees us, and fixes the wrong in the past so that its consequences are politically 'undone.'

Clearly acts of forgiveness, however magnanimous, have no supernatural or counterfactual abilities. They cannot literally undo the events of the past. Neither does Arendt imagine forgiveness to be an act of historical amnesia, in which past traumas are covered over and ignored completely. While she describes forgiveness as the opposite of vengeance, she also calls it an alternative to punishment, "but by no means its opposite."[57] Both forgiveness and punishment have the same function, Arendt argues: to put an end to cycles of violent reaction. But if forgiveness is relevantly like punishment, it cannot forsake responsibility and accountability for the past – this would defy the purpose of retributive punishment altogether. Nor would an amnesiac response be in keeping with Arendt's respect for narrative and shared history.[58] So the 'release' that Arendt takes forgiveness to offer is not relief from the very fact of our actions, nor is it relief from our accountability for them. Instead, an act of forgiveness is an act that prevents the past from continuing to wholly determine the present (as it would in an ongoing cycle of revenge and retaliation) and which thus returns us to a condition of relative freedom (a condition for the possibility of politics, in Arendt's eyes).

In forgiving, Arendt claims, "*what* was done is forgiven for the sake of *who* did it."[59] Forgiveness allows us to assume identities beyond the restrictive 'victim' and 'wrongdoer' identities created by the original (wrongful) act. In a political context, where both sides may see themselves as 'victim' and the other as 'wrongdoer,' such identities may freeze debate in an endless litany of wrongs done on each side. Forgiving does not mean that the deed vanishes from public memory, however this new, revelatory act shifts its original meaning. Just as an apology by the wrongdoer can change the initial significance of a wrongdoing, in the eyes of the victim, so too can forgiveness by the injured party alter the relationship between the two. As Andrew Schaap explains, Arendtian readiness to forgive displays a willingness to re-enter the sphere of political debate with former enemies and combatants, forsaking the apolitical methods of vengeance and violence.[60] Forgiveness returns the actor and the act to the shared political realm. It does not signal an end or final reconciliation, therefore, but – like all Arendtian political action – a new beginning.[61]

---

57 Ibid, 241.

58 She cites the creation of meaningful narrative as the only appropriate product of political action.

59 Ibid, 241.

60 Schaap 2005, 75–78.

61 "Forgiving...tries the seemingly impossible, to undo what has been done, and succeeds in making a new beginning where everything seemed to have come to an end." Arendt 1994, 308.

In other words, what Arendt refers to as acts of forgiveness are the renewals of trust required to sustain a political space of verbal and not violent disputes. They are grounded in our ongoing commitment to political society as well as our respect for those who are our co-participants in it and, as a result, our willingness to trust them enough to enter into a space of political action. Arendt describes the appropriate relation of political respect as something akin to Aristotle's *philia politike* (political friendship) and also as analogous to love in the private sphere; just as appropriate private relationships express love, so too do appropriate political relationships express respect.[62] Since it concerns our personhood as speaking and acting beings, such respect is sufficient ground – Arendt believes – to forgive others when necessary, and it sits alonside the presumable awareness that we, ourselves, will eventually need forgiveness in turn and the trust that it too will be offered.[63] A culture of mutual political respect is also a method of sustaining the *personal* aspect of the political; Govier acknowledges Arendt's insight that so long as "public life does not become completely depersonalized and maintains a basis for respectful relations…we can make sense of forgiveness in public life."[64] Respect, defined here as the willingness, however grudgingly, to continue to share an intersubjective political world together, can legitimately ground political acts of forgiveness. As a reason grounding decisions to forgive, Arendtian respect lies somewhere between realist determinations of sheer necessity and the demand that forgiveness not take into account any need to negotiate co-existence, that it be somehow 'purified' of any political consideration.

Admittedly, Arendt's conception of politics is itself highly agonistic. Political citizens live with one another, but not necessarily for one another and will, in fact, strive to distinguish themselves against others (in both word and deed). Therefore forgiveness cannot represent political closure; total harmony would mean the end of politics, and the ongoing commitment to politics is what grounds and motivates political forgiveness in the first place. In other words, the political sphere cannot, and perhaps ought not, achieve the same kind of close reconciliation that some acts of interpersonal forgiveness may – though they certainly need not – initiate. Acts of political forgiveness release us just enough to be able to move forward, together. The *meaning* of the wrong is fixed in the past, so that it no longer continues to determine and dominate the present in cycles of violence.

---

62 Arendt 1958, 243.

63 Of course this respect, and the forgiveness it engenders, is not an all-encompassing solution to political violence. Arendtian commentator Michael Janover (2005) comments that while "respect…may be a possible grounding for forgiveness in political situations of conflict… we stand in greatest need of the circuit-breaker of forgiveness when the ground of respect itself has been shattered by intra-communal violence and hatred" (230) – the difficulty is that such respect may have vanished just when forgiveness is most needed.

64 Govier 2002, 80. Digeser also acknowledges Arendt in his account of political forgiveness.

The relative merit of acts of forgiveness depends, in part, on their relationship to and expression of other important moral values: moderation and restraint in retaliation, trust, compassion, the alleviation of suffering, moral sensitivity and self-reflection. Particularly important in a political context are trust and the moderation of anger and revenge. Arendtian forgiveness-as-release certainly contributes to a political culture of greater trust, insofar as it attends to public records and official history, new political beginnings, willingness to live with one another. Charles Villa-Vincencio, national director of research for the South African TRC concluded, regarding the potential limitations of the Commission's mandate, "it is important that we all treat one another in the best possible manner – that even if we are not fully reconciled to one another, we do not kill one another."[65] In other words, the regeneration of trust is a gradual, relative matter. Political forgiveness may represent the beginning of such a restoration, rather than its conclusion.

According to the Emotional Model, concessions like this cannot be genuine forgiveness, because they fall short of its expressed goal: the eradication of all resentment and angry feeling, and the restoration of goodwill. But this is a deeply problematic political goal and, if we are honest, often an unrealistic personal one. In accepting that we forgive to various degrees of reconciliation and restoration, and that our forgiveness is compatible with a certain degree of ambivalence, recalcitrance, and anxiety, the multidimensional account generates an understanding of political forgiveness that is at least amenable to liberal concerns of dissent, free expression, and autonomy. Insofar as we understand that forgiveness, in any realm, is not immune from considerations of interest, security and calculation, the possibility of political negotiation and strategy entering into political decisions to forgive does not prevent us from recognizing them as both politically and morally valuable. Furthermore, an account of mutual political respect, like Arendt's, explains how political relationships can be sufficiently 'personal' to ground and motivate decisions to forgive.

9. CONCLUSION

The multidimensional account offers a workable definition of political forgiveness that sits within the same framework as discussions of forgiveness in everyday life. The standard objections to political forgiveness – that it violates the victim's prerogative, that it is essentially illiberal, that we cannot make sense of forgiveness between groups – either do not apply to the multidimensional approach, or are left as cautions to policy-makers, and not conceptual obstacles. There is nothing in the concept of forgiveness, understood as a determinate range of moral practices, which prevents its cautious application to political conflicts.

65 Elshtain 2001, 51.

In fact, considering forgiveness in social-political contexts reveals that any sharp distinction between 'political' and 'personal' acts of forgiveness is perhaps more problematic than is ordinarily recognized. Failing to acknowledge the extent to which our interpersonal conflicts are politicized risks idealizing interpersonal forgiveness as a spontaneous, unmeasured act of utterly disinterested generosity, even while caricaturing political forgiveness: either as a radically illiberal effort to impose emotional states on large groups of people or as a cynical calculation of power. This caricature not only fails to be faithful to the multiple meanings of forgiveness, but also ignores many ways in which political leaders, institutions, and even collectivities, *are* capable of assuming the role of forgiver: in individual acts and ceremonies, in policy choices, in the values governing widespread policy, and the social consequences of political change. If the political sphere retains the common respect Arendt describes, and at least some minimal will to continue to share political institutions, forgiveness is potentially both a politically legitimate and a morally valuable option for political reconstruction and renewal.

REFERENCES

Amstutz, M. R. (2005). *The Healing of Nations. The promise and limits of political forgiveness*. Lanham, MD: Rowman & Littlefield.

Anderson, R. (1997). Non-obligatory forgiveness: Supererogatory or Impermissible? *Auslegung* 22 (1), 39–47.

Andrews, M. (1999). Truth-Telling, Justice and Forgiveness: A Study of East Germany's "Truth Commission". *International Journal of Politics, Culture and Society* 13 (1), 107–124.

Arendt, H. (1958). *The Human Condition*. 2nd edition ed. Chicago: University of Chicago Press.

— (1963). *On revolution*. New York,: Viking Press.

— (1994). *Essays in understanding, 1930–1954*. Edited by J. Kohn. New York: Harcourt Brace & Co.

Ash, T. G. (1997). True Confessions. *New York Review of Books*, July 17, 36–37.

Derrida, J. (2001). *On cosmopolitanism and forgiveness*. New York: Routledge.

Digeser, P. (2001). *Political forgiveness*. Ithaca, N.Y.: Cornell University Press.

Elshtain, J. B. (2001). Politics and Forgiveness. In: *Burying the Past*, edited by N. Biggar. Washington: Georgetown University Press.

Govier, T. (2002). *Forgiveness and Revenge*. New York: Routledge.

Griswold, C. L. (2005). *Forgiving the Unforgivable*, Boston University Institute for Philosophy and Religion.

— (2007). *Forgiveness: A Philosophical Exploration*. Cambridge: Cambridge University Press.

Gutmann, A. and D. Thompson (2000). The Moral Foundations of Truth Commissions. In *Truth v. Justice: The Morality of Truth Commissions*, edited by R. I. Rotberg and D. Thompson. Princeton: University of Princeton Press.

Haynor, P. B. (2001). *Unspeakable Truths: Facing the Challenge of Truth Commissions.* New York: Routledge.

Janover, M. (2005). The Limits of Forgiveness and the Ends of Politics. *Journal of Intercultural Studies* 26 (3), 221–235.

Jaspers, K. (2000). *The Question of German Guilt.* New York: Fordham University Press.

Kraybill, D. B., S. M. Nolt and D. L. Weaver-Zerche (2007). *Amish Grace: How Forgiveness Transcended Tragedy.* New York: Wiley and Sons.

Lamb, S. (2002). Women, Abuse and Forgiveness: A Special Case. In *Before Forgiving: Cautionary Views of Forgiveness in Psychotherapy*, edited by S. Lamb and J. G. Murphy. Oxford: Oxford University Press.

MacLachlan, A. (2006). An Ethic of Plurality: Reconciling Politics and Morality in Hannah Arendt. In *History and Judgment*, edited by A. MacLachlan and I. Torsen. Vienna: IWM Junior Visiting Fellows' Conferences.

— (2008). Forgiveness and Moral Solidarity. In *Forgiveness: Probing the Boundaries*, e-book [978-1-904710-62-2]. Oxford: Inter-Disciplinary Press.

— (2009). Practicing Imperfect Forgiveness. In *Feminist Ethics and Social and Political Philosophy: Theorizing the Non-Ideal*, edited by Lisa Tessman. New York: Springer.

Minow, M. (1998). *Between vengeance and forgiveness: facing history after genocide and mass violence.* Boston: Beacon Press.

Montiel, C. J. (2000). Constructive and Destructive Post-Conflict Forgiveness. *Peace Review* 12 (1), 95–101.

Moon, C. (2004). Prelapsarian State: Forgiveness and Reconciliation in Transitional Justice. *International Journal for the Semiotics of Law* 17, 185–197.

Murphy, C. (2010). *A Moral Theory of Political Reconciliation.* New York: Cambridge University Press.

Murphy, J. G., and J. Hampton (1988). *Forgiveness and Mercy.* Cambridge: Cambridge University Press.

Norlock, K. (2009). *Forgiveness from a Feminist Perspective.* Lanham: Lexington Books.

Orr, W. (2000). Reparation Delayed is Healing Retarded. In *Looking Back, Reaching Forward: Reflections on the Truth and Reconciliation Commission of South Africa*, edited by C. Villa-Vicencio and W. Verwoerd. Cape Town: University of Cape Town Press.

Pettigrove, G. A. (2004). The Forgiveness We Speak: The Illocutionary Force of Forgiving. *Southern Journal of Philosophy* 42(3), 371–392.

— (2009). The Standing to Forgive. *Monist* 92(4), 583–603.

Radzik, L. (2009). Moral Bystanders and the Virtue of Forgiveness. Paper presented at Forgiveness: Probing the Boundaries (Second Global Conference), Salzburg, Austria.

Renteln, A. D. (2008). Apologies: A Cross-Cultural Analysis. in *The Age of Apology: Facing Up to the Past.* Edited by Mark Gibney, Rhoda E. Howard-Hassmann, Jean-MarcCoicaud and Niklaus Steiner. Philadelphia: University of Pennsylvania Press.

Ricoeur, P. (2004). *Memory, History and Forgetting.* Translated by K. Blamey. Chicago: University of Chicago Press.

Rigby, A. (2001). *Justice and Reconciliation: After the Violence.* Boulder: Lynne Rienner.
Schaap, A. (2005). Forgiveness, Reconciliation and Transitional Justice. In *Hannah Arendt and International Relations*, edited by A. F. Lang and J. Williams. New York: Palgrave MacMillan.
Shklar, J. (1984). *Ordinary Vices.* Cambridge: Harvard University Press.
Shriver, D. W. (1995). *An ethic for enemies: forgiveness in politics.* New York: Oxford University Press.
— 2001. Where and When in Political Life is Justice Served by Forgiveness? In *Burying the Past*, edited by N. Biggar. Washington: Georgetown University Press.
Tavuchis, N. (1990). *Mea Culpa: A Sociology of Apology and Reconciliation.* Stanford: Stanford University Press.
Torpey, J. (2001). Making Whole what has been Smashed: Reflections on Reparations. *The Journal of Modern History* 73, 333–358.
Villa-Vicencio, C., and W. Verwoerd (2000). *Looking Back, Reaching Forward: Reflections on the Truth and Reconciliation Commission of South Africa.* Cape Town: University of Cape Town Press.
Williams, G. (1998). Love and Responsibility: A Political Ethic for Hannah Arendt. *Political Studies* 46 (5), 937–950.

FORGETTING, REMEMBERING, FORGIVING, AND THE MUNDANE LEGAL ORDER

Wouter VERAART

1. INTRODUCTION*

What is the function of law, or, more precisely, legal institutions, in response to historic injustice? A period of injustice and violence can be followed by an urge to forget what has happened or indeed specifically to remember it or alternatively to seek reconciliation and forgiveness. Sometimes the legal system takes it upon itself to forget, to remember or to forgive.

This article is based on the assumption that collective processes of forgetting, remembering and forgiving are related to societal efforts of structuring time in response to historic injustice. In the figure of remembering, the past is "relived", whereas in the figure of forgetting the present is (temporarily) disconnected from its relationship with the past. In the figure of forgiving the relationship with the past is released, while the future is being anticipated.

Although these three collective figures, with their respective strong points and weaknesses, continue to play their roles as markers of historic changes, it will be argued that the specific role of legal institutions is primarily of a mundane, workaday nature. Legal institutions are well-equipped to keep some distance from the collective urges to forget, to forgive or to remember. On the one hand these bodies have to ensure that historical injustice is not ignored, while on the other hand they need to be able to take binding decisions on such injustice that will bring conflicts of the past to legal closure and will be accepted by those involved. By allowing people access to legal action, providing finite answers to injustice, a system of law can help counteract the possibility of historic injustice creating permanent victimhood.

This article is structured as follows. Firstly the relationship between the legal order and the collective duties to forget or to remember the past is discussed in

* This article is part of the research project "Time, Restitution and the Law", for which a Veni grant has been awarded by the Netherlands Organisation for Scientific Research (NWO).

sections 2 to 4. Secondly I examine the relationship between law and the collective duty to forgive in sections 5.1 to 5.4. The conclusion follows in section 6.

2. A COLLECTIVE DUTY TO FORGET

Do we actually have a legal duty to forget? For a long time I associated a duty to forget with the attempts at falsifying history that totalitarian states in particular are so good at.[1] That was before I discovered that liberal, secular societies such as the Netherlands also started out from a basis of legal texts containing wording that imposed a duty of forgetting. These texts – mainly treaties – brought an end in law to the wars of religion that had caused such torment to Europe in the sixteenth and seventeenth centuries. At the same time, however, they also marked the start of a new constitutional order in Europe, in which the separation of church and state, and the model of the state as the guardian of individual liberties, became more and more manifest. A good example of this phenomenon can be found in one of the articles of the Edict of Nantes of 1598. This Edict, which was issued by Henry IV of France, sought to bring the bloody civil war between French Catholics and Huguenots (Calvinist Protestants) to an end by allowing freedom of conscience and the freedom to practise religion. However, provisions such as this were standard at the time and can also be found in the peace treaties that brought an end to other wars of religion, such as the 1648 Treaty of Westphalia, which ended the Thirty Years' War, and the related Treaty of Münster, which was also signed in 1648 and brought the Eighty Years' War to an end.[2] And this practice continued in Europe until well into the eighteenth century.[3]

---

1 See Todorov 1995: pp. 9–12; Rév 2005: pp. 5–6.

2 See Lesaffer & Broers 2007: p. 40; Biehler 1994, pp. 131–133.

3 In his classic work *Le Droit des Gens ou Principes de la Loi Naturelle* the Swiss legal philosopher M. de Vattel refers to the amnesia clause in peace treaties as standard practice between states. See Vattel 1758, p. 266 (Vol. II, bk. IV, ch. II, § 20 and § 21): "L'*Amnistie* est un oubli parfait du passé; et comme la Paix est destinée à mettre à néant tous les sujets de discorde, ce doit être là le premier Article du Traité. C'est aussi à quoi on ne manque pas aujourd'hui. Mais quand le Traité n'en diroit pas un mot, l'*Amnistie* y est nécessairement comprise, par la nature même de la Paix.
Chacune des Puissances qui se font la guerre prétendant être fondée en justice, et ne pouvant juger de cette prétention [...]; l'état où les choses se trouvent, au moment du Traité, doit passer pour légitime, et si l'on veut y apporter du changement, il faut que le Traité en fasse une mention expresse. Par conséquent, toutes les choses, dont le Traité ne dit rien, doivent demeurer dans l'état où elles se trouvent lors de sa conclusion. C'est aussi une conséquence de l'*Amnistie* promise. Tous les dommages causés pendant la guerre, sont pareillement mis en oubli; et l'on n'a aucune action pour ceux, dont la réparation n'est pas stipulée dans le Traité: Ils sont regardés comme non-avenus."

The provision I am referring to can be found in the first article of the Edict of Nantes and [translated] reads as follows:

> "First, that the recollection of everything done by one party or the other, between the beginning of March 1585 and our accession to the crown, and during all the preceding period of troubles, remain obliterated and forgotten, as if no such things had ever happened."[4]

"As if no such things had ever happened." That was how Catholics and Huguenots were expected from then onwards to deal in public with the terrible events of the past. Normality had to be re-established by starting with a clean slate. And the second article of the Edict goes on to confirm this by instructing citizens to live together peacefully as "brothers, friends and fellow countrymen" and in no way to seek to renew the memory of or start new disputes about past events. Anyone trying to re-open the past would be punished as a disturber of the public peace.

By imposing this collective loss of memory the French king was able to adopt a completely neutral position and to act as if nothing had happened. In other words, he did not have to say that one party was right or to decide on who was the moral winner of the religious conflict, and this helped to create a basis for introducing freedom of conscience and freedom of religious belief. The logical result of this compulsory public amnesia was a collective amnesty[5] for all those who had committed acts of violence and crimes against other people or other people's property. From a civil law perspective, any damage caused remained as it was because it is difficult to hold someone liable for something that, as far as the law is concerned, never took place.[6]

It is hard for me now, in 2011, to accept the first two articles in the Edict of Nantes. There is something particularly dangerous in any legal attempt to selectively wipe the memories of a whole society as this leads to a loss of identity. How can people ever manage to come to terms with traumatic experiences if what they experienced is made taboo and publicly considered not to have existed? How can a society learn from that?[7]

---

4 The original text, which can be found on <elec.enc.sorbonne.fr/editsdepacification/>, is as follows: "Premierement, que la memoire de toutes choses passées d'une part et d'autre, depuis le commencement du mois de mars mil cinq cens quatre vingtz cinq jusques à nostre avenement à la couronne, et durant les autres troubles preceddens et à l'occasion d'iceulx, demourera estaincte et assoupie, comme de chose non advenue."

5 The word 'amnesty' comes from *amnèstia*, the Greek word for oblivion.

6 The second sentence of the first article, the actual amnesty provision, prohibits legal action (public or private) on matters that should be forgotten, with some substantial exceptions to this rule in the subsequent articles. See Margolf 1996, p. 401: "Many of the edict's subsequent articles *both reinforced and undermined* this stated policy of obliterating or ignoring the conflicts of the later sixteenth century." Emphasis WV.

7 See Ricoeur 2006: pp. 454–456.

On the other hand, however, agreeing to bury the hatchet ('forget it all ever happened') seems to a certain extent to be unavoidable if you want to move from a state of war to a state of peace, based on tolerance.[8] There is also a link between the strong need to forget and let the past go and the mundane, workaday base underlying the system of law. In other words, the need to create a basic framework of conditions allowing people to live in a peaceful, pluralist society now and also offering them assurance for the future. The system of law also intervenes in all sorts of ways to prevent us continually allowing 'old sores' to guide the operation of law because otherwise society would become intolerable. I am thinking in this respect of concepts such as immunity from prosecution because of the passage of time, the principle of *ne bis in idem*,[9] the binding nature of court decisions[10] and the principle of *lites finiri oportet*, whereby legal disputes cannot go on for ever. The need to let the past rest and bygones be bygones is obviously far stronger in the period immediately after a civil war.

3. A COLLECTIVE DUTY TO REMEMBER

It was in the twentieth century that the turnaround in views came. The horrors of the two world wars were simply too great to forget. Whereas tolerance and individual freedoms were once based on a legal duty to forget the past, the preamble to the Universal Declaration of Human Rights of 1948 specifically refers to "barbarous acts which have outraged the conscience of mankind." This was a clear reference to the horrors of the Second World War, and specifically the Holocaust. The shocked "conscience of mankind" is used here as a way of justifying the proclamation of universal human rights. Here, the foundations on which these human rights are based – in other words, a world community of states offering individuals peace, dignity and freedoms – are linked to memories of what happened in the past. In the West, Auschwitz has served in the post-war period as what has been referred to as a "negative myth of origin of the modern age."[11] In other words, values such as tolerance, freedom and equality find their origins today in the memory of the negative, traumatic experience of Auschwitz (as a symbol of the greatest evil). The legal prohibition of Holocaust denial is in

8 According to E. Renan in his famous *Qu'est-ce qu'une nation* lecture of 1883 (see Renan 1887, pp. 284–285): "L'oubli, et je dirai même l'erreur historique, sont un facteur essentiel de la création d'une nation, et c'est ainsi que le progrès des études historiques est souvent pour la nationalité un danger. L'investigation historique, en effet, remet en lumière les faits qui se sont passés à l'origine de toutes les formations politiques, même de celles dont les conséquences ont été les plus bien-faisantes. L'unité se fait toujours brutalement (.)."

9 This is the principle whereby a person cannot be tried or punished twice for the same crime.

10 For the finality of court decisions, see also Van Klink 2010, pp. 67–68.

11 See Margalit & Motzkin 1996, pp. 80–81. By calling the Holocaust a myth they do not mean that it did not take place, but that (p. 80) "it serves a mythic function in society."

turn the mirror image of the duty to forget (and, therefore, to deny) the past as contained in the first article of the Edict of Nantes of 1598.

Whereas the Edict of Nantes tries to bury, with some exceptions, the possibility of any form of persecution or condemnation for past wrongdoings under the legal duty to forget events of the past[12], it is our remembering of the past that makes it most difficult to achieve *legal closure* in the widest sense of the word. It is because of the belief that law must always remain available to deal with perpetrators of the ultimate evil that genocide, crimes against humanity and war crimes cannot in international law be barred by the passage of time.[13] In recent decades, there have also been calls for a more flexible approach to statutes of limitation in civil law, specifically in situations involving injustice relating to the Holocaust. Sometimes people have gone a step further and claimed that post-war court rulings and settlements relating to injustices of this nature should be reviewed if the decisions prove to be unfavourable to the victims from a perspective of current-day morality. Lastly, there is the phenomenon of claims relating to historic injustices (as seen, for example, in class actions in the United States), which have assumed a life of their own and are no longer bound by any temporal or spatial limits in law.[14]

Accepting a duty not to forget the past, but to remember and commemorate it, opens the way, both for victims and for society as a whole, to come to terms with historical injustice, in what Ricoeur referred to as a *travail de mémoire*.[15] Here, too, just as in the case of the duty to forget, the duty to remember also calls on a function of a mundane, workaday system of law. Tribunals judging those accused of war crimes, and also the special procedures that allow victims to seek legal rehabilitation or compensation for what was taken from them or done to them during the period of injustice, are both grafted on to the normal procedures for independent courts, which have to treat people fairly and equally and can hear witnesses. This is because the system of law is not designed only to bring conflicts to an end, but also to establish what happened in the past.[16]

At the same time, *unlimited* litigation in cases of historical injustice places heavy demands on a mundane system of law, particularly if the nature and extent of the claims are such that honouring them would affect the social fabric of the society or give rise to new injustice. The passage of time, and particularly changes in circumstances, can also create additional problems when we attempt to resolve historical injustices through the legal system.[17] If the binding force of court

12 The edict did not proclaim *complete* oblivion, neither legally, nor socially: see Margolf 1996, p. 401.
13 For an illustration of this view, see Jankélévitch 1986. See also Ricoeur 2006, pp. 472–473.
14 For critical views, see Garapon 2008, pp. 255–262; McInnes 2009, pp. 133–136.
15 See Ricoeur 2006, p. 456.
16 For a discussion of the complex relationship between legal and historical truth, see Winkel 1994, pp. 20–25.
17 For an analysis of this problem in a South African context, see Veraart 2009, pp. 45–60.

decisions or settlements is no longer accepted and claims keep on coming back time and time again, a situation can arise in which it is impossible to deal with what happened in the past in an objective and disinterested way. And a 'compensation claim culture', dominated by looking back at the past, is also something I have mixed feelings about.[18]

4. EARTHLY JUSTICE AND THEOLOGICAL MOTIVES

Let me try to summarise. Our liberal, secular state, going back to the Early Modern era, was founded on the basis of a legal duty to forget the past. The turnaround came in the twentieth century: since the two world wars it has been specifically the memory of the greatest evil committed in the past that has created the foundations for a society based on tolerance and individual liberty.

There is something rather contrived in the way that both concepts – that of forgetting and that of remembering – are reflected in law. Are remembering and forgetting not typical phenomena of everyday life that the law has no hold on (and on which it also should not seek to have any hold)? As the Dutch author Cees Nooteboom famously said, "Memory is a dog that lies where it pleases." In the same vein, the philosopher Avishai Margalit writes that "We cannot be morally or ethically praised for remembering, or blamed for failing to remember, if memory is not under our control. [..] Remembering and forgetting may, after all, not be proper subjects for moral or ethical decrees and evaluations."[19]

What I learned from the Marc de Wilde's excellent doctoral thesis on political theology in the work of Carl Schmitt and Walter Benjamin is that the concepts of remembrance and forgetting, as they are applied in their legal forms, refer to theological motives. According to De Wilde, the legal duty to forget can be seen [translated] as "the ideal order-creating moment – the moment at which lawlessness is averted by the sovereign."[20] In averting lawlessness, the sovereign – according, for example, to the controversial constitutional lawyer Carl Schmitt – takes on the role of the historical force that, in Christian theology, has to oppose the appearing of the anti-Christ and the start of the end of time.[21]

De Wilde also sees a theological motive in the concept of remembrance. The left-wing intellectual Walter Benjamin, for example, believes that it is important

---

18 For an overview of the 'politics of war trauma' in Europe, in the aftermath of World War II, see Mooij & Withuis, 2010, pp. 327–331.

19 See Margalit 2002, p. 56. Our memory is also highly unreliable. According to French, Garry & Loftus 2009, p. 48, "Contrary to popular belief, memory tends to decay over time, forgetting the past is normal."

20 See De Wilde 2008, p. 122.

21 See De Wilde 2008, pp. 106–107.

(and here I quote De Wilde [translated]) "consciously to drag past violence out of oblivion [...] so as to bring the 'claims' of previous generations back to life and to submit the current order to radical discussion."[22]

The critical issue for Benjamin is that by recalling memories of past injustice, we can enforce claims today that can have a radical impact on the existing legal order. Benjamin, too, attributes a theological significance to the act of remembering. For him, according to De Wilde, the concept of remembrance has a "weak Messianic power", where by rekindling the past – so as to seek, in the present, to remedy an injustice from that past – we can gain a glimpse of another order. In other words, that of eternity, when mankind will be redeemed and where true justice will prevail because justice will then be done to each individual moment.[23] The concept of remembrance, as it is reflected in law, can also, therefore, be linked to theological concepts.

What these theological images show is that the legal concepts of forgetting and remembrance each draw strength from references to forms of justice that are ultimately not of this world (transcendent). This also explains why these concepts, when they appear in their radical form in a mundane, workaday system of law, can create the problems that I briefly referred to earlier.

When we are forced by law to publicly forget, as in the case of the Edict of Nantes, or when law accepts violence or injustice by pretending in essence that it never happened, we are getting close to creating fiction. In such situations, the law, acting in the name of a higher justice (in other words, seeking to create a sovereign order to avert catastrophe), consciously ignores the facts, as if waving a magic wand to make them disappear. However, any attempt to break with the past by denying that it ever happened is doomed to fail. People can certainly make a new start time and time again, but they never make this new start with a clean slate.[24]

It is ultimately useless trying to maintain the legal fiction that the past did not happen. Reality is far more stubborn and persistent. Although the Edict of Nantes did manage for some decades to maintain the peace that it set out to achieve, in the end the Huguenots once again had many of their rights taken from them. And in 1685 the Edict of Nantes was formally revoked. Once again, it became illegal to be a Protestant and, as a result, huge numbers of Huguenots fled France and went to countries such as the Netherlands. A single legal document is not enough to create a pluralist society based on a value such as tolerance. Instead, such a society is shaped by trial and error within its social reality.

22 See De Wilde 2008, pp. 123.

23 See De Wilde 2008, pp. 123, 169.

24 Hannah Arendt's concept of 'natality', understood as the human being's ability to start afresh in order to create something new out of the old, is relevant in this context. See Arendt 1969, p. 82.

On the other hand, however, we come up against all sorts of other problems if we make remembrance of past injustice our absolute guiding principle in law. Being called on not to forget past injustices, but to keep them alive and constantly to seek to enforce claims arising from them, including those of previous generations, can potentially result in court decisions being subject to review time and time again because they can never be sufficiently just. This is a matter of principle: earthly forms of justice (court rulings and settlements, for example) are incapable of putting right the indescribable and incomprehensible acts of injustice committed in the past, and specifically in the twentieth century. For those who demand the highest form of justice, earthly forms of justice (with their periods of limitation, statutory limitations and limited opportunities for appeal, and the fact that those taking the decisions are human) are more of a hindrance than the start of a solution. And that means having to come to terms with the paradox that claimants continue demanding justice within the existing systems of law, but at the same time reject the binding force of the court decisions that these systems produce.[25]

Both the concept of forgetting and that of remembrance mark the start of a new era after a period of injustice and violence. If we look at it from its most positive angle, the concept of forgetting can symbolise focusing on the present, letting go of the past and deciding to bury the hatchet. The concept of remembrance on the other hand enables us to see the founding values of a new constitutional order that is being created as a clear and specific response to violence and injustice of the past and to acknowledge what has happened in the past. Remembering and commemorating, and having the opportunity to bear witness to the past, all help society to arrive at a point where it can establish the truth, come to terms with what has happened and provide compensation and satisfaction, both from a legal perspective and in other ways. The South African Truth and Reconciliation Committee is obviously the most well-known example of an alternative approach.[26]

In my view, the concepts of forgetting and remembering can best be seen as two sides of a dynamic process, where one (the concept of forgetting) stands for those moments when we leave the past behind us, and the other (the concept of remembrance) enables us to keep on looking back at the past from our position in the present.[27] In that way, the thoughts I outline here can be seen as a warning against blocking either of the two routes – even though the urge to opt for one or the other of them tends to be very strong after a period of great injustice. The system of law should never be allowed to prevent people going back to the past (or, as we put it today, the 'right to know'), but similarly should not allow us to cling to the past to such an extent that people are effectively prevented from

25 See Garapon 2008, p. 257.
26 See the following section.
27 See Ricoeur 2006, p. 504.

making a fresh start.[28] In both cases, there is a danger of creating permanent victimhood, which will be passed on from generation to generation: in the one case because the system of law structurally refuses to acknowledge that people have suffered, and in the other case because the system of law is never able to do enough to satisfy victims.

5. A COLLECTIVE DUTY TO FORGIVE

5.1. BACK TO DAMHOUDER

So far I have tried to show that forgetting and remembering both have their role to play in the foundation of a mundane legal order. I have also argued that the role that law can play in dealing with past injustices is by necessity limited and imperfect. The legal system is dependent on the general acceptance of the binding force of its court decisions and settlements.

If there is some scope within law for remembering and forgetting, is there not also a place for forgiving? There are similarities. Forgiving, just as remembering and forgetting, is a concept that relates to theological motives.[29] As we know from European legal history, the connection between a religious (Christian) practice of forgiving and a mundane system of law is firmly entrenched in the canon law tradition, as shown in the following provision from *De regulis iuris* of the *Liber Sextus* (1298 AD): "Sin shall not be forgiven, unless that which was taken away will be returned."[30] This principle of law demonstrates that earthly justice takes precedence. *Firstly* there needs to be legal restitution (of the property that has been looted or otherwise taken), and only *subsequently* is forgiveness possible.

In the history of criminal law, there is also a clear connection between forgiveness and legal practice. Legal forms of punishment imposed from the late Middle Ages right up into the Early Modern era cannot simply be seen as acts of public vengeance, as opposed to acts of forgiveness. On the contrary, the strongly ritualized legal procedure leading to capital punishment was carefully staged as a process in which confession, penance and forgiveness each had their successive roles to play and gave a deeper significance to the enforcement of the punishment.[31]

An elaborate example of this phenomenon can be found in the Latin version of a famous textbook on criminal law in the southern Netherlands, *Praxis Rerum*

---

28 See Waldron 2002, pp. 157–158.
29 See Margalit 2002, pp. 184–200.
30 Translation of "Peccatum non dimittitur, nisi restituatur ablatum", *Corpus Iuris Canonici 1881*, col. 1122.
31 See Van Caenegem 1954, pp. 19–20.

Criminalium, by the Flemish jurist Joost de Damhouder (first published in 1555). In chapter 150 Damhouder states the following in respect of the confession of crimes:[32]

> "In this, however, the [various local practices] are similar, in that they elevate the convict whose corporeal life they are going to take away, to spiritual life, that they bring about penitence, atonement for committed crimes and hope of forgiveness."[33]

The day before the execution, the condemned person was led to a clergyman who heard his confession and had to convince him that his punishment was in fact a blessing in disguise:

> "[The father confessor] has to convince the patient that it is the work of the highest divine charity that he has come in the grasp and power of justice, while God has not permitted that he would die in a fight or in some other sudden disaster; but that God has organized his salvation in such manner, that he, by this – only temporary – confusion, sorrow, and pain *will return to the heart* and that punishment will open the eyes of his mind which were before closed by his guilt, and in this way he will stimulate the patient to thank God from the bottom of his heart for such a great benefaction."[34]

In the same spirit the father confessor later accompanies the 'patient', as Damhouder refers to the condemned person in his Dutch works, to the scene of the execution:

> "Arrived at the scene, he has to encourage the patient to ask almighty God's forgiveness in the best tone of voice he can produce, for those he has hurt in their possessions or in their body, irrespective of their presence or absence, and finally to ask for Justice itself [i.e. the execution]. Let him, thereupon, beg for the prayers and support of the bystanders, and subsequently prepare himself for death, reciting the Lord's Prayer, the Ave Maria and the profession of faith. And after he has invoked the Holy Virgin, his guardian angel and all saints, he will commend his soul to God saying the words: "In your hands, Lord, I commend my spirit", or "Lord Jesus, accept my spirit." And in order to sweeten and facilitate the process, they put an image or a small statue of the crucified Christ in his hands, and they constantly remind him of

32 I am very grateful to Dr. J.B.M. van Hoek, who brought these fragments to my attention and whose working translations I have to a large extent used.

33 Damhouder 1562, p. 424: "In hoc autem pene omnes conveniunt, ut reum, quem sua vita corporali privabunt, eundem ad vitam spiritalem promoveant, & ad resipiscentiam & ad commissorum poenitentiam & in spem veniae erigant." Translation: JvH/WV.

34 Damhouder 1562, p. 424: "Persuadeatque illi opus esse summae misericordiae divinae quod in manus & potestatem iustititiae devenerit: & non permiserit Deus illum vel pugna vel alio quovis subitaneo perire periculo: hocque modo Deum habuisse rationem salutis ipsius ut hac scilicet temporali confusione, tristitia, & dolore, *rediret ad cor*, mentisque oculos aperiret poena quos prius culpa cluserat unde & illum moneat ut pro tanto beneficio Deo ex corde gratias agat." Italics: WV. Translation: JvH/WV.

> the bitter and extremely humiliating suffering of this Christ, while trying to prepare the soul that is going to migrate for a state of glory and to gain it for Christ, in this way, that they will not leave the patient before he has paid with his life by being subjected to the death penalty."[35]

What is especially interesting in this sixteenth-century account of criminal justice is that the well-known, particularly gruesome practice of a public execution of a convict derives its contemporary meaning and coherence from an underlying account of confession, penance, and forgiveness. It is not simply a matter of retribution, but of a 'return to the heart', or, to put it in more modern terms, the releasing of the 'patient' from his sins[36] and their consequences and the reforming of him into a person capable of better.[37]

The importance attached by the community went further than concern for the well-being of the individual convict's soul. The 'return to the heart', as referred to above, referred not only to an internal transformation of the convict (in other words, a return to sense and reflection), but also – and primarily – a return to the heart of the community, the Church as the mystical body of Christ.[38] Danielle Celermajer explained in a recent study how a sinner's return to the heart of the community was needed in order to reconstitute this community, which derived its unity and reason for existence from its normative orientation:

> "[R]epentance was not simply about bringing the individual back into the community, but *reconstituting the community itself*, because the community only existed as God's body by virtue of the fidelity of the individuals who composed and affirmed it."[39]

---

35 Damhouder 1562, p. 425: "[...] ubi cum venerit admoneat eum ut meliori qua possit voce roget Deo omnipotenti veniam, illis quos laesit in re vel in corpore, sive praesentes sint, sive absentes, denique Iustitie ipsi, nec pudeat illum hoc facere, quia caedet ei in maximam satisfactionis partem. Deinde imploret preces & suffragia astantium: quo facto paret se ad mortem, recitando orationem Dominicam cum salutatione Angelica, & fidei symbolo: & invocata Diva virgine, Angelo custode, & sanctis omnibus, commendet animam suam Deo dicens: In manus tuas Domine commendo spiritum meum. Vel Domine Iesu accipe spiritum meum. Quae omnia ut faciat foelicius ac facilius imaginem aut statua parvam Christi crucifixi ipsius manibus inserunt, & ad eiusdem Christi acerbam, atque ignominiosam passionem assidue erigunt & ad foelicem statum animam emigraturam praeparare, & Christo lucrifacere contendunt, adeo ut ipsum reum non deserant prius, quam mortis supplicium vita persolverit." Translation: JvH/WV.

36 See Ricoeur 2006, p. 459.

37 See Verwoerd 2007, p. 142.

38 With thanks to Van Hoek for this clarification. See also Celermajer 2009, pp. 114, 117 and 120.

39 Celermajer 2009, p. 117. [Italics: WV]. Interestingly, Celermajer demonstrates that the Christian practice of repentance has over the centuries increasingly (and not only as a result of the Reformation) been 'privatised'. See also Weber 2009, pp. 102–103. This aspect is not discussed in this article.

Just like the duty to forget, the primary concern, in a theological sense, in the duty to repent and beg for forgiveness – as highlighted in the above practice of criminal law – was to restore the unity (broken by sin) of the community, in which the relationship with God ultimately had its foundations.[40] The belief that the very health and well-being of the community was at stake explains why the gallows, which is where the greatest sinners were executed, have featured so prominently in matters of repentance and forgiveness over the centuries and why proceedings at the gallows have been accompanied by so many rituals; it was precisely at moments such as these that the community needed to emerge chastened (and not battered) from the exactitudes of the ceremony.

5.2. FORGIVENESS AND TRANSITIONAL JUSTICE

The Early Modern example of forgiveness being based in practice on penal law and having a highly religious element consequently shows two things. Firstly that punishment and forgiveness do not have to be mutually exclusive, while secondly that forgiveness need not be limited to individuals in relation to other individuals, but can also have a significance for the community as a whole. In respect of the first element, current discussions on the place of forgiveness as a possible response to historic injustice are often compared with reactions such as revenge,[41] anger or rage[42] or retributive justice.[43] Although most authors do not exclude the possibility of forgiveness *in the wake of* legal expressions of retributive justice, they tend to present it as a process in which victims are invited not only to forgive their wrongdoers, but also to accept that these wrongdoers will usually go largely unpunished. Forgiveness, in these present-day accounts, is a phenomenon closer to the legal concept of amnesty than to retribution as a legal form of punishment. Martha Minow, for example, writes that

> "[…] in practice, forgiveness often produces exemption from punishment. Especially when a governmental body adopts a forgiving attitude towards offenders, the

40 Celermajer 2009, p. 117: "[T]he relationship with God was grounded in the constitution of the Church as the Community of God. If we assume a hard conceptual or ontological distinction between the abstract transcendence of the divine and the materiality and mundane character of the ecclesial community, we will miss this inter-penetration. […] [T]he existence of the community and its normative orientation are not two separate moments, where the community exists first and then it acquires a normative character. Rather, the church was constituted as a distinct community only insofar as it is the ethical orientation of actual people."

41 See Minow 1998.

42 See Brudholm 2008.

43 See Verwoerd 2007.

> instrument often takes the form of amnesty and pardon, pre-empting prosecution and punishment."[44]

Conceptually, however, forgiveness is much closer to remembering than to forgetting: in order to be able to forgive, we need to know what has happened and who is morally accountable for it.[45] In this way, forgiveness is closer to law that has run its course – ideally in the form, for example, of court decisions in which past wrongs are legally acknowledged and settled and in which a perpetrator is punished and compensation awarded – than to a situation in which justice is pre-empted or even withheld in advance, as happens when a general amnesty, which is akin to legal forgetting, is announced?[46]

In the specific context of post-apartheid South Africa, however, amnesty and amnesia cannot be equated. On the contrary, it was specifically the process of truth-finding by the Amnesty Committee of the Truth and Reconciliation Commission that encouraged the collective process of reconciliation. Wilhelm Verwoerd, for example, points out that accountability, as a key principle of justice, was not sacrificed within the proceedings of the Amnesty Committee since, in order to apply for amnesty, perpetrators were required to make full disclosure of their crimes.[47] The opportunities for reconciliation and forgiveness were enhanced by the public acknowledgement of past wrongs by particular perpetrators[48], not by the granting of amnesty that generally followed.[49]

In current accounts of forgiveness, especially in a context of transitional justice, forgiveness is most often understood in a practical, secular sense. Whereas in previous centuries in Europe, as discussed earlier, the primary purpose of forgiveness was to heal the soul, with a view to the hereafter, and to reconfirm the community as the Church of God, these days forgiveness is often

44 Minow 1998, p. 15.

45 See Wolterstorff 2008, pp. 105–106.

46 Although this obviously does not exclude forgiveness, it makes it more difficult in practice, particularly in cases in which perpetrators and victims come across each other on a daily basis and the possibility of new violence cannot be excluded.

47 See Verwoerd 2007, p. 17. In the same context, see Ost 1999, p. 147. The Constitutional Court of South Africa also made this unambiguously clear in its ruling in the *Azapo* case (*The Azanian Peoples Organization (Azapo) and others* v. *The President of the Republic of South Africa and others*, South Africa Constitutional Court, 27 July 1996, Judgment Mahomed DP, section 32): "*The amnesty contemplated is not a blanket amnesty against criminal prosecution for all and sundry, granted automatically as a uniform act of compulsory statutory amnesia.* It is specifically authorised for the purposes of effecting a constructive transition towards a democratic legal order. It is available only where there is a full disclosure of all facts to the Amnesty Committee and where it is clear that the particular transgression was perpetrated during the prescribed period and with a political objective committed in the course of the conflicts of the past." Italics: WV.

48 They are not actually required to show regret or remorse.

49 The amnesty regulations were the result of political negotiations that allowed apartheid to be brought to an end. Generous amnesty provisions were a precondition for the white regime, which otherwise would not have cooperated to achieve peaceful transition.

of a secular and highly individualised nature, where the emphasis is no longer on the hereafter, but instead on a new beginning in this (mortal) life. The concept has become individualised because forgiveness is often seen as a private matter for the individual victim in his relationship with the individual perpetrator, and which is in principle of no concern to the community.

Both aspects can be seen in the way in which Wilhelm Verwoerd enumerates five central elements occurring within any instance of 'forgiveness' and which focus primarily on the position of the victim:

> "(a) the *affective* element of overcoming of negative feelings toward the perpetrator; (b) the *releasing* element of giving up the moral claim against the perpetrator as a result of his or her wrongdoing; (c) the *reframing* element of conceptualizing the perpetrator as a person capable of better; (d) the *ethical* element of reasserting moral values; and (e) the *temporal* element of locating of the wrongdoing in the past."[50]

Sometimes, victims are encouraged to forgive only for therapeutical reasons, specifically when the perpetrators deny past wrongs and are reluctant to cooperate in any way. This can be seen in 'unilateral' or 'invitational' forgiveness, where victims forgive perpetrators, possibly in the hope that the perpetrators will in future acknowledge their past wrongs and may then offer their apologies.[51]

On a more fundamental level, however, forgiveness is still conceived of as a complex process that aspires to release victims *and* perpetrators from the grip of a violent past. For victims because they are invited to leave their negative feelings towards the perpetrators behind them, and for perpetrators because they are given the opportunity to ask victims for forgiveness, to accept their forgiveness and ultimately also to forgive themselves, and thus to see themselves as a person capable of better. Once released from the hold that the past has on them, victims and perpetrators can then enter a new era in their lives, albeit no longer with a clean sheet.

In its aspiration to 'overcome' the past, to locate the past in the past and to enable both victims and perpetrators to make a new start as transformed human beings, forgiveness also cannot be seen completely free of its religious origins. In relation to historic injustice, forgiveness is marked not only by a desire for a variant of transcendence[52] in a worldly form (in other words, transforming the victims and perpetrators in order to prepare them for a new beginning), but also by the belief that forgiveness contributes in this way to the *constitution* of a

50 Verwoerd 2007, p. 142.

51 See Verwoerd 2007, p. 168. See also Govier elsewhere in this volume.

52 What has become known as the 'epilogue' of the South African Interim Constitution of 1993 makes explicit reference to the 'transcending' of past injustice: "[...] The adoption of this [1993] Constitution lays secure foundation for the people of South Africa to *transcend* the divisions and strife of the past [...]."[Italics: WV].

society that primarily sees itself as a community of values in which the same recognition is available to *everyone*. And that is precisely why the phenomenon of forgiveness (alongside remembering and forgetting) is also attractive to a nation struggling with a legacy of extreme injustice and searching for transformation and a new beginning.[53]

5.3. TUTU AND HIS CRITICS

In post-apartheid South Africa it has been above all Desmond Tutu, as chairman of the Truth and Reconciliation Committee and as a highly respected clergyman, who has championed the spirit of forgiveness as a major force for overcoming the feelings of anger and revenge associated with the unjust past.

The Danish researcher Thomas Brudholm criticized Tutu in a recent analysis of the latter's comments on anger and forgiveness. Brudholm has little time for Tutu's praise of forgiveness and his consistent rejection of negative feelings such as resentment and anger. According to Brudholm, negative feelings such as sustained anger can also constitute a healthy response to injustice and demand full respect. As Brudholm sees it, Tutu fails to appreciate this because he has a naïve view of the world:

> "[...] the problem lies with Tutu's highly positive evaluation of an apolitical and amoral notion of frictionless social harmony. We live in a social and historical reality where intentional wrongdoing is part of the game. One may agree with Tutu that resentment does, indeed, disrupt 'social harmony', but disagree with his absolute appreciation of this harmony."[54]

Brudholm's criticism centres on the view that Tutu's dream of a frictionless society is not of this world. Brudholm's view is that we will never live in a society without conflict, and so need the freedom to be angry and to refuse to forgive someone: feelings of anger can also be a virtue in certain circumstances. But is Brudholm's criticism of Tutu fair? What exactly is wrong with Tutu's dream of a South Africa that is able to come to terms with its legacy of historic injustice? Tutu's appeal for forgiveness would seem primarily designed to offer the hope of a 'new' South Africa, which has to establish its unity and cohesion on the basis of certain fundamental values that have been constitutionally anchored in the South African constitution of 1996. The preamble to this constitution, which starts "We, the people of South Africa", deals in one fell swoop with the issue of acknowledging past injustice, honouring those who have suffered for justice and

---

53 For the complex relationship between the individual and the collective in this context, see Augé 2001, pp. 79–81; Celermajer 2009, p. 223 ff.

54 Brudholm 2008, p. 48.

freedom, *and* expresses the belief that South Africa belong to *all* those who live there, unified in their diversity.

> "We, the people of South Africa",

as it states later on in the preamble,

> "[...] heal the divisions of the past and establish a society based on democratic values, social justice and fundamental human rights."

With this promise to 'heal' the divisions of the past as the basis for a society unified in diversity around a number of shared values, the South African constitution circumvents both the duty to forget the past, as seen earlier in the Edict of Nantes, and the Western world's post-Auschwitz commandment to remember. The norm of tolerance does not refer solely to the present – as in Nantes in 1598, where the past was suppressed – or primarily to the past – as in the case of Western Europe in the decades since the Second World War. Here, the norm looks primarily to the future in the promise to overcome past injustice, while also continuing to recognise and acknowledge it.[55] And it is only within the paradigm of forgiveness, in which the *dissolution* of the obligations tying us to the past is the central issue and not *fulfilment* of those obligations,[56] that we can live up to that promise.[57]

In light of this analysis Brudholm's criticism of Tutu no longer seems justified. By calling on people to forgive each other Tutu seems not to be seeking a world

55 Sometimes forgiving is reduced to forgetting, as, for example, in Ellian 2003, pp. 626–627 [translated]: "What do we do if we forgive? We intentionally forget what the particular person has done to us [...]." This view is sterile. Not only because, as we have seen earlier, it is humanly impossible 'intentionally' to forget something, but primarily because forgiving does not automatically imply forgetting, and vice versa, and so the two cannot be deemed equivalent. A process of forgiveness specifically seeks to make it *possible* for someone to go back to the past, along the route of remembering, to that specific injustice from the past, but without feelings of anger or revenge towards those who caused that past injustice. Although South African society is admittedly focused on reconciliation and forgiveness of the political injustice and violence of the apartheid era, it is not seeking to erase that injustice, as the impressive Apartheid Museum in Johannesburg so clearly demonstrates.

56 For an in-depth discussion, see Ost 1999, p. 113 ff.

57 It is interesting that these three ways in which a community can relate to a historical injustice have parallels with three traditional figures of structuring and managing time that Marc Augé encountered in many African rituals. Augé distinguishes between three concepts. Firstly the concept of the 'return' (cf. remembrance), in which the past is relived, while the present is forgotten in, for example, the case of a person temporarily 'possessed' by the spirit of an ancestor. Secondly the figure of 'suspension' (cf. forgetting), in which the present is temporarily disconnected from its relationship with the past and the future; this is a phase in which various social role inversions can occur as, for example, at carnival time. And lastly there is the figure of 're-beginning' (cf. forgiveness), in which the relationship with the past is let go and the future is anticipated by creating new relationships in the form of rituals. The best known example of this is the initiation rite. See Augé 2001, pp. 75–79.

entirely free of conflict nor to be seeking to put an end to feelings of anger and rage. What he is seeking to create is a society able to come to terms with past injustice. This explains why he has so persistently and tirelessly emphasised the need to focus on forgiveness. It would be no exaggeration to state that the South African constitution tacitly assumes that the mindset of all South Africans is one of forgiveness towards the past, just as the Edict of Nantes was based on the principle of forgetting the past and the foundations of the Universal Declaration of Human Rights on a call to remember it.

The fact that Tutu's rhetoric and enthusiasm have a clear Christian component – and one that is recognisable to everyone – forms another possible ground for objection. The type of forgiveness that Tutu is pleading for is clearly, however, of a completely open nature and can equally well be associated with other religions,[58] as well as with non-religious philosophies and local and native traditions. In South Africa, the call on people to forgive has been clearly associated, including by Tutu himself, with the African concept of *ubuntu*, which bases itself on the idea of a deep interconnectedness between human beings.[59]

Purists attaching great importance to the principle of the separation of church and state may continue to object to the prominent role of the Anglican archbishop Tutu in the South African process of reconciliation. The answer to this view is that it may well be impossible for a country to reinvent itself after so many decades of injustice without using all the resources (whether religious or otherwise) available to the society on a day-to-day basis.

A more pertinent criticism of Tutu's praise of forgiveness is that members of the Truth and Reconciliation Committee (TRC) sometimes went too far in their endeavours to encourage victims to forgive their wrongdoers.[60] Some victims felt they were put under excessive pressure to forgive and felt angry about this afterwards. Here we come up against the problem mentioned earlier in respect of the duty either to forget or to remember the past. The collective interest in reconciliation and in being able to forgive each other can sometimes be so great that it can become a blanket that is rolled out across the population and from which individuals, depending on the circumstances, can hardly escape.

As mentioned earlier in respect of forgetting and remembering, forgiveness obviously cannot be legally enforced. Any process of forgiveness should be based on voluntary participation because forgiveness, in all directions, both for victims and perpetrators, is a personal and often complex and difficult process, of uncertain duration and with an uncertain outcome.

---

58 South Africa is predominantly Christian. For a discussion of repentance and forgiveness in Judaism, see Celermajer 2009, pp. 65–107; for a discussion of repentance and forgiveness in Islam, see, for example, Mensia 2004, pp. 107–123; Goldziher 1981, pp. 15–19; 24; 41–43.

59 See Tutu 1999, pp. 31–32; Brudholm 2008, pp. 46–47; Ellian 2003, pp. 171–176.

60 Brudholm 2008: p. 55 ff; Verdoolaege 2006, pp. 74–76.

5.4. THE CONSTITUTION AND STRUCTURING TIME

Has the final word on this subject now been said? Was it *wrong* that the members of the TRC presiding over the hearings in which victims were given the opportunity to tell their accounts of the injustice they suffered (in the words of researcher Annelies Verdoolaege):

> "[...] *were more or less obliged* to limit the victims' freedom of expression to establish a reconciling atmosphere, crucial for the future well-being of the nation of South Africa [...]?"[61]

Here, the collective interest in reconciliation and forgiveness clashes with the interest of the individual in freely deciding whether or not to pursue that route. Essentially we see here the same theoretical issue as in Damhouder. In other words, where the collective forces the condemned individual to repent and to beg for forgiveness because the constitution or, in other words, the normative unity of the Christian community is at stake. This aspect was fortunately much milder in the South African context; in this respect the comparison simply does not apply. However, what the two situations do have in common is that the committee hearings at which victims of apartheid were heard were *convened* in order to encourage and ideally also achieve reconciliation and forgiveness because this attitude was considered crucial for the constitution of the new South Africa, or rather its unity and identity as a political community of values.

Is this *modelling* (or *framing*)[62] wrong? To answer this question, we first need to examine a different question. Can we and should we generally speak of 'right' or 'wrong' in respect of the three basic responses to historic injustice – forgetting, remembering and forgiving – discussed here? What I would warn against is the temptation to turn these concepts into legal concepts. In my view, a *legal duty* to forget, to remember or to forgive is wrong as what is at stake is a phenomenon that cannot be forced into a legal framework, even if only because the individuals themselves who are subject to the law have too little control over these often intangible processes.[63]

As the anthropologist Marc Augé explains, figures such as those discussed above are ways of structuring and coming to terms with time. The characteristic aspect of these figures is that they are applied within social processes in which the distance between the individual and the collective has to be put into perspective.[64] This ties in with the intuitive feeling that forgetting, remembering and forgiving are phenomena primarily seen in the arena of day-to-day reality,

---

61 Verdoolaege 2006, p. 75. [Italics: WV].

62 'Emotional framing' is the term used by Verdoolaege (2006, p. 76).

63 As Lon Fuller comments, rules of law cannot demand the impossible from their addressees without losing their meaning. See Fuller 1969, p. 39.

64 See Augé 2001, p. 81. See also footnote 57.

in which individuals seek to give meaning to their lives in their relationships with others, partly by passively adapting themselves, but also by actively constituting that reality.[65]

For many years day-to-day reality in South Africa was poisoned by racism. The racist motive constituted a reality in which the vast majority of the population was excluded, at all conceivable levels, from equal access to the system of law. Essentially the system of law had been divided into an 'ordinary' system of law participated in by those citizens of South Africa with full rights (in other words, the white population) and into a parallel universe in which the political aim was to withhold the normality applying to citizens with full rights from the rest of the population. Those in the population who were discriminated against (in this case, the black and coloured parts of the population) consequently faced a day-to-day reality that, at least in legal and political terms, was anything but normal.

The South African constitution locates this period in the past via the figure of forgiveness: a new era is beginning in which the mundane system of law will from now on be available to everyone. As a result of the social and historical formation process that enabled this constitution to come about, and in which certain individuals may have made the difference,[66] the identity of the inhabitants of South Africa is no longer determined by race, but by the fundamental equality of each person, irrespective of their race, gender, religion, origins, sexual orientation and so on.

The factor heralding the new constitutional era was not primarily the *process* of reconciliation and forgiveness itself, but rather the *declaration* that the inhabitants of South Africa were willing to reconcile and forgive.[67] This is a vital presumption. The *example* set by some (Mandela, Tutu) challenges others to follow. Indeed the new era had already started by the time the TRC started its work in 1995. The South African constitution of 1996 was preceded by the

65 In a reflection on the concept of *Dasein* in Karl Jaspers, Celermajer described what I loosely see as workaday, mundane practices as follows (Celermajer 2009, p. 224): "[By *Dasein*, Jaspers understood] a field of meaning, an ongoing process of political cultural production, through which context is folded into the identity of individual members of the nation, at the same time as the judgements, actions, and aspirations of individuals form the context in which the institutions of the nation take shape."

66 It is fairly generally assumed that the transition would have proceeded considerably less peacefully, or would even have resulted in civil war, if, after his release, Mandela had not so unconditionally forgiven his oppressors.

67 It is this presumption that legitimizes "We, the people of South Africa", the opening words of the South African Constitution of 1996. For a philosophical analysis of 'first-person plural legislation' in general, see Van Roermund 2003, pp. 245–249; for the relationship between constitution and temporality, see Lindahl 2010, p. 36: "As legal norms are posited from the first-person plural perspective, they situate human behaviour in the temporal arc spanning the past, present and future of a collective. These modes of time are irreducible to calendar time."

Interim Constitution of 1993.[68] In what is referred to as the 'epilogue' of this Interim Constitution it had been decided to respond to the extreme injustice of the past on the basis of the belief:

> "[...] that there is a need for understanding but not for vengeance, a need for reparation but not for retaliation, a need for ubuntu, but not for victimization [...]."[69]

Victims given the opportunity to appear in front of the committee dealing with violations of human rights[70] and to tell of the injustice and violence they experienced, enter into a *setting* that is already focused on reconciliation and forgiveness. Provision has already been made for a mindset looking to forgive. And for some people that feels like a trap. Anyone seeking to oppose this comes up against a performative contradiction, and this in turn can create a sense of impotence or injustice.

This difficult situation is to a certain extent unavoidable. Breathtaking historical shifts occur at strongly felt collective moments, and although these are most often moments that we individually undergo more or less passively, they also mean that, from that moment on, we as individuals will view the past, present and future differently. The activities of the TRC form a bridge between the collective aspirations of the new constitutional order and day-to-day practice, in which the figure of forgiveness has to find its own path and acquire a new significance in each specific, individual case.[71] There can be said to be an interaction in that, although the constitution 'constitutes' the new order, it is the way in which citizens give shape to the new order on a day-to-day basis that further elaborates and feeds that constitution. Without meaningful context, therefore, the constitution itself does not (yet) have sufficient meaning. This was very clearly appreciated by the German political scientist Hermann Heller, who stated the following [translated] in *Staatslehre*, which was published posthumously in 1934:

---

68 The first non-racial elections were held in 1994.

69 The Constitutional Court of South Africa took this 'epilogue' to be a legally binding element of the Interim Constitution of 1993 and applied it in its ruling in the *Azapo* case of 27 July 1996 (see also footnote 47 above). According to the Court, this epilogue should be seen as 'holistic' (Judgment Mahomed DP, section 48): "It expresses an integrated philosophical and jurisprudential approach."

70 The hearings at which victims were given the opportunity to speak were chaired by members of the Truth and Reconciliation's Human Rights Violations Committee. These hearings were held between April 1996 and June 2000.

71 The assertions that Luigi Corrias makes as regards the following of rules (Corrias 2011, p. 112) also apply here in respect of 'copying' a model for reconciliation and forgiveness: "Following a rule 'as we do it' means that, going from case to case, the meaning of the rule itself is at stake, time and again. In other words, meaning is formed in the practice of following, i.e., meaning is 'originating'. The meaning of a rule does not exist independent from its application as if it were some kind of ideal reality."

> "The constitution grounded in a basic legal norm never consists exclusively of rules of law authorised by the state, but for its application always requires supplementing ['*Ergänzung*'] by non-normed and extrajudicial constitutional elements. [...] It is [...] the whole natural and cultural milieu, the anthropological, geographic, national, economic and social normalities with or in combination with which the constitution grounded in a basic, legal norm must form a single whole, which concretizes its content and determines its individuality."[72]

Here we touch on the views of Ernst-Wolfgang Böckenförde, another German political scientist, who expressed the view that whatever it is that binds a free, pluralistic society can never be enforced by the state.[73] A constitution that implies a collective promise of reconciliation and cohesion must be 'aligned' in some way or another with the world to which it relates.[74] And this means it must be supplemented by the pluralistic and polyphonic practices of the social reality.[75] In that delicate and complex process, there is increasing scope for correspondence *and* contrast. The TRC sought to mediate directly and publicly between the highly symbolic, collective level, and the individual case. Given the special nature of this task, the fact that it exercised a limited degree of 'constitutional' pressure on parties to bring about reconciliation and forgiveness has been inevitable. However, as long as both the TRC and the society at large still leave room for refusal and anger and *also* offer recognition and respect to those who are not (yet) prepared to reconcile or to forgive, this symbolically relevant attitude cannot reasonably be held against the committee.

6. TASKS OF THE MUNDANE LEGAL ORDER

If forgetting, remembering and forgiving are three figures that enable people, both collectively and individually, to make the transition to a new era, with the 'choice' for one or the other depending very much on contextual factors and circumstances,[76] this can provide a partial answer to the question of how a

72 Heller 1970, p. 255: "Die rechtlich normierte Verfassung besteht niemals bloss aus staatlich autorisierten Rechtssätzen, sondern bedarf zu ihren Geltung immer einer Ergänzung durch die nicht normierten und durch die ausserrechtlich normierten Verfassungselemente. [...] Es ist [...] das gesamte Natur- und Kulturmilieu, die antropologischen, geographischen, volklichen, wirtschaftlichen und sozialen Normalitäten, mit welchem oder gegen welchen die rechtlich normierte Verfassung ein Ganzes bilden soll, welche ihren Inhalt erst konkretisiert und ihre Individualität bestimmt."

73 See Böckenförde 1991, p. 112.

74 The relationship is almost physical, comparable with the relationship between an icon and reality. For a discussion of this relationship, see Moyaert 2007, pp. 123–124.

75 This also applies in respect of the legal application of constitutional rules in the specific case. See Tans 2009, pp. 21–22.

76 Obviously there were all sorts of special historical, political and social factors that led to the decision in Nantes in 1598 to 'choose' to forget, to the decision in Western Europe after 1945

pluriform, deeply divided society can attain social cohesion. This is because social practices characterised by remembering, forgetting or forgiving allow people to gain access to the constitutional order of a political community, with all the shared values that this entails.

The constitution of a society based on the equality of people and tolerance is shaped by its relationship with these practices in, to paraphrase Albie Sachs, a "strange alchemy between life and law."[77] Here, individuals participate in collective aspirations that herald the transition to a new era for society as a whole. This movement always goes hand-in-hand with social and political pressure and makes the individual a part of a greater whole.

However, a mundane legal system in such a society has been shown to create a certain distance with regard to remembering, forgetting and forgiving and thereby primarily to serve as a means of unburdening and release. What I mean by this is that the mundane system of law seems primarily fit to focus on keeping open for everyone, or at least not permanently blocking, the transitions (in both directions) between past and present, and present and future. If it performs this task well, the legal system can help prevent permanent victimhood and thus help achieve cohesion in society.

Mundane legal institutions can perform this function only if they avoid becoming all too closely associated with the task of forgetting or continuously remembering the past. On the one hand, the judicial system should never *completely* block off access to the past by being all too committed to the duty to forget the past. It is particularly in situations involving historic injustice that, sooner or later, a legal or pseudo-legal body needs to be able to respond to that injustice. The precise legal form that this takes will depend very much on the context and sometimes require political and legal imagination.

On the other hand, legal institutions also need to avoid becoming too devoted to the duty continuously to remember historic injustice. Otherwise they will no longer be able to rule definitively on matters and bring them to legal closure, as it will be impossible to conceive of a court decision or settlement that will *truly* do justice to what has happened in the past. As previously stated, both situations involve the danger of creating permanent victimhood: in the first case because victims cannot gain political and legal acknowledgement of their suffering, while in the second case the legal battle for acknowledgement and recognition is no longer able to come to an end.

Similarly, it can be said in respect of the duty to forgive that, on the one hand, legal and pseudo-legal institutions should never *oblige* victims to forgive, and neither should they be able to *compel* perpetrators to ask their victims for

---

to remember (and this tendency is increasing) and to the decision in South Africa in the 1990s to seek reconciliation and forgiveness. These factors are not discussed in this article.

77 See Sachs 2009. Sachs was one of the high-profile judges at the South African Constitutional Court and retired in October 2009.

forgiveness. On the other hand, given the above, the system of law should not be shaped in a way that seriously impedes the opportunities for reconciliation or forgiveness, either for victims or perpetrators.

This impediment can occur if legal institutions close their eyes completely to past injustice in an attempt to achieve legal oblivion. As outlined in section 5.2, forgiveness is conceptually closer to law that has run its course than to a situation in which justice is pre-empted or even withheld in advance. It is easier to let go of feelings of anger once a perpetrator has been convicted and punished, just as it is easier to forgive a thief after he returns what he has stolen.

Secondly, legal institutions can stand in the way of reconciliation if they deny people the opportunity of transformation by imposing sanctions on them that are so severe that they effectively withhold from them any prospects for the future (in this life). Obvious examples of such sanctions are the death penalty and sentences of life imprisonment without any credible prospect of early release. Punishments such as these chain perpetrators to their past as they make it totally impossible for them to make the transition to a new beginning, no longer as perpetrators, but as former perpetrators, no longer purely as victims of their 'perpetratorship', but as individuals who are capable of better.

A humane and mundane system of law has to ensure that conditions can be maintained in which remembering, forgetting and forgiving can in practice remain elements of significance and in turn increase cohesion in a society characterised by individual freedom and plurality. By providing a limited, finite response to infinite injustice from the past, the mundane system of law not only creates scope for many different, non-judicial approaches to dealing with what has happened in the past, but also offers the prospect of a future for all those within its sphere of influence.

REFERENCES

Arendt, H. (1969). *On Violence*, New York: Hartcourt, Brace & World.

Augé, M. (2001). *Les Formes de l'oubli*, Paris: Payot & Rivages.

Biehler, G. (1994). *Die Bodenkonfiskationen in der Sowjetischen Besatzungszone Deutschlands 1945 nach Wiederherstellung der gesamtdeutschen Rechtsordnung 1990*, Berlin: Duncker & Humblot.

Böckenförde, E-W. (1991). Die Entstehung des Staates als Vorgang der Säkularisation, in: E.-W. Böckenförde, *Recht, Staat, Freiheit. Studien zur Rechtphilosophie, Staatstheorie und Verfassungsgeschichte*, Frankfurt am Main: Suhrkamp, 92–114.

Brudholm, T. (2008). *Resentment's Virtue*, Philadelphia: Temple University Press.

Celermajer, D. (2009). *The Sins of the Nation and the Ritual of Apologies*, Cambridge: Cambridge University Press.

Corpus iuris canonici, II, Friedberg, E. (ed.) (1881), Leipzig: Tauchnitz.

Corrias, L.D.A. (2011). *The Passivity of Law. Competence and Constitution in the European Body Politic*, Heidelberg: Springer.

Damhouder, J. de (1562), *Praxis rerum criminalium iconibus materiae subjectae convenientibus apud Ioannem Bellerum*, Antwerp: J. Beller.

De Wilde, M. (2008). *Verwantschap in extremen. Politieke theologie bij Walter Benjamin en Carl Schmitt* (diss. Amsterdam UvA), Amsterdam: Vossius Pers.

Ellian, A. (2003). *Een onderzoek naar de Waarheids- en Verzoeningscommissie van Zuid-Afrika* (diss. Tilburg), Nijmegen: Wolf Legal Publishers.

French, L, M. Garry & E. Loftus (2009). False memories: A kind of confabulation in non-clinical subjects, in: W, Hirstein (ed.), *Confabulation. Views from neuroscience, psychiatry, psychology and philosophy*, Oxford: Oxford University Press 2009, 33–66.

Fuller, L.L. (1969). *The Morality of Law*, New Haven/London: Yale University Press.

Garapon, A. (2008). *Peut-on réparer l'histoire? Colonisation, esclavage, Shoah*, Paris: Odile Jacob.

Goldziher, I. (1981). *Introduction to Islamic Theology and Law*, Princeton NJ: Princeton University Press.

Heller, H. (1970). *Staatslehre* [1934], Leiden: A.W. Sijthoff.

Jankélévitch, V. (1986). *L'imprescriptible. Pardonner? Dans l'honneur et la dignité*, Paris: Édition du Seuil.

Lesaffer, R. & E-J. Broers (2007). Private Property in the Dutch-Spanish Peace Treaty of Münster, Tilburg University Legal Studies Working Paper No. 002/2007, <papers.ssrn.com>.

Lindahl, H. (2010). A-Legality: Postnationalism and the Question of Legal Boundaries, *The Modern aw Review*, 73 (1), 30–56.

Margalit, A. (2002). *The Ethics of Memory*, Cambridge Mass./London: Harvard University Press.

Margalit, A. & G. Motzkin (1996). The Uniqueness of the Holocaust, *Philosophy & Public Affairs* 25 (1), 65–83.

Margolf, D.C. (1996). Adjudicating Memory: Law and Religious Difference in Early Seventeenth Century France, *The Sixteenth Century Journal* 27 (2), 399–418.

McInnis, M. (2009). Resisting Temptations to "Justice", in: R. Chambers et al. (eds.), *Philosophical Foundations of the Law of Unjust Enrichment*, Oxford: Oxford University Press, 100–146.

Mensia, M.A. (2004), Théories du répentir chez les théologiens musulmans classiques, in: A. Destro & M. Pesce (eds.), *Rituals and Ethics. Patterns of Repentance. Judaism, Christianity, Islam. Second International Conference of Mediterraneum*, Paris/Louvain: Peeters, 107–123.

Minow, M. (1998). *Between Vengeance and Forgiveness. Facing History after Genocide and Mass Violence*, Boston: Beacon Press.

Moyaert, P. (2007). *Iconen en beeldverering. Godsdienst als symbolische praktijk*, Amsterdam: Sun.

Ost, F. (1999). *Le temps du droit*, Paris: Odile Jacob.

Renan, E. (1887). Qu'est-ce qu'une nation?, in: E. Renan, *Discours et Conférences*, Paris: Calmann Lévy.

Rév, I. (2005). *Retroactive Justice. Prehistory of Post-Communism*, Stanford: Stanford University Press.
Ricoeur, P. (2006). *Memory, History, Forgetting*, Chicago/London: The University of Chicago Press.
Sachs, A. (2009). *The Strange Alchemy of Life and Law*, Oxford: Oxford University Press.
Tans, O. (2009). De fictie van de constitutie. Over de maatschappelijke functie van ontwerp-denken, *Recht der Werkelijkheid* 2009, 1, 11–26.
Todorov, T. (1995). *Les abus de la mémoire*, Paris: Arléa.
Tutu, D. (1999), *No Future without Forgiveness*, New York: Image.
Van Caenegem, R.C. (1954). *Geschiedenis van het strafrecht in Vlaanderen van de XIe tot de XIVe eeuw*, Brussels: Paleis der Academiën.
Van Klink, B.M.J. (2010), *Rechtsvormen. Autonomie van recht en rechtswetenschap* (speech at VU University Amsterdam), The Hague: Boom Juridische Uitgevers.
Van Roermund, B. (2003), First-Person Plural Legislature: Political Reflexivity and Representation, *Philosophical Explorations* 2003, 6, 235–250.
Vattel, M. de (1758). *Le Droit des Gens ou Principes de la Loi Naturelle, Appliqués à la conduite & aux affaires des Nations & des Souverains*, Vol. II, London.
Veraart, W.J. (2009). Redressing the Past with an Eye to the Future. The Impact of the Passage of Time to Property Rights Restitution in Post-Apartheid South Africa, *Netherlands Quarterly of Human Rights* 27 (1), 45–60.
Verdoolaege, A. (2006). Managing Reconciliation at the Human Rights Violations Hearings of the South African TRC, *Journal of Human Rights* 5 (1), 61–80.
Verwoerd, W. (2007). *Equity, Mercy, Forgiveness. Interpreting Amnesty within the South African Truth and Reconciliation Commission*, Louvain: Peeters.
Waldron, J. (2002). Redressing Historic Injustice, *University of Toronto Law Journal* (52), 135–160.
Weber, M. (2009). *Die protestantische Ethik und der Geist des Kapitalismus*, Cologne: Anaconda.
Winkel, L.C. (1994). *Themis en Clio. Bondgenoten of vijanden? Een beschouwing over waarheid in recht en geschiedenis* (speech in Rotterdam), Deventer: Kluwer.
Withuis, J. & A. Mooij (2010). Conclusion, in: A. Mooij & J. Withuis (eds.), *The Politics of War Trauma. The aftermath of World War II in Eleven European countries*, Aksant: Amsterdam, pp. 323–331.
Wolterstorff, N. (2008). *Justice. Rights and Wrongs*, Princeton & Oxford: Princeton University Press.

TIME BEYOND TIME – TIME BEFORE TIME: COMMENTS ON RICOEUR*

Bert VAN ROERMUND

The Epilogue of Ricoeur's *Memory, History, Forgetting*[1] is entitled 'Difficult Forgiveness', indicating that forgiveness is neither easy nor impossible. As the common horizon of memory, history and forgetting, it is always attracting but never reached. Ultimately its two dimensions diverge: below the awareness of guilt, above the gift of forgiveness. There is no conceptual middle ground between them. Neither can we construe a form of reciprocity between the demand of being forgiven and the offer to forgive, nor build on the symmetry between an agent binding herself to an action (as in promising) and releasing her from this bond (as in forgiving). Forgiveness points to a realm beyond established social relationships, a realm where an agent is regarded a priori as a moral subject, i.e., as someone capable of rejecting what she did wrong in the name of the good. Both a negative and a positive consequence follow from that. The negative one[2] reads that there is no public dimension in forgiveness, that 'the people' cannot be the agent of forgiving, and that there cannot be political institutions of genuine reconciliation. While individuals can, polities cannot pose as agents summoned by a moral norm. In other words, they are unable to

* To a considerable extent this paper overlaps with a draft chapter for a book I have been co-authoring since 2004 with Scott Veitch, Emilios Christodoulidis, and Johan VanderWalt. Writing this book was (and in fact still is) part of a project on 'Law, Time and the Politics of Reconciliation' that went through various conferences and workshops, ushering in (Veitch 2006) and (Du Bois and Du Bois-Pedain 2008) while the monograph still has to be finalised. I hugely profited from discussions with most of the contributors to these volumes, in particular with Andrew Schaap, Carrol Clarkson and the three colleagues mentioned above. The collaboration was so intense that it is not always possible to attribute credits for arguments and terms with the accuracy that is normally required, for which I apologise. Also on behalf of my co-applicants I gratefully acknowledge funding by the Leverhulme Trust and the British Academy for this project, as well as additional financial support from the Law School of the universities of Glasgow, Edinburgh, Johannesburg, Cape Town and Tilburg.

1 Cf. the English translation (Ricoeur 2004). For the thesis discussed here see the introduction to the Epilogue, and in particular part II, section 2–3, and part V.

2 A tantalising thesis which Ricoeur derives from Klaus-Michael Kodalle. the former professor of legal philosophy at Jena. Cf. (Kodalle 1994). This is an appropriate occasion to thank him for inviting me to deliver a guest lecture in 2003, for most rewarding discussions and for copy-editing my German text afterwards.

relate the wrongness of their actions to their selfhood. In the final analysis they can neither bear nor lift moral guilt. What they can do is to engage in 'a culture of considerateness', moderation, or clemency, in order to normalise their relationships. Certain public gestures can further this disposition to considerateness on a public scale, but this does not amount to public forgiveness. The positive thesis is that forgiveness can only be thought in a time beyond time, in the optative mode of wish and hope rather than in the indicative mode of description or the imperative mode of prescription. For this anticipation of a memory that will once turn out be unequivocally 'blessed', Ricoeur uses the theological term 'eschatology', though in a radically philosophical (rather than a theological) sense.

In an equally philosophical vein I propose to ask what is the protology correlate with this eschatology? What is the 'beginning' of times, or the 'time before time', that is both preparing for and recaptured by 'the end of times', or the 'time beyond time'? And if there is such a protology conceivable, does it have implications for the Ricoeur/Kodalle thesis that, on the brink of becoming public, forgiveness has to go 'incognito'; that political institutions can do no more than contribute to a culture of considerateness; and that 'the people' cannot be the agent of forgiving by dint of its falling short of moral selfhood? The argument will take the following steps. In the first section I revisit an argument made earlier that the concept of reconciliation is predicated on two sequences rather than one. It is not only the end of a political process, but also the beginning. In the second section I develop the notion of 'proto-politics' as the vestigial memory of a polity about its origin. In the third section I return explicitly to Ricoeur's thesis as set out above, arguing that *Ubuntu* as a concept rooted in African culture may give form and substance to such memory in ways that are functionally equivalent to, but conceptually different from, Western practices of reconciliation. While the latter is based, ultimately, on political theology, the former is best conceived as a political ecology.

1. FORGIVENESS AND RECONCILIATION

In a contribution to *Lethe's Law*, drawing on the South African TRC experiences, I argued that reconciliation is constitutive of a dignifying past for the victims of oppression, in so far as it involves an aporetic back and forth between two sequences.[3] One we could call a practical sequence, as it represents a reasonable order of doing things. The other we could call an anthropological sequence, as it reflects how one sees the human condition. When it comes to their inner temporal orders, the latter sequence is the exact inversion of the former. Let me explain.

3 Van Roermund 2001.

Predominant in accounts of reconciliation is the former sequence.[4] On these accounts, in order for a process of reconciliation to succeed, it is necessary, first of all, that the facts of violent oppression in the past are revealed, the names of the responsible agents or agencies disclosed, and the stories of survivors heard. To uncover the suffering of the past is the first step. It is of the utmost importance that perpetrators step forward from their own free will to join this initial stage of the process. In any case, confession and repentance from the side of the perpetrators should follow as a second step. Thirdly, truth and guilt established, perpetrators should show repentance by adopting and sharing the victim's perspective on the past in a respectful way and by offering reparations. Indeed, there repentance will not be credible until they have promised to pay, as it will also lack credibility unless they have joined the process of truth finding by their voluntary disclosures. The last step in this order of things is forgiveness: the victims of the former oppression can offer a new social bond for the future, on the basis of the perpetrators' repentance rather than their actual payments.

This sequence is not a false picture at all by any standard. I submit though, on the basis of some salient evidence, that it is an incomplete one with regard to reconciliation. I propose to focus on another sequence of exactly the same steps in reverse order. This sequence is not a better account of the process of reconciliation, but rather one that is at work here *at the same time*, i.e. at the time this practical sequence takes place. According to this second sequence forgiveness would come first as a decision made by the former victims of oppression. It would make repentance possible, and then repentance would appeal to the perpetrators' confession. Let me start with an example. On July 12th, 2008 all national newspaper in the West reported about the interview Ingrid Betancourt had given in hotel Le Meurice in Paris, one week after her release from the Colombian jungle, where she was held hostage by the FARC. She explained that at that point in time she was not ready yet to describe the facts of physical and psychic 'torture and humiliation' she had gone through. One day she would outline the truth, she promised. 'I know that I have to give testimony about all the things I lived,' she said. 'But I need time ... The only thing I've settled in my mind is that I want to forgive, and forgiveness comes with forgetting.' I will come back to the relationship between forgiving and forgetting at a later stage of my argument. Here I would only like to underline that for Betancourt there is an initial decision to forgive, and it precedes any account of the facts, let alone confession or repentance from her torturers. In this respect her statement is similar to that of Babwhala Mhlauli, the mother of one of the Craddock Four, before the South

4 In earlier versions of their website, the International Centre for Transitional Justice (ICTJ) indicated five phases that process of transitional justice would go through. 1: Fact finding; 2: Prosecution of perpetrators; 3: Compensation for victims; 4: Institutional reform; 5: Reconciliation. They now prefer to speak of five 'key elements' in transitional justice that must be integrated in a 'holistic approach'. In most documents, however, reconciliation is mentioned last – a remnant of a phase theory left behind. Cf. www.ictj.org/en/tj/.

African TRC: 'We want to forgive; but whom should we forgive?' Here again, to the extent that forgiving is the core of reconciliation, it precedes the process of truth seeking. The decision to forgive is not conditional on specific behaviour on the part of the former perpetrators. Prior to confession, repentance and reparation it reaches out to them as an invitation to step forward and receive what they cannot possibly expect: to be forgiven. Let me emphasise once more that this second sequence does not reflect a 'better' approach to reconciliation in any practicable way. As a practical device it would be sheer non-sense: one cannot forgive 'whatever may turn out to have been the case'. Apparently, reconciliation is based on following both temporal sequences, one in which truth comes first and forgiveness last, another in which forgiveness comes first and truth last.[5]

Not only are the two sequences equi-primordial, they are also, and more importantly, mutually conditional.[6] According to the practical sequence, there cannot be reconciliation without truth. What this means in practice is that there will be no decision to forgive unless the former victims can be sure that under the new regime their story will be heard. The point of the anthropological sequence is that they do not wait until indeed it has been heard. They *anticipate* the moment that it will have been heard. And perhaps not even that, since their 'anticipation' is based on hope rather than stochastics. It faces the possibility that this moment will not materialise, but it takes the risk. Thus the anticipation is best captured in a counterfactual mode: the former victims of oppression act as if their stories *would* have been heard. According to this sequence, forgiveness prior to any disclosure creates a space of hope in which perpetrators can feel repentance[7] so that they can come forward and reveal their wrongdoings on their own account. Short of such space of hope there is no possibility for perpetrators to look at themselves from an angle that would go beyond self-preservation and that would enable them to let any distinction between good and bad count against them.

This double logic of reconciliation seems largely in line with Ricoeur's view on forgiving as set out in his monograph on *Memory*. The keystone of the argument there is 'the final paradox proposed by the religions of the Book', as Ricoeur calls them. The paradox consists in the circular interdependence of forgiving and repentance: a unique circle '(…) by reason of which the existential response [i.e. of repentance; BvR] to forgiveness is implied, as it were, in the gift itself, while the antecedence of the gift [i.e. of forgiving; BvR] is recognized at the

5 Thus, one tries to uncover and cover the truth of the past, rubbing it off and rubbing it on the surface of this desperate vow 'never again'.

6 As a consequence I doubt whether 'invitational forgiveness' as an alternative practical scenario or account makes much sense.

7 The more proper word here, I suppose, would be 'remorse'. Cf. (Bankowski 2008) I keep the term 'repentance' in order to maintain the picture of inversed sequences.

very heart of the inaugural gesture of repentance.'[8] Ricoeur emphasises that this interdependence is not a transaction[9] between a gift and a counter-gift exchanged over time in mutual expectations. Indeed, the idea of a transaction would lend support again to there being 'a common ground' between victims and perpetrators. The decisive difference between the economy of the exchange and the paradox that Ricoeur has in mind is precisely the asymmetry of the temporal modes that forgiving and repentance are involved in. The offer of forgiving 'permits neither before nor after'[10], as Ingrid Betancourt's and Babwhala Mhlauli's phrases make clear: it is unconditional with regard to the various stages of what I called the practical sequence. The response of repentance or remorse, on the other hand, given either suddenly (as in certain spectacular conversions) or gradually (in the course of an entire life), comes after the offer to forgive. But this response is not given in exchange of this offer, as if the offer were a condition that the agent of the response could set in advance.[11]

The only way in which one can conceive of this circle being actually lived through by either victims or perpetrators is in the various forms an agent can be 'dissociated' from his or her wrongful acts. One may try and tease out the gap between what a person did and the person she or he is. For Ricoeur, the basis of such dissociation would be 'an act of faith' and 'an act of confidence'. This faith would regard this person's capacity as a moral subject. It holds on to the belief that, in spite of all the wrong she did, she is able to turn to the good, at least in the sense that once she will acknowledge the wrong even if she remains unable to change her behaviour. Thus, her personhood is not exhausted by the various ways it has inscribed itself in the course of the world by acting as it did in the past. The final moral stance is the hope that the guilty person is capable of disapproving of his crimes. This is why we may say that the guilty agent is 'dissociated', i.e. cut loose from his deeds. Dissociation, therefore, is the opposite of 'demonization'. By calling Saddam Hussein a devil, the then president of the United States implied that Saddam Hussein coincided with his wrongdoings. In contrast, by explaining 'the banality of evil', Hannah Arendt implied that Eichmann did not. This is not to say that she did not want to see him held to account in a court of law. On the contrary, precisely by dissociating Eichmann from his deeds during the nazi regime, she pointed to the possibility that, in retrospect, he might have confessed to have been deeply wrong – which he did not. So the dissociation of agent and actor takes the form of a normative counterfactual. Moreover – and this is crucial – the counterfactual takes the form of a first person agent. We hope that a wrongdoer will say 'I should have

8 (Ricoeur 2000), 490–491.
9 P. 490.
10 P. 491.
11 Ibid.: 'The paradox is precisely that of the circular relation between what "remains" forever and what comes to be in each instance'. Ricoeur points to the dogmatic battles fought between Christian religions on 'grace' being primary or conditional on free human initiative.

done otherwise.' In her statements of July 2008, Betancourt told that her captors treated her with exceptional malice, partly because the Marxist guerillas saw her as coming from an established political family, and partly because of their own treatment in Colombian jails. She said her treatment had shown that every human being had an 'animal' inside them. She learned how 'in any situation like the ones I experienced, perhaps any of us could do those kind of cruel things. For me it was like understanding what I couldn't understand before, how for example the Nazis, how (things like that) could have happened.' Betancourt was certainly neither justifying nor explaining nor demonizing her captors' behaviour. By mentioning 'the animal' inside all of us, she did not hold a plea for excuses; she opened up a space for reconciliation that would not be predicated on excuses but on unconditional forgiveness. Again, as an advice for action this is totally meaningless. All action in society would stop if we could always 'dissociate' ourselves from our actions. But as an underlying presupposition of social action it makes sense: social action would equally stop if we would radically identify one another by our actions.

At the public scene of politics and law, however, Ricoeur argues[12] that the most we can do in virtue of such dissociation is to retreat to the 'incognito' mode of considerateness.[13] Considerateness in the sense of thoughtfulness rather than respect should be the attitude that governs our public dealings with oppressive wrongdoing. This public context of reconciliation is a derivative one compared to reconciliation based on forgiving. Genuine forgiveness can only occur in the direct social relationship between former victims and perpetrators both transcending the wrongdoings of the past. In Ricoeur's conception of things the offer of forgiveness can only come from a Third Person under the guise of a transcendent God, as 'the religions of the Book' picture Him. This offer is made to persons, not to polities.

But – and here I begin to hesitate – should we see Babwhala Mhlauli, then, as a priest or a prophet, the representative of a transcendent realm or an eschatological time? Should we admit that it is true, after all, that forgiveness is offered 'in the end', and that the moral awareness of fault is 'at the beginning'? Have we substituted the anthropological sequence by a metaphysical one, only to reiterate the time order of the practical sequence? It certainly is the logic of reconciliation which we feel attracted to, a logic we apply immediately as soon as we believe to detect the anthropological sequence in reconciliation at work. For instance, the same newspapers that reported Betancourt's readiness to forgive were also quick to call her 'France's new Joan of Arc'[14], that is, to picture her as a saint. Betancourt herself had only confessed her growth in faith, not her role as

---

12 As said, with Klaus-Michael Kodalle who wrote extensively on reconciliation between 'the two Germanies' after the fall of the wall.

13 P. 493; cf. 476f.

14 See www.theage.com.au/world/i-want-to-forgive-says-betancourt-20080711-3dqm.html, accessed July 13th, 2008.

a representative of the eschaton. The problem is how we can stay critical towards both sanctification and demonization as one another's mirror images?

2. THE PROBLEM OF THE POLITICAL

My first concern with Ricoeur's view, then, is with his most embracing time frame: the eschaton, i.e. the time beyond time. One way to phrase the question – perhaps a too grandiloquent one – is this: if the final philosophical perspective of forgiveness is an eschatological one, what is the protology that can bear this eschatology? What 'time before time' would support 'a time beyond time'? A simpler one is this: if there is an ethical perspective for a society that cannot be evaded, what is the viewpoint from which this perspective can appear as an appeal? Or even: why would we be interested in forgiveness in the first place? If Ricoeur says, with Levinas, that the voice declaring that 'there is' forgiveness, is the voice of the Third (*illéité*), one cannot evade the question why it is that we would hear it? Why would we not only hear it, but also *attend* to what we are hearing? Why would we listen to what we hear? Even if we decide not to care, aren't we responsive to the extent that we turn away from what at least registered?[15] How could we contemplate this responsiveness prior to conceptualising it? Answering these and similar questions amounts to narrating a beginning of time that is unimaginable and yet undeniable; a story of how the human condition came about. Without claiming, at this stage, that there is no account of such a protology in Ricoeur whatsoever, I would stipulate that a protology would not suffice if it would only relate evil. If humans would have been borne in nothing but evil from the start, hope of forgiveness would not speak to them at all. This is why I propose to return to a phenomenology of reconciliation and ask the question if its time structures are completely covered by what Ricoeur has taught us? We may have overlooked its very beginnings in search of what it takes in the end. If we did, we may have reason to also revisit the thesis that public forgiveness is impossible.

There are two interrelated points I would like to make. The first concerns the doubt I have with regard to the thesis that reconciliation is exclusively bound up with forgiveness, and forgiveness, in turn, with 'a religious heritage that we could call "abrahamic" if we were to gather judaism, christianisms and islams'.[16] I think it is premature to claim that, as a matter of cultural fact, a process of reconciliation is exclusively dependent on the vertical dimension of divine

15 On responsiveness in this sense, see (Waldenfels 1994) and on attentiveness as a sequel to it see (Waldenfels 2004). My question to Ricoeur is not new, I suppose. In many ways, it is Derrida's question to Levinas in the essay on violence and metaphysics in (Derrida 1978).

16 (Ricoeur 2000), p. 606, where he quotes Derrida's piece 'Le siècle et le pardon' in *Le Monde des débats*, décembre 1999. The translation is mine. One may be surprised to find the term 'judaism' not in the plural.

forgiveness that these 'abrahamic' categories embody, and on the religious culture in which they are entrenched. For instance, notwithstanding the impact of the 'religions of the Book' on the South African TRC-process, the fact that the road to reconciliation was primarily understood in terms of *ubuntu* as an African topos[17] should make us hesitant about the quasi-universal character of the 'abrahamic' claim. *Ubuntu*, as far as I understand, invokes the oblique awareness of being committed to a horizontal togetherness (oneness and wholeness)[18] of 'the living'. Rather than an 'idea', it is the sense of being part of an incessant process of regeneration involving 'the living-dead' (ancestors) and the 'yet-to-be-born' (offspring).[19] It is this relational context which '(...) always conceals and reveals the potentialities of the individual'.[20] From a 'western' point of view, we might say that *ubuntu* is basically both pre-political and pre-moral. It finds home in religion, but this is a religion without a God; Or rather, without what theologians call a God.[21] Justice Yvonne Mokgoro – a judge in the South African Constitutional Court – says that ubuntu

> '(...) in its most fundamental sense represents personhood, humanity, humaneness and morality; a metaphor that describes group solidarity where such group solidarity is central to the survival of communities with a scarcity of resources, where the fundamental belief is that "motho ke motho ba batho ba bangwe/umuntu ngumuntu ngabantu" which, literally translated, means a person can only be a person through others. (...) In other words the individual's whole existence is relative to that of the group: this is manifested in anti-individualistic conduct towards the survival of the group if the individual is to survive. It is a basically humanistic orientation towards fellow beings.'[22]

In what I believe to be a similar vein, Antjie Krog, a close watcher and incisive commentator of the TRC at the time, submits that reconciliation is in fact not based on 'mysterious' jewish-christian ideology[23], but on what she calls 'survival instinct', lived out in nitty-gritty negotiations and trade-offs between groups, circling around each other in a process of articulating and adjusting new

17 Cf. (Ramose 1994). (Ramose 1995), and in particular (Ramose 1999), where one find a wealth of other references.

18 (Ramose 1999), 49 ff.

19 Ibid., 62.

20 Ibid., 139.

21 Ibid., 63: 'According to the *ubuntu* understanding of being, the world of metaphysics is the world of *u-nkulu-knulu*: the greatest of the great; the ineffable. (...) Therefore, it is best to remain quiet about the unknowable and simply recognize the ineffability of (...) *unkulunkulu*. This, it is submitted, is a basic starting point, to explain why *ubuntu* philosophy and religion have no theology.'

22 (Mokgoro 1998). But note that 'humanistic' here captures predicates like 'human' and 'humane' rather than a specific western, secular, world view called 'humanism'.

23 As no doubt bishop Tutu would have it.

identities.[24] This is perhaps a deliberately blunt way of putting it. But it does bring out that there may be a supplementary account of reconciliation, not based on the vertical disparity (as again Ricoeur calls it[25]) between the guilty wrongdoer down here and the divine legislator up there, but rather on the horizontal parity in self-regeneration that in western culture is perhaps best rendered by the primary meaning of the term 'economy': self-reproduction under alternating conditions of scarcity and abundance. This is not necessarily, as Ricoeur seems to think at times, reducing forgiving to giving-and-taking. Demand, supply, market price and exchange come to the economy only as tributaries to a river already carrying water. Economy in the basic sense of the word is about reproducing one's existence (self-regeneration indeed) in a sustained metabolism with one's environment.[26] That is to say, the economy is primarily about sustaining the household, the *oikia*, and therefore predicated on ecology rather than economics. It is not unthinkable that in non-abrahamic cultures reconciliation is rooted in political *oiko-logy* rather than political *theology*. It is not unthinkable either that in abrahamic cultures theology is the preferred form of political oikology. Salvation, after all, is about survival and regeneration, even if it is not about the typically 'modern' issue of self-preservation. But an African ubuntu account of reconciliation does not necessarily have to join these preferences.

My second concern is related to the first one, as it purports to express the philosophical worry underlying the culture-theoretical observation just made. It is with Ricoeur's thesis that reconciliation can only be understood within a conceptual framework that goes 'beyond the legal and the political'[27]; a framework that focuses on the interrelationships between humans as moral subjects or persons. In the public dimension of the social sphere, Ricoeur argues, forgiveness will always yield to crime and punishment, i.e., if and when there is a crime that can be imputed to a certain agent and legal consequences follow from this imputation. This, again, is possible only if and when there is a violation of a rule that was established (in the final analysis) for the sake of the commonwealth. But in that case it would be highly unjust to forgive rather than

---

24 (Krog 2000), which is the Dutch edition of *Country of my Skull* (1998); one finds the observation in the Postscript to the Dutch edition.

25 (Ricoeur 2000), 457.

26 'Die Natur ist der unorganische Leib des Menschen, nämlich die Natur, soweit sie nicht selbst menschlicher Körper ist. Der Mensch lebt von der Natur, heißt: Die Natur ist sein Leib, mit dem er in beständigen Prozeß bleiben muß, um nicht zu sterben. Daß das physische und geistige Leben des Menschen mit der Natur zusammenhängt, hat keinen anderen Sinn, als daß die Natur mit sich selbst zusammenhängt, denn der Mensch ist ein Teil der Natur.' (Marx 1844 [1971]) 566. [Nature is the non-organic body of man, to wit nature in so far as it is not human body itself. 'Man lives from nature' means: nature is his body, with which he has to stay intertwined in order not to die. That the physical and psychic life of man is linked up with nature only means that nature is linked up with itself, for man is part of nature. My trans. BvR].

27 P. 469. Although it can be politically used and abused.

to punish, unless the fault cannot be attributed to the agent. Forgiving will boil down to accepting excuses. Hence 'the impossibility of genuine political institutions of forgiveness'.[28] This is why real forgiveness has to reach beyond the realm of law and politics, indeed beyond the realm of morality to the extent that morality is often pre-formatted by the very same categories as law and politics.

As for Ricoeur, philosophical ethics should be less averse to theological infiltration, or rather to spirituality[29], as it could help to enter this post-legal and post-political realm. This is also why he cannot appreciate Hannah Arendt's position. He believes that Arendt is wrong in arguing that, where human plurality is primitive, the ability to forgive and the ability to promise are symmetrical faculties. He does not believe that both are on a par in coming to the rescue of human plurality by making up for its in-built weaknesses.[30] What is missing from her political interpretation of forgiving, he says, is precisely the possibility of dissociation mentioned earlier on: i.e., the possibility to release the agent from his or her act, as a precondition for bringing perpetrator and victim together.[31] With Derrida[32], Ricoeur's positive thesis is that forgiving, if it is to mean anything at all[33], should pertain to the unforgivable. In other words, it should pertain to things that do not fit into the categories we are familiar with, i.e., the kinds of evil we know well enough to deal with them in rules. Forgiveness therefore is a gift of charity (*agape*) that is to be received in a realm 'beyond the political'.[34] This is the realm where a person is regarded as a moral subject – the moral subject being the highest stage of 'l'homme capable'[35] – capable, that is, of orienting himself to the pole of the good in making and objectifying the distinction between good and evil.[36] Forgiveness is tantamount to this mode of regarding a person.

The central question, then, is, whether forgiveness in this sense is the only possible mode of such dissociation, i.e. the only mode to release the agent from his or her act? I submit that this is not the case. Even if Arendt is too quick in finding a parallel between promising and forgiving, her concept of 'natality' points to the kind of dissociation that Ricoeur is (rightly) demanding. The difference is that she locates it in the political as the heart of the human

28 P. 459; 470; 488–489.

29 P. 466.

30 P. 486ff. For a different appreciation of Arendt's philosophy with regard to reconciliation, see (Schaap 2005).

31 P. 486; cf. 489ff.

32 For a most intriguing effort to come to terms with reconciliation in a Derridean vein, see (Van der Walt 2005), ch. 8.

33 P. 468.

34 P. 468; 488.

35 '(...) the capable being' (p. 491). I am rather hesitant about this translation.

36 P. 491ff.

condition.[37] For Arendt it is part of a political anthropology or protology, one might say – while Ricoeur refers it to a realm beyond the political, to a time beyond time that is the ultimate perspective of morality. But note that natality as a protological concept is as much about dissociation as the eschatological account of forgiveness can be: 'The fact that man is capable of action means that the unexpected can be expected from him, that he is able to perform what is infinitely improbable.'[38] African Bantu-culture may well provide us with a thicker notion of natality than Arendt herself was able to. While she grounded natality in the 'uniqueness of each man', *ubuntu* – without denying individual uniqueness – points to a social ground that encompasses both past and future of a community, thus making it intrinsically political. Something new can be expected from individual men, precisely because they are held to account not only by those who are present (their fellow human beings), not only by one who remains absent (a transcendental God), but also, and even primarily, by those who are present in their absence (those who gave them birth and those to whom they will give birth). Again, this makes natality more rather than less political.[39]

Let us listen, once more, to Babwhala Mhlauli's phrase 'We want to forgive, but whom should we forgive?' Conceded that this phrase expresses the core of reconciliation, does her use of 'we' have political reference? And if it does, in what sense precisely? I submit that it does[40], as she makes the offer and asks the question on behalf of a group that is already involved in the political process, complying with the 'logic' of the political discourse. She delineates them as the victims of oppression, as distinct as can be from the perpetrators of oppression. She claims to represent this group in pursuit of a common well-being. This claim is voiced in the representational and inclusive first-person pronoun 'we'. The offer of reconciliation made on behalf of the formerly oppressed cannot but comply with the logic of representation that is inherent in the political constitution of society. The pronoun 'we' is not the 'we' of an offer in unisono; it is the 'we' to which an offer is attributed by a plurality of agents posing as (claiming to be) representatives of a collective: *the* victims, *the* oppressed, *the* people. Such collective is represented as able to relate to itself: it has reflexive capacity, selfhood, or, as Ricoeur would probably call it, *ipseity*.[41]

---

37 Cf. (Arendt 1958), 9: '(…) since action is the political activity par excellence, natality, and not mortality, may be the central category of political, as distinguished from metaphysical, thought.' Cf. 177–8.

38 Ibid., 178.

39 What Ricoeur / Kodalle and Arendt do have in common, though, is a justified suspicion towards political *institutions*. Cf. (Arendt 1958) 191: 'The frailty of human institutions and laws and, generally, of all matters pertaining to men's living together, arises from the human condition of natality and is quite independent of the frailty of human nature.' But that is a different, though important, matter.

40 See for further arguments (Van Roermund 2001).

41 The reference is, of course to (Ricoeur 1990).

3. PUBLIC FORGIVENESS?

As we saw, Ricoeur chooses to follow Kodalle in that a people cannot forgive because 'the collectivity does not have a moral consciousness'.[42] But the force of this argument is entirely dependent on how one conceives of 'consciousness', in particular whether it is a precondition for reflexivity or a mode of reflexivity. If 'to have consciousness' is a precondition for a self, there cannot be a collective self, i.e. there cannot be reflexivity or *ipseity* in the plural at all. But ipseity in the plural, I would venture, has to make *some* sense, otherwise one could not understand words like 'together', 'co-operation', 'general interest', 'self-determination', and their ilk. All of these contain a reflexive element that cannot be reduced to individual self-awareness. One should only acknowledge that these plural forms of reflexivity are 'wired' in ways different from the ones that we associate with individual consciousness. As Michael E. Bratman has argued[43], they mainly feed on patterns of *reciprocal* individual behaviour, which may range from very cooperative to very competitive without losing their basic property of being shared intentional action. Least of all they commit us ontologically to a super-mind embracing all individual minds, or a super-body that is independent of the life and behaviour of individuals, or a super-consciousness of whatever make-up.

One can easily imagine individual agents *sharing*, by way of mutually responsive behaviour, the kind of recognition Ricoeur is pointing to in his analysis of reconciliation, in such a way that we can say that the *groups they belong to*, rather than the individuals composing them, are in the process of reconciling. After the lofty phrases about forgiveness, descriptions of these goings-on may sound almost trivial. And indeed, they have to do with sustaining everyday life, and with living the sheer proximity of bodies that comes with it. Yet, this is what a political ecology boils down to, and trivial as it may sound, it is by no means easy to do.[44] Nor, however, is it impossible. Here are just a few examples: if some former victims and former perpetrators start out to farm or to do business on an honest basis, if some leading historians and poets of the polity write about the suffering and meet with applause from a mixed audience, if rituals of mourning are taken part in by some who confessed guilt, if some secular and religious authorities are unanimous in their call to future peace, if some beneficiaries of the violent past purport to do their share in restoring the damage that was done, or prove convincing in expressing their awareness that the harm cannot be made undone, then, in virtue of these and other reciprocal

42 P. 467ff.

43 (Bratman 1999); see also (Van Roermund 2003).

44 For dramatic details on how difficult this is, see e.g. (Hatzfeld 2008), from the original French book *La Stratégie des antilopes* (Paris, Du Seuil, 2007) on living together in Rwanda after the genocides.

gestures, these societies, though perhaps not all of their individual members, are involved in reconciling. The crucial point, then, is not that consciousness is an exclusive ability that allows agents to be reflexive, i.e. to represent themselves qua selves in various contents of thinking, speaking and doing. The point is that there is reflexivity, i.e. a subject taking its very subjectivity as an object; that this formal structure can be accounted for by various sets of terms: physical, mental, or social terms; and that the plural mode is not derivative of the singular mode. Terms of reciprocity are particularly apt to give an account of reflexivity for collective subjects or groups.

But Bratman's account of shared intentionality can only be used to question the argument underlying Ricoeur's thesis on the supra-political character of reconciliation. It does not address the thesis itself. And indeed, the problem with Bratman's account of shared intentions is that it ignores the very political element it seems to presuppose. For in order to establish, from an agent point of view, a reciprocal relationship, one has to determine the terms of the relationship, i.e. the group of agents involved. This, in turn, cannot be done unless one goes by factual proximity rather than a normative criterion. It is difficult to see how the full-blown political moment of 'founding' the polity could be conceived of without some representational form of self-inclusion building on this proximity. As soon as the political basis of a society is made explicit, it turns to the notion of a purely decisive act, which by definition cannot be shared by all those who would *like* to be involved. So Ricoeur is right in so far as his thesis entails that reconciliation has to be conceived of as conceptually *prior* to political institutions, including the polity as an institution overarching the addressors and the addressees of Babwhala Mhlauli's phrase. But he is not right in so far as his thesis would include that the collective vow made in the offer of reconciliation can be conceived without the presupposition of a polity of addressors *already* instituted. The 'we' in Babwhala Mhlauli's phrase, therefore, is a genuinely political 'we', expressing the self-enclosure that is characteristic of politics by virtue of the logic of representation. And it seems to me also that the act of addressing the representatives of the former oppressor, performed so generously by Babwhala Mhlauli as a representative of the former victims, obliquely invokes a more embracing 'we' of a polity-yet-to-be-established[45] that would include the former perpetrators now registering as excluded. But then – in virtue of this registering – this act in itself has to be regarded as proto-political, in the sense of being not framed by the political institutions but itself framing (instituting) the polity. It is an act that maps the instituted polity represented in its content on to the yet-to-be-instituted polity of its performance. We might perhaps also say, slightly twisting Ricoeur's formula, that it is self-regeneration in the plural, and therefore a form of political ecology. This form of politics is neither prior to inclusion, as it presupposes a polity already in place; nor is it posterior to inclusion, as it

45 Cf on the gerundival forms implied in *ubuntu*, see Ramose, ibid.

invokes[46] a 'we' not yet included. This 'we' can only obliquely be pointed to.[47] It is never present, as any political action immediately destroys it by virtue of the inevitability of self-inclusion. It can only be re-presented, i.e. to be 'staged' as present in spite of its sustained absence. Alternatively we might say that this 'we' invokes an economy that is 'prior' to politics in spite of its being also 'posterior' to politics. This priority may well amount to the 'protology' – or the 'political anthropology' for one who eschews theological vocabulary – we were looking for as the necessary supplement of Ricoeur's eschatology.

REFERENCES

Arendt, H. (1958). *The Human Condition.* Chicago – London, Univ. of Chicago Press.

Bankowski, Z. (2008). The risk of reconciliation. In *Law and the Politics of Reconciliation*, edited by S. Veitch. Aldershot: Ashgate.

Bratman, M.E. (1999). *Faces of Intention. Selected Essays on Intention and Agency.* Cambridge, Cambridge University Press.

Derrida, J. (1978). *Writing and difference.* Transl., with an introd. and add. notes by A. Bass, London.

Du Bois, Fr., and A. Du Bois-Pedain, eds. (2008). *Justice and Reconciliation in Post-Apartheid South Africa.* Cambridge: Cambridge University Press.

Hatzfeld, J. (2008). *De strategie van de antilopen. Daders en slachtoffers van de Rwandese genocide.* Amsterdam: De Bezige Bij.

Kodalle, Kl.-M. (1994). *Verzeihung nach Wendezeiten? Über Unnachsichtigkeit und misslingende Selbstentschuldung.* Erlangen – Jena, Verlag Palm & Enke.

Krog, A. (2000). *De kleur van je hart.* Amsterdam: Mets en Schilt – Novib. Original edition, *Country of My Skull* (1998).

Marx, K. (1844) [1971]. Zur Kritik der Nationalökonomie – ökonomisch-philosophische Manuskripte. In *Karl Marx Frühe Schriften, Bd I*, edited by H.-J. Lieber and P. Furth. Damstadt: Wissenschaftliche Buchgesellschaft.

Mokgoro, Y. (2008). *Ubuntu and the Law in South Africa.* The EcoPort Foundation 1998 [cited July 14th 2008 2008]. Available from http://epf.ecoport.org/appendix3.html.

Ramose, M.B. (1995). Specific African thought structures and their possible contribution to world peace. In *H. Beck – G. Schmirber, Kreative Friede durch Begegnung der Weltkulturen.* Frankfurt a.M., P. Lang, 227-251.

— (1994). The concept of life as a universal wholeness. In E. Schadel – U. Voigt (eds), *Sein -Erkennen – Handeln. Interkulturelle, ontologische und ethische Perspektiven. Festschrift für Heinrich Beck zum 65. Geburtstag.*

— (1999). *African Philosophy Through Ubuntu.* Harare, Mond Books.

Ricoeur, P. (1990). *Soi-même comme un autre.* Paris, Du Seuil.

— (2000). *La mémoire, l'histoire, l'oubli.* Paris: Du Seuil.

46 Cf. (Schaap 2005).

47 Bankowski 2008.

— (2004). *Memory, History, Forgetting.* Translated by K.B. a. D. Pellauer. Chicago – London: The University of Chicago Press.

Schaap, A. (2005). *Political Reconciliation.* London – New York: Routledge.

Van der Walt, J.W.G. (2005). *Law and Sacrifice. Towards a Post-Apartheid Theory of Law.* London: Birkbeck Press.

Van Roermund, B. (2001). Rubbing Off and Rubbing On: The Grammar of Reconciliation. In E. Christodoulidis – S. Veitch (eds.), *Lethe's Law. Justice, Law and Ethics in Reconciliation.* Oxford – Portland (Or), Hart Publishing: 175–190.

— (2003). First-Person Plural Legislature: Political Reflexivity and Representation. *Philosophical Explorations* 6 (3):235–250.

Veitch, S., ed. (2006). *Law and the Politics of Reconciliation, Edinburgh Centre for Law and Society.* Aldershot: Ashgate.

Waldenfels, B. (1994). *Antwortregister.* Frankfurt a. M.: Suhrkamp.

— (2004). *Phänomenologie der Aufmerksamkeit.* Frankfurt a.M.: Suhrkamp.

A QUESTION OF FORGIVING WORDS

Erik Doxtader

> [T]he smallest act in the most limited circumstances
> bears the seed of the same boundlessness,
> because one deed, and sometimes one word,
> suffices to change every constellation.
> Hannah Arendt

> To save time, just ask unanswerable questions.
> Jacques Derrida

1. SPEAKING, TO A QUESTION

What if the question remains? Amidst all the public discussion of forgiveness, there is the question of the inquiry with which it begins, the question that appears in the name of beginning anew – *Will you forgive me?* Charged if not loaded, the very sound of this question resonates. Asked in time, it strikes us as an opening, a moment of potential given to (re)turning history from fate. Posed in the wake of that which changes everything, however, the inquiry smacks of contrivance, an artifice that recalls if not (re)inflicts a hollowing wound. Between a gesture of redress and an unthinking affront...this variation is telling. Addressed to a subject that has suffered a particular wrong, a transgression whose precise depth may touch the very limit of articulation and defy complete knowledge, the question of forgiveness is never quite the same even if its grammar is altogether familiar. Its inquiry composes a unique imposition, a posing with (dis)respect to an event, a posture that makes reference even as it has neither the comprehension nor the standing needed to refer to that which it addresses. Before a reply, the captivating problem of whether forgiveness is permissible and perhaps even desirable, there is then the matter of hearing the question, of listening to what it renders questionable. Without promise, the question of forgiveness arrives already divided, an inquiry caught between its own expression and its query as to what remains (in)expressible. A speech act that troubles the action of speaking – in public and perhaps for publicity's sake –

the question of forgiveness asks *after* the (im)potentiality of (its) speak-ability and inquires into our experience of (its) language.[1]

In how many ways does the (un)speakable haunt the question of forgiveness? We do not always remember – we may not be able to remember – that the question appears in the aftermath, a moment in which the capacity to ask and the capacity to answer are not given. As it emerges from the folds of transgression, conflict, and trauma, the question arrives in moment in which there may be no stable place to stand, no shared ground for argument, no common time for narrative. A public call for forgiveness may thus echo across a landscape in which the public lacks for words and reverberate within a moment in which the public is fundamentally not itself.[2] In the wake of violence that distorts the fabric of language, that tears word from experience and leads institutions to homogenize norms of interpretation in the name of restoring the past or moving forward, the problem of "deep division" may well be defined by the matter of what can be spoken, who can(not) speak, and how to reconstitute the capacity for speech.[3] If so, the occasion which heralds the 'need' for forgiveness may be an exigence that fundamentally disrupts the conditions of its performance. In the face of the imprescriptable offence, a crime so heinous as to defy the law's prescriptive (or pre-scripted) words of redress, the mere suggestion of forgiveness is muted by

---

1 By the concept of "publicity," I do not mean the act of making something public, an assertion or advance that is frequently considered a mode of advertisement or a mechanism of public relations. Rather, the concept refers to the rhetorical process whereby a public finds or invents its voice as public. In this sense, publicity is a mode of action dedicated to discerning and defining the rules and norms of public discourse and argumentation. See Doxtader 2001.

2 In such a context there are significant risks involved in defining forgiveness as a "public good." Behind this appellation, forgiveness is turned from inquiry to procedure, an exchange whose conditions are pre-defined and capable of being plotted over time. The form of the equation varies. Its consistent appeal, however, is the formal-pragmatic stability of the public sphere, a grounding of public discourse in validity conditions that imbue forgiveness with the aura of a rule and defer basic theoretical matters such as whether it is important to differentiate (and relate) *public* forgiveness and public *forgiveness* – a distinction that may bear directly on the promise of beginning (again) that inheres in both publicity and forgiving. This conferral of methodological status to forgiveness also affords an evidently comforting alternative to reconciliation, particularly given that the latter's ambiguities are often viewed more as a threat to mutual understanding than as an opening to think the limits of the word's unifying power in those very moments of *stasis* that are held out as the occasion for forgiveness.

3 For all of the talk about the importance of ensuring that the drowned out subaltern, the silenced margin, and the mute victim can come to voice, gain a hearing, and receive due recognition, the fields of restorative and transitional justice, in which so much of the discourse of forgiveness is contained, show a marked tendency to discount the value of inquiry into the conditions, dynamics, and value of speech. Reflecting a traditional view that speaking is neither a trustworthy nor legitimate form of action, this neglect is curious insofar as the advocacy of human rights discourse has long relied on the classical dicta that the human being *is* the speaking being and that narrating subjectivity – *homo narrans* – is a (pre)given form of life. For an important discussion of the ways in which discourses of transitional justice and human rights frequently fail to acknowledge their own discursive quality, see Kennedy 2004. Also see, Ricoeur 2006: 464; Ross 2003; Minow 1999.

the presumption that expiation is an impossible wrong. *How dare we speak of forgiveness in the wake of an attack on humanity!* Beyond this limit, the question of forgiveness may go unheard in the midst of legal violence, a form of subjection "justified" by a logic of exception whereby law discounts forgiveness with an endless promise to undo the damage done in a future yet to come. *Do not ask of forgiveness but wait for salvation!* And in situations where forgiveness is deemed a legitimate option, the dilemma is no less stark: the speech action of forgiving – as a question and answer – may proceed only by forgetting the subject's potential (in)capacity for self-expression, the ways in which ethical life may turn on a recognition of the inability of an "I" to give an account of itself or, as Hannah Arendt understood so well, the ways in which the self-certain action of speech inflicts unexpected wounds.[4] *You know not what you ask! You know not what you have given in reply!*

Does forgiveness ask too much or not enough? Operating on the verge of the unspeakable, it appears without "proper" justification and defies a "standardized" reply. Its inquiry rests on inarticulable grounds that appear to undercut its own meaning at the same time that its expression opens space to consider the (un) binding power of language. As Paul Ricoeur put it, the question of forgiveness both pronounces an interest in discovering "gestures incapable of being transformed into institutions" and discloses the need for "greater semantic vigilance" with respect to the ways in which speech action turns enmity towards friendship.[5] An indication of why forgiveness is neither theoretically simple nor practically straightforward, this dynamic merits consideration. At the most basic level, it underscores that forgiveness must be asked. This much must be clear and left unencumbered by analytic games that would have us define the work of language as so much clutter at the cost of grasping how philosophy's holy war against expression contributes to the conflict that it promises to overcome.[6] In the name of a beginning, forgiveness is dependent on an interrogative mode of speech; it begins with the formulation and utterance of a question. Yet, as Ricoeur suggests, the asking of this question does not fully disclose that which is being asked. Composed without the banister of *topoi* and posed to an other in a manner that calls attention to the contingency of its own terms, the question of forgiveness appears to conceal something of its precise request.

The question of forgiveness is a rhetorical question. By this, I mean something well beyond the thin view of an interrogative utterance for which there need be no reply. In the pages that follow, my wager is that the rhetorical question of forgiveness is rhetorical precisely as its expression both performs and troubles

---

4 I turn to Arendt shortly. On the former point, see Butler 2005.

5 Ricoeur 2006: 458, 469. For other carefully argued reflections on the discourse of forgiveness, see Sanders 2007; Schaap 2003; Oliver 2003.

6 Required reading in this regard: McKeon 1944 and Cassin 2000. For an extended treatment of McKeon's work and its implications for the contemporary discourse of human rights, see Doxtader 2010.

the question-ability of (its) language. Working from within Hannah Arendt and Jacques Derrida's respective accounts of how the action of speaking marks an occasion for human being to utter the question of whether they might be forgiven, my aim here is to grasp something of how the particular interrogative expression with which forgiveness begins contains a general inquiry that calls language itself into question. Before a reply, the question of forgiveness *asks after* and it *asks for* a suffering (of) language; it inquires into the ways in which the word subjects being to violence and how the redress of this violence hinges on an experience of language as such, an experience of relinquishing the grounds of self-certain expression and abiding in the (im)potential of the word's contingency. Within the fold of its question, forgiveness asks us to turn within and (re)turn to language, a double movement of theory, a discovery addressed to the words that stand between us, the words that constitute and negate human (inter)action.

2. ASKING FOR FORGIVENESS: THE (IM)POTENTIALITY OF LANGUAGE

We request forgiveness. On the grounds that it cannot be presumed, we request, for our being, to be forgiven. We ask for the favor of forgiveness, an agreeable or agreement-making reply that arrives without reason, as a gift that opposes and perhaps breaks the bonds of fate. If governed less by statute than calling, forgiveness begins with the question of faith in words that we have no right to expect but which are felt to hold the power to render us as we are not. That the query which inaugurates forgiveness surprises – and shocks – is not all that surprising except perhaps as it yields a question of its own, one put well by Horace Bushnell in 1874: "How shall a man be able to entirely and perfectly forgive his enemy, so as to forever sweeten the bitterness of his wounded feeling and leave no sense of personal revulsion?"[7] Before its reply, the asking of forgiveness yields if not imposes the question of its question-ability.

The expression of the question brings us to a question of expression. For Hannah Arendt, this point was crucial, an indication of how forgiveness expresses and reflects the ontological problem of the word's (non)relation to being's becoming. As "a life without speech and without action" is a life that has "ceased to be a human life because it is no longer lived among men", Arendt's argument begins with the claim that "with word and deed we insert ourselves into the human world, and this insertion is like a second birth".[8] Beyond cause, it is a springing; with the potential to begin again, to discover and invent, *zoe* is thrown towards *bios* with(in) the "initiative" of speech-action that brings being to appearance, into a shared space in which beings "appear to each other" and

7 Bushnell 2009: 10.
8 Arendt 1958: 176.

become human as they reveal who they are – with one another. And it is the action of speech that underwrites this shared work of self-revelation. Absent the word, Arendt suggests, action "would lose its [human] subject." It is with(in) the "doing" of speaking that we enter the domain of "inter-est", the space of the "in-between" wherein we inaugurate beginnings, experience the "'web' of human relationships," and fashion forms of public life.[9]

If words make a difference, perhaps even a unity in difference, they do so with a contingency that speaks to the fragility of our condition. Neither ephemeral nor instrumental, according to Arendt, the action of speech is an (im) potentiality, a kind of power that may or may not come to be and whose actuality holds within it the 'seeds' of its absence.[10] Necessary but lacking necessity, the word itself abides and moves "in-between" such that its action is a shuttling which blurs what its appearance *is* and what it *is not*. Within the movement of speech, the human capacity to begin anew beckons a subject at the cost of self-certainty. In the most straightforward sense, Arendt takes this to mean that "he who acts never quite knows what he is doing" and that the "ideal of uncompromising self-sufficiency is contradictory to the very condition of plurality".[11] With(in) the word, we are indeed caught between; we are caught between the speech-action of the promise whose force enables us to "act in concert" and the way in which the promise's expression "seems to entangle its producer to such an extent that he appears much more the victim and the sufferer than author and doer of what he has done."[12] In the work of becoming with(in) language, the initiative that emerges with the word's appearance comes at the expense of others; the irreversible and unpredictable power of expression leaves us guilty of damaging the very relationships to which they are dedicated.

In the human condition, we suffer language. We suffer (from) the potentiality and the impotentiality of the words that underwrite our becoming human. If this experience is frequently taken as a warrant to dismiss the importance of speaking and "reason enough to turn away with despair from the realm of human affairs", Arendt claims that it is better understood as the fundamental occasion of forgiveness. As the "sovereign" actor discerns the (self-inflicted) wounds of its words, the possibility of life beyond bare life comes to rest on the faculty of forgiving:

> Without being forgiven, released from the consequences of what we have done, our capacity to act would, as it were, be confined to one single deed from which we could

9 Arendt 1958: 182–3, 198.

10 Arendt 1958: 236. For a full discussion of potential (*dunamis*) as it emerges in Aristotle and informs his definition of rhetoric, see Agamben 2000.

11 Arendt 1958: 233.

12 Arendt 1958: 233–34.

> never recover; we would remain the victims of its consequences forever, not unlike the sorcerer's apprentice who lacked the magic formula to break the spell.[13]

It seems that there is magic in the mix, a mysterious power that may strike us as a miracle but which is "one of the potentialities of action itself," a capacity for speech to undo what (its) words have done, a potential for expression to interrupt the irreversible force of (its) action.[14] As such, as a surprising and "mutual release," Arendt holds out forgiveness as a constitutive (inter)action and an event whose word "acts anew" to put an end to the damage done – not least by language – and recuperate the "promising ground" of collective life.[15] But how? How does forgiveness work in the moment? How does its expression exceed – if only temporarily – the human condition's suffering (from) language?

Arendt's reply is unexpectedly indirect. With a warning that it remains "without reality" if attempted in solitude or secrecy, her account of the "faculty" and dynamics of forgiving is implicit in the claim that it "depend[s] on plurality, on the presence and acting of others". It depends then on speech. And, as it appears in the moment in which the articulation of a promise simply compounds the injury, it rests on the expression and utterance of a question. It is a question that begins the work of beginning (again) with forgiveness: *Will you forgive me?* This is an inquiry into what might remain between us, what bond of words might yet abide in the name of (being's) being together. In asking to be forgiven, self-certain expression is interrupted by an interrogative voice that concedes the contingency of expression, the provisionality of the grounds on which to assert, propose, and narrate. In this way, as a question, forgiveness discloses the (im) potentiality of language as such, the contingency of the "taking place" of language that is obscured in the pragmatic terms of everyday life.[16] Addressed to the word that has devolved to force, the questioning with which forgiveness begins is an act of speech that confesses to the unknowable basis of speech-action.

With the hope of a beginning that brings individuals to the cusp of public life, the human(izing) action of speech holds out a question of forgiveness that recalls and perhaps redresses the violence of the word's (im)potential, a power that we cannot fully claim to know and to which we are all vulnerable. For Arendt, however, this expiating revelation has a limit, a point beyond which the question of forgiveness may not be asked, an offence that undoes our capacity to undo the deeds of words. Confronted with the commission of "radical evil", she famously contends, "all we know is that we can neither punish nor forgive such

13 Arendt 1958: 237.

14 Arendt 1958: 236–7.

15 Arendt 1958: 240–1, 244. Soon enough, this recovery of the capacity to promise occasions, once more, the need of forgiveness, a dynamic that underwrites Arendt's case even as she does not detail the precise interplay of the forgiving and promising word.

16 Here, I draw from Agamben 1991.

offenses and that they therefore transcend the realm of human affairs and the potentialities of human power, both of which they radically destroy wherever they make their appearance."[17] Now linked to law, what Arendt describes as a structural limit of forgiveness amounts to a crime against potentiality, the possibilities of becoming (human) that exceed knowledge.[18] Whether negated or folded into a logic of exception that marks the beginning of "legal violence", the collapse of this "in-between" power yields only the "tranquility of the cemetery", a silence that heralds the relegation of *bios* to *zoe* and thus strikes down the hope that forgiveness might "put an end to something that without interference would go on endlessly".[19] And, at just this moment, Arendt turns from the word and its loss to the loss demanded by the Word: "It were better for him that a millstone were hanged about his neck, and he cast into the sea."[20]

Perhaps there is nowhere else to turn. In a human world where the "political realm rises directly out of acting together" *and* the public is prefaced by law in the name of assuring that deeds and stories will not perish, the barbarism (literally: without the capacity to speak) of radical evil leads Arendt to the command that forsakes its perpetrator. And then, it leads her to the corollary problem: what to do with the "current conviction that only love has the power to forgive" and the attending Christian principle that with love we arrive "to the point of being always willing to forgive" regardless of what has been done.[21] While it may take forgiveness as a given, Arendt holds that the irony of such goodness is that it has no place in the world. Incapable of being seen, of entering into the scene of human appearance, love "destroys the in-between which relates us to and separates us from others".[22] Thus, she claims, the unity of love forecloses the question of forgiveness. Leaving nothing between us, it closes the gap on which the question's expression depends; it affords no space to ask after the doing *and* the undoing of those words that compose the human condition's "unity in difference."

Addressed to the ways in which "we are dependent upon others, to whom we appear in a distinctness which we ourselves are not able to perceive", the question of forgiveness would appear to begin with(in) a struggle for recognition.[23] Here, as she concludes that love precludes the very question that it seeks to answer, Arendt's account of forgiveness both borrows and breaks from the young Hegel's reflection on the spirit of Christianity, an essay that is often overshadowed by the *Phenomenology* but which has much to say about how law (dis)figures the limit

17 Arendt 1958: 241.
18 For two very relevant reflections on the connection between law and forgiveness see Benjamin 2003 and Derrida 1992.
19 Arendt 1958: 241.
20 Arendt 1958: 241.
21 Arendt 1958: 242–3.
22 Arendt 1958: 242.
23 Arendt 1958: 74, 242.

of forgiveness. The initial resonance appears with Arendt's claim that forgiveness puts a stop to the fate of speech action, the "chain reaction contained in every action to take its unhindered course".[24]Absent forgiveness, the word's transgression beckons a bad infinity that is felt, according to Hegel, as the power of life turning hostile to itself.[25] Forgiveness undertakes to cancel this endless *stasis*, a force that otherwise renders us alien not only to each other but to ourselves. Such an 'undoing' is not intuitive, particularly given that it requires that the victim "no longer stands on the right acquired in opposition to the offender."[26] From the 'good word', Hegel's claim is thus that the occasion of forgiveness is a moment in which we are left with the question of the word before law, a *logos* that names the potential for being to become in(to) relation but does so within a love that "pronounces no imperatives".[27] Thus, while Arendt links law and forgiveness and refuses love on the grounds that it risks the collapse of public life, Hegel seeks to expose the limit of law's duty (and our duty to it) by way of love's demonstration that law is a contingent "fragment of human nature" and unable to redress those transgressions that destroy the "friendliness of life".[28] Revealing that law arises out of man – as constitutive speech action, in Arendt's terms – love prompts the question of how forgiveness is called to work in excess of law's jurisdiction. Taken as an objective (alien) power, law is not simply powerless to redress the "causality of fate" – whereby "through the killing of life" one stands having "perverted life into an enemy" – it is also a means of its instantiation, a rendering alien of the word whose love is first a recognition of the need to question, to sacrifice the isolation of acting and judging consciousness in the name of standing "naked and impotent" before the (im)potential of an "expressive relation".[29]

If forgiveness abides between the assumption and negation of the subject as it appears in (and for) relation, the habitation of this "middle space" does not assure an existence with(in) a mean(ing); there is no bright line that differentiates the release of self-certainty which conditions (asking) forgiveness and the abject subjection which holds only a paralytic silence. For both Arendt and Hegel, this ambiguity amounts to the problem of how to explain the *grounds* of forgiveness. While forgiveness may depend on its surprise, Arendt does not presuppose that it appears *ex nihilo*. In public and for the public, the law indemnifies and contains forgiveness. Thus, as the limit of the law's ability to punish demarcates the limit

24 Arendt 1958: 240.

25 Hegel 1948: 228–9, 231.

26 Hegel 1948: 237.

27 Hegel 1948: 246–7.

28 Hegel 1948: 229.

29 Bernstein 1996: 62–3. As Bernstein puts it, forgiveness stands (without standing) before the law in the name of asking after the "'unwritten law' which inscribes my originary debt to the other," the question of what words might work to both "express my particularity and renounce it."

of forgiveness, Arendt's case amounts to a defense of *public* forgiveness, a mode of (inter)action that stems from and remains tied to a given grammar of collective life. For Hegel, however, forgiveness rests on the word of love that defies law's 'common space' in the name of forging a "living link", a life in relation that unfolds only as "man has found himself in another".[30] On the latter view, it is only through a process of public *forgiveness* that human beings exceed the given terms (*topoi*) of the commons and undertake to account for its violence.

Between Arendt and Hegel, there is an unspoken question about speaking. Between a forgiveness grounded in the expression of publicity and a unity in difference borne of a forgiving word, there is a muted disclosure that speaks to the dilemma of defining the limit of forgiveness and why efforts to discern the threshold at which the (im)potential of forgiveness devolves to an unjust(ified) force are rooted less in given standards of morality than the question of how to conceive the gift of language. Drawing the line in the face of radical evil, Arendt reserves forgiveness for transgressions that remain within the sphere of a common and shared vocabulary, a limit that leads her to resist the 'reduction' of forgiveness to love, a private language that may promote an extra-legal absolutism. Yet, as Hegel contends, the risk that love's inexpressible goodness will yield an opaque politics of the heart, must be juxtaposed to a consideration of whether the strictures of legal precedent leave forgiveness in fate's corner, a position in which it is barred from disclosing the law's public (making) violence against life. In other words, the constitutive rhetorical "surprise" – the expression of a (re)inventing word – that Arendt attributes to forgiveness may be prematurely given away to the degree that it is prefigured or conditioned by its larger discourse, the underlying historical fabric of publicity through which forgiveness is expressed and understood. Still, even if Arendt cannot fully explain how the potentiality of the unexpected word resists being turned into a banal inevitability, she is attuned to the way in which Hegel's forgiving *logos* of love radicalizes the word into an experience of language as such, a language that renders us fully present in relation but does so at the cost of the historical referent needed to determine whether such interaction is – in any sense – meaningful. At this threshold, at the point where its (im)potentiality appears equally enlivening and threatening, the question of forgiveness held between Arendt and Hegel is a rhetorical question, a query that Adorno cast as the tension between the barbarism of writing poetry after Auschwitz and the fact that societies turn barbaric when they steady themselves with a "stern hostility" to rhetoric.[31]

What can(not) be asked of forgiveness? The question turns and returns, a shifting problem of the threshold beyond which forgiveness cannot inquire in the name of making a beginning. In it, everything may seem at stake, at least as the question struggles between an inquiry that aims to wrest being from the

30 Hegel 1948: 278.
31 Adorno 1973.

violence of (its) fate and a recognition of the unquestionable evil that betrays the potential of ethical life. Here, at this trying nexus, Derrida approaches the "address of forgiveness" and contends that it appears and operates in a "zone of hyperbole, of aporia and paradox".[32] If "forgiveness must be asked", he suggests, the question remains "heterogeneous to any determination in the order of knowledge." It is a question composed of:

> a tension or a contradiction between the hyperbolical ethics that tends to push the exigency to the limit and beyond the limit of the possible *and* this everyday economy of forgiveness that dominates the religious, juridical, even political and psychological semantics of forgiveness, a forgiveness held within the human or anthropo-theological limits of repentance, confession, expiation, reconciliation, or redemption.[33]

Does the question of forgiveness rest on the (un)conditionality of its inquiry? On Derrida's reading, it stands – perhaps without standing – between the "power of the impossible" that asks what cannot be asked in the name of an "ethics beyond ethics" and a quotidian logic that governs the question with a calculus that binds it to "the judiciary as penal order".[34] It is not then that forgiveness is impossible or that it is "real" only as it undertakes to address the unforgiveable. Rather, it is that if forgiveness must be asked, if its asking expresses "a hope for a word to come – or not", the question of forgiveness holds out the question of asking itself; with the question thought to inaugurate forgiveness there appears a "question of the word" and its (im)potential:

> Must forgiveness pass through words or must it pass (beyond) words? Must it pass through word-verbs or must it pass (beyond) them, those word-verbs? Can one only forgive or ask forgiveness when speaking or sharing the language of the other, that is to say, by already identifying sufficiently with the other for this, and, by identifying with the other, making forgiveness both possible and impossible? Must one refuse the experience of forgiveness to whoever does not speak? Or, on the contrary, must one make silence the very element of forgiveness, if there is such a thing?[35]

These are not analytic but rhetorical questions, which is to say that they are questions of forgiveness that appear with(in) its performance, with(in) the performativity of its inquiry, an inquisition into the possibility of asking after words that have (yet) to come and which are (yet) defiled by necessity.

Such inquiry affords few comforts. In the puzzling moment to which it is "given," Derrida contends that the question of forgiveness marks the anguishing

32 Derrida 2001a: 42. Also see Derrida 2001b.
33 Derrida 2001a: 29.
34 Derrida, 2001a: 29, 45.
35 Derrida, 2001a: 47.

"experience of language itself, always as the other".[36] Such experience amounts to a double problem. On the one hand, it means that the question throws us into words that are not our own, a vocabulary and grammar with which we have no experience, no history of exchange, and whose meaning would appear to rest on the very gift of forgiveness itself. On the other, the expression of the question seems to beckon if not reel us back into the word's fold, into a "sharing [of] language" that addresses the unique event which occasions forgiveness at the same time that it sets the work of address – the asking of the question – into a "law of iterable unicity," a statute that indemnifies the unhinged moment of forgiveness with precedent, a (shared) ground for the word in the face of the singular transgression for which there are no words.[37]

Derrida leaves us between. And he does so in a way that sheds useful light on the dilemma that inheres within the gap which energizes Arendt's account of forgiveness. In the question of forgiveness, we are left between the loss of words that mark the (in)capacity to ask forgiveness and the gathering of a word that underwrites the (un)questioning power of interrogative address. If it does more than articulate an incomprehensible promise of that which is always to come and if it is less than a doctrine that banks on the historicity which it seeks to exceed, the question of forgiveness is a question that asks "must forgiveness pass through words or must it pass (beyond) words?" Thus, the defining aporia of forgiveness, the obstacle that provokes and precludes thought about its threshold, is that the question of its asking hinges on asking after the question-ability that inheres within it. The beginning of forgiveness is an experience of language as such, the experience of an interrogative expression that pronounces the contingency of its own terms, a contingency that renders every posing of the question premature and every reply too late. Put in a slightly different way, if it must be asked, it is not certain that the question of forgiveness can be asked.

Will you forgive me? Made in the name of beginning (again), this inquiry rests on the question of whether and how to begin inquiry – Will you forgive a question? Can you hear let alone listen to a question that cannot be fully understood or justified in the moment of its utterance, a question that has no standing and which promises to set us into an unmooring experience of language, an encounter with the word that may trouble meaning and the history that it embodies? In the aftermath of transgression, can you forgive the hypocrisy of a question, a query that can only take itself back to the extent that its asking points to the need to dismiss its apparent coherence and discover words about the words that might allow us to (re)make the grounds of (inter)action? From within a persisting wound, can you relinquish the narrative that affords a measure of self-certainty and cede to a question that exceeds and likely forecloses any *right* of last reply?

---

36 Derrida, 2001a: 38.
37 Derrida, 2001a: 46.

Perhaps these are impossible questions. At the very least, they are questions that defy formulaic reply. From Derrida's vantage, this difficulty is an indication that the difference between the forgivable and the unforgiveable is not defined by declaration – a propositional mode of speech action that would constitute a banal repetition and a trite overlooking of the particular transgression under consideration. Instead, the threshold of the forgivable appears only through or by way of the question that asks forgiveness and which does so in a manner that dismantles the conditions and meaning of its own inquiry, that discloses how the aftermath of transgression is a moment – a *stasis* – in which the question of what we can do with words coincides with the question of what words do with us. In Derrida's controversial terms, it is such that:

> We constantly struggle in the snares of an aporia whose abstract and dry form, whose logical formality is an implacable as it is indisputable: There is only forgiveness, if there is such a thing, of the un-forgivable. Thus forgiveness, if there is such a thing, is not possible, it does not exist as possible, it only exists by exempting itself from the law of the possible, by impossibilizing itself, so to speak, and in the infinite endurance of the im-possible as impossible.[38]

If there is such a thing as forgiveness it is that which holds a power to turn against itself. Its question moves (us) only as it turns toward and takes in (or, in more Derridian terms, remains hospitable to) the indescribable cost of (its own) expression. Here, if we can hear the resonance between the unforgiveable and the un-forgiveable *and* the impossible and the im-possible, there is no (moralizing) demand that forgiveness address and redress the unforgivable. In Derrida's view, the task is not to breach a norm but to step back and ask after the "*law* of the possible" that codifies the norm and which thus delineates the threshold of forgiveness through a procedure that he sees as all to quick to forget the "trial of decision" held within the question of forgiveness itself, the choice of whether (and how) to move between a question offered in a given language and the question of giving language (back to itself).

For a moment, it is useful to linger with this idea. Derrida is not contending that forgiveness cannot occur or that it is literally no-thing – two common renditions of his position that follow from a failure to distinguish between the "impossible" and the "im-possible." Nor is he proposing that forgiveness rests on the performance of a somehow superhuman effort. Rather, *if it is possible*, if it not simply fated and if it is not simply presupposed to already *actually* exist in the wake of a *particular* transgression, forgiveness comes (in)to being through an exemption, an exception to the law that not only governs but distorts its possibility, a law that delineates a set of conditions which, if met, do not produce forgiveness so much as ensure that it *can* occur in principle, that there is nothing

[38] Derrida 2001a: 48.

impossible about forgiveness.[39] Recalling something of Arendt's case, the problem with this conditioned or conditional form of forgiveness is that by barring the impossible it cannot make good on its founding promise – the appearance of the new, a (re)turn to the question of beginning (again). More precisely, it is the play between the impossibility and possibility of forgiveness that yields its im-possibility, that is, its (im)potentiality, the modality of power (*dunamis*) in which a thing's coming-to-be contains and in fact never transcends the chance that it may not-come-to-be. Thus, for Derrida, an exception to the "law of the possible" is a gesture that returns the impossible to the im-possible. It is an effort that resists a methodological-juridical maneuver in the name of grasping "an im-possible that is the very experience of the possible" or, to put it in a slightly different manner, the way that "the impossibility of forgiving must continue to haunt forgiveness".[40]

Rather than bicker over whether this is a "practical" idea (a favorite retort from those committed to locating transitional justice "on the ground"), the better path is to ask how Derrida's concern for the (im)potentiality of forgiveness (we could equally say im-possibility) leads him back to its question, the problem of the question with which forgiveness begins. *Will you forgive me?* Faced with this question, a beginning of forgiveness that appears to rest on the "juridical-political" register that it claims to render questionable, Derrida asks. He asks: "Is it true that for forgiveness to be granted or even only envisaged, it must be asked for and asked for on the basis of confession and regret?"[41] It is important that we hear both of these inquiries – Must forgiveness be asked? Must its request rest on a basis? The latter, as it constitutes the law of possibility, affords the ground on which to stand, the quotidian words that support the making of an inquiry for forgiveness within an economy of "repentance, confession, expiation, reconciliation, or redemption".[42] The former, however, sets us before the word itself, the language in which we have no necessary standing; it is a question that opens a way to the experience of language without condition, a power to disclose the impossibility of the law that underwrites its utterance. Corresponding to the conditional and unconditional forms of forgiveness, Derrida contends that the two 'sides' of his double question are linked: "The unconditional and conditional are, certainly, absolutely heterogeneous, and this forever, on either side of a limit, but they are also indissociable. There is in the movement, in the motion of the unconditional forgiveness, an inner exigency of becoming-effective, manifest,

39 A different way of making the same point is that the fact that forgiveness is necessary, in Arendt's ontological sense, is too often mistaken for the legitimacy of procedures that promise forgiveness as something 'automatic'.

40 Derrida 2007a: 453–4.

41 Derrida, 2001a: 45.

42 Derrida, 2001a: 29. More simply, the expression of the question, as a question offered or submitted, is a speech act whereby the "guilty party mortifies himself, confesses himself, repents, accuses himself by asking for forgiveness" (Derrida, 2001a: 28).

determined, and in determining itself, bending to conditionality."[43] Far from a retreat to compromise or a normative mean, this suggests that the (im) potentiality of forgiveness moves within the question (of the question) of forgiveness. If it admits to "no theoretical *statement*", the question of forgiveness, as a rhetorical question, composes a proteptic gesture; it is an expression that begins the work of theory, a mode of inquiry that amounts not to method or problem-solving but a movement that opens a way to question language in the face of (its) aporia and which proceeds outside the given strictures of (its) law.[44]

3. THE PUBLIC QUESTION OF FORGIVENESS

What is the (im)potential of asking (after) the question of forgiveness? Two questions then, a double question: what power abides in the making-request with which forgiveness begins *and* what does the request for forgiveness make of the power that abides in a beginning? To this, we might add a third: in what way are these public questions? For Arendt, human beings make the request for forgiveness in the name of (re)constituting the potential for the words with which they appear to one another and establish the basis for collective action; the speech-action of the question follows from and endeavors to repair the wounds that attend the acting performed by the speaking that enables and sustains public life. The difficulty, however, is that such expression unfolds within the very language that it endeavors to purify. As Derrida makes plain, the promise of this question, the request that promises an opportunity to begin again in relation, sits in tension with its asking, at least insofar as its motivating transgression, if it is indeed forgivable, throws publicity into rather stark relief; the question as such is either incomprehensible given that it is posed at a moment when norms of shared (and sharable) meaning are disputed (perhaps deeply) or its conceptual and grammatical integrity is indemnified by a form of law that silently backs public discourse with *topoi* that overwrite the historical rupture which occasions the request for forgiveness in the first place.

With the public question of forgiveness, we are confronted with an inquiry that involves both the word's potential to make and the invention of potential-making words. As a question, the question appears and moves between a speech act of inquiry that opens the potential for new (inter)action *and* an act of asking after how the asking of forgiveness figures the possibility of beginning through a ritual repetition in which it is impossible to live. In this way, as it depends on the operativity of interrogative words at the same time that opens them to scrutiny, the rhetorical question of forgiveness opens an important theoretical space.

43 Derrida, 2001a: 45.

44 For accounts of theory (*theoria*) that set its movement over its ocular quality, see Nightingale 2004 and Gadamer 1994.

Before it invites reply, its expression figures an *aporia*, a blockage of (its own) movement that marks the occasion of theory – the question that asks whether forgiveness *will* be given is first the question of whether it *can* be given, at least insofar as the question has not been reduced to one element of an (automatic) procedure, a decision calculus that contains a prior definition regarding the relative necessity of affirming or refusing the question. As the question of forgiveness speaks to the (im)potential for forgiving, the problem of defining the threshold of the (un)forgivable is held within the question as a call for theoretical inquiry, a setting out toward or a discovery of the question as an expression and experience of 'suffering language'. In its rhetorical-proteptic terms, the public question of forgiveness is thus a response to the suffering of damage *to* the word and *by* the word; the transgression that occasions the question of forgiveness is both an attack on the word's promising (shared) power and a disclosure of how promising words turn violent.

Facing a language (of) suffering, one that may or may not be articulate or articulable, the question of forgiveness does not propose a solution but asks how the constitutive (im)potential of the word, the contingent rhetorical power to begin again, may turn on a suffering (of) language, an experience of giving over to language as such. This experience may have several interlocking dimensions. First, the question of forgiveness pronounces the vulnerability of the speaking subject. As a request made at the limit of language, the question expresses both a loss of words and a loss of control over them. Absent the capacity to *propose*, a power underwritten by a historically grounded grammar that may be indistinguishable from the transgression that occasions forgiveness, the question of forgiveness does not then fate a confession given to an accounting of what the questioning subject has done so much as it first discloses the subject's displacement from language and its inability to give an account of its (given) self.[45] For the victim, in the wake of an offence, the submitting of the question is thus not only a presumptuous intrusion but a request for a certain submission; backed by no good reason, the inquiry is a request to hear (and perhaps listen to) baseless words and expend time – literally – on the work of (re)constituting the grounds for (inter)action. That there may be a desire to hear the question does not deny that its receipt comes at the potential cost of a 'surviving narrative'.[46]

Second, the question of forgiveness interrupts the given ends and means of (hermeneutic) interpretation. If a request for forgiveness asks for something with respect to something – *What is forgiveness to be given for?* – the nature and meaning of the offence that constitutes the 'object' of the question is often opaque and frequently contested. While the human rights community may wish it

45 Here, I rely somewhat on Butler (2005).

46 Moreover, when the question of forgiveness is posed *in* public, when it moves and appears outside its immediate context and is taken up as a matter of collective interest, the parties issuing and addressed by the question are themselves reduced to objects of scrutiny if not intense debate.

otherwise, the acts that occasion requests for forgiveness are more often rooted in diverging historical norms about what counts as justifiable action than acts that break from laws about which there is no (interpretive) disagreement. There is a crucial but altogether blurry line between a request for forgiveness that speaks to "an act that I thought was right which *went* wrong", and "an act that I thought was right which *is* wrong".[47] If some will entertain the former, others will not. The difference often hinges on historical interpretations of whether the question of forgiveness can legitimately (meaningfully) proceed from the view that an offence can mean otherwise or if the question entails giving up and renouncing justifications for action that were previously taken for granted.[48] A hint as to the banality of slogans about the dangers of forgiving and forgetting, the question of forgiveness may well function to recollect the question of whether and how to recall, particularly with respect to the ways in which language's power is codified over time and how best to interpret the (non)relation of announced justifications for action and their (un)expected consequences. This would also pertain to the very idea of forgiveness itself, not least if its meaning hinges on the discernment of the sacred Word. As a question of what history's words can and do mean, the question of forgiveness marks an exigence in which parties to the question are called to the work of translation, an interchange between languages and discursive registers of action in which none may be able to claim the status of 'original'.[49]

Third, the question of forgiveness opens space in which to invent the constitutive grounds of interaction and argumentation. Far more than forgetting, the danger of forgiveness may be an enforced silence – the answering of the question such that there is nothing left to say and no basis for generating what might (yet) be said. In this light, the proteptic function of the question underscores that a forgiveness which simply serves to "clear the register" may yield a discursive vacuum. If so, as it may cut against its own hope for a certain harmony – whether ontological or political – the question of forgiveness holds out the problem of how its parties might (re)learn to (dis)agree. Aligned closely with the work of interpreting interpretation, it signals the need if not an interest in talking about talk, a process that involves confronting the shared limits of language and asking what to make of the word's risk, the costs that attend the rhetorical invention which holds the (im)potential of initiative and collective

47 The matter of the question's object underscores Derrida's conclusion as to how the conditional and unconditional forms of forgiveness are indissociable. A concrete example of this ambiguity might well be found in F.W. de Klerk's ambivalent statements about his view of South African apartheid.

48 Things are complicated further when the question is presumed to ask forgiveness of the person and not the deed, a distinction that may beg the question in situations where historical rationales for action are tied to (self) definitions of identity. See Derrida 2001a: 23.

49 Along with Benjamin's well known reflection on the dynamic of translation, also see Gadamer 1994.

modes of power. In public, the issue is what can and should count as publicity; if they are not self-generating, what are the grounds and rules of discourse dedicated to fostering shared understanding and productive dispute? In contrast to a number of accounts, including Derrida's, this work of the question sets it in league with reconciliation, where the latter is not the outcome of forgiveness but a process in which the (im)potential for a "unity in difference" emerges through the work of constituting a language of shared opposition from within the throes of paralytic conflict.[50]

The question of forgiveness asks after the experience of language. At the cost of the proposition which pronounces a self-certainty blind to the violence of its expression, the question inaugurates a suffering (of) language in the name of recognizing hypocrisy. The question's provocation is the wound rendered by the word that is other than it seems to be but which is incapable of being otherwise. Thus, the question's categorical reply is not an answer, particularly if one recalls that hypocrisy in the ancient Greek is not simply a term of moral condemnation but a speaking from another place, an expression whose grounds are not disclosed to us and to whose terms we are subjected.[51] In this light, it is the question – as a question of the word's question-ability – that holds a power to initiate a discovery of the human condition's mutual vulnerability in language. The grounds of the word are not steady even as they may prove decisive. If so, as it plays between contingency and fate, the question of forgiveness is that query which asks *after* the power of forgiving words in the name of setting their (im) potential *before* us. What we might say in reply thus becomes the question – a shared thinking of the question – of what, if anything, can be said *now*.

REFERENCES

Adorno, T. (1973). *Negative Dialectics*. New York: Continuum.

Agamben G. (1991). *Language and Death: The Place of Negativity*. Minneapolis: University of Minnesota Press.

Agamben, G. (2000). *Potentialities: Collected Essays in Philosophy*. Palo Alto: Stanford University Press.

Arendt, H. (1958). *The Human Condition*. Chicago: University of Chicago Press.

Arendt, H. (1965). *On Revolution*. New York: Viking Press.

Benjamin, B. (2003). The Critique of Violence. In M. Bullock (ed.) *Walter Benjamin: Selected Writings, Vol. 1*. Cambridge: Harvard University Press, 236–252.

50 For an extended discussion of reconciliation's constitutive rhetorical quality, see Doxtader 2009.

51 There is then a crucial connection between Arendt's account of forgiveness and her reflection on the nature of the hypocrite. See Arendt, 1965. For a reflection on the role of hypocrisy in human rights discourse, see Doxtader 2010.

Bernstein, J.B. (1996). Confession and Forgiveness: Hegel's Poetics of Action. In R. Eldridge (ed.), *Beyond Representation: Philosophy and Poetic Imagination*. Cambridge: Cambridge University Press, 34–65.

Bushnell, H. (2009). *Forgiveness and Law*. New York: Bibliofile.

Butler, J. (2005). *Giving an Account of Oneself*. New York: Fordham University Press.

Derrida, J. (1992). Force of Law: The Mystical Authority of Justice. In D. Cornell (ed.) *Deconstruction and the Possibility of Justice*. London: Routledge.

Derrida, J. (2001a). To Forgive. In J. Caputo (ed.) *Questioning God*. Bloomington: Indiana University Press, 21–51.

Derrida, J. (2001b). *On Cosmopolitanism and Forgiveness*. New York: Routledge.

Derrida (2007). A Certain Impossible Possibility of Saying the Event. *Critical Inquiry* 33, 441–461.

Doxtader, E. (2001). In the Name of Reconciliation: The Faith and Works of Counterpublicity. In R Asen (ed.) *Counterpublics and the State*. Albany: SUNY Press, 59–85.

Doxtader, E. (2009). *With Faith in the Works of Words: The Beginnings of Reconciliation in South Africa*. Lansing: Michigan State University Press.

Doxtader, E. (2010). The Rhetorical Question of Human Rights – A Preface. *Quarterly Journal of Speech*, 96, 353-379.

Gadamer, H.G. (1994). *Truth and Method*. New York: Continuum.

Hegel, G.W.F. (1948) The Spirit of Christianity and its Fate. In T.M. Knox (ed.) *On Christianity: Early Theological Writings*. New York: Harper, 182–301.

Kennedy, D. (2004). *The Dark Sides of Virtue: Reassessing International Humanitarianism*. Princeton: Princeton University Press.

Minow, M. (1999). *Between Vengeance and Forgiveness: Facing History after Genocide and Mass Violence*. Boston: Beacon Press.

Nightingale, A. (2004). *Spectacles of Truth in Classical Greek Philosophy*. Cambridge: Cambridge University Press.

Oliver, K. (2003). *Forgiveness and Subjectivity*. Philosophy Today, 47, 280–292.

Ricoeur, P. (2006). *Memory, History and Forgetting*. Chicago: University of Chicago Press.

Ross, F. (2003). *Bearing Witness*. Cape Town: Pluto Press.

Sanders, M. (2007). *Ambiguities of Witnessing: Law and Literature in the Time of Truth Commission*. Palo Alto: Stanford University Press.

Schaap, A. (2003). Political Grounds for Forgiveness. *Contemporary Political Theory*, 2, 77–87.

SYMPATHY AND INSEPARABILITY

Nir Eisikovits

1. SYMPATHY AND POLITICAL RECONCILIATION[1]

In a series of recent writings[2], I have offered an account of political reconciliation as the process combining the resolution of formal questions between adversaries (e.g. who has a right to what) with the inculcation of sympathetic attitudes. I use 'sympathy' in its philosophical signification, as the ability to imaginatively switch places with others and view the world from their perspective. This definition is arrived at by way of elimination. There is surely more to reconciliation than the cessation of hostilities. After all, no one would claim that the fighting factions in Iraq have reconciled just because they stopped shooting at each other for a while. There is also more to reconciliation than two or more enemies reaching a fair agreement on how to settle their claims and how to distribute disputed resources. Israel and Egypt reached such an agreement rather quickly in the late 70's. The Sinai peninsula was returned to the Egyptians, prisoners were exchanged, the war dead exhumed and shipped back home. Since then Israelis and Egyptian have had few claims against each other. They have also wanted nothing to do with each other. Can this state of affairs count as political reconciliation?

Reconciliation, then, involves more than the cessation of hostilities and more than the fair settlement of mutual claims. But what more is needed? Is forgiveness the missing element? I have argued elsewhere that it is not. Since this volume centers on the idea of political or "public" forgiveness, let me reiterate the contours of that argument.[3]

It has become fashionable of late to speak about the importance of forgiveness in politics. The most prevalent argument in favor of political forgiveness concerns its potential to release victims and wrongdoers from the effects of vindictiveness. A desire for revenge, so the argument goes, can generate a never-ending violent cycle, trapping both sides in a dynamic of blow and response, eventually destroying all those involved. As Ghandi famously put it, "an eye for an eye can

1 Thanks to David Lyons for comments and to Peter August for research assistance.

2 Eisikovits 2010, Eisikovits 2006, Eisikovits 2004.

3 For a detailed account see primarily Eisikovits (2004). My summary here draws on that article.

make the whole world blind". The argument is intuitively compelling, but forgiveness is not the only way to quell the desire for revenge. We can steer clear of revenge without forgiving. Victims might seek legal rather than private justice. They might agree to institutionalize their vindictive passions through the use of the courts.[4] Victims can (and often do) simply move away from the scene of the trauma rather than seek revenge or engage in forgiveness. Most Holocaust survivors, uninterested in revenge or forgiveness, simply moved thousands of miles away from the sites of their horrific memories and swore never to set foot in the countries that had persecuted them. Others replace revenge with commemoration, dedicating themselves to the creation and maintenance of monuments and museums. Thus, for example, some of those handing out the ID cards at the Holocaust Museum in Washington D.C. are holocaust survivors, as are many of the guides in Jerusalem's Yad Vashem memorial. Vengeance can, indeed, be a very dangerous thing. But one does not have to advocate forgiveness in order to avoid it.

There are other difficulties with making forgiveness into a political goal. Many commentators assume that forgiving is the exclusive prerogative of victims. On this view, it is problematic to define a process of political reconciliation in terms of forgiveness, because forgiving is a very private business that cannot be promoted as a policy.[5] Furthermore, a policy encouraging victims to forgive those who have harmed them risks adding insult to their injuries; it can induce a sense of moral inadequacy (due to an inability to forgive) on top of the devastation already suffered. In such cases demands for forgiveness might exacerbate rather than quell resentment – both towards the offender, to whom the victim does not want to owe a moral debt, and towards the state that makes such demands.

Finally, it is worth remembering that forgiveness is a deeply Christian notion. The term does have an important role in both Judaism and Islam, but its status in these faiths is more ambivalent. While Judaism does, under some conditions,

---

4 On this see, e.g., Minow 1998: 11.

5 Elsewhere I have offered what may be labeled the 'fading prerogative' view of political forgiveness: While forgiving is not exclusively up to victims, it certainly makes less sense to talk about forgiveness the further away we move from the partly directly injured. If X gets hurt in a bus bombing, she might forgive the person who planned the attack. It can make sense for her parents to forgive him too, though it is not obvious that they would be forgiving the same thing (the nature of the parents' injury is different from X's: the extent of her physical pain was greater than theirs; the degree of their emotional anguish might have well been higher than hers). It would be more problematic to speak of X's neighbors forgiving the bus bomber for X's injuries, and even more problematic to speak of people whom X has never met forgiving the bomber. Forgiveness, then, might not be the exclusive prerogative of victims, but the entitlement to grant it certainly seems to fade as we move away from them. There is, in other words, a limited radius in which it makes sense to speak of forgiveness. This does not, of course, mean that we cannot think of political reconciliation in terms of forgiveness. It only means that such an approach would exclude a (potentially) significant part of the community from the process. See Eisikovits 2004: supra, note 2.

impose a duty to forgive, it is not clear whether this duty must be exercised towards non-Jews. Furthermore, Judaism, unlike Christianity, discourages unconditional forgiveness. Islamic doctrine does state that forgiveness is superior to revenge, but permits retributive practices, and even feuding under some circumstances. The Koran also makes a division between forgivable and unforgivable sins, mentioning the trespass of *shirk* – the recognition of divinities other than Allah – as a prime example of the latter category. Finally, both Judaism and Islam allow for forgiveness without the resumption of relations between victim and offender, while Christianity insists that the possibility of full restoration of previous relations be left open. Since the demands and centrality of forgiveness vary between the different faiths, it might be problematic to include the term as part of our notion of political reconciliation, especially in cases of inter-religious conflict.

We are better off thinking about political reconciliation in terms of what Adam Smith called 'sympathy' – the ability to imaginatively enter the minds of others. For Smith, to sympathize with someone is to understand her sentiments or actions on the background of the circumstances she operates in. It is to think that I might have felt or done the same under similar circumstances. Our sympathetic ability, he claims, is crucial for making meaningful moral judgments. We only judge an action or emotional response morally right if we imagine we would have acted or felt similarly if placed in a similar situation. As Smith puts it: " If, upon bringing the case home to our own breast, we find that the sentiments which it gives occasion to, coincide and tally with our own, we necessarily approve of them as proportioned and suitable to their objects; if otherwise, we necessarily disapprove of them, as extravagant and out of proportion"[6]. To sympathize with X, then, is to imagine myself in X's circumstances, and to try to think, as independently from my own contingent attributes as possible, what I would have felt and done in his place. This results in a suspension of moral judgment of another's actions or emotional comportment until after an imaginary exchange has been attempted.

Importantly, such sympathy depends on exposure to details, on familiarity with particulars. To project myself into the circumstances in which somebody else operates, I need to know as much as possible about those circumstances. Sympathizing involves an imaginary projection, As Smith insists. But the imagination needs something to work with. It needs data. An imagination uninformed by details is bound to produce shallow romanticized versions of the realities on which it reflects.[7]

Sympathy between adversaries is not a naïve fantasy. Enemies can, and have sympathized with each other for centuries. From Achilles' gesture, allowing Priam to burry his son during the siege of Troy, to the famous Christmas Truce

6 Smith 1976: Section I.i.3.9.

7 For a detailed account about the operation of sympathy see Eisikovits 2010: Chapter 1.

in December 1914, when French, German, and English soldiers fraternized in the trenches of the Western Front, combatants have always been able to see the world through the eyes of their rivals.

Sympathy is useful for thinking about political reconciliation because it makes our enemies more concrete. It transforms the villains of propaganda into flesh and blood human beings. As she ruminates about the process of writing, Briony Tallis, the heroine of Ian McEwan's *Atonement*, arrives at the following insight: "It wasn't only wickedness and scheming that made people unhappy, it was confusion and misunderstanding; above all it was the failure to grasp the simple truth that other people are as real as you..."[8] War ends only when combatants understand that their enemies are 'real'. That they are not part of an 'Arab World', 'Black Culture' or a 'Jewish conspiracy'. That they are not 'Islamo-Fascists', 'Tutsi Cockroaches' or 'Godless Communists' either. That they are, rather, human beings with complicated wants, loves, hates, priorities, desires.

Every act of mass killing in living memory has been preceded by a campaign of de-individuation, allowing killers to perceive their victims as faceless stand-ins for an entire group. War is made possible by, and then sustained through, moral blindness. By the propensity to look through human beings and see abstractions instead. In the Balkans, Hasan Agic is transformed from neighbor, colleague, poker-partner to 'Bosnian Muslim', a direct descendent of a collectivity that humiliated the Christian Serbs in the battle of Kosovo in 1389. In Rwanda Paul Mutaboba, a modest concession stand owner from Kigali, is altered into part of a Tutsi ploy to dispossess the Hutu. The Ten Commandments of the Hutu, published in the magazine Kangura in 1990, warn his neighbors that: "All Hutus must know that all Tutsis are dishonest in business. Their only goal is ethnic superiority."[9] Sympathizing with an enemy – imagining in detail what it is like to be him- counteracts the most basic martial impulse: the readiness to look through individuals.

If sympathy is effective in offsetting such moral blindness, it is also valuable for thwarting moral absolutism – the assumption that we fight on the side of the angels, that our cause is entirely just, rooted in authentic historical grievances, and that, therefore, we should settle for nothing short of a full acceptance of our demands. Sympathy requires us to think what we would have done in the place of our enemies, thus complicating moral judgments. It asks us to supplement our reliance on stern principles with the employment of the imagination. This exercise allows us to consider not only whether we are right, but also what life would look like if we acted on being right. By doing so, sympathy checks the self-righteousness that so often fuels war. The Palestinians, to give one example, may be morally entitled to return to the lands from which they were expelled in 1948. But what of those living in the houses to which they are to return? What would

8 McEwan 2001.

9 *Kangura,* December, 1990 (6th issue).

their lives look like if the "right of return" were implemented? "From the place where we are right," wrote Israeli poet Yehuda Amichai, having witnessed everything extraordinary and wicked in his country's violent history, "flowers will never grow in the spring. The place where we are right is hard and trampled like a yard." It is sympathy that helps us understand Amichai's warning: steadfast insistence on getting everything we deserve often leaves us with nothing worth having.

In this essay I argue that the inculcation of sympathy is particularly important in the case of physically inseparable enemies. Such adversaries must *reconcile* rather than simply resolve their material disagreements. After investigating the political significance of inseparability, I make my case by looking at two examples: the relationship between Israeli Jews and Israeli Arabs and the enmity between Israelis and Palestinians.

2. INSEPARABILITY

"When you cannot avoid living side by side with all others", writes Kant in the *Metaphysics of Morals*, "you ought to leave the state of nature and proceed with them into a rightful condition, that is, a condition of distributive justice".[10] Jeremy Waldron calls this Kantian directive "the principle of proximity". In his adaptation it reads: "people have a natural duty to enter into political society with those with whom they find themselves in a condition of unavoidable coexistence…"[11]. Waldron insists that the principle cannot be used to legitimize land grabs. An occupier cannot invoke it to demand that those she has dispossessed make an effort to coexist with her. This is due to the fact that such an occupier puts herself, rather than *finds* herself, next to those she occupies. The situation might, however, be different for the occupier's decedents: "if [the option of leaving] has evaporated over the centuries, then coexistence must be treated as a brute fact…that means we must form and sustain a political society among us – all of us – whether we like one another, or the circumstances under which we came into another's company or not".[12]

10 Kant 1996: 451–452.

11 Waldron 2002: 137–138.

12 Ibid.: 138. In an article from 1992 titled "Superceding Historical Injustice", Waldron (1992: 4) argues for a 'Supersession Thesis'. The thesis states that there are cases in which historical injustice might be overcome or superseded given a sufficiently thoroughgoing change of circumstances. For Waldron the Supersession Thesis is a product of the principle of proximity. He writes: "the spirit of the Supersession Thesis is that people who are thrown, in Kant's phrase, unavoidably side by side, have no choice but to share the resources that surround them justly among themselves, as though they were a new community, even if the presence of some of them in that situation is a result of injustice" – See Waldron 2003: 36.

> The Principle of Proximity captures a fundamental insight: Geography matters immensely in understanding political conflict. The very fact of closeness, can both create moral obligations that do not exist for more distant parties, and, at the same time, suggest the kind of relationship that it is prudent for proximate groups to develop. Nevertheless, the Principle of Proximity does not provide sufficient instruction. What, for example, is the relevant sense of proximity, which activates the special duty Kant speaks of? Two groups can be geographically proximate, but also clearly separable from each other, as are France and Spain, or Israel and Egypt. On the other hand, two societies can be literally enmeshed or entangled – both proximate and inseparable – as are Israelis and Palestinians in the West Bank. If these two kinds of cases are different, is the Kantian concern with entering a 'state of distributive justice' equally important in both?

It might be useful to distinguish between three kinds of geographical relations: distance, proximity, and inseparability. The Falklands war, between England and Argentina, was a conflict between *distant* groups – by which I mean two political entities that either do not share a common frontier, or are located in separate geographical regions. The 1973 war in the Middle East, between Israel on one side, and the Egyptian-Syrian coalition on the other, was a war between *proximate*, but separate entities. The three countries shared borders, but could very easily be told apart. The Jim Crow era in the United States, the war between Israelis and Palestinians and Apartheid in South Africa all involved (or still involve) strife between *inseparable* groups. These kinds of conflicts rage between two groups that are not merely close to each other but, rather, entangled with each other.

Our analysis of peacemaking requires a variation on Kant's proximity principle, one that takes the geographical categories just offered into account. Perhaps we might call this variation the *Inseparability Principle*. The general point of the modified principle is simple enough: the harder it is to physically separate between rival sides, the more important it is to try and make them sympathize with each other. Stated a bit more formally the inseparability principle reads: " When two groups (whether or not they are part of the same political entity) are physically inseparable, the inculcation of sympathetic attitudes between their members is at least as important as the fair resolution of questions concerning distributive justice"[13].

As an introduction to the argument justifying the Inseparability Principle, let us retreat for a moment and consider a domestic analogy. Four people in their early thirties share a house in Brookline, Massachusetts. Abby works as a junior prosecutor at the Suffolk County DA's office. Bob is a graduate student in political science, finishing up his dissertation. Carry is a second grade teacher at a private

13 I am assuming that by 'questions of distributive justice' Kant means something close to what we have labeled the 'formal' aspects of peacemaking – the concerns with who has a right to which resources.

school in nearby Newton. Dieter is a visiting scholar from Germany, in town for a period of one year, in which he plans to complete his first book. After 6 months of peaceful living, the relations between the roommates are turning sour. Dieter is demanding that the existing arrangement according to which the Cable Television bill is split up into four equal parts be re-examined, since Bob watches significantly more television than the others. Bob wants to reconfigure the equal division of the rent, because his room is directly above the service alley, and he is woken up at least twice weekly by the garbage truck. Carry is becoming impatient with both Bob and Dieter, who cannot seem to remember washing the sink after they shave, or respect the division of space agreed upon in the joint refrigerator. Abby has to work for two hours every evening on her cases for the next day, and she is growing annoyed at the scuffles between the other roommates, which hinder her concentration. Several times in recent weeks she has stepped out of her room and yelled at them to shut up. Life in the handsome Brookline Colonial is getting unbearable.

It might be useful to point out some aspects of this situation – attributes that can help explain how it became so bad: 1. The four roommates cannot completely avoid each other. They live in the same house, and necessarily bump into one another all the time. Assuming that breaking the lease is not an option, each of them is forced to interact with someone they dislike on a daily basis. This friction implies two further problems: 2. It is pretty easy for the roommates to annoy or hurt each other. Thus, for example, the refrigerator, with its fragile division, is always nearby if anyone wants to upset Carry. The den, with its big screen TV, is close to Abby's room, and anyone who turns it on too loudly can disrupt her work. 3. The results of any disagreement between the tenants are immediately present and easy for all to spot: Dieter hears the TV every night and is reminded of Bob's parasitism very often. Carry has no choice but to open the refrigerator every morning, and thus cannot help but notice the infringements by the others. The fourth and last point is that arguments about the formal arrangements between the roommates tend to become personal. All too often they turn into claims about the very character of those involved: Dieter thinks Bob is a free rider since he watches more TV than anyone else but refuses to pay his fair share. Abby accuses Bob of being selfish for watching it too loudly. Bob tells Dieter he is cheap, since he is capable of fighting over a meager 10 dollars a month; Bob also thinks that Carry is obsessive and petty because of her insistence on each square inch of refrigerator space.

This story is meant as a device for illustrating some of the factors complicating the relationship between people living in intimate closeness. I realize, of course, that tensions between groups are more complicated than tensions between roommates. Nevertheless, the four factors mentioned here are descriptive of what makes the relationship of inseparable groups problematic. The combination of constant friction, vulnerability, the visibility of injuries, and the tendency of arguments about resources to turn into statements about one's identity, makes these relationships especially explosive. The existence of these factors often renders the fair resolution of questions concerning distributive justice between inseparable groups into a lengthy and problematic process. When it is impossible to avoid seeing your enemy, when he can easily hurt you at any given moment, when you are constantly reminded of how he has wronged you, and when any argument between you potentially points to something disturbing about your very identity – peacemaking can be a very arduous task indeed. In such cases sympathy can work as a cushion or safety valve, moderating the reactions of the different parties. Stated differently, when inseparability makes it hard to quickly settle questions of distributive justice, sympathy might make life bearable in the interim.

The examination of two case studies, each involving the kind of inseparability I have spoken of, may be useful for spelling out this point. The first case deals with the relationship between Israeli Jews and Israeli Arabs. The Second concentrates on the Israeli-Palestinian conflict.

3. ISRAELI JEWS AND ISRAELI ARABS

The Middle East war of 1948 resulted in the establishment of the state of Israel and in the creation of a massive Palestinian refugee population. Approximately 700,000[14] Arab inhabitants were either forcefully expelled or fled from the areas that were to become the Jewish State. About 170,000 Arabs remained in their towns and villages, and became citizens of the newly founded state. The Arab citizens of Israel were discriminated against from the get go. The state's basic constitutional documents (its Declaration of Independence and all of its 'Basic Laws') describe it as "Jewish and Democratic" rather than simply "Democratic". Arabs are excluded from some special benefits and protections granted exclusively to Jews by the naturalization and property laws. There is a vast disparity in the level of government investment in education, infrastructure, and social services between Israeli and Arab communities. Arabs cannot, by and large, join the IDF, which is still one of the main avenues of social integration and mobility in Israeli society, and they are much less likely than Jews with equal qualifications to find jobs or receive decent pay. When one adds all of this to the fact that many Israeli Arabs bear grudges for the removal of their relatives from

14 The precise figure has been the subject of some debate. Some Israeli sources speak of a lower number, approximately 520,000, while some Palestinians claim that it was as high as 1,000,000. For a good discussion See Morris 2001: 252–258.

Israel, and many of them identify wholeheartedly with the Palestinian cause, the resulting picture is grim.[15]

Needless to say that all of the factors complicating the relationship between inseparable groups are present: since Arabs make up a fifth of the state's population, and since they are not exclusively concentrated in one region, the degree of friction between both populations is high. It is extremely hard for Jews and Arabs to avoid each other inside Israel, and extremely easy for them to hurt each other. Failures in distributive justice are visible and unmistakable. Whenever an Israeli Arab travels to a Jewish community (and most do so on a daily basis for purposes of work, shopping, or higher education) they encounter better roads, more stoplights, more road signs, better kept schools, neater houses, newer cars, and so on. Finally, the claims both sides have against each other relate to the very legitimacy of their respective group identities: the Arab demand that Israel renounce its 'law of return', for example, calls into question the state's official raison d'etre – namely the creation of a safe haven for Jews. On the other hand, the accusations against Israeli Arabs claiming that their support for the Palestinian cause makes them into a fifth column, also touches on the very essence of their collective identity – since many see themselves as Palestinians with Israeli citizenship.

And yet, in spite of these horrific starting conditions, in spite of the massive power differential between them, Israeli Jews and Israeli Arabs coexist relatively peacefully. Relations have been damaged by the two Intifadas, but nowhere as significantly as one might expect. Rather than asking, as many do, how things got so bad between Arabs and Jews in Israel, I would like to suggest a more unusual, controversial question: how, in spite of everything, did relations stay so good?

I suspect that the coexistence is not simply a result of disparities in power. It cannot simply be explained by the fact that Israeli Arabs are too weak to make trouble. The growth of asymmetrical warfare in the second half of the twentieth century speaks volumes about the violent possibilities open to the weak. Rather, one of the main reasons for the relatively benign relationship between Israeli Jews and Arabs inside Israel is the existence of widespread personal ties between Israeli Jews and Arabs, and the relative prosperity of Israel's Arab citizens (relative, that is, to the condition of Palestinians in the territories or to the living standards of Arabs in many neighboring countries). The existence of personal ties means that each party has had detailed exposure to how the other lives: a very large percentage of Israeli Jews and Arabs have seen the inside each other's homes. Many of them have been invited to the weddings of friends or colleagues from the other group. Many more have had college classmates of the other

15 David Grossman's meditation on the status of Israeli Arabs is a very good starting point: Grossman 2003. Other sources on the status of Israeli Arabs are: Landau 1991, Smooha 1990: 389–413.

ethnicity, and even more have shopped extensively in grocery stores and markets operated or owned by members of the other group. The relatively high living standard enjoyed by Israeli Arabs has significantly increased similarities in life style between the two communities. Such specific knowledge of the conditions under which others live, and the existence of similarities in lifestyle, are conducive for the creation of sympathetic dispositions. It is easier to see the world through they eyes of those whose life is not opaque. It is easier to sympathize with those who are like us.

Take the university of Haifa as an example. The institution is home to the nation's largest Arab student body. Jews and Arabs take the same classes, participate in the same reading groups, and share the same recreational facilities. To a growing degree, the differences in the way they dress, in the accessories they use, and the popular culture they consume are shrinking. Needless to say that close interactions and the existence of such similarities do not guarantee civic equality. Arab graduates of the University of Haifa are still much less likely to find jobs than their Jewish colleagues. But these interactions and the resulting sympathy do decrease the likelihood of ethnic violence. There is one significant exception to this conclusion in recent Israeli history. But a close look at it bolsters the analysis offered here.

In October of 2002, 13 Israeli Arabs were killed by Israeli Police, during riots that broke out on the background of the second Palestinian Intifada. Immediately after the killings, the government asked the legislature to set up a national commission of inquiry – the highest investigative body allowed for by Israeli law. Such commissions are quite rare (one of the instances in which one had been created was to investigate the nation's greatest collective trauma- the intelligence failures that led to the outbreak of the 1973 war). The commission, headed by Supreme Court Justice Or, issued a seething criticism of the way in which the police handled the events. The report concluded with harsh personal recommendations about the Minister of Police, Shlomo Ben Ami, and several senior commanders under his authority.[16]

All of this is to say that the killing, by Israeli police, of 13 Israeli Arab citizens was *a big deal* for Israeli Jews and for the Israeli Jewish establishment. The deaths were taken seriously. This was not due to fear of negative publicity, nor was it a result of pressures applied by the international community. Israel has shown, time and again, that it is largely indifferent to such pressures. I suspect that a large part of the reason these killings were viewed so severely was that the people killed were not faceless. Some of them had Israeli friends. Their parents had Israeli friends. They cheered for some of the same soccer teams Israelis cheered for. They wore similar clothes. Perhaps they even had similar, fashionable plastic

---

16 The official summation of the commission's report can be accessed here: www.haaretz.com/hasen/pages/ShArt.jhtml?itemNo=335594&contrassID=2&subContrassID=1&sbSubContrassID=0&listSrc=Y.

covers for their cell phones. They were, in short, natural objects of sympathy for Israeli Jews.

4. THE ISRAELI PALESTINIAN CONFLICT

The Israeli Palestinian conflict offers a different picture all together. The two groups certainly qualify as inseparable: Jerusalem has virtually merged with Ramallah and its surroundings. Kfar Saba, a suburb of Tel Aviv, is less than five minutes by car from Kalkilya in the West Bank. The passage between the West Bank and the Gaza strip, the two areas in which some Palestinian self-rule has been instituted, involves traveling through Israel. The West Bank is peppered with dozens of Israeli settlements and army bases, which make it impossible for the two sides not to interact with each other. And yet, a preponderance of their mutual actions and attitudes display what I have earlier labeled 'moral blindness' – a refusal to acknowledge the impact of one's actions on specific, flesh and blood human beings.

The Israelis impose indiscriminate closures on entire populations in response to specific threats, though more intelligent and selective methods are available. They build separate roads for settlers and Palestinians in the West Bank, to make sure the former don't suffer because of movement restrictions imposed on the latter. They uproot entire fields and destroy residential building blocks to eliminate potential cover for militants. They engage in 'targeted' killings, regardless of the fact that these often claim the lives of civilian bystanders. They have systematically used, with lethal results, excessive means for crowd control, though more benign technologies exist. They have built a wall or "security barrier" which literally blocks out life in the West Bank from most Israeli eyes. Palestinians, on the other hand, have long engaged in the indiscriminate killing of civilians in the center of Israeli towns. Mosques regularly propagate the kind of blood libels that make the Protocols of the Elders of Zion seem like beach reading. Senior Palestinian officials engage in Holocaust denial, and sanctify a 'right of return', to towns and houses populated with people who had nothing to do with their dispossession.

In short, Israelis and Palestinians, the most intimate of neighbors, see through and talk past each other. The killing of 13 Israeli Arabs outraged an entire country. On the other hand Israelis and Palestinians have been killing each other in great numbers for many years with complete impunity. Scores of women and children are blown to smithereens on both sides and neither launches a serious investigation or even bothers to wholeheartedly condemn the deaths. Fathers carrying their dead toddlers in Dir al Balah, workers collecting body parts in a Jerusalem cafés regarded with the same indifferent, fatalistic shrugs, sometimes with open joy.

At least part of this unbearable lightness of killing can be attributed to the fact that the dead are faceless, as far as those on the other side are concerned. Most often, they and their families have no acquaintances among members of the opposed ethnic group. Each party to this conflict lives under conditions the other knows little about. The ignorance is not accidental. It is a matter of principle. The Israeli newspaper Haaretz is regularly accused of treachery for running columns on the hardship of everyday life in the occupied territories. Recalling some of the reactions to her stories, Journalist Amira Hass, who reports from Gaza and Ramallah, says: "I get messages saying I must have been a kapo [a Jewish camp overseer for the Nazis] in my first incarnation. Then I'll get an e-mail saying: 'Bravo, you have written a great article – Heil Hitler!' Someone told me they hoped I suffered breast cancer. 'Until we expel all Palestinians, there will be no peace,' some of them say. I can't reply to them – there are thousands of these messages."[17]

Palestinians schools regularly remove Israel from their geography Atlases. Many teachers refuse to include a discussion of the Holocaust in their history curriculums, claiming that the traumas and fears of the Jews are of no interest to them. In 2003, a group of Israeli Jews and Arabs took a joint educational trip to Auschwitz. A Television news program tried to solicit some responses from Palestinian educators. Naim Abu'l Humus, the Palestinian Minister of Education, conceded that the Holocaust was a historical fact. He added that he was not versed in the number of Jews that had been killed in it, and that he did not see himself as obligated to teach about other peoples' troubles. Anya Alhamisi, the head mistress of a high school in Ramallah replied: "the Jewish Holocaust? We are concerned with the Palestinian Holocaust". Young teachers attending a workshop in Ramallah opined that the figure of Six Million Jews was a lie:

> "Six Million? Where would six million come from? Perhaps One million; perhaps two thousand [were killed]".[18]

The Israeli Palestinian conflict is an example of what happens when failures of distributive justice are compounded by failures of sympathy. Neither side has honored its formal contractual obligations under the Oslo accords. In addition, neither community has made an effort to think of the other as constituted of ordinary, actual, flesh and blood people. There are, in this conflict, far too many 'Jews' and 'Palestinians' and far too few Haims and Ahmeds. Under these conditions, the four characteristics of inseparability mentioned earlier – friction, vulnerability, visibility of harms, and the connection between mutual claims and collective identity, have made life unbearable on both side of the Green Line.

---

17 Published on Sunday, August 26, 2001 in the Independent/UK.

18 Channel 1, Mabat Sheni News Magazine: "The Arabs and the Jewish Holocaust" August 9th, 2003.

5. CONCLUSION

I hope to have established that inseparability carries a special potential for explosiveness. The importance of sympathy under such conditions is two fold: first, inseparability can make it harder to reach a fair resolution of formal questions. The resources up for distribution are likely to be especially important for both sides, each is likely to claim some special relationship to them, and there are almost never enough of them to go around. While such formal questions are in the process of being resolved, the existence of de facto sympathies can avert disaster. In fact, the relationship between Israeli Jews and Arabs suggests that sympathy has the potential to prevent calamity even when questions of distributive justice are likely to persist unresolved. This might raise the objection that sympathy is essentially a pain reliever that allows for abject injustices to remain un-addressed. I am skeptical of this objection. Averting violence is, in itself, a good thing. A bearable life is still superior to no life. Furthermore, and perhaps more importantly, the existence of such sympathies can bring about a desire for change just as it can generate complacency. Knowing someone intimately not only makes it harder to kill her, it also makes it easier to promote her interests.

Second, even when fair formal arrangements are in place, their enforcement is a question of motivation more than it is one of procedural justice. A personal acquaintance with those who are the prospective recipients of the formal protections can be a powerful reason to make sure they are extended. The claim that fair, rational arrangements are not self-sustaining by virtue of being fair and rational is not new. My argument here is that something like sympathy, something like the conscious attempt to familiarize one's self with the details making up another's life, can be instrumental for such sustenance.

The importance of sympathy in cases of inseparability is not the result of a substantive preference about what constitutes a good life. It does not, in other words, turn on any latent communitarian commitments. For the reasons I have provided above, the inculcation of sympathetic dispositions between the members of such groups is not a question of 'living well'. It is, rather, a question of living, period. Insofar as sympathy is part of the definition of reconciliation, it is a matter of life and death for inseparable groups to reconcile. It is a matter of life and death for those making peace between such groups to put in place post war policies that can promote sympathy.[19]

This is not necessarily so in other cases. When two groups are physically separate the importance of sympathy is reduced. Here straightforward questions of distributive justice can take priority, and their resolution might, even without the inculcation of mutual sympathetic dispositions, suffice for creating stable

19 For a detailed account of the kind of transitional policies that promote sympathy see Eisikovits 2010: Chapters 4–5.

and satisfying life conditions. To the degree that sympathy is still lacking, we might not be able to claim that the two groups in question have reconciled. But it might not be as important to aim for reconciliation in these instances.

As the failure of the Oslo Accords has shown us, when it comes to inseparable groups, a formalistic approach to conflict resolution wherein parties focus on resolving their disagreements about resources and security arrangements while neglecting their hostile mutual attitudes won't do. In one of the first instances of conflict resolution in the Bible we read about Abram (Abraham before the Lord renames him) and his nephew, Lot, who have grown very rich in livestock and gold. The two men set themselves up in central Canaan but the area where they settled cannot sustain the flocks of both, and this creates "strife between the herders of Abram's livestock and the herders of Lot's livestock".[20] Abram decides to eliminate the tension: "Let there be no strife between you and me, and between your herders and my herders; for we are kindred," he tells Lot. "Is not the whole land before you? Separate yourself from me. If you take the left hand, then I will go the right; or if you take the right hand, then I will go the left."[21] Abram was correct. The two clans did not have to fight. But what happens when we cannot block our adversaries out, when we cannot move away, when we cannot separate to the left and right? When it comes to political Siamese Twins, the adversaries have no choice but to change the way they relate to each other. In such cases we must, to paraphrase Auden, sympathize with one each other or die.

REFERENCES

Eisikovits, N. (2004). Forget Forgiveness: On The Benefits of Sympathy for Political Reconciliation, *Theoria,* 52 (1), 31–63.

Eisikovits, N. (2006). I am the Enemy you Killed, My Friend: Rethinking the Legitimacy of Truth Commissions, *Metaphilosophy* 37 (3/4), 489–514.

Eisikovits, N. (2010). *Sympathizing with the Enemy: Reconciliation, Transitional Justice, Negotiation*, Leiden, Brill Academic Publishers.

Grossman D., (2003). *Sleeping on a Wire: Conversations with Palestinians in Israel,* Picador.

Kant, I. (1996). *The Cambridge Edition of the Works of Immanuel Kant – Practical Philosophy* Cambridge, Cambridge University Press.

Landau, J. (1991). *The Arab Minority in Israel: 1967–1991*, Oxford, Clarendon.

McEwan, I.(2001). *Atonement*, London, J. Cape.

Minow, M. (1998). *Between Vengeance and Forgiveness,* Boston, Beacon Press.

Morris, B. (2001). *Righteous Victims: A History of the Zionist Arab Conflict,* New York, Vintage Books.

20 *Genesis* 13:7.

21 *Genesis* 13: 8–9.

Smith, A. (1976). *The Theory of Moral Sentiments.* Oxford, Oxford University Press. Section I.i.3.9.
Waldron, J.(2002). Redressing Historical Injustice, *University of Toronto Law Journal*, 52 (1), 135–160.
Smooha, S. (1990). Minority Status in an Ethnic Democracy: The Status of the Arab Minority in Israel, *Ethnic and Racial Studies* 13 (3), 389–413.
Waldron, J. (1992). Superseding Historical Injustice, *Ethics*, 103 (1).
Waldron, J. (2003). The Supersession Thesis: The Process and Legacy of Settlement – a paper given at the *Conference on Israeli Settlement and Related Cases* – Minerva Center for Human Rights, Tel Aviv University, June 1–2.

PART 2

PUBLIC FORGIVENESS IN POLITICAL AND RELIGIOUS CONTEXTS

POLITICAL FORGIVENESS, PROMISE, AND THE "UNDERSTANDING HEART" IN HANNAH ARENDT'S THEORY

Catherine GUISAN

1. INTRODUCTION

Hannah Arendt's theorizing of forgiveness has become a frequent reference in conflict resolution literature and has rightly prompted many commentaries by theologians and political theorists.[1] The concept itself is controversial, and this chapter reviews some of the critical comments addressed to Arendt. However, the chapter's main purpose is to offer a theoretical complement to the interpretations of Arendt's contribution to theories of peace-making, and a three-fold empirical illustration of this argument.[2] Most discussions of Arendtian forgiveness fail to take into account the other human capacity that palliates the irreversibility and unpredictability of action: promising. The connection between forgiveness and promising is what endows forgiveness with its political character and secures justice. Moreover, although Arendt was wary of the political impact of self-improvement efforts, she theorized reconciliation as the attempt to understand one's place in the world, a kind of pondering that admits of self-reflection, but is quite unlike forgiveness. This rather idiosyncratic form of reconciliation as a process of understanding, which stimulates political judgment, is crucial to empower the public actor. The "gift of the understanding heart," as Arendt called it poetically, like the connection between forgiving and promising, has provoked few academic commentaries.[3] To make the most of Arendt' contribution to the theorizing and practices of conflict resolution requires taking into account her analyses of three key political concepts –

1 See *inter alia* Bar-Siman-Tov 2004; Brudholm 2008; Enright and North 1998; Shriver 1995; Wink 1998.

2 In *On Violence*, Arendt describes peace as an unattainable "absolute," but undoubtedly her life-long concern for politics as a set of agonistic, but non-violent practices implies the possibility of peace-making. Arendt 1970: 51. Yet Arendt never couched her politics in terms of conflict resolution or peace-seeking, two fields of scholarship, which have grown enormously, but mostly after her death in 1975.

3 Arendt 2004: 308 and 322–3.

forgiving, promising and reconciliation as "understanding" – *jointly* rather than discretely. The first part of the chapter develops this argument by examining Arendt's theorizing and the critiques leveled especially against her discussion of political forgiveness. The second part discusses three real life examples to illustrate why this theoretical argument matters to politics: Arendt's concepts, taken together, can work as analytical categories to decipher and assess empirical processes of conflict resolution. The chapter examines the role of promising and forgiveness in the launching of the 1952 European Coal and Steel Community and the deficit of understanding; in the South African Truth and Reconciliation Commission and the deficit of promising; and the deficit of forgiveness and understanding in some of the early Iraqi and US reconciliatory attempts.

2. THE THEORETICAL ARGUMENT

2.1. FORGIVING AND PROMISING IN ARENDT'S POLITICS

Eleven pages in Arendt's *The Human Condition* offer a theory of promise and forgiveness that has struck the imagination of thinkers and actors alike.[4] Because men act under conditions of plurality (they are many) and natality (they usher in the new), their political initiatives carry consequences that are both irreversible and unpredictable. No one can predict with total certainty how her action will affect others; and no one can erase the consequences of her act. In other terms political action does not guarantee justice and the protection of basic human rights. How then to overcome the temptation to "palliate" such costly consequences of freedom, and avoid withdrawing from the political sphere or bending to an authoritarian sovereign? Arendt's response is to conceptualize forgiving and promising as two "remedies", which form an integral part of the human capacity for action. Political forgiveness is the epitome of natality, freeing both victim and victimizer from the paralyzing consequences of past deeds: it is "the exact opposite of vengeance…the only reaction which does not merely re-act, but acts anew and unexpectedly, unconditioned by the act which provoked it." Promising, a more usual concept in politics (i.e. constitutions, laws and treaties) creates "certain islands of predictability…in which certain guideposts of reliability are erected."[5] Taken together promising and forgiving represent a small price to pay for freedom and the continuation of politics.

The concept of promising, which has inspired a great variety of contract theories, features in discussions of political legitimacy since Roman times. Because of its relatively uncontroversial nature, it does not call for more

4 Arendt 1958: 236–47.
5 Ibid.: 240–1 and 244.

commentary in this short essay.[6] On the other hand, by *politicizing* forgiveness, Arendt breaks boldly with an old tradition, and she was well aware of it.[7] The more usual objection leveled against her brief discussion of forgiveness is that it does not meet the requirements of justice. Thus Paul Ricoeur, an admirer of her work whose Christian ethos admits of interpersonal forgiveness, doubts whether forgiveness can ever be political: it cannot be institutionalized except as a state amnesty, which constitutes most often a travesty of justice: "Pay the debt, I shall say, but also inventory the heritage."[8] For George Kateb also, "Forgiving and being forgiven cannot withstand the overwhelming force of consequences."[9] Moreover Arendt's definition is too inclusive: "no one is entitled to forgive me for the wrong I have done except the person to whom I have done wrong."[10] Other critics note that Arendt's rejection of "interest-based" politics makes her appear strangely insensitive to concerns of justice.[11] It is important to note, however, that Arendt does not theorize forgiveness as the opposite of punishment.[12] Nor is she discussing institutions of forgiveness, such as amnesty; she casts forgiveness in terms of natality as the breaking free from the vicious cycle of revenge and as a political experience; it is precisely because of the "intractability of injustice even in the best regimes that we should consider the appropriateness of forgiving." According to Peter Digeser, forgiveness contributes a supplement to procedural justice, and frees both wrongdoer and victim to act again.[13]

Since the end of the Cold War forgiving and reconciliation have become part and parcel of academic and political discourse. This is new.[14] Scholars draw from Arendt to support their narratives of political reconciliation although some argue against forgiveness and for resentment that preserves the victim's dignity and animates protests against injustice.[15] But most, like Julia Kristeva, discuss Arendt's concept of forgiveness primarily in terms of moral emotions.[16] Shin Chiba argues that, "even her [Arendt's] notion of *political* forgiveness does not seem to make sense, unless it presumes a certain quality, an attitude, or an ethos of *agape*, such as contrition, repentance, kindness, altruism...".[17] There is little discussion of kindness, contrition, or altruism, however, in Arendt: forgiving is not a moral or spiritual affect, but a singular act that liberates doer and sufferer

6 Arendt 1958: 243–4. For an interesting discussion of the tension between promise and natality in Arendt's thought, see Keenan 1994.

7 Arendt, *op.cit.*: 238–9 and 243.

8 Ricoeur 2004: 89 and 452–6.

9 Kateb in Villa 2000: 143.

10 Kateb 1984: 35.

11 Sitton in Hinchman and Hinchman 1994; Pitkin in ibid.

12 Only punishable acts can be forgiven; the radical evil manifested in Nazism is beyond the scope of forgiveness. Arendt 1958: 241.

13 Digeser 1998: 707; Digeser 2001: 43–55.

14 Digeser 2001: 66; and Prager in Prager and Govier 2003: 1.

15 See note 1: 1; and Brudholm 2008.

16 Kristeva 2001: 232–4; also Shriver 1995: 114.

17 Chiba 1995: 526.

from the "relentless automatism of the action process" for the sake of both.[18] Elizabeth Young-Bruehl defines it as the human faculty for "undoing – or reversing – deeds and words that have been done and spoken" in the public realm.[19] In an interesting discussion of political forgiveness between citizens and the institutions which govern them, Digeser argues that forgiveness is not about eradicating resentment, which may be "too demanding or too intrusive for politics," but about restoring a relationship which has gone wrong. "Perhaps what should count in politics is not the sentiment behind forgiving, but the act itself." Forgiveness "entails a particular kind of conduct."[20]

Arendt deserves credit for secularizing the concept of forgiveness; her Jesus of Nazareth who "discovered the role of forgiveness in the realm of human affairs", is a historical figure, not the Son of God, and the power to forgive is a "human", not a divine power.[21] Thus Jesus can serve as an "exemplar" for non-religious actors also.[22] Arendt's forgiving safeguards the wondrous human capacity for natality, but has little to do with affect. This is a theoretical move, which Ricoeur resists partly by coupling forgiveness with repentance, a process of self-reflection unbinding the agent from his act.[23] Repentance, however, does not feature in Arendt's considerations, whose understanding of political ethics is intensely cerebral,[24] also for autobiographical reasons. Her confrontation with Nazism convinced her that in times of urgency only courageous political action matters: Christian Germans failed to stand up against Hitler in spite of their commitment to love.[25] Her comments on forgiveness and promise categorically exclude love from the public sphere because of its privatizing impact on the lovers, whose passion makes them oblivious to the larger concerns of the republic. For Arendt respect, a kind of esteem practiced from a distance, is the emotion appropriate in politics.[26] No one can judge another person's motivations from the outside; indeed, it is difficult enough to assess one's own and therefore best to accept "the human heart" as a "place of darkness", whose intimate struggles should remain hidden from public scrutiny.[27] Arendt's discourse on the inner life remains ambiguous: she critiques "modern psychology and

18 Arendt 1958: 241.
19 Young-Bruehl 2006: 96–7 and 105.
20 Digeser 1998: 701 and 703–4.
21 Arendt 1958: 238–9.
22 Arendt was fond of illustrating her thought with "exemplars." For instance, Solomon exemplified sound political judgment and the gift of an "understanding heart." Arendt 2004: 322–3. For more on this, see Guisan 2011, 131–2.
23 Ricoeur 2004: 489.
24 Reshaur 1992: 724.
25 See Canovan 1992: 197. Arendt's misgivings regarding Christianity may also explain why she did not take seriously the commitment to principled politics professed by Christian Democrat leaders, Robert Schuman in France, Konrad Adenauer in Germany and Alcide De Gasperi in Italy, after the war.
26 Arendt 1958: 242–3.
27 Arendt 2006: 86–7.

sociology" for "explaining away the responsibility of the doer in terms of this or that kind of determinism", but recommends the inner Socratic dialogue and self-examination.[28] She may give too short shrift to "ostensibly praiseworthy emotions" such as love and compassion[29] although she acknowledges that victims have to free themselves of "fanatical hatred" and victimizers of the guilt of complicity in order to act anew.[30] After the war Arendt chose to set things "straight again with a lot of people" in Germany.[31] Still politics are to be assessed on the basis of their concrete outcomes in the public sphere, not the emotions professed by actors. There is no space to account more fully for the interesting controversies sparked by Arendt's concept of political forgiveness. What matters here is that Arendt found an original way to draw a politically relevant "moral code… inferred from the faculties of forgiving and of making promises" from a specific religious tradition and the Roman legacy, but in a non-exclusive mode.[32] Her historical discussion of Jesus and forgiveness does not call upon religious identity or faith to persuade, but on reason and the commitment to non-violent politics.

In Arendt's mature work, the political bond between people forms around promising, not love.[33] Surprisingly there is a dearth of commentaries on the tight connection between Arendtian forgiving and promising in the vast and excellent literature on Arendt.[34] If Arendt can be a "frustrating theorist in that her originality and insights are not developed in concrete examples",[35] she did write extensively on promise in *On Revolution*, her homage to the American Revolution and its web of lasting covenants, a work which "illustrates" *The Human Condition*.[36] Yet there is no mention of forgiveness in that book. Should we then think of these two faculties discretely? Arendt's biographer Elizabeth Young-Bruehl seems to think so: she mentions the South African Truth and Reconciliation Commission as an example of Arendtian forgiving and the European integration process as an illustration of promising.[37] This essay argues to the contrary that forgiveness implies promising and the reverse also, taking Arendt at her word that these two faculties "belong together".[38] Promising acts like a guarantee against the risks of acting anew while forgiving opens up the

28 On this see Arendt 2003: 90–92. Arendt had little regard for psychoanalysis. Young-Bruehl 2006: 85.
29 Kateb 1984: 25–8.
30 Arendt 2004: 214.
31 Ibid.: 14.
32 Arendt 1958: 238.
33 Leah Bradshaw 1997: 370.
34 See *inter alia* Canovan 1992; Dietz 2002; Hill 1979; Hinchman and Hinchman 1994; Kateb 1984; Villa 2000; Young-Bruehl 1994 and 2006.
35 Lang and Williams 2005: 226.
36 Young-Bruehl 2006: 84.
37 Young-Bruehl 2006: 114–21 and 143.
38 Arendt 1958: 237.

future for promising to turn into practices, which eventually coalesce into a new political tradition.[39]

2.2. RECONCILIATION AS UNDERSTANDING AND THE HERMENEUTICAL PATH OF STORY-TELLING

Arendt takes pains to distinguish reconciliation from forgiving and promising: whereas these two human capacities manifest themselves through singular acts directed toward specific actors, reconciliation consists in the unending search for "understanding", a coming to terms with one's fate that prompts action instead of resignation. To understand is the attempt to make oneself at home in the world, to seek meaning: it is an open-ended exercise with no final conclusion.[40] This form of cognition, which has to do with knowledge, but even more with common sense and conscience, "becomes the other side of action". Arendt's illustration is Solomon who prayed for the gift of "an understanding heart". The understanding heart, "far removed from sentimentality…not mere reflection or mere feelings, makes it bearable for us to live with other people, strangers forever, in the same world, and for them to bear with us." It is also the "only thing in the world" that can bear the gift of action, of making a new beginning. In less biblical terms it corresponds with the faculty of imagination that helps us see others and the world from the proper distance, neither too close nor too distant, and to become "reconciled with what unavoidably exists".[41]

Arendt's notion of the understanding heart is both evocative and elusive: it calls on the mind rather than the emotions in order to act. The way to meaning is through story-telling, which need not establish causal relationships, but make sense.[42] Arendt adopts storytelling as "the point of departure for her concept of political thinking" because it is one form of thinking that does not trump acting.[43] She called herself a "phenomenologist of sort", but eschewed theoretical self-definitions.[44] Arendt's methodology, at least in *On Revolution*, is hermeneutical, going back to the speech and deed of actors in order to retrieve meaning out of their self-understandings. There is no space here to elaborate

---

39 For an interpretation of the tight connection between forgiving and promising in European integration see Guisan 2003.

40 Some scholars who mistrust the liberating power of forgiveness discuss reconciliation in similar terms. Brudholm 2008: 116. In *On Violence* Arendt calls peace an "absolute", that is an end in itself, although periods of peace have "nearly always" been shorter than periods of warfare in recorded history. Arendt 1970: 51. So peace may be simply unattainable in a world of unpredictable and irreversible actions.

41 Arendt 2004: 308–11 and 321–3.

42 Ibid., 318–320.

43 See Hill 1979: 287. For another thought-provoking discussion of understanding and reconciliation, see Prager in Prager and Govier 2003: 197–219.

44 Young-Bruehl 2004.

further on this except to say that the examination of practices that follow in the second part of this essay is inspired by Arendt and Paul Ricoeur's action-oriented hermeneutical inquiries.[45] It probes the relevance of the Arendtian categories of forgiveness, promise and understanding to reconciliatory practices in post conflict contexts by recalling stories. The first set of narratives about the founding of the European Coal and Steel Community (1950–2) is already quite old, and enough time has passed for a considered assessment, which constitutes the core of this essay's empirical discussion. The second narrative concerns the South African Truth and Reconciliation Commission, which has already stimulated extraordinarily rich political and academic debates, and this commentary should be taken as a modest footnote to the existing literature; the third story is still unfolding in Iraq and can only suggest tentative comments. It is important to note at the outset that Arendt did not distinguish between grassroots and "elite" actors except to say that in politics the elite selects itself by its willingness to engage in the public sphere for the sake of the common good.[46] Likewise this essay's narratives do not respect the usual scholarly distinctions between top-down and down-top processes of reconciliation;[47] in the "web of human relations" these interact with each other ceaselessly.[48]

3. THE PRACTICES OF POLITICAL FORGIVENESS, PROMISE AND UNDERSTANDING: THREE STORIES

3.1. THE FOUNDING OF THE EUROPEAN COAL AND STEEL COMMUNITY (ECSC): A DEFICIT OF UNDERSTANDING

Today few remember the 1952 Treaty of Paris on the ECSC, yet it was one of the starting points of the European reconciliation process.[49] The 1950 French Schuman Plan offered to the Federal Republic of Germany (FRG), and all other European countries willing to participate, the opportunity to create a limited but supranational "community" of equals to manage their coal and steel industries. Its purpose was unequivocal: to eliminate "the age old opposition of France and Germany" and contribute to "world peace", by making war "materially impossible".[50] Peace has featured in all major treaties on European integration since, but it is only recently that the word reconciliation entered EU public and

45 Arendt 2004 and Ricoeur 2004. For more on this see Guisan 2011, 2–3.

46 Arendt 2006: 278–81. See the excellent commentary of Jeffrey Isaacs 1994.

47 Bloomfield 2006: 25–6.

48 Arendt 1958: 181–8.

49 Within a few years the less supranational European Economic Community had upstaged the ECSC.

50 Fontaine 2000: 36.

academic rhetoric.[51] The ECSC, and the May 9, 1950 Schuman Declaration, which announced it, can be interpreted as manifestations of political forgiveness and promise.[52] Forgiving breaks with the past by acting "anew" and thus "can never be predicted".[53] The Schuman Declaration came as a shock: "nobody expected an initiative of this kind".[54] Upon hearing of it, "Dulles told Acheson, this was what Marshall and he had talked about in Moscow in 1947 but assumed that the French would never do...the obvious break with the past concerned the commitment with Germany. Five years after the war, the very idea was threatening... Many French politicians had talked of something like a Schuman Plan. But words are one thing, actions another."[55] Only if forgiveness and promise are actions, not feelings or motivations, can they be ascertainable and meaningful in the public realm. Like Arendt, the European founders believed in the virtue of institutions to check human nature.[56] The willingness of the French to put themselves under a common authority with the Germans is what convinced other countries such as Netherlands to sign the first European Community treaty.[57]Assessments of the ECSC's economic benefits vary greatly.[58] Some call it a success because production and trade in coal and steel increased considerably among the six partners;[59] others a failure because it did not succeed in dismantling the German steel cartels.[60] But even if "the ECSC actually delivered on only one of its promises", it was "the most important one: it advanced the integration process" and "substituted for a peace treaty with Germany".[61] The ECSC High Authority replaced the International Authority on the Ruhr under which the Germans had chafed, and the new relationship between former enemies facilitated the French withdrawal from the Saar after its people voted to join the FRG in 1955.

That a treaty would represent political promise is uncontroversial in legal and political theory. This is not the case for political forgiveness, which deserved more attention here. The European founders were well aware of the "psychological" barriers between the nations of Europe.[62] But Jacques-René Rabier and Max Kohnstamm, two of Monnet's closest collaborators, are reluctant

---

51 Diez et al. 2008; Gardner Feldman 1999; Guisan 2003; Mink and Neumayer 2007; Tocci 2004 and 2007.

52 Other practices played a part also: the willingness to acknowledge wrongs. Maritain 1993; Schuman 1964; Adenauer 1966; the pursuit of material interests; and the security guarantee by the US. Gillingham 1991; Milward 1992. See also Guisan 2003: 28–65.

53 Arendt 1958: 241.

54 Schuman 1964: 144.

55 Duchêne 1994: 203.

56 Monnet 1955: 45.

57 Duchêne 1994: 205.

58 Steiner in Jarausch and Lindenberger 2007.

59 Daltrop 1982: 10.

60 Gillingham 1991a: 355.

61 Gillingham 1991b: 154; Milward 1984: 420.

62 Duchêne 1994: 224.

to analyze their states of mind in 1950, and reject the idea that the ECSC should be understood as a symbol of forgiveness although they endorse the interpretation of promising.[63] In spite of harrowing experiences in a German concentration camp Kohnstamm thinks like Kateb: "Forgiveness is a personal act. To speak of forgiving the Germans in general is already the beginning of the Holocaust, a dangerous abstraction." As a young Dutch diplomat, traveling through German cities, which had been totally destroyed, he would see little children emerging from the ruins: "To speak of forgiving these innocent young people would have been ridiculous... Reconciliation is better than forgiveness."[64] How was reconciliation in Europe possible without forgiveness after WWII? Kohnstamm responds that the requirements of justice were satisfied by the Nuremberg trials, by the denazification programs imposed by the occupiers, and by the sizable reparations Germany paid to war victims. The Germans atoned for their past by renouncing dictatorship, adopting a democratic constitution, and accepting the leadership of men like Adenauer who had not been compromised with the Nazi regime. "We trusted Adenauer and if a few of his collaborators were former Nazis, we accepted it. All this would have been unthinkable if we had not been entirely turned toward the future. We had much to accomplish together." Did promising then replace forgiveness? The desire for revenge could lurk. Kohnstamm, whose two aunts had died in Auschwitz, recalls vividly an incident after he became ECSC secretary-general in Luxembourg: "The window of my office opened right above a bridge crossing a very deep ditch in the middle of the city. One day I was eating my sandwich when I saw a young German walking alone, in a raincoat, which resembled a Nazi uniform. The thought flashed through my mind: 'Why not push him in the ditch!' I was shocked by my reaction."[65]

If forgiveness is conceptualized as an action, a breaking from the past, treating former enemies in an amicable way and daring to "act in concert" with them, as Arendt and Digeser both argue, why should the ECSC founding not be interpreted as emblematic of this human capacity also? Senior actors were less leery of acknowledging the forgiving element of the process than Kohnstamm and Rabier. Thus French Foreign Affairs minister Robert Schuman, who spent the war years in a German prison and in hiding, recommended for France and Germany "a detoxification from history books". He did not minimize the difficult relationship with Germany, "which will remain perpetually dissatisfied, history

63 Rabier 1999; Kohnstamm 1999. The Frenchman Jacques-René Rabier was Jean Monnet's *directeur de cabinet* at the French Planning Commission and at the ECSC. He became head of Directorate X at the EEC Commission and helped create the euro-barometers upon retirement.
The Dutch diplomat Max Kohnstamm helped negotiate the ECSC Treaty and became the first ECSC Secretary-General. He was also the first president of the Florence European Institute.

64 Kohnstamm 1999.

65 Ibid.

has proved it,"[66] but acknowledged France's dynastic and ideological ambitions and Napoleon's wars of aggression. Both countries had to overcome "painful memories" to move "from hate to esteem and mutual trust" on the basis of equality.[67] Schuman chose to "extend our hand to our enemies not simply to forgive, but to build together the Europe of tomorrow", which was an "undertaking of peace" beyond "antagonism and resentments".[68] German Chancellor Konrad Adenauer, who was arrested several times during the war and whose wife died in the late 1940s following her internment in a Gestapo camp, was deeply convinced of the need for Germans to atone for their war crimes: "We [Germans] had to search our conscience."[69] To carry political meaning this search had to become action also, and Adenauer, as soon as he became FRG chancellor, started to negotiate with Israel sizable compensation for the "eternal suffering" the German nation had inflicted upon the Jewish people.[70] The negotiations were so controversial in both countries that they took place in the Netherlands, and Adenauer barely escaped an assassination attempt there, but an agreement was concluded between Israel and the FRG in 1952.

In the early years of European integration, the ECSC was theorized as a rational elite and technocratic process of neo-functionalism.[71] Little attention was paid to the role of affects; and resistance to theorize emotions in international relations persists.[72] There were no philosophical conversations around Monnet who refused to waste time on abstract debates, according to his collaborator Jean Fourastié. The ECSC High Authority's first president focused on political, administrative and economic problems, already a considerable undertaking, although he behaved as a man very conscious of the tragic side of the human condition. "The point was to try, starting from the tensions between men…to limit the dramatic, disorderly character of life."[73] In hindsight both Rabier and Kohnstamm wonder whether "enough was explained". The core meaning of the enterprise was obfuscated and decades later senior bureaucrats, politicians and public intellectuals do not get it.[74] French philosopher André Glucksmann questions the European founders' motivations who acted in deafening "silence." Meanwhile, the new peace has yet to be thought through.[75]

Without the engagement of countless grassroots activists, it is doubtful whether the French-German reconciliation could have been institutionalized in the ECSC and other treaties that followed; by the same token grassroots

66 Schuman 1964: 49 and 88.
67 Ibid.: 91 and 106.
68 Ibid.: 44 and 26.
69 Adenauer 1966: 39.
70 Adenauer 1967: 127.
71 Haas 1958.
72 Moïsi 2009.
73 Fourastié 1981.
74 Guisan 2003: 13–14.
75 Glucksmann 1997: 32 and 34; and 19. All texts in French translated by the author.

initiatives may have gone nowhere but for the political decisions at the highest level. Most often elite and grassroots initiatives were uncoordinated, yet they were compatible. In post WWII Europe grass roots movements manifesting a "spontaneous reconciliatory tendency" promoted forgiving as a healing of negative emotions and emotional reconnection.[76] Thus the participation of French and German coal industry representatives from labor and management in meetings at the international center of Caux, Switzerland was strong and dovetailed with the launching of the ECSC in a "classic case of serendipity."[77] But adequate theorizing of the European narratives of self-transformation, which might stimulate an Arendtian exercise in understanding, has been lacking so far; such narratives have remained semi-confidential and often couched a quasi-religious language that has attracted little scholarly and popular attention unfortunately.[78] Arendt mourned the loss of the tradition of public engagement in the US by calling it a "lost treasure."[79] The legacy of post War II popular and elite processes of forgiveness and promise in Europe is another political "lost treasure," which more critical understanding might have kept in existence.

3.2. THE SOUTH AFRICAN TRUTH AND RECONCILIATION COMMISSION: A DEFICIT OF PROMISING

In contrast with the European experience the South African democratic transition does not lack narratives, thanks in part to the Truth and Reconciliation Commission, which gathered over 22.000 testimonies, or "stories," on human rights violations.[80] The TRC encouraged something akin to a gigantic exercise in Arendtian reconciliation, a collective process of seeking "understanding." This essay probes briefly this experiment by drawing from one of its most famous narratives, Desmond Tutu's *No Future without Forgiveness*.[81] It could be argued that the state proposal for the TRC illustrates Arendtian forgiveness, an action, not an affect or attitude, initiated for the sake of the new political community.[82]

76 Mink in Mink and Neumayer 2007: 34.
77 Luttwak 1994: 51.
78 For autobiographical accounts see Hovelsen 1959 and 2008; Piguet 1985. For a few academic accounts see Luttwak in Johnston and Sampson 1994; Montville 1991; Guisan 2003 and 2011. Guisan focuses on the theorizing of the speech and deed of witnesses, 1946–2010. A new literature on reconciliation is appearing in EU studies, with its main focus on the EU as an *external* agent of reconciliation rather than on the founding experiences of self-reconciliation within the European Communities. See Diez, Albert and Stetter 2008; Rumelili 2007; Tocci 2004 and 2007. Elizabeth Pond, on the other hand, describes European self-reconciliations since 1989, but in a more journalistic vein. See Pond 2002 and 2006.
79 Arendt 2006: 210.
80 Henderson 2000: 457. Annelies Verdoolaege argues in this volume that the intensity and inclusiveness of discourses opened South Africa to the possibility of reconciliation.
81 Tutu 1999.
82 Young Bruehl 2006: 112–22. On this, see also Ricoeur 2004: 483–5.

The TRC was also the fruit of promises in the South African democratic transition: the interim constitution and its postscript, which established the TRC on the ground "that there is a need for understanding but not for vengeance";[83] and subsequently the Promotion of National Unity and Reconciliation Act voted by Parliament. The South African leaders offered conditional amnesty in exchange for truth, and institutionalized the process by setting up three committees on violation of human rights, amnesty and reparations. As Tutu acknowledges the whole process was contentious from start to finish even among the Commission members, but he justifies the conditional amnesties offered to fully confessing perpetrators by the TRC in the most rational way: Nuremberg-style trials or "victors" justice would have been too expensive for South Africa and left dangerous resentment; moreover this was a negotiated settlement and the whites still controlled the guns during the transition. Contrary to the Allies who went home, "we in South Africa had to live with each other".[84] "Restorative" rather than retributive justice was served: victims could not sue the perpetrators in civil courts, and the state took responsibility for the reparations "indispensable to counterbalance amnesty".[85] Promises made by the state to the Commission and the victims, however, were not kept: by 2000 only a few "urgent interim reparations" had been paid.[86] By 2002 the victims were still not being compensated adequately.[87] Contrary to Sierra Leone where victims got meaningful reparations, "in South Africa, where the TRC accomplished much, except notably the provision of meaningful reparations, it has engendered deep and bitter disappointment among the population it was designed to assist".[88]

Tutu argues for the positive political impact of forgiveness in a fledging democracy of ethnically diverse and economically unequal citizens. The forgiveness expected from the victims was promoted in terms of abandoning hatred, and resentment, not as a set of new political initiatives to undertake together for the sake of the community. Public exercises in confession and interpersonal forgiving are liable to psychoanalytical considerations, whose self-centeredness renders them apolitical, and Tutu acknowledges the sarcastic nickname given the Commission as the "Kleenex Commission".[89] Because the state did not deliver fully on its promise of reparations, the victims were not provided adequate support and opportunities to become engaged citizens in the new republic. Too few "islands of stability", which promises help establish, emerged in South Africa. Tutu mentions only one perpetrator, the policeman Brian Mitchell "actively involved in reconstructing" the Trust Feed Farm

83 Tutu 1999: 45.
84 Ibid.: 20–1.
85 Ibid.: 54–5 and 58.
86 Tutu 1999: 62.
87 Du Plessis in Fobelts and von Trotha 2004: 186–7.
88 Daly and Sarkin 2007: 229.
89 Tutu 1999: 163.

community he helped destroy. "Perhaps this kind of reparation should have been a required condition for amnesty to be granted."[90] It might have offered an opportunity to South Africans of all backgrounds to engage in a process of promising, thus weaving the new "web" of human relationships even if the government did not deliver on its promises for compensations. Nevertheless the Commission, by providing a space for South Africans "to come together and tell their stories," created an "event" where limited reconstruction across deep socio-economic divides could take place.[91] Was it a successful exercise in Arendtian understanding? Time will tell whether the therapeutic side of the TRC process, which Arendt might have frowned upon as apolitical and best handled in the intimate space of private relationships, will carry the hoped-for political import.

3.3. IRAQI AND US RECONCILIATORY PROCESSES AND THE DEFICITS OF FORGIVING AND UNDERSTANDING

It would take knowledge of the Arabic language to delve rigorously into the peace-making efforts under way, which Iraqi and non-Iraqi, elite and grassroots, have initiated in the last half-decade. But even a cursory overview of English-language resources posted on the Internet allows some preliminary comments. The stress on political measures ascertainable in the public realm is Arendt-like: fair political processes, protection of human rights, support for the return of refugees, reintegration in the national life of supporters of Saddam Hussein. There is little mention of forgiveness as an affect or moral attitude in these projects, although the 17 point statement signed by 33 Iraqi leaders in May 2009 urges the Iraqi state to apologize to its citizens, and perpetrators of the worst crimes to do likewise.[92] As in the European process it is grassroots movements that may be best equipped to deal with changes of attitude. University professor Ghada Hussein Al-Almy organizes street theater performances at the sites of deadly bombings since 2007 to counter the terrorist attacks on the Iraqi minds, enlisting the participation of well-known Iraqi artists. "You will not take our way of life or our culture away," is the message. One actor yells: "Sunni, Shiite… whatever ethnic group – I don't care! Spurn each other's hand no longer. Long life and success – to both of you!" Other Iraqi women have set up non-sectarian welfare and education programs in spite of the threats by extremists.[93] Foreign

90 Ibid.: 176–7.
91 Du Plessis in Foblets and von Trotha 2004: 193.
92 Giovannini, N. Successful Conclusion of the Conference on Reconciliation and Accountability in Iraq organized by the International Alliance for Justice and No Peace without Justice, Erbil, May 11, 2009. www.npwj.org. Downloaded December 21, 2009.
93 Edward O'Connor and Cheryl Benard, "In Iraq, a different kind of drama stages a message of reconciliation." Christian Science Monitor. December 18, 2008. www.csmonitor.com/2008/1218/p09s02-coop.html. Downloaded December 21, 2009.

NGOs and governments attempt to assist the process. Thus the Norwegian Institute of International Affairs gathered a group of ethnically diverse Iraqi academics and professionals in February 2009 to talk and write about Iraqi future.[94] The UN Assistance Mission for Iraq (UNAMI) runs projects designed to foster dialogue and address unresolved conflicts between ethnic and religious groups, a mandate laid down in 2007 UN Security Council Resolution 1770.[95]

Iraqis have made promises since the 2003 US invasion, which delivered them from Saddam Hussein's rule, starting with the Constitution approved in an October 2005 referendum with the caveat that it might be amended later. A contentious and protracted process led to the new Election Law on December 6, 2009 that will allow the second parliamentary election since 2005 to proceed in March 2010. In order to accommodate the grievances of Sunnis and Kurds for more representation the Parliament will enlarge from 275 to 325 seats, with eight at large seats to represent Christian and other minorities and seven additional at large seats to be distributed by the top vote getters. The votes of Iraqis abroad will count in their provinces of origin.[96] In a "surprising move" the Iraqi government even announced on February 25, 2010 that it would reinstate 20,000 officers who served under Saddam Hussein.[97] Arendt credited the situation of relative economic abundance in the US for the possibility of covenanting. That a constitutional process and rule making should happen at all in an ethnically divided country, with 4 ½ million displaced persons, after years of dictatorship is admirable.[98]

But promises are not enough to guarantee the continuation of politics as both Iraqi and regional leaders have acknowledged.[99] Therefore the Arab League in 2005 and Iraqi Prime Minister Nouri al-Maliki in 2006 initiated two top-down processes of "reconciliation". Although the Arab League project ended up in a stalemate partly because of the spring 2006 attack on the Samarra's Shiite shrine,[100] the second process built on the first by drawing on committees, which had already been set up. The Maliki Reconciliation and National Dialogue Plan offered amnesty to insurgents who condemned violence and would support the state; reintegration of Saddam Hussein's officers and soldiers in the Iraqi armed

94 Report, "More than 'Shiites' and 'Sunnis': How a Post Sectarian Strategy Can Change the Logic and Facilitate Sustained Political Reform in Iraq." Oslo, April 3, 2009. www.nupi.no/Publikasjoner/Boeker-Rapporter. Downloaded June 5, 2009.

95 UNAMI sent a Kurdish delegation to Northern Ireland on a "lesson-learned mission." Graeber, D. UNAMI reviews Irish Reconciliation for Kirkuk. May 15, 2009. www.upi.com. Downloaded December 21, 2009. For more on UNAMI: www.uniraq.org.

96 New Iraqi Election Law Approved. December 6, 2009. www.news.bbc.co.uk/2/hi/8398377.stm. Downloaded December 22, 2009.

97 The news was greeted with skepticism by political rivals of the Prime Minister al-Maliki Marc Santora. "Iraq plans to reinstate 20,000 ex-officers. Herald Tribune, February 26, 2010.

98 Arendt 2006: 99–105. She compared the US situation with France where the *malheureux* crying for bread encouraged Robespierre to rule by force under the sway of necessity (*ibid.*).

99 Al-Marashi and Keskin 2008: 247.

100 Ibid.: 252.

forces; and material compensations to the victims of violence.[101] The Iraqi parliament approved several reconciliation laws in 2007 and 2008, whose implementation is still incomplete; a parliamentarian Reconciliation Committee and a Ministry for National Dialogue were set up. The withdrawal of Sunni parties from Parliament in 2007 to protest the state's inability to rein in the militias stalled the Maliki Plan. According to Ibrahim Al-Marashi and Aysegul Keskin, both plans suffered from some of the same weaknesses: they lacked credibility with some major players and were perceived as biased.[102] Although the South African example was held as a template and several senior Iraqi politicians traveled to South Africa, there was no plea for forgiveness and accountability. The public display of private emotion, of forgiveness and apology, was perceived in the Iraqi cultural context as potentially damaging to the honor of the victim and the accused.[103]

On the US side, a bipartisan Commission was appointed by the US Congress to look into the Iraq conflict and issue proposals for solving the stalemate in 2006. Its *The Iraq Study Group Report* (2006) should be considered as another important narrative of reconciliation. Indeed "reconciliation" featured as a core concept starting with the executive summary. The Report, conceived by a blue-ribbon bipartisan ten-member committee and headed by Republican former Secretary of State James A. Baker, III and Democratic former congressman Lee H. Hamilton, assigned different responsibilities to the US and the Iraqi governments. The US should engage all neighboring countries, including Iran, in crafting a comprehensive peace plan, and help Iraqis achieve the milestones set by the Maliki government on security, governance and national reconciliation; and it should withdraw all its troops by December 2011. The recommendations to Iraqis included the speedy approval of the provincial Election Law, of the Petroleum Law that would guarantee a fair sharing of the oil resources on a per capita rather than ethnic basis; the approval and implementation of the De-Baathification Law and Militia Law that would complete the reintegration of Baathists and Arab nationalist into national life.[104]

The important question of the effectiveness of recommendations on reconciliation by an occupying power is left aside here.[105] The main points are that the Report did not define the term reconciliation, and left the emotional, or private, aspect of reconciliatory processes unmentioned as well. It focused on proposals for concrete action in the public realm. It could be theorized as an exercise in "understanding" on the US' part, given the extensive consultations the study group engaged with expert working groups and 169 individual experts

---

101 Ibid.: 254.
102 Ibid.: 255.
103 Ibid.: 248 and 254; 256.
104 Baker and Hamilton 2006.
105 The US encouraged a French initiative toward the FRG in 1949 and supported the 1950 Schuman Plan, but was not its author.

and leaders, including 35 Iraqi leaders and 21 foreign officials, although the group included mostly establishment figures. Sadly the Report was never seriously discussed in the US although its publication had been preceded by much publicity. Thus it failed to stimulate a national process of attempting to "understand" the difficult consequences of a war of choice. Albeit understanding was not the primary intent of the congressional mandate to the Study Group, which asked for concrete proposals, the Report remains a missed opportunity.

4. CONCLUSION

Each of the three cases examined above deserves much more consideration. But, as they are, these narratives provide ample material to ponder the meaning of Arendt's categories of political forgiveness and promise, two human capacities that have little to do with the heart's emotions, and of reconciliation as a process of understanding. These stories illustrate the reconciliatory potential of these practices; the main point is that *only together,* not singly, can they deploy their full effects in the public realm. Political theory should speak to concrete practices: Arendt's original reflections help us think anew the intricate connections between forgiving, promising, and the "gift of the understanding heart," as they impact post conflict contexts.

Interviews by the author:
Max Kohnstamm, Brussels, March 19, 1999.
Jacques-René Rabier, Brussels, March 3, 1999.
Interview by Antoine Marès:
Jean Fourastié, Paris, May 6, 1981

REFERENCES

Adenauer, K. (1966). *Memoirs.* Vol 1. Trans. Ruhm von Oppen, B. London: Weidenfeld and Nicolson.
Adenauer, K. (1967). *Mémoires.* Vol 2. Trans. Teissèdre, G. and Chatenet, G. Paris: Hachette.
Al-Marashi, I. and Keskin A. (2008). Reconciliation Dilemmas in Post-Ba'athist Iraq: Truth Commissions, Media and Ethno-sectarian Conflicts. *Mediterranean Politics,* 13 (2), 243–259.
Arendt, H. (1958). *The Human Condition.* Chicago: Chicago University Press.
— (1970). *On Violence.* Orlando, FL: Harcourt Brace Jovanovich Publishers.
— (2003). *Responsibility and Judgment.* Ed. Kohn, J. New York: Shocken Books.
— (2004). *Essays in Understanding 1930–1945: Formation, Exile and Totalitarianism* (2nd ed). New York: Schocken Books.

— (2006). *On Revolution* (4th ed.). New York: Penguin Books.
Baker, J. A. III & Hamilton, L.H. co-chairs (2006). *The Iraq Study Group Report.* New York: Vintage Books.
Bar-Siman-Tov, Y. (ed.) (2004). *From Conflict Resolution to Reconciliation.* Oxford: Oxford University Press.
Bloomfield, D. (2006). On Good Terms: Clarifying Reconciliation, *Berghof Report*, 14, 1–33.
Bradshaw, L. (1997). Communion with Others, Communion with Truth. *The Review of Politics*, 59 (2), 368–371.
Brudholm, T. (2008). *Resentment's Virtue: Jean Améry and the Refusal to Forgive.* Philadelphia: Temple University.
Canovan, M. (1992). *Hannah Arendt: A Reinterpretation of Her Political Thought.* Cambridge: Cambridge University Press.
Chiba, S. (1995). Hannah Arendt on Love and the Political: Love, Friendship, and Citizenship. *The Review of Politics*, 57(3), 505–535.
Daltrop, A. (1982). *Politics and the European Community.* Harlow, Essex: Longman.
Daly, E. & Sarkin, J. (2007). *Reconciliation in Divided Societies: Finding Common Ground.* Philadelphia: University of Pennsylvania Press.
Digeser, P. (1998). Forgiveness and Politics: Dirty Hands and Imperfect Procedures. *Political Theory*, 26 (5), 700–734.
— (2001). *Political Forgiveness.* Ithaca: Cornell University Press.
Dietz, M. G. (2002). *Turning Operations: Feminism, Arendt and Politics.* New York: Routledge.
Diez, T., Albert, M. & Stetter, S. (eds.) (2008). *The European Union and Border Conflicts: The Power of Integration and Association*, Cambridge, UK: Cambridge University Press.
Duchêne, F. (1994). *Jean Monnet: The First Statesman of Interdependence.* New York and London: W. W. Norton & Company.
Du Plessis, W. (2004). The South African Truth and Reconciliation Commission: 'The Truth will set you free.' in Foblets, M-C. and von Trotha, T. (Eds.) *Healing the Wounds: Essays on the Reconstruction of Societies after War.* Oxford: Hart Publishing, 169–200.
Enright, R.D. & North, J. (eds.) (1998). *Exploring Forgiveness.* Madison, WI: The University of Wisconsin Press.
Fontaine, P. (2000). *A new idea for Europe: The Schuman declaration 1950–2000.* Luxembourg: Office for Official Publications of the European Communities.
Gardner Feldman, L. (1999). Reconciliation and Legitimacy: Foreign relations and enlargement of the European Union. In Banchoff, T. and Smith, M.P. (eds.), *Legitimacy and the European Union: The contested Polity,* London and New York: Routledge, 66–90.
Gillingham, J. (1991a). *Coal, steel and the rebirth of Europe, 1945–1955.* Cambridge and New York: Cambridge University Press.
— (1991b). Jean Monnet and the European Coal and Steel Community: A Preliminary Appraisal. In Douglas Brinkley and Clifford Hackett (eds.). *Jean Monnet: The Path to European Unity.* New York: St Martin's Press, 129–62.

Glucksmann, A. (1997). *Le Bien et le Mal: Lettres immorales d'Allemagne et de France.* Paris: Robert Laffont.
Guisan, C. (2003). *Un sens à l'Europe: Gagner la paix* (1950–2003). Paris: Odile Jacob.
— (2011) *A Political Theory of Identity in European Integration: Memory and Policies.* Oxford and New York: Routledge.
Haas, E. B. (1958). *The Uniting of Europe: Political, Social and Economic Forces, 1950–1957.* Stanford, CA: Stanford University Press.
Henderson, W. (2000). Metaphors, Narrative and 'Truth': South Africa's TRC. *African Affairs*, 99, 457–465.
Hill, M. (1979). *Hannah Arendt: The Recovery of the Public World.* New York: St Martin's Press.
Hinchman, L.P. and Hinchman, S.K. (eds.). (1994). *Hannah Arendt: Critical Essays.* Albany, NY: State University of New York Press.
Hovelsen, L. (1959). *Out of the Evil Night.* Trans. Morrison, J. London: Blandford Press.
— (2009). *Durch die Mauern: Wege zur Versöhnung.* Lüdenscheid: Asaph GmbH.
Isaacs, J. (1994). Oases in the Desert: Hannah Arendt on Democratic Politics. *American Political Science Review*, 88(1), 156–68.
Kateb, G. (1984). *Hannah Arendt: Politics, Conscience, Evil.* Totowa, NJ: Rowman & Allanheld.
— (2000). Political action: its nature and advantages. In Dana Villa (ed.). *The Cambridge Companion to Hannah Arendt.* Cambridge, UK: Cambridge University Press, 130–148.
Keenan, A. (1994) Promises, Promises: The Abyss of Freedom and the Loss of the Political in the Work of Hannah Arendt. *Political Theory*, 22 (2), 297–322.
Kristeva, J. (2001). *Hannah Arendt.* Trans. Guberman, R. New York: Columbia University Press.
Lang, A. F., Jr. and Williams, J. (eds.) (2005). *Hannah Arendt and International Relations: Reading Across the Lines.* New York: Palgrave MacMillan.
Luttwak, E. (1994). Franco-German Reconciliation: The Overlooked Role of the Moral Re-Armament Movement. Appendix by Steele, D. (pp. 37–63). In Johnston, D. & Sampson, C. (eds.). *Religion, The Missing Dimension of Statecraft.* New York and Oxford: Oxford University Press.
Marcel, G. (ed.) (1971). *Plus décisif que la violence.* Paris: Plon.
Maritain, J. (1993). *L'Europe et l'idée fédérale.* Paris: Mame.
Milward, A. (1992). *The European Rescue of the Nation-State.* Berkeley: University of California Press.
Mink, G. and Neumayer, L. (eds.). (2007). *L'Europe et ses passés douloureux.* Paris: La Découverte.
Mink, G. (2007). Introduction. In Mink and Neumayer, 11–35.
Moïsi, D. (2009). *The Geopolitics of Emotions: How Cultures of Fear, Humiliation and Hope Are Reshaping the World.* New York: Doubleday.
Monnet, J. (1955). *Les Etats-Unis d'Europe ont commencé: La Communauté européenne du charbon et de l'acier, Discours et Allocutions 1952–1954.* Paris: Laffont.
Monnet, J. (1978). *Memoirs.* Trans. Mayne, R. New York: Doubleday.
Piguet, J. (1985). *For the Love of Tomorrow: The Story of Irène Laure.* Trans. Sciortino, J. London: Grosvenor.

Pitkin, H.F. (1994). Justice: On Relating Private and Public. In Hinchman L.P. and Hinchman, S.K. (Eds.), *Hannah Arendt: Critical Essays*. Albany, NY: State University of New York Press, 261–288.
Pond, E. (2002). *The Rebirth of Europe*. Washington, DC: Brookings Institution Press.
— (2006). *Endgame in the Balkans: Regime Change, European Style*. Washington, DC: Brookings Institution Press.
Prager, C. A. L. (2003). Introduction and Aspects of Understanding and Judging Mass Human Rights Abuses, in Prager, C.A.L. and Govier, T. (eds.), *Dilemmas of Reconciliation*. Waterloo, Ontario: Wilfrid Laurier University Press, 1-26 and 197–219.
Ricoeur, P. (2004). *Memory, History, Forgetting*. Trans. Blamey, K. and Pellauer, D. Chicago: The University of Chicago Press.
Reshaur, K. (1992). Concepts of Solidarity in the Political Theory of Hannah Arendt. *Canadian Journal of Political Science / Revue canadienne de science politique*, 25(4), 723–736.
Rumelili, B. (2007). Transforming Conflict on EU Borders: The Case of Greek-Turkish Relations. *Journal of Common Market Studies*, 45(1), 105–126.
Schuman, R. (1964). *Pour l'Europe*. Paris: Nagel.
Shriver, D. (1995). *An Ethics for Enemies: Forgiveness in Politics*. New York and Oxford: Oxford University Press.
Sitton, J.F. (1994). Hannah Arendt's Argument for Council Democracy. In Hinchman L.P. and Hinchman S. K. (eds.), *Hannah Arendt: Critical Essays*. Albany, NY: State University of New York Press, 307–329.
Steiner, A. (2007). Economics of West European Integration? Proving the Benefits 1952–1973. In Jarausch, K.H. and Lindenberger, T. (eds.), *Conflicted Memories: Europeanizing Contemporary Histories*. New York and Oxford: Berghahn Books, 194–2005.
Tocci, N. (2004). *EU Accession Dynamics and Conflict Resolution: Catalysing Peace or Consolidating Partition in Cyprus?* Aldershot, UK and Burlington, VT: Ashgate.
— (2007). *The EU and Conflict Resolution: Promoting peace in the backyard*. London and New York: Routledge.
Tutu, D. M. (1999). *No Future without Forgiveness*. New York: Doubleday.
Villa, D. R. (Ed.). (2000). *The Cambridge Companion to Hannah Arendt*. Cambridge: Cambridge University Press.
Wink, W. (1984). *When the Powers Fall: Reconciliation in the Healing of Nations*. Minneapolis: Fortress Press.
Young-Bruehl, E. (2004). *For Love of the World*. (2nd ed.). New Heaven and London: Yale University Press.
— (2006). *Why Arendt Matters*. New Haven and London: Yale University Press.

VICTIMHOOD, TRUTH RECOVERY, AND PUBLIC FORGIVENESS IN NORTHERN IRELAND

Some interdisciplinary reflections

Margaret E. Smith

1. INTRODUCTION

Public forgiveness in Northern Ireland, if it has a place at all, still lies in the future. The Northern Ireland Executive's recent policy statement, *Strategy for Victims and Survivors,* once again kicks the can down the road with regard to deciding on a definition of who was a victim and on a truth recovery process. *Strategy for Victims and Survivors* lowers expectations for reconciliation and proposes that victims discuss and give input on the character of a future truth process. Is this tantamount to concluding that no process leading to public forgiveness will happen in Northern Ireland? This paper explores this question, highlighting the deeply divided nature of Northern Ireland society, which provoked the conflict in the first place, reduces the likelihood of a truth commission, and hobbles those in leadership from making reconciliatory gestures. Paradoxically, public forgiveness in Northern Ireland will have to come from the grass roots, given the challenges of Northern Ireland's "consensus" politics.

2. NORTHERN IRELAND AFTER 1998

The Good Friday Agreement of 1998 found a formula, through power-sharing, by which two long opposed parties engaged in a zero-sum conflict could work together. It did not, however, represent new found political solidarity. Both parties retain, unaltered, political goals that are antithetical to one another. These political goals are shored up by narratives that draw on a rich history of successive violent events. From both perspectives, victimhood is part of the political narrative. Though nationalists view the 1998 plan more positively than unionists because they see power-sharing as a way-station en route to the eventual unification of Ireland, neither politicized group considers the current constitutional arrangements to be a long term solution to its aspirations.

Tensions got so bad in 2002 that Westminster took back into its own hands the running of Northern Ireland. The Stormont government was restored in 2007, with the Reverend Ian Paisley as First Minister and former IRA operative Martin McGuinness as Deputy First Minister. Paisley has now given his place to a younger colleague, Peter Robinson.

Despite political tensions, the work of rehabilitating the society after its thirty years' war continues, by many measures quite effectively. Foreign investment and job creation have helped lift the economy despite persistent high unemployment in certain areas most associated with the conflict. Grassroots cross-community efforts to break down barriers include cycling and other sports events, joint church services, drama workshops, and art shows.[1] Dialogue groups attempt to keep in the forefront of people's minds the idea that neither community has a monopoly of suffering. Interfaces in Belfast now claim a reduction in violent conflict through the use of cell phone communication between community leaders on both sides. Optimists would say that trust-building is a gradual process and that Northern Ireland has made a start in that direction.

Four salient issues regarding the completion of what was signed onto in the Agreement have remained on the table since the Stormont government resumed in 2007: decommissioning of the last paramilitary weapons, devolution of authority over policing and justice from Westminster to Stormont, processing the facts of the past, and supporting the victims. In the opening weeks of 2010, the first of these reached an advanced stage of resolution when the last significant paramilitary groups announced they had disarmed.[2] With regard to the second issue – devolution – on February 5, 2010, parties involved announced agreement on handing policing and justice back to Northern Ireland's jurisdiction from Westminster, and devolution took place April 12.

The status is different for the two remaining issues. The third issue on the table is the process of unearthing the facts about the deaths of over three thousand people killed in the thirty year conflict that ended in 1998. The idea of a truth commission has been much discussed but, so far, not pursued. A series of government funded formal inquiries have been and are being pursued to investigate possible culpability of the state with regard to particular killings during the conflict. The Police Service of Northern Ireland (PSNI) has, in addition, launched its own truth recovery process, the Historical Inquiries Teams, reopening the files on nearly all the deaths during the Troubles, to allow

1 One Small Step Campaign.

2 The Ulster Defense Association (UDA) announced full decommissioning January 6, 2010. The Official Republican Movement (ORM), a faction of the Official IRA, revealed February 8, 2010, that it had put its weapons beyond use. Its statement came just under an hour after the Irish National Liberation Army (INLA) announced it had decommissioned its weapons.

families to have access to what is known. And community-based story telling projects have attempted to allow victims some form of catharsis.

The other live issue in the Northern Ireland post conflict process is the response to victims' needs. While efforts to help victims have proceeded, coordinated policy for service delivery and reparations has been slow to emerge. Victims' issues and truth recovery have remained a barometer of the two communities' ongoing view of post-conflict realities. They have been described as among the "most highly contentious issues and key 'sites of struggle' within civil society and the wider political arena."[3]

3. TRUTH RECOVERY

Because the Good Friday Agreement came so soon after the launching of South Africa's Truth and Reconciliation Commission, discussions of a possible truth commission for Northern Ireland popped up repeatedly in the 1990s. At the same time, reflections on the South African process already were pointing to the fact that South Africa's truth recovery was more successful in helping the society move on than it was in helping individual victims get their needs met.[4] This introduced the idea that a "victim centered" truth recovery process was needed for Northern Ireland. A second, and not unrelated, criticism of the South African process has been its narrow focus, where individual violations were investigated rather than structural, socio-economic injustices.[5] A third matter of debate highlighted the tradeoff between truth and justice on the one hand, and stability, reconciliation and "pragmatic politics" on the other.[6] All these issues have been live in Northern Ireland's societal debate on a possible truth commission.

Research in 2001 found that 64.7% in Northern Ireland favored a truth commission.[7] By 2007 this number had dropped to 49.6%.[8] The later research found that the idea of a truth commission is relatively more important to nationalists than to unionists, though this division by party affiliation is less strong than some might expect.

Republicans – the more extreme wing of Northern Ireland nationalists – have been the most vocal of any group in their call for a broad truth recovery process. They insist that an exploration of the past not be limited to individual injurious acts committed since 1966, but should also examine structural abuses and intergroup patterns of behavior that go back to the earlier troubled history of the

3 Lundy and McGovern, 322.
4 Hamber, 2001, 135.
5 Mani, R. (2002). *Beyond Retribution. Seeking Justice in the Shadow of War.* Oxford: Polity Press. Cited by Lundy & McGovern, 322.
6 Biggar, 6–22; Lundy & McGovern, 322.
7 Cairns and Mallett, 12.
8 Lundy and McGovern, 326.

region. Many non-Republicans who might otherwise be attracted to a truth commission find this maximal vision impractical and counter- productive, with the potential to arouse more inter-communal antipathy than understanding. Unionists demonstrate less overall enthusiasm for a truth recovery process. While the fears they express – that it would be very expensive and the money could be better used elsewhere, or that the guilty will go free – are the same ones nationalists express, more unionists than nationalists express these concerns.[9]

The body with the greatest power to encourage or launch a truth commission would be the British government. After holding extensive hearings on the matter, the Northern Ireland Affairs Committee (NIAC) in the House of Commons decided in 2005 that it was "too soon" for such a process.[10] Transcripts of those hearings indicate that high-profile members of Northern Ireland's "peacemaking" community agree with this stance,[11] though nationalists would view the NIAC decision as one more example of the British tendency to be more in sympathy with unionist than nationalist goals.

The British army and the police force in Northern Ireland – formerly called the Royal Ulster Constabulary (RUC) but now, having undergone reforms, called the Police Service of Northern Ireland (PSNI) – were the two official bodies responsible for maintaining civil order during the conflict, and their views on truth recovery are very similar. They understood their task during the conflict as one of bringing to heel the most sophisticated terrorist organization known to date – the IRA – and they believed at the time and subsequently that the means to do so inevitably required going beyond what the ordinary public would understand to be normal forms of law enforcement. The police and army paid a high price in injury and loss of life for their efforts to restore civil order, and their families are now some of the most outspoken with regard to victims' concerns. The police and the army recognize that a full inquiry into the events of the Troubles would be a murky and expensive business; neither have any intention of allowing their records to be inspected by others.

INQUIRIES INTO COLLUSION

The matter of truth recovery remains center stage in part because nationalist accusations of criminal behavior by British authorities during the Troubles have spawned legal action. The Stephens Inquiry and the Cory Inquiry, which delivered their reports in 2003 and 2004 respectively, were both directed at the

9 Lundy and McGovern, 334.

10 NIAC. This decision came after then Secretary of State for Northern Ireland, Paul Murphy, looked into the matter with some thoroughness, including making a trip to South Africa to study the process there. See Smyth 2007 for an extensive critique of the NIAC hearings.

11 Smyth.

matter of "collusion" between the British security forces[12] and loyalist (Protestant) paramilitaries. Allegedly the security forces turned a blind eye when they knew Protestant paramilitaries were targeting civilians with IRA sympathies. Indeed in some cases army members and the Northern Ireland police are accused of tipping off the paramilitaries about "desirable" targets. The Cory Report found that four of the eight cases it considered pointed to a need for a fuller investigation of collusion. Three further inquiries are currently in progress.

Another formal inquiry reopened the matter of what happened on "Bloody Sunday," January 30, 1972, that led to the deaths of fourteen Catholics in Derry at the hands of British paratroopers. Catholics believe the British paratroopers decided ahead of time to fire at Catholics to "teach them a lesson," when they had no evidence that people in the crowd were armed or had any intention of firing weapons. This inquiry, led by Lord Saville, delivered its report on June 15, 2010, announcing the historic decision that the paratroopers *were* at fault. The announcement was followed by an official apology by Prime Minister David Cameron.

HISTORICAL ENQUIRIES TEAMS

In order to demonstrate good will, and to satisfy the desires of many of the families of those who died in the conflict, the Chief of the PSNI from 2002 to 2009, Sir Hugh Orde, explored various approaches to dealing with the past that would be short of a truth commission but serve similar ends. The result is the Historical Enquiries Teams (HETs), a project undertaken by the PSNI to re-open the files on 3,258 deaths, and to meet with the families of those who died to tell them all that is known about the cause of death.

A thorough critique of the HET process has been published by sociologist Patricia Lundy, who points out the problem of having the police supervise a process of investigation, when nearly half the population views the police as having been complicit in the abuses of the conflict itself.[13] In certain circles it is axiomatic that the HETs need to be taken out of the hands of the police and be placed under the jurisdiction of a more objective body.

12 This blanket term is used in the parlance of Northern Ireland to include the Northern Ireland police – known during the conflict as the Royal Ulster Constabulary (RUC); police auxiliaries known as B-Specials (disbanded in 1970); a local Northern Ireland regiment of the British Army – the Ulster Defense Regiment (UDR); British army regiments from mainland Britain, including specialized forces; and various arms of British intelligence. All these groups were perceived by nationalists to have a stake in the preservation of the status quo.

13 Lundy.

STORYTELLING

One cross-community, non-government initiative worthy of particular note, the Healing Through Remembering Project,[14] embarked on an extensive consultation, beginning in 2001, which asked individuals, organizations and communities "How should people remember the events connected with the conflict in and about Northern Ireland and in so doing, individually and collectively contribute to the healing of the wounds of society?" "Storytelling" proved to be the most popular of the options people recommended in the survey.[15]

"Storytelling" is understood as an unofficial form of truth recovery, springing from the grassroots. It addresses some of the downsides of official truth processes for victims – victims' stories having to be framed according to a predicted narrative form, victims having to subject their stories to sterile cross examination in court. Some see it as a benign, uncontroversial way to deal with truth recovery. But storytelling, like victimhood or truth recovery, is addressed differently depending on each community's understanding of the conflict.[16] Most storytelling projects are pursued within a single community.[17] Storytelling is therefore not as "benign" as might be imagined, because it goes beyond personal catharsis and lends itself to articulation of ongoing politicized outlooks.[18] Catholic/nationalist victims come from a community committed to challenging the predominant culture and readily embark on storytelling because it offers them one more form of agency in challenging hegemonic discourse. Unionists tend to be much more reticent in speaking about what happened to them than nationalists, probably because a high percentage of the victims in this community were linked with the security forces, who adopted stoicism and refusal to speak about their experiences to strangers as part of their professional persona.[19] In addition, unionists who served the state in the police or army fear that their contribution will be forgotten if nationalists, with their anti-state narrative, are given a voice. This makes unionists less supportive of storytelling.

14 Healing Through Remembering is a limited company with charitable status operating through independent funding which has been sourced internationally.

15 Healing Through Remembering continues to work, from the non-government side, towards the realization of the goals enumerated here. Its Day of Reflection is observed on June 21st each year.

16 Hackett and Rolston, 366.

17 Ardoyne Commemoration Project; Falls Community Council's Dúchas.

18 Hackett and Rolston, 355–356.

19 Hackett and Rolston, 367.

MEMORIALIZATION

Another aspect of dealing with the past – memorialization of the victims – has been the subject of considerable discussion. In 2001, seventy percent of people in Northern Ireland believed that victims should be remembered in some way. Catholics/nationalists were more supportive of remembrance gestures than Protestants/unionists, but this research indicated no sign that victims themselves were more or less likely to support such projects than non-victims.[20] Thus, it seems, memorialization serves society in general more than it serves victims. Memorials have been created, though mostly in a single community context. Finding meaningful cross-community memorials has been a taxing exercise, with little success. A book composed of a list of all those who died in the Troubles, with a paragraph of biographical information on each person, has been dubbed the most successful cross-community remembrance project.[21]

4. VICTIMS IN THE NORTHERN IRELAND CONFLICT

Between 1969 and 2003, 3,725 people were killed and 47,541 injured[22] in a population of 1.7 million. In addition to these "primary" victims, "secondary" victims would include family members and ongoing care givers. "Tertiary" victims would be members of the wider society who were exposed to the conflict.[23]

The first comprehensive research project to capture the situation of victims of the conflict, The Cost of the Troubles Study, published in 1999, concluded that about 30% of those who had been exposed to violence associated with the Troubles had needs approximating to Post Traumatic Stress Disorder.[24] A 2003 study found psychological well being in Northern Ireland had not been as broadly affected as the earlier study indicated, but did find that the twelve percent of the population that self-described as victim showed a strong correlation with "poor psychological well-being".[25] In 2005 a government funded mental health report announced that people who reported being affected a lot by the Troubles "were almost twice as likely to show signs of possible mental health problems (thirty-four percent) as those who had not been affected much (eighteen

20 Cairns and Mallett, 11.

21 David McKittrick, Seamus Kelters, Brian Feeney and Chris Thornton. *Lost Lives: The stories of the men, women and children who died as a result of the Northern Ireland troubles.* Edinburgh: Mainstream Publishing Company Ltd, 1999.

22 Conflict Archive on the Internet (CAIN).

23 See Govier for this categorization of victims.

24 Smyth and Morrisey.

25 Cairns and Mallett, 20.

percent).[26] Suicide trends between 1997 and 2007 showed a twenty-seven percent increase in Northern Ireland compared to a nine percent decrease in the UK generally; rates of depression and anxiety among teenagers increased by seventy percent between 1982 and 2007.[27] Overall, Northern Ireland has a twenty-five percent higher incidence of mental health problems than other parts of the UK, a fact which can be directly related to the Troubles.[28]

That suicide rates were increasing during a period that largely postdated the Good Friday Agreement, shows the ongoing legacy of the conflict even after violence had ended. This is borne out in other research that indicates that the ceasefires did not lead to a notable change in psychological well being.[29] One explanation for this is that during the conflict people were more likely to bond together and help each other. Once the conflict was deemed "over", informal supportive practices were undermined by the new social realities.[30]

The Community Relations Council, as late as 2006, criticized the adequacy of support services for those caring for victims. "Whilst there has been recognition of the existence of this group, and an acknowledgement of the support they provide, there is still a conspicuous lack of cohesive and comprehensive inclusion at strategic levels and in the shaping and delivery of support services."[31]

5. EMERGENCE OF VICTIMS' GROUPS

The Victims' Liaison Unit of the Northern Ireland Office[32], created in 1998 to oversee the needs of victims, encouraged community groups to develop discussions about the needs of victims. The groups that formed were usually designed for particular localities, and on the whole represented people from one community or the other.

Unionist victims' groups demonstrated a narrative that matches with a wider unionist view: We were the defenders of Northern Ireland against an onslaught of terrorism. Civilians and those who were part of the state security apparatus who died at the hands of republican terrorists are the only true victims. If you died at the hands of the state security forces while you were associated with a terrorist organization, you brought that on yourself, and you do not deserve to be dubbed a victim.

Thus, for unionists, definition of the word "victim" has become a huge preoccupation.

26 Bamford Review.
27 Bamford Review, 7.
28 Community Relations Council.
29 Cairns and Mallett, 21.
30 Bamford Review.
31 Community Relations Council.
32 This body was superseded by the Victims Unit of the OFMDFM in 2005.

Republican victims have their narrative also, which mainly consists of a push for more inquiries into the questionable acts of the British state in addressing the Troubles. This view of things lines up with republicans' long-standing focus on British imperial policies as the real cause of the conflict. Republican victims' groups are the ones who have lobbied for inquiries into collusion between the security forces and loyalist (i.e. protestant) paramilitaries. Republicans criticize unionists' concept of a "hierarchy of victims".

Some victims' coalitions have emerged, most notably in the organization WAVE, which serves victims of both communities from a center in North Belfast. But such cross-community victims' groups are rare.

The definition debate reached its most intense level in spring 2009, upon the publication of a report by the cross-community Consultative Group on the Past, which will be discussed below. In autumn 2009, Jeffrey Donaldson, a prominent unionist politician, proposed legislation in Stormont to support the exclusivist definition of "innocent victims". Donaldson has pulled back, but this development made the strong connection between the definition issue and broader unionist mobilization quite clear.

6. THE CONSULTATIVE GROUP ON THE PAST

Events described up to this point, and those that follow, demonstrate the deliberate caution with which any pubic issue that touches on the conflict gets treated in Northern Ireland. The inclination to delay decisions is pervasive, because the alternative, actually reaching agreement on something, is so painfully difficult.

Power-sharing is more than a form of government, it is a mentality that trickles down to all levels of decision making. Everything becomes a matter of finding consensus. Matters of concern get handed on to committees, often drawing people from the grassroots. No single person wants to stand alone to take a decision on an issue of controversy.

In order to maintain the integrity of a public discussion about handling victims' affairs and dealing with the past, a Consultative Group on the Past was launched in 2007. It was headed by freelance journalist and former Catholic priest Denis Bradley, and former Church of Ireland (Anglican) Primate Robin Eames and composed of six other respected individuals from the two communities as well as two international observers. After twenty-four months of broad consultation, the Group made their recommendations in January 2009.

The most controversial of their proposals was the recommendation that the nearest relative of every person who died as a result of the conflict from 1966 to 1998 should receive a payment of £12,000. This proposal was disliked by nearly everyone, many viewing it as a drain on money that could be better spent on improvement of infrastructure and community services. In addition the proposal proved to be a lightning rod for the "definition of victims" issue. The proposal has since been, effectively, dropped.

The Consultative Group also proposed a Reconciliation Forum, composed of a cross section of citizens, "to tackle certain societal issues", including encouragement of educational projects, remembrance projects and storytelling.

Thirdly, the Consultative Group proposed the creation of a Legacy Commission, to be chaired by an international commissioner, that would handle a future truth recovery process, taking over the work of the Historical Enquiries Teams and the Police Ombudsman's Unit, as well as examining, through private hearings, themes arising from cases that raised broad public concern, e.g. paramilitary activity and collusion. A corollary of creating this commission was that no new public inquiries would be permitted. The Legacy Commission was to last for five years, and was to propose how Northern Ireland would draw a line under truth recovery at that point.[33]

While unionist responses focused mainly on the definition and compensation issue, nationalists expressed unhappiness with the vagueness of the truth recovery proposals and the requirement that examinations of patterns of violence be held in private. Sinn Fein counterproposed an international truth commission that would be "independent of the state, combatant groups, political parties, civil society and economic interests".[34]

7. STRATEGY FOR VICTIMS AND SURVIVORS – THE NEW GOVERNMENT PLAN

Drawing on many of the Consultative Group's recommendations, the Northern Ireland Executive launched a definitive policy paper on victims and survivors, *Strategy for Victims and Survivors – November 2009.*

The plan was built around three bodies. The four-person Commission for Victims and Survivors was to advise the Office of the First Minister on policy matters and ensure that feedback about victims' needs reaches the Executive. The Commission was, in addition, to develop a comprehensive needs assessment and oversee further discussions of truth recovery. Secondly, a Victims' and Survivors' Service was given the task of standardizing service delivery, ensuring continuity of funding, efficiency and transparency. Thirdly, a Victims and Survivors Forum (based presumably on the recommendations for a Reconciliation Forum in the Consultative Group's proposal) was to continue "grass-roots" discussion of ongoing issues, such as definition, through a body of twenty-six people representing all points of view.

33 See Duffy (2010) for an in depth critique of the report of the Consultative Group on the Past.
34 Sinn Fein.

The policy paper acknowledges the strong sense of grievance felt towards specific individuals or organizations that committed injuries, and proposes that, because of this, local communities will have to move towards reconciliation at their own pace. The report tries to create a forward-looking tone, making the point that "it is important that the work of the Forum, while recognizing the suffering of the past, does not become locked in the past," and speaks of building a shared future. It goes on to say that "an over emphasis on reconciliation between communities in the context of victims and survivors work can be misplaced... [The reconciliation process] must take account of the broad range of feelings and sensitivities which exist. Everyone must be allowed to move at his or her own pace and should not be made to feel excluded."[35]

As far as addressing the past is concerned, a section headed "The Past" consists of a single paragraph (number 36) out of fifty numbered paragraphs in the report:

> The Commission (in liaison with the Forum) will be tasked with developing advice to government and contribute to the broader consideration of ways to deal with the 'past' as an essential element of transition. Key issues will include recommendations on truth recovery and justice, story-telling, acknowledgment, memorials, inquiries and the work on historic cases. It is important for specific objectives to be achievable within defined timescales.

In addition, Paragraphs 10 and 11 express the goal to give victims and survivors the chance to play a central role, if they so wish it, "as part of wider society in addressing the legacy of the past".[36]

The value of the *Strategy for Victims and Survivors – November 2009* is in offering a stronger and more cohesive approach to addressing the injuries of people through mental health services, job training, and other support services that can assist their wellbeing. It has created institutions tasked, among other things, to address the debate on the definition of victim and the matter of truth recovery. The report's lack of *parti pris,* however, on either the definition issue or truth recovery, is a reminder of how fraught these matters are, and therefore how limited are the possibilities for leadership by a consensus government.

One is left with the sense that *Strategy for Victims and Survivors* abandons a certain idealism that used to exist with regard to dealing with the past. The formula it points to for truth recovery falls back on the private catharsis of storytelling and educational and remembrance projects. Any more public process seems further from realization than ever. Its language also dampens expectations about reconciliation. The idea that a common commitment to truth will unite a divided people, or that confronting the past is a healing endeavor, is absent.

35 OFMDFM, November 2009.
36 Ibid.

Perhaps belief in a truth recovery process that would effectively help the society move forward dissipated long ago, but this report seems to endorse that view.

8. PUBLIC FORGIVENESS IN NORTHERN IRELAND

The term "public forgiveness" suggests recognition, amongst those who think about these things, that a societal process for healing and moving on should be understood differently from a personal experience of moving on. Nonetheless, the term implies that the dynamic of forgiveness has something to offer societies in restoring relations at the political, and not just the personal, level.

Amstutz's definition of political forgiveness[37] suggests a close correlation between personal and societal forgiveness. His preconditions for public forgiveness are admission of culpability and remorse from the side of the perpetrators and an expression of empathy from the side of the victims. He therefore places an act of public apology front and center. He believes that a truth recovery process is necessary to help offenders to "confront their culpability and express remorse"; that contrition is needed to "develop an alternative moral discourse rooted in mutual respect and empathy"; and that victims need acknowledgement and remorse to open themselves to forgiving the perpetrators. Without a truth recovery process, he argues, it will be difficult to create a "peace rooted in the restoration of humane communal ties".[38]

Digeser establishes a much greater separation between public forgiveness and private forgiveness. He distinguishes between a purposive action to relieve debt (which describes forgiveness in the public sphere) with a motivational action (which describes forgiveness in the personal sphere) and suggests that a public act of apology or forgiveness doesn't need to contain the same level of emotion as a private act, because it is being made on behalf of a public entity. He does not require remorse or repentance for public forgiveness. He nonetheless does require an act by which the party with authority to do so relieves the other party of a deserved debt.[39]

Arendt proposes that a society can draw a line under its past and move on without any official apology, contrition, or a stated exemption of a group from punishment for its misdeeds. For Arendt, the forward looking nature of the ongoing political process is synonymous with public forgiveness.[40]

By any of these definitions, traces of public forgiveness are few and far between in Northern Ireland. If public forgiveness requires a public statement of

---

37 I use the terms "political forgiveness" and "public forgiveness" interchangeably, as those who coin the terms seem to mean pretty much the same thing by them.

38 Amstutz, 182–184.

39 Degiser, 18–30.

40 For Arendt, the very existence of politics implies the willingness to forgive. Schaap, 67–80.

forgiveness by someone who speaks for a larger group, it is entirely absent. By Arendt's definition, Northern Ireland's political situation might be called public forgiveness, though politics is hobbled in ways Arendt might never have imagined.

Several public apologies have been expressed. In 1994 at the announcement of the loyalist ceasefire, Gusty Spence, former Ulster Volunteer Force commander and Progressive Unionist Party Politician, spoke on behalf of the Combined Loyalist Military Command, reading out a statement which included the following:

> In all sincerity we offer to the loved ones of all innocent victims over the past 20 years abject and true remorse. No words of ours will compensate for the intolerable suffering they have undergone during the conflict.[41]

The IRA delivered an apology on July 16, 2002, the thirtieth anniversary of Bloody Friday, an event in Belfast when the IRA were responsible for the deaths of nine people:

> While it was not our intention to injure or kill non-combatants, the reality is that on this and on a number of other occasions, that was the consequence of our actions. It is therefore appropriate on the anniversary of this tragic event, that we address all of the deaths and injuries of non-combatants caused by us. We offer our sincere apologies and condolences to their families.[42]

The fact that neither paramilitary group had yet put its weapons beyond use might be one reason that these apologies drew little response. Research on the impact of the IRA apology shows that most unionists chose not to accept it. Some believed that acceptance would mean conferring legitimacy on the IRA. Victims of the IRA were the most strongly rejectionist. At best, unionists said they wanted to see it followed up by actions.[43]

Some of the instances of forgiveness most cited in Northern Ireland demonstrate acts of magnanimity by people whose background connects them less strongly with the conflict than the background of typical members of the unionist or nationalist community. Gordon Wilson, whose daughter Marie was killed at Enniskillen in 1987, spoke to the BBC immediately after her death, saying that he did not bear ill will, and forgave those who were responsible. His generosity of spirit halted at least one planned act of retaliation. It is interesting to note that Wilson was brought up in County Leitrim in the Republic of Ireland, and belonged to the Methodist church, a church with a liberal reputation that has never been as strongly identified with unionist politics as the Presbyterian

41 Combined Loyalist Military Command Statement.

42 Irish Republican Army.

43 Ferguson et al., 105–109.

church. Likewise, some of the Catholic priests most involved in reconciliation work come originally from the Republic.

Research tells us that a favorable attitude to intergroup forgiveness in Northern Ireland correlates with more outgroup contact, more outgroup perspective taking, higher outgroup trust, collective guilt with regard to the actions of one's own group, and less strong ingroup identification.[44] Forgiving would be more likely if there were public acknowledgment of the wrong and if perpetrators expressed remorse.[45] A survey from 2001 indicates that of the twelve percent of the population who self-identified as victims, fifty percent said they believed in forgiveness, and of the other eighty-eight percent who did not self-identify as victims, sixty-four percent believed in forgiveness. Thus in 2001 over half the population did support intergroup forgiveness. Those least likely to favor forgiveness were victims, those living in close proximity to violence, or Protestants. Seventy one percent of Protestant self-identified victims did not favor forgiveness. Catholics demonstrated a willingness to forgive irrespective of whether they were victims. This correlates with considerable evidence that Catholics as a group are more tolerant to outgroups than Protestants.[46]

The particularly unforgiving attitude of protestant victims' groups has been attributed to a higher level of traumatic injury than has been officially acknowledged.[47] These people are concentrated in South Armagh, a region that, along with North and West Belfast and Derry, experienced the highest levels of violence during the Troubles. Dawson's assertion of this is backed by empirical research that demonstrates that the amount of violence to which people are exposed correlates with their ability to forgive.[48]

The aforementioned facts and the considerable discussion that surrounds them lead us to several conclusions about public forgiveness. 1) The nature of the conflict has a bearing on capacity for public forgiveness. 2) Leaving it to victims (and I use the word *victims* in its broader, inclusive sense) to develop a societal truth recovery process reduces the likelihood that reconciliation and public forgiveness will be given the highest priority, since victims are the least likely to be forgiving. 3) Northern Ireland is unlikely to have a comprehensive truth recovery process. More minimalist approaches – private, cathartic interactions, or giving more information to families on particular cases may go forward. But the stalled discussion pretty much guarantees that a societal approach to truth recovery will not happen. 4) Public forgiveness, if it is to happen at all in Northern Ireland, will have to come from the "bottom up" rather than the "top down". It will be modeled by private initiatives that manage to gain public notice.

---

44 Hewstone, 211–212.

45 McLernon et al., 137.

46 Cairns and Mallett, 26.

47 Dawson, 131.

48 Hewstone et al., 209.

9. NATURE OF THE CONFLICT – NORTHERN IRELAND AS A CONTESTED STATE

One way to elaborate on the proposition that the nature of the conflict affects a society's capacity for public forgiveness is to create ideal types of conflicts which yield different post-conflict realities.

Interstate conflicts represent the way war was waged in seventeenth, eighteenth and nineteenth century Europe. Their peace treaties may involve some change of territory, but this territorial change affects relatively few people in the population. The Geneva Conventions address the conduct of such wars, regulating the treatment of prisoners and the treatment of civilians in order to reduce the number of people affected on the long term. Many of our ideas about war derive from this type of war, but in fact, since 1945, wars have resembled this model less and less.

Challenging authoritarian or totalitarian regimes. In these intrastate cases of human rights abuse, one side in the conflict is responsible for most of the abuses. This is not absolutely true, because victims can find themselves doing horrible things to address their situation that they would not have otherwise done. But it is axiomatic to such conflicts that the victims never succeed in mobilizing sufficiently to do great harm to members of the regime. Possibly, in such conflicts, individuals within the authoritarian regime who felt forced to collaborate with the regime also consider themselves victims, an interesting category of victim that almost inevitably means that the victim was also a perpetrator. Such conflicts come to an end when the regime changes, either because an outside power intervenes, or the regime implodes. Chile and Argentina are good cxamples.

In *contested states*, another form of intrastate conflict, those challenging state authority mobilize sufficiently to cause injury to those defending the state. While human rights are significant, the deeper issue is the definition of the state itself, and this has ramifications for personal as well as political identity. Such conflicts produce victims on both sides, but these victims perceive their situation in asymmetrical ways. Northern Ireland would fall into this category, as would Kosovo/a-Serbia, Bosnia and Herzegovina, Israel-Palestine and Cyprus.

These three types of conflict differ in the degree that physical and psychological boundaries are threatened after the peace is made. In the first, physical boundaries are represented by international borders, and are secure at the end of the conflict. National identity is not being redefined for the majority of people, so psychological boundaries are not greatly threatened. In the second, the dispute centers on level of democracy, inclusion and rule of law. These sources of conflict introduce only moderate psychological strains with regard to identity. A person does not need to alter his or her sense of group belonging in order to participate in a more democratic regime.

In the third, the state that follows from the conflict must knit together groups that were fighting about the identity of the state itself. Unless a conflict of this type produces a definitive winner who can dictate the peace, the peace will involve a power-sharing constitution to include all parties. But this very arrangement introduces a sense of psychological danger, because the protagonists need some boundary between them, whether physical or emotional. The peace process, far from reinforcing boundaries, as we see happening after an interstate conflict, has issued in a situation of reduced psychic security, even if the physical security is enhanced through the absence of violence. The "solution" to such conflicts is a constitution that tries to work with the irreconcilable goals of the different players. Their lack of consensus over the future means that creation of trust and a sense of common purpose after war is exceedingly difficult.

Contested societies that issue in power-sharing regimes have a number of characteristics in common: the absence of an overarching narrative, the absence of a leader who embodies a common future, and tenacious group identifications based on rhetorical memories and a strong sense of victimhood at the hand of the chosen "other".

ABSENCE OF A SUPERORDINATE IDENTITY OR NARRATIVE

Essential to the process of state creation is the articulation of a narrative that includes touchstones of a common sense of history, a foundation myth, and an accompanying set of values, which, in combination, tell the political community who "we" are. Societies that manage to move on from civil war do so when they produce a narrative or discourse that works for most people. This narrative is more than a forgiveness narrative, though the narrative might include or imply acts of acknowledgment and forgiveness. It has been described as a common act of forgetting, whereby the society fastens onto elements of its history that give it coherence and ignores the rest.[49] Crucially, the society needs an articulation of "who we are and how we got here" that resonates.

In Northern Ireland, it is logical to search for the emerging new narrative, the superordinate sense of identity, that can be the framework for good relations between the two communities. This is highly relevant to public forgiveness, because experimental evidence shows us that increasingly inclusive categorization is a critical determinant of an increased ability to forgive. For this to occur, the new superordinate identity does not need to replace completely alternative identities, but it does have to become the primary sense of identity. Once the ingroup identifies itself with a broader category, people's minds will have the capacity to be more open to the idea that their victimhood is not unique and this

49 Anderson, 6.

is what makes them more willing to forgive.[50] In other words, a sense of common ground or common identification could be considered a prerequisite, rather than a result, of public forgiveness.

In a post-civil war society, creating a common narrative is particularly difficult and cannot be taken for granted. The closer in numbers the constituent groups are to each other, the more difficult this task of articulating a common narrative becomes, because respect for the will of the majority proportionately diminishes. And the longer the conflict has been going on, the greater the number of traumatic incidents that enter the discourse. In a post-civil war society where the formerly warring groups are of similar size, have long-standing memories, and, additionally, have mutually exclusive group narratives and visions of the future, this task is gargantuan.

South Africa was able to transition to a new narrative fairly easily because blacks were able to cast their struggle as a struggle for democracy rather than a struggle about identity. Nobody wanted to abandon their South African identity; rather, they wanted to expand South African identity to be more democratic. Because they were the overwhelming majority, black South Africans provided what political scientists refer to as a *staatsvolk*,[51] one group that clearly predominates and thus gives the state a characteristic face. In addition, black South Africans were represented mainly by one political party, the ANC, which played a role, somewhat analogous to the Congress Party in India's independence struggle, in unifying the mindset of a majority of the citizenry.

LEADERSHIP

The crucial role of leadership in the development of a common polity after a civil war must not be underestimated. In most post-civil-war situations one party was the victor, and the new leader represents that party. Lincoln's magnanimity in his Second Inaugural Address demonstrates public forgiveness as an act of leadership. Lincoln articulated a vision of the future that included the people of the South, and urged Americans to move on in a forgiving spirit. But magnanimity in the wake of a civil war involves enormous personal risk. Gandhi comes to mind – an example of a magnanimous leader who paid a price for his outlook. Mandela was of course helped in his task by coming from the oppressed group. This fact may point us towards a fertile ground for processes of political forgiveness: the oppressed group articulating a future in which all can share. It works when the "oppressors" have some sense of contrition or culpability about the past, or at least are greatly outnumbered.

50 Wohl and Branscombe, 299.
51 O'Leary.

GROUP IDENTITY, POLITICS, AND VICTIMHOOD

Another aspect of deeply divided society, which is not easy for those who do not live in such a society to imagine fully, is the interconnection between people's sense of self and their political outlook. A sense of self is composed of two elements: the personal and the social. Depending on context, social identity can take on a greater role in creating a sense of self than personal identity. Social identity starts as a means to biological need fulfillment: identification with the mores and ideology of a group is a means by which the infant gains control over his life and environment so that his basic needs can be satisfied. Thus the historical narratives, cultural symbols and behaviors that define the group early on become crucial to meeting an individual's basic needs. In deeply divided societies, the social self is constantly salient.

As our social identity develops, we abstract recurring themes and shape these into dimensions of awareness which psychologists refer to as "constructs".[52] We resist the alteration of these constructs because such alteration challenges our core sense of self.

> If an individual comes upon new information that elicits a construct basically incompatible with or invalidating to the core sense of self, it is likely that the new information will be rejected or redefined in order to fit the existing, rather impermeable constructs. It is also likely that this process of rejection and redefinition (called "aggression" by Kelly, 1955) will be characterized by a high emotional charge and a great sense of urgency. In a sense, if one's core sense of self, the identity, is threatened by the demands, behavior or identity of another person, then psychic or even physical annihilation will seem to be imminent.[53]

A sense of victimization can therefore be experienced in several different ways. First comes the trauma itself, then the group solidarity that it enhances, and finally the development of a core construct of victimization. People's sense of self is thus profoundly rooted in a particular view of past events, and they will feel deeply threatened if someone tries to make them see these events differently. The core construct of victimhood provides a frame for the interpretation of other events. Over time, in a deeply divided society, groups co-opt more and more events and ideas to support the core construct that holds them together and gives their life meaning.

Both communities in Northern Ireland have a core construct of victimhood that they acquired through historical events. For the Catholics this goes back to the arrival of English and Scottish Protestants who pushed Catholics off their land and asserted their authority over the region. For Protestants, their sense of

52 Northrup, note 44.
53 Northrup, note 45.

being settlers under siege and subject to attack undergirds a mindset of persistent determination despite persecution. These outlooks are often described as "narratives", and are equated with the two political outlooks in Northern Ireland. But the word "narrative", arising from discourse theory, suggests that these thought systems can easily be substituted by new thought systems. In fact, once narratives become core constructs within the psychological makeup of people, they acquire a degree of permanence not easily shaken.

Group identifications gain further tenacity when co-opted for political causes. Mobilized group identifications work well in politics because they serve both instrumental and emotional functions. They resonate with people's personal outlook, and assist in meeting practical goals by underlining communitarian bonds. People who are asserting a political identity have little or no motivation to abandon emotions that are both bound in with their political goals and provide a core construct of their personal identity.

Montville suggests that a sense of victimhood arises from unacknowledged or unreconciled historical losses, the belief the aggression was unjustified, and fears that it will be repeated.[54] However, the picture is really more complicated. While we do know that unacknowledged personal trauma can have a long term effect on the human psyche,[55] we have little evidence or research to show whether acknowledgement of long term historical losses is enough to remove deep-set constructs of victimhood. What we do know in Northern Ireland is that Catholic self-described victims are more likely to be forgiving than protestant self-described victims.[56] It is arguable that Catholic victims actually feel some empowerment through the struggle that engaged them and the fact that the Agreement takes them further on the path to attain their goals. A sense of new empowerment might be more important than recognition of historical loss for intergroup forgiveness, though this needs further examination.

10. NO TRUTH COMMISSION FOR NORTHERN IRELAND

A truth commission is unlikely for Northern Ireland. Some people have known this for a long time.[57] To state this baldly is politically problematic, however, because the nationalist community is eager to have such a process. Hence, for those in authority, it is more politically expedient to keep talking about it, while moving forward with investigations on an individual basis and advocating catharsis through private storytelling. Reaching agreement on the parameters of

54 Montville, 113.
55 Herman.
56 Cairns and Mallett, 26.
57 Hamber, 1998; McCaughy, 260.

a truth commission seems outside the bounds of what is politically possible in Northern Ireland's power-sharing polity.

But power-sharing also locks in a spirit of non-forgiveness by reinforcing communal boundaries at all levels of decision-making. Research tells us that a strong sense of identification with one's own group is a strong predictor of non-forgiveness, and indeed that ingroup identification is a stronger reason not to forgive than perception of the perpetrator's motives.[58] Thus a power-sharing government decreases the likelihood of a person feeling a sense of forgiveness.

The absence of a truth commission lets both groups off the hook in terms of being forced to confront the results of their actions. In addition, the victimhood element in each group's narrative prevents a sense of wider responsibility or collective guilt.[59] Thus we have a constellation of characteristics that leads to an unforgiving attitude, each of which plays off the others.

11. PUBLIC FORGIVENESS FROM THE BOTTOM UP

It has been argued that contested states are not amenable to processes of political forgiveness: that they must arrive at an agreed political identity before truth processes, remorse and compassion can emerge.[60] The psychic change implied in forgiveness does not easily overcome deeply held constructs of social and political identity. This stark reality throws a damper on enthusiasts who believe that the power of truth or a change of heart can break through a political impasse.

One of the other contributors to this volume, Nir Eisikovits, speaks of *sympathy* – the ability imaginatively to switch places with the other – as the needed extra ingredient for producing co-existence between warring but inseparable groups. Much of what is written above explicates just why sympathy is so difficult to produce in Northern Ireland. In order to have sympathy, people entrapped in core constructs of identity that negate the other need to find some way to begin to dismantle those core constructs. No one has expressed this more succinctly than Senator George Mitchell himself, when he spoke of the need for a "decommissioning of mindsets" in Northern Ireland. Research cited here links the ability and willingness to forgive with measures of toleration of the outgroup, with outgroup perspective taking, flexibility of ingroup identification, increasingly inclusive categorization, and public acknowledgement of remorse. Eisikovits's sympathy, presumably, would likewise correlate with these measures.

We might reasonably hope that a truth commission could serve the purpose, quite apart from establishing the facts of what occurred, of helping people from

58 Hewstone et al., 211.
59 Amstutz, 185.
60 Amstutz, 186.

each mindset develop greater knowledge, and hence sympathy, for the other. But the reverse could also be the case – that in the setting of a truth commission, the groups become more defensive and more assertive of their own narratives. The likelihood that this would happen in NI is high, which is why many of those most dedicated to peace and reconciliation are not pushing for it.

Can we imagine other ways that the mindsets could be dismantled? In this setting, taking the perspective of the other, particularly in public, is an act of courage. If it is to occur, it might more easily happen through a person's new articulation of the group narrative within his or her own community. Another approach might be to articulate the two narratives simultaneously, demonstrating that taking the perspective of the other group need not be a negation of the perspective of one's own group.

I prefer not to infer from all of the above that public forgiveness is impossible in Northern Ireland. But to have a societal process of forgiving, Northern Ireland requires models of forgiveness that come from sources other than the public domain. This introduces an interesting paradox into discussions of public forgiveness. While, by some people's definition, public forgiveness can only come about through official leadership in deeply divided societies, the only hope of a public forgiveness process emerging is if gestures of magnanimity, contrition and forgiveness are modeled by private initiative and compellingly made public so that people are forced to pay attention. The arts are a promising arena in which this could be pursued.

But this also brings us back to the question of what, really, *is* forgiveness? As a term that has found much credence in the spiritual realm, personal forgiveness implies a recognition of shared humanity that releases in the forgiver a certain generosity of spirit, a feeling of "there, but for the grace of God, go I". It correlates with a personal sense of empowerment.[61] But it is an experience of the transcendent, not easily examined in rational discourse. Perhaps it is a kind of energy that, when released into the ether, sends out waves that can be felt by others. Because our understanding of the nature of spirituality is so limited, we can only take an agnostic position with regard to forgiveness, and hope that in some stumbling fashion, we bump into the formula that brings this source of energy alive.

12. FINAL THOUGHTS

The facts of the situation in Northern Ireland are well known to all who study the literature of transitional justice, and Northern Ireland itself has produced top-notch social scientists whose research illuminates the characteristics of their province. In its political life, this society, which has suffered entrenched divisions

61 Smith, 2008.

over centuries, has almost no middle ground, and finding a sense of shared future is extremely hard when the groups involved are profoundly committed to maintaining the tenets of their own group identity. When seen in this light, Northern Ireland's progress towards a functional power-sharing society seems remarkable. This is not to say that a leadership that could speak with contrition about the past or articulate a shared future would not be welcome. Various bodies in Northern Ireland have been trying to express precisely this vision.[62] A human rights and citizenship discourse tries to open the public space for a civic identity that stands separately from the ethno-political identities. But this is a long, slow road, and the people of Northern Ireland deserve our admiration for the tenacity with which they have been pursuing the journey.

To the degree that Northern Ireland can illuminate our understanding of political forgiveness, I put forward a few modest propositions: the nature of the conflict has a bearing on a society's capacity for political forgiveness; victims' ability to come up with a societal process of healing is likely to be limited, because this group, with its historically developed core construct of suffering at the hands of the other, is less likely than others in the society to be forgiving; while theoretically a truth recovery process might seem the best path for a society emerging from war, in practice this might not be the case; and, paradoxically, public forgiveness, if it is possible at all in societies emerging from intractable conflicts, has to emerge from non-official quarters.

REFERENCES

Amstutz, Mark (2005). *The Healing of Nations.* Lanham, MD: Rowman and Littlefield Publishers Inc.

Anderson, Benedict (1983). *Imagined Communities.* London: Verso.

Arendt, Hannah (1958). *The Human Condition.* Chicago: University of Chicago Press.

Bamford Review of Mental Health and Learning Disability (2005).

Biggar, Nigel (2001). Making Peace or Doing Justice: Must we Choose? In Nigel Biggar (ed.) *Burying the Past: Making Peace and Doing Justice after Civil Conflict.* Washington, DC: Georgetown University Press, 6–22.

Bloom, William (1990). *Personal Identity, National Identity, and International Relations.* Cambridge: Cambridge University Press.

Cairns, Ed and Mallett, John, with Christopher Lewis and Ronnie Wilson (2003). *Who are the Victims? Self-assessed victimhood and the Northern Irish Conflict.* NIO Research and Statistical Series Report No. 7., Belfast: NIO Statistics and Research Branch. http://cain.ulst.ac.uk/issues/victims/index.html.

Cehajic, Sabina, Brown, Rupert, & Castano, Emanuele (2008). Forgive and Forget? Antecedents and Consequences of Intergroup Forgiveness in Bosnia and Herzegovina. *Political Psychology* 29(3), 351–367.

62 Community Relations Unit.

Community Relations Council (2006). *Who Cares for the Carers – A Study into the Issues Affecting Carers of Victims of the Northern Ireland Conflict.*

Community Relations Unit, OFMDFM (2003). A Shared Future: A Consultation Paper on Improving Relations in Northern Ireland. http://cain.ulst.ac.uk/issues/community/cru03.htm.

Combined Loyalist Military Command (CLMC) Statement (1994). http://cain.ulst.ac.uk/events/peace/docs/clmc131094.htm.

Conflict Archive on the Internet (CAIN), RUC/PSNI statistics: Table NI-SEC-05: Persons injured (number) due to the security situation in Northern Ireland (only), 1969 to 2003. Available at http://cain.ulster.ac.uk/ni/security.htm#05.

Dawson, Graham (2003). Mobilization Memories: Protestant and Unionist Victims' Groups and the Politics of Victimhood in the Irish Peace Process. In Paul Gready (ed.), *Political Transition: Politics and Cultures.* London: Pluto Press, 127–147.

Digeser, P.E. (2001). *Political Forgiveness.* Ithaca, NY: Cornell University Press.

Duffy, Aiole. (2010). A Truth Commission for Northern Ireland? *International Journal of Transitional Justice* 4(1), 26–46.

Fay, M.T., Morrisey, M. and Smyth, M.B. (1999). *Northern Ireland's Troubles: the Human Costs.* London: Pluto Press.

Ferguson, Neil, et al. (2007). The IRA Apology of 2002 and Forgiveness in Northern Ireland's Troubles: A Cross National Study of Printed Media. *Peace and Conflict* 13(1), 93–113.

Govier, Trudy. (2006). *Taking Wrongs Seriously: Acknowledgement,Reconciliation and the Politicsof Sustainable Peace.* Amherst, NY: Humanity Books.

Hackett, Claire and Rolston, Bill (2009). The burden of memory: Victims, storytelling and resistance in Northern Ireland. *Memory Studies* 2(3), 355–376.

Hamber, Brandon. (1998). Conclusion: A Truth Commission for Northern Ireland? In Brandon Hamber (ed.), *Past Imperfect: Dealing with the Past in Northern Ireland and Societies in Transition.* Derry/Londonderry: INCORE. www.brandonhamber.com/.../Chap%207%20-20SA%20&%20NI%20Brandon%20Hamber.pdf.

Hamber, Brandon. (2001). Does the Truth Heal? A Psychological Perspective on Political Strategies for Dealing with the Legacy of Political Violence. In Nigel Biggar (ed.), *Burying the Past: Making Peace and Doing Justice after Civil Conflict.* Washington, DC: Georgetown University Press, 131–148.

Hamber, Brandon and Wilson, Robin (eds.) (2003). Recognition and Reckoning: The Way Ahead on Victims Issues. Report No. 15. Belfast: Democratic Dialogue.

Healing Through Remembering Report (2002) Retrieved from www.brandonhamber.com/resources-htr2002.htm.

Healing Through Remembering (2006). International Experiences of Days of Remembering and Reflection. Ensor, Kathleen Rose and Maria Truno I Salvado. Belfast: Healing Through Remembering Project. http://healingthroughremembering.info/day_of_reflection/publications/.

Herman, Judith (1997). *Trauma and Recovery.* New York: Basic Books.

Hewstone, Miles et al. (2004). Intergroup Forgiveness and Guilt in Northern Ireland: Social Psychological Dimensions of 'The Troubles.' In Nyla R. Branscombe and

Bertjan Doosje, (eds.). *Collective Guilt: International Perspectives*. Cambridge: Cambridge University Press, 193–215.

Irish Republican Army (IRA) (2002). Apology, July 16. http://cain.ulst.ac.uk/events/peace/docs/ira160702.htm.

Schaap, Andrew (2005). Forgiveness, Reconciliation and Transitional Justice. In Anthony F. Lang, Jr. and John Williams (eds.) *Hannah Arendt and International Relations: Readings Across the Lines*. New York: Palgrave Macmillan, 67–94.

Lundy, Patricia (2009). Can the Past be Policed?: Lessons from the Historical Enquiries Team Northern Ireland. *Law and Social Challenges* 11, Spring/Summer 2009, 109–156.

Lundy, Patricia and McGovern, Mark (2007). Attitudes towards a Truth Commission for Northern Ireland in Relation to Party Political Affiliation. *Irish Political Studies* 22(3), 321–338.

McCaughy, Terence (2007). Northern Ireland: Burying the Hatchett, not the Past. In Nigel Biggar (ed.), *Burying the Past: Making Peace and Doing Justice after Civil Conflict*. Washington, DC: Georgetown University Press, 254–268.

McLernon, Frances et al. (2003). Memories of Recent Conflict and Forgiveness in Northern Ireland. In Ed Cairns and Mícheál Roe (eds.), *The Role of Memory in Ethnic Conflict*. Basingstoke and New York: Palgrave Macmillan, 125–143.

Montville, Joseph (1993). The healing function in political conflict resolution. In Dennis Sandole and Hugo Van Der Merwe (eds.), *Conflict Resolution: Theory and Practice: Integration and Application*. Manchester, UK: Manchester University Press, 112–127.

Northern Ireland Affairs Committee (NIAC). Ways of Dealing with Northern Ireland's Past: Interim Report – Victims and Survivors. Government Response to the Committee's Tenth Report of Session 2004–05. www.publications.parliament.uk/pa/cm200506/cmselect/cmniaf/530/53002.htm.

Northrup, Terrell (1989). The Dynamics of Identity in Personal and Social Conflict. In Louis Kriesberg, Terrell Northrup and Stuart Thorson (eds.), *Intractable Conflicts and their Transformation*. Syracuse: Syracuse University Press, Chapter 4.

Office of the First Minister and Deputy First Minister (OFMDFM) (January 2009). *Report of the Consultative Group on the Past*. Robin Eames and Denis Bradley, (Co-Chairs). www.cgpni.org/.

Office of the First Minister and Deputy First Minister (November 2009). *Strategy for Victims and Survivors*. www.northernireland.gov.uk/news/news-ofmdfm/news-ofmdfm-091209-strategy-for-victims.htm.

O'Leary, Brendan (2003). An iron law of nationalism and federation?: A (neo-Diceyian) theory of the necessity of a federal *Staatsvolk*, and of consociational rescue. *Nations and Nationalism* 7(3), 273–296.

One Small Step Campaign. www.onesmallstepcampaign.org/.

Philpott, Daniel (ed.). (2006). *The Politics of Past Evil: Religion, Reconciliation, and the Dilemmas of Transitional Justice*. Notre Dame, IN: University of Notre Dame Press.

Rolston, Bill (2006). Dealing with the Past: Pro-State Paramilitaries, Truth and Transition in Northern Ireland. *Human Rights Quarterly* 28(3), 652–800.

Rolston, Bill and Scraton, Phil (2005). In the Full Glare of English Politics: Ireland, Inquiries and the British State. *British Journal of Criminology* 45, 547–564.

Secretary of State for Northern Ireland (1998). *We Will Remember Them: Report of the Northern Ireland Victims Commissioner.* Sir Kenneth Bloomfield (Chair).

Smith, Margaret E. (2005). *Reckoning with the Past: Teaching History in Northern Ireland.* Lanham, MD: Lexington Books.

Smith, Margaret E. (2008). An Exploration of Forgiveness, Empowerment and the Journey of Healing. In Stephen Bloch-Schulman and David White (eds.), *Forgiveness: Probing the Boundaries.* Ebook. www.Inter-disciplinary.net. www.inter-disciplinary.net/wp-content/uploads/2009/11/Forgiveness-Draft-One.pdf

Smyth, Marie Breen (2007). *Truth Recovery and Justice after Conflict: Managing Violent Pasts.* London: Routledge.

Smyth, Marie Breen and Morrisey, M. (2002). *Northern Ireland After the Good Friday Agreement: Victims, Grievance and Blame.* London: Pluto Press.

Sinn Fein (2009). Submission to British and Irish Governments on Truth Recovery.

Wilke, Christiane (2007). Recognizing Victimhood: Politics and Narratives of Rehabilitation in Germany. *Journal of Human Rights* 6(4), 479–496.

Wohl, Michael J.A. and Branscombe, Nyla (2004). Importance of Social Categorization for Forgiveness and Collective Guilt Assignment for the Holocaust. In Nyla Branscombe and Bertjan Doosje (eds.), *Collective Guilt: International Perspectives.* Cambridge: Cambridge University Press, 284–305.

FORUMS OF APOLOGY AND FORGIVENESS

Sanderijn CELS

1. INTRODUCTION[1]

In 1974, the Irish Republican Army bombing of pubs in Guildford and Woolwich led to the wrongful jailing of eleven Irishmen. The individuals were arrested by the British police based on evidence that was later discredited. In 2005, Prime Minister Tony Blair apologized to the surviving victims and their families. Mr. Blair had been expected to make his statement in the House of Commons, but Members of Parliament did not offer him that opportunity. Instead, he recorded a TV statement immediately afterwards from his office and after that, he spoke in private chambers with the families of the victims without any press present, repeating the statement he just had made.[2]

There had been a "miscarriage of justice", Mr. Blair said in this statement. "I recognize the trauma that the conviction caused the (...) families and the stigma which wrongly attaches to them to this day. I am very sorry that they were subject to such an ordeal and such an injustice. That's why I am making this apology today. They deserve to be completely and publicly exonerated".[3]

Gerry Conlon, one of the Irishmen who were wrongly jailed for the bombings, stated to the press afterwards that "[the Prime Minister] went beyond what we thought he would, he took time to listen to everyone. He exceeded our expectations in apologizing, he said it was long overdue." Conlon added that Blair spoke with sincerity and that "...the good thing is that he has acknowledged it, and he accepts that we are in pain, that we are suffering terrible, terrible nightmares and terrible post-traumatic stress disorder".[4] Mr. Conlon concluded that he had got all he had wanted from Mr. Blair "and more".[5]

1 The author would like to thank Mr. Patrick Field Mcp (managing director Consensus Building Institute) and prof. dr. Barbara Oomen (University of Amsterdam and Roosevelt Academy, the Netherlands) for their support.

2 Millar 2005.

3 Lane 2005.

4 Graham 2005.

5 Millar 2005.

2. PUBLIC FORGIVENESS

Can this official apology be seen as an act of public forgiveness? If we understand public forgiveness as (a) a mutual process of transformation: a change of mind and heart on the part of the victim and the wrongdoer to end a cycle of offense and resentment[6] that (b) takes place in an open, accessible forum, then the aforementioned apology seems to match the definition. Mr. Blair's statement evoked a positive reaction; Gerry Conlon, one of the victims who personally suffered from the wrongdoing, responded with gratitude to the Prime Minister. Furthermore, since the process of offering and accepting the apology statement took place in a public setting, one could very well argue that the exchange as a whole can indeed be labeled as an act of public forgiveness.

This point of view is in correspondence with a prominent body of apology-literature in which the concepts of apology and forgiveness are tied together in a productive relationship. They are both regarded as parts of a "bridging discourse".[7] Apologies can contribute to forgiveness: forgiveness may depend upon apology. "Apologies explicitly acknowledge wrongdoing and afford victims the chance both to forgive or to refuse to forgive," writes Martha Minow for example.[8] This point of view also corresponds with another common outlook, in which the official apology is regarded as part of the phenomenon of public or "political forgiveness", a phrasing that has been coined by P.E. Digeser.[9] This phenomenon refers to the emerging practice of apologies in the public or political realm. Some scholars even speak of an "age of apology",[10] since the number of remorseful gestures has recently grown significantly. To summarize the apology of Mr. Blair to the alleged IRA-member as an act of public forgiveness would be in correspondence with current views in academic literature today.

After a second look, however, the case raises some questions. The formal happening left no room for the surviving victims and their families to respond openly. They may have uttered words of thankfulness in the press forum afterwards, but that was not part of the official stage for the wider public. In fact, in this case, three distinct apology forums can be distinguished: the official forum in which the statement was delivered by Prime Minister Blair on camera; the private forum of intimate exchange by the Prime Minister and the victims; and the press forum in which the latter were able to react in public.

It was only in the last forum that Mr. Conlon and other victims were able to show their change of mind and heart publicly. So did the official apology really offer room for the receiving party to openly forgive? Or was their moral

6 Lazare 2004: 231.
7 Barkan 2006: 25.
8 Minow 1998: 116.
9 Digeser 2001.
10 Gibney et al 2008.

contribution destined for another time and place – before the press corps, in the aftermath of the formal happening? It is exactly this separation in forums, hindering an instant public response by the victims, that leads to the main questions examined in this chapter.

3. QUESTIONS

This chapter is concerned with two theoretical questions: when are official apologies indeed acts of public forgiveness? To be more precise: which conditions does the public act of official apology have to meet, in order to reflect a process of mutual transformation in which both apologizer and victim take part? And what are the possible consequences for the meaning of official apologies, if these conditions are *not* met? At the end of each theoretical exploration, I will apply the insights that have been derived to the practice of official apologies. Two apology-cases will serve as illustrations throughout the text.

To answer the first question, it is necessary to determine which conditions constitute forgiveness. I will focus on one of these conditions, drawing mainly on the theory of Charles L. Griswold. Griswold makes clear that the process of forgiveness is a dyadic undertaking; both parties have to do part of the "moral work".[11] If this insight is translated to the practice of official apologies, one can conclude that the event has to allow for moral activities of both apologizer and victim.

In order to answer the second question, I will look into one of the possible consequences of the absence of such moral symmetry, using philosopher Nick Smith's insights on the meanings of apologies.[12] I will argue that if the apology event does not provide for room for the victims to respond to the official statement, for example because separate forums do not provide them with the opportunity to do so on the public stage, official apologies run the risk of failing to deliver on one of their moral promises: the establishment of a designated moral community to which both offender and victim belong.

The focus of this chapter is on events that include an apologetic statement of a government leader on behalf of the state addressed to a receiving party present at the scene. This aspect makes the apologies "bilateral" cases in which two parties are involved, according to the classification that Trudy Govier has presented in this volume. They take part, either actively or passively, in a moral exchange. The events take place in a public forum: they are accessible to spectators and press, and therefore to a broad audience. The statement by the government leader must at least include an acknowledgement of a wrongdoing, for which the offender

11 Griswold 2007: 47–48.
12 Smith 2008.

takes responsibility on behalf of the collective that he (or she) represents, accompanied by an expression of remorse.

I consider whether the leader is the actual perpetrator or a symbolic one, who has no personal involvement with the wrongdoing for which he apologizes, to be irrelevant.[13] The same issue concerns the victim: this word will be used for any receiving party, whether it consists of the actual victims, their surviving relatives, or other persons involved, such as leaders of a disenfranchised minority group. Both parties can be collective subjects.

4. MORAL DEPENDENCY

Which conditions constitute forgiveness? Philosopher Charles L. Griswold has recently examined the meanings, conditions and norms of forgiveness.[14] In order to understand what forgiveness is, he has analyzed seemingly trivial and basic components of the mutual act of forgiving and being forgiven in an everyday situation[15], thereby laying out the groundwork for a basic but profound set of conditions for a "paradigmatic interpersonal case" – a dual act in which offender and victim both undergo a transformation.[16] I will not discuss Griswold's whole framework, but single out the aspects that are relevant for the argument at issue.

The paradigmatic case consists of an exchange between two parties in each other's presence. One expresses regret over an injury and asks for forgiveness. In doing so, he may undergo a transformation that signals that he, for example, genuinely experiences and expresses regret and that he repudiates his misdeeds. The other party might indeed forgive the agent (not the deed). If he (or she) does, he may undergo a transformation that Griswold describes as a "change of heart, and seeing the offender and oneself in a new light". This change includes, for instance, a recognition of the shared humanity of the victim and the offender.[17]

There are no third parties involved: in Griswold's interpersonal model, forgiveness is offered by the person who bears responsibility for the injury to another person who owns a moral right to forgiveness. When the first asks for

13 I propose that it is sufficient that the symbolic perpetrator acknowledges that he has, in effect, ceased to endorse the wrongful deed that was committed in the name of the entity he represents (Govier & Verwoerd 2002b: 70), and that the standing and position of the statesman allows for such representation.

14 Griswold 2007.

15 Of course, an everyday situation differs from the political (or public) realm in which official apologies are offered. Forgiveness is often divided into "exclusive categories of 'interpersonal' and 'political'", writes Alice MacLachan in her chapter, and therefore, is even argued by Griswold himself, insights that are derived from the first cannot be smoothly applied in the second (Griswold 2007: 142). MacLachan has discussed this matter sufficiently in her contribution to this volume. Some conceptual frameworks, such as Griswold's, can be very helpful to deepen the understanding of the moral exchange in the political realm.

16 Griswold 2007: 47–48.

17 Ibid.: 53, 79.

forgiveness, the latter may be willing to grant that, if certain conditions are met. Griswold further analyzes these conditions and develops an understanding of the transformation that both parties have to go through, in order to qualify their exchange as an act of forgiveness.

An important aspect of this process is the moral dependency of the two parties. Both of them have to do a good share of the "moral work" in order to forgive and to be forgiven.[18] The offender, for example, has to repudiate his deeds; the victim, for instance, has to be willing to revise his judgments.[19] "One of the striking consequences of this interdependence is that each party holds the other in its power, in this sense: the offender depends on the victim to be forgiven, and the victim depends on the offender in order to forgive. This interdependence is part of the logic of forgiveness…".[20]

The address of the offender can be understood as a call upon the injured party to react; it is a request to be forgiven. The address is, simply put, just one part of a two-way communication. A univocally positive response to it can help both parties accomplish the ethical goals involved. Moreover, a lack of response can easily be understood as a refusal of the remorseful statement and can ruin the whole process, because "the lack of symmetry (…) would presumably be understood by the offender as the withholding of forgiveness…"[21]

Griswold's scheme reveals that there is a form of suspense present in the exchange, that I will call 'anticipation anxiety'. Suspense is built up during the address of the offender because of the interdependency. He may well do his best to meet all conditions necessary for a favorable response, but it remains to be seen if the victim is willing to accept the moral gesture. Will he let go of resentment? Or will he turn his head away and leave the scene?

A second notion that I will call 'acceptance power' is hereby introduced: the receiving party has the ability to choose between accepting and refusing the moral gesture that the offender has made. The victim has the power to grant forgiveness. If he is forced into forgiving, the moral interdependency between both parties would vanish and this deficit would undermine the whole process – one can safely state that there cannot be any forgiveness in this situation at all, since the heart does not support the change.

To conclude, forgiveness can be seen as a dyadic undertaking that requires an open exchange, consisting of a request and a response. The offender delivers an apologetic statement that is unmistakably connected with an answer of the victims who have the power to reject or to accept. Based on this interdependency, a mutual transformation process is then set in motion. So both parties are not

---

18 Ibid.: 47–48.

19 Ibid.: 38–69.

20 Ibid.: 49.

21 Ibid.: 58.

only present, they also have a role to play in the exchange – each by doing their own share of the moral work.

5. PRACTICE OF APOLOGIES

What does this condition imply for official apologies? What are the implications of the concept of moral interdependency, and the related notions of suspense and power, for these public performances? I will now translate the insights above to the practice of government apologies, thereby focussing on the forum in which they are offered.

Following the aforementioned argument, an official apology can be regarded as an act of public forgiveness if the event somehow allows for moral symmetry: it has to be a dyadic undertaking in which both parties can contribute. It must provide room for the victims to express themselves and the freedom for them to do as they please. To be more specific, the apology event has to meet two conditions: first, the forum in which the statement is delivered has to provide for space for the display of morality of both apologizer and victim. Secondly, it has to allow for the possibility of the refusal of the gesture by the receiving party. For this, the latter needs not only the room to respond, but also the power to do as he sees fit.

An example can illustrate how this can be realized in practice. When Prime Minister Harper of Canada offered apologies in June 2008, the party to whom the apology was addressed took actively part in the exchange and was present in the same forum in which the remorseful statement was delivered. PM Stephen Harper offered formal apologies in the House of Commons for "a sad chapter in our history". This chapter was concerned with the mistreatment of aborigines in his country, and especially referred to the residential schools which forced 150,000 aboriginal children to learn English and adopt Christianity. The schools were part of a federally financed program and overseen by the Department of Indian Affairs. They fit into the government policy of assimilation at that time.

"Mr. Speaker, I stand before you today to offer an apology to former students of Indian residential schools," PM Harper said. "...Today, we recognize that this policy of assimilation was wrong, has caused great harm and has no place in our country." Harper was surrounded by a group of aboriginal leaders and former students. Other politicians spoke up as well, confirming the apology.

After that, victims were allowed to speak on the record in the House of Commons as part of the official happening. Press reported that this was a last minute decision by House leaders[22] and that opposition parties had demanded it.[23] This was a break with tradition, since this was unheard of in the history of

[22] CBC News 2008.
[23] Gillies 2008.

the parliament.[24] Among the speakers was, for example, Assembly of First Nations Chief Phil Fontaine, in native headdress, who had attended a residential school and had been sexually abused during his studentship. He stated that the apology "testifies nothing less than the accomplishment of the impossible." All aboriginal speakers also praised the gesture of the government.

If the House leaders had decided not to allow the victims to speak their truth, then the apology would have ended up as a one man show. However, the stage was now taken by the offender and the victim, allowing the receiving party the room and the power to react in the official public forum.[25] Nevertheless, such apologies are rare. When one takes a closer look at government apologies in the last 6 years, one will notice immediately that it is more common for victims not to participate.[26] Victims either stand aside as "extra's", are invisible or absent from the formal happening (as recorded by large television networks), or they fulfill another passive yet symbolic role. Such official apologies run the risk to become sheer displays of the morality of the apologizer, not of the morality of the victims.

Let's turn to the case of the Australian apology for the mistreatment of aborigines to develop a practical understanding of this particular situation. This gesture was similar to the aforementioned apology in Canada, but the performance was different. In February 2008, Prime Minister Kevin Rudd offered formal apologies to aborigines in his country with a special referral to the Stolen Generations – aboriginal children who had been removed from their families by government agencies according to the law at that time without establishing (good) reasons for their removal. These actions had been part of a policy of assimilation that had lasted from the 19th century to the late 1960's.

PM Rudd apologized for laws and policies that "inflicted profound grief, suffering and loss". He added: "To the mothers and the fathers, the brothers and the sisters, for the breaking up of families and communities, we say sorry".[27] In fact, PM Rudd made a speech supporting the an apology-motion in parliament. Rudd spoke on behalf of this political body in the Member's Hall of Parliament House: "We the Parliament of Australia respectfully request that this apology be received in the spirit in which it is offered as part of the healing of the nation." The motion would be passed unanimously.

---

24 Austen 2008.

25 Suspense, however, the related notion, can be present at such occasions, but it will probably concern the display of emotions. Suspense can be built up during the dramatic performance of the apologizer; for example, the (TV) viewers of the spectacle can anxiously anticipate an emotional climax: will the apologizer cry at the end of his statement?

26 In 4 of 32 apology-cases that the Consensus Building institute has studied so far, victims actively participated.

27 BBC 2008a.

The BBC reported that "Australia has no Aboriginal members in parliament, but 100 leaders of the community and members of the Stolen Generations were present for the historic apology."[28] These people had been invited by the PM as special guests of the Government.[29] They remained passive: no representatives from the side of the victims had an active role on the floor in parliament.

6. CONSEQUENCES

What are the consequences of such an asymmetrical performance for the meanings of apologies? Can they still deliver on their ethical promises? Is a contribution of the victims absolutely necessary or can we do without them? In this section, I will argue that a 'bare' apology, solely consisting of a statement by a government leader, can miss out on something. Apologies can have many meanings, but the realization of an important one – the establishment of a shared moral discourse between offender and victim, and possibly between the collectives that they can represent – can become problematic. To create that discourse, you need the victim's voice as well.

In the body of apology-literature, several understandings of the meanings of (official) apologies have been developed.[30] One of those meanings concerns the "assurance that both parties have shared values", in the words of Aaron Lazare.[31] I will focus on this particular meaning of apologies and refer to it as their 'moral meaning'. Central to this concept is the idea that an apology reaffirms the membership of both offender and victim of a designated moral community.[32]

"By apologizing," Lazare writes, "the offending party reaffirms his or her commitment to the rules and values implicit in the relationship".[33] Before the apology was offered, the offender did not respect the victim as a moral equal, but as a worthless tool that he could oppress, harm, exploit – or, as was the case in the apology of Prime Minister Blair, put behind bars without fair trial. By apologizing, the offender comes to treat the victim with dignity again; his apology is an acknowledgement of "the moral worth of victims", in the words of Govier and Verwoerd.[34] Indeed, "the offender reaches out to the victim in a gesture of respect," according to Kathleen Gill. "More specifically, the apology involves a recognition of the injustice of the harm done to the victim, a

28 BBC 2008b.

29 PM Office 2008.

30 See Tavuchis (1991), Lazare (2004), Celermajer (2008), Smith (2008), Gibney et al (2008). In these contributions, the word apology usually refers to the statement of the offender, not to the event as a whole.

31 Lazare 2004: 93.

32 Tavuchis 1991: 7.

33 Lazare 2004: 93.

34 Govier & Verwoerd 2002a: 69.

confirmation of the moral worth of the victim and the value of what has been lost".[35]

But how exactly is this shared morality established? Is simply telling another person in a respectful way that he is indeed an agent of the same moral discourse – and therefore part of the same moral community – enough? This question has not received much consideration in apology-theory so far. If just telling someone that he is indeed a moral equal suffices, then an apologetic statement without response is adequate. Thus, an official apology event has to include an address by the offender in which he shows an esteem of the victim as a full member of that same community. As long as the statement serves as an indicator of a shared moral orientation between offender and victim, and as long as it pays homage to the victim as an equal, one can argue that the moral bond is re-established, because the party who violated the alliance has carried out the requisite repairs.

The rehabilitation of the victim as a moral agent then requires just telling him in a considerate manner that he is an equal and should have been treated differently. That can already be satisfactory for this purpose. A promise to never repeat the mistake again can be a valuable addition and an extra confirmation that the offender, and the collective that he stands for, are really on the right track towards a just future. But for this future to be realized, instant two-way communication is not necessary at all.

A second look on the matter, however, may cause some doubts whether such a bare apology statement is indeed satisfactory for fulfilling its moral goal. When we turn to the work of Nick Smith, a philosopher who recently wrote an extensive study on the meanings of apologies, we may start to doubt the unidirectional approach. In his analysis, Smith describes several meanings that an apology can have and by exploring those meanings, he makes a rare contribution to apology-theory by proposing a profound notion of what it means to be moral equals.

Smith describes the process that actually takes place when the offender treats the victim as moral equal. The apologizer, Smith writes, comes to recognize and treat him as a "moral interlocutor", worthy of engaging in a common moral discourse.[36] An interlocutor is someone you are having a conversation with and in this case, this conversation is a moral one. In this role of interlocutor, the victim can "become the primary conversant in the offender's task of re-examining and maintaining her core values. (…) The offender finds the victim worthy of engaging in such an intimate and identity-defining conversation."[37] Again, we find ourselves amid a dyadic undertaking.

Smith emphasizes that this is different that just treating the victim as a moral agent: instead, he argues, he becomes "my moral peer". Apologies therefore

35 Gill 2000, 24.
36 Smith 2008: 141.
37 Ibid.: 65.

"foreground a dialectical relationship with the other constitutes my own sense of meaning, value and self". The apologizer makes clear that he can get straight with himself only by getting straight with the other.[38] Both parties engage together in the process of revealing and shaping their values: "victim and offender become equals at the most basic level as they try to explain what has meaning and value and recognize when one has strayed from those beliefs".[39] In other words, it boils down to *engaging* the victim, not just telling him that from now on, he is allowed to take part in a moral conversation again.

The notion of engagement has a profound consequence for the actors involved in the apologetic exchange. Because of the dependency on the other and his ability to talk back, the offender becomes vulnerable. Not only because of the possible sanctions that may follow the admittance of a wrongdoing, Smith writes, but because the apologizer turns to the person he has alienated most by his wrongful actions – a move that exposes his moral flaws to their full extent.

What are the consequences of this insight for the practice of government apologies and for their meaning? What does the above argument imply for these public events? In this section, I will apply the notions of engagement and vulnerability to the official performance, again focussing on the forum in which the offender's statement is delivered.

First, let's consider the consequences of the notion of vulnerability. By engaging the victim, the offender becomes vulnerable, because he turns to the person who can most expose his moral flaws. It is exactly this kind of profound vulnerability that is absent in an official apology forum that is solely occupied by a government leader who delivers his statement in front of the cameras, looking in the distant eye of the TV spectators. He avoids looking at the victim, engaging him and in doing so, exposing himself. Instead, he chooses to turn towards another audience, far away.

This does not mean that there is no vulnerability at stake. The apologizer can be in a very vulnerable position, and could even be lauded for deliberately choosing this spot, because he runs the risk of being slashed by comments from the media and from TV spectators at home, or by undermining remarks of his political opponents who use every opportunity to attack him – all possible threats that can be damaging. But these harms are linked to the peculiarities of the public realm in which interests, power and public relations play a part, and this realm is, by far, not the same as the inner circle in which the intimate and identity-defining conversation takes place to which Nick Smith was referring.

There are probably well-thought-out reasons for the selection of this particular audience. If a leader discloses the genuine, inmost conversation, and the victim refuses the gesture or chooses to respond in another unwelcome way

38 Ibid.: 65.
39 Ibid.: 66.

– for example, because he is so traumatized that he is just not capable of a prompt positive reply – the whole show turns against the statesman. Therefore, politically speaking, a one man show is a sound choice, since it enables the statesman to control the damage and to protect his interests. Nevertheless, for moral reasons, a choice for a distant, instead of an intimate setting is not the most adequate one.

Secondly, if the interlocutor is not engaged in a conversation, it undermines the essence of his role as primary conversant. The apologizer may very well treat the victim as worthy of engaging in a moral conversation, but his effort can best be described as a monologue – and that is, after all, not a conversation.[40] Moreover, the victim, if not allowed to speak up, cannot contribute to a common discourse – at least, not in the open, official forum. He may have had extensive conversations, even negotiations, with the apologizer behind closed doors before an official statement is delivered, therefore influencing the public outcome, but the audience at large will never know that, unless the offender chooses to quote the victim explicitly. In other occasions, however, the speechless victim does not noticeably participate in the establishment of a joint discourse.

To conclude, if victims are not capable of doing their share of the moral work in the open, side by side with the offender in the same forum, the public apology may miss out on one of its moral promises.[41] It has the potential for true engagement, leading to a full acknowledgment of the victim as a moral interlocutor, but only when the notion of a conversation is translated to the apology event by offering the victim, in one way or the other, a chance to publicly fulfill his role as primary conversant.

7. OTHER MEANINGS

Are bare apologies then useless? Does a statement of a government leader lack meaning, when he does not openly share the official stage with the persons who own the moral right to respond? Ultimately, an apology event does not have to include an instant response of victims to have meaning. Even if it only consists of an official address by the statesman, it can still be meaningful without anyone talking back.

---

40 We can speculate on the lack of social impact of a public apology when the moral work of the victims remains unnoticed. For example, if they openly show their difficulties in letting go of their resentment, one can imagine that members of the collective they represent, who are also filled with resentment towards the offender, can identify themselves better with their inner struggle.

41 This suggestion has been made before, by, for example, Meredith Gibbs and Janna Thompson (Gibney et al, 2008) but it did not receive mature, theoretical consideration so far.

Such a bare public apology can, for example, convey moral substance as a value declaring statement. Such statements can be considered as articulations of "relevant values for the perpetrator group or for society in general, including possible future victims."[42] As "value declaring statements", they "may nourish public normative discourse by articulating our values and recognizing their violation", in the words of Nick Smith.[43]

This meaning can be realized without the response of victims; a value declaring statement does not need an answer from anyone. It serves to openly announce the values of the speaker and to recommit him and the collective he represents to honoring these principles. It makes clear that, from now on, the community should treat the victims as equals again, worthy of having a moral conversation with. The apologizer himself however, is not serving as an example of this while being on stage, but rather fulfils the role of the announcer of the official proclamation.

To strengthen this meaning, an apology can be accompanied by promises of forbearance and even practical measures to prevent repetition. The active contribution of victims, however, is not necessary. They can be present in a purely symbolic role and remain passive. In fact, you may very well argue that the apology is not aimed at them, but that the primary target group is the collective upon which the apologizer calls, since its members should act upon his proclamation.

8. CONCLUSIONS

To conclude, official apologies are often labelled as examples of public or political forgiveness, without serious consideration of the concepts that are involved in such a qualification. Many authors have linked the concepts of forgiveness and apology so eloquently and fruitfully that the need to further investigate them seems redundant. However, if we understand forgiveness as a mutual process of transformation in which both offender and victim take part, a second look at official apology cases remains necessary to cautiously analyze whether the conditions which such a dyadic process demands, are actually met in practice.

Furthermore, in literature today, official apologies are often analyzed without attention directed towards their performative features. This is unfortunate, because these aspects can express multiple meanings as well: just as textual aspects do. The staging, scripting and setting of apologies can be conceptualized, analyzed and connected to existing theories, such as the ones of Griswold and Smith. However, researchers tend to focus upon linguistic features, such as the phrasing of the apologetic statement, to explain the meanings of the act.

42 Govier & Verwoerd 2002a: 157.
43 Smith 2008, 248.

Apologies are usually defined as speech acts, according to Searle's and Austin's classifications[44] and this point of view merely draws attention to the textual account – "what is said" matters most. "How and where it is said" remains a new field of interest that calls for further exploration.

A last conclusion concerns a consideration for practitioners involved in processes of demanding, offering and accepting moral repair. Based on the theoretical study above, the argument can be made that a bare apology without response of the victim runs the risk of failing to live up to at least part of its moral potential. If it aims to establish a shared moral discourse of victim and offender – and, indirectly, within the broad community to which the offender and victim belong, a public contribution of both parties is somehow required. An asymmetric performance can fall short, if a victim cannot speak up publicly as primary conversant. Only if the public apology forum allows for a full rehabilitation of the victim as moral interlocutor, and only if it openly reflects the morality of both offender and victim, can it deliver on this moral promise. Let us not miss out on this grand opportunity.

REFERENCES

Austen, I. (2008). Canada Offers an Apology for Native Students' Abuse. *The New York Times*, June 12. www.nytimes.com Accessed: April 10, 2010.

Barkan, E. (2000). *The guilt of nations: restitution and negotiating historical injustices*, Johns Hopkins paperbacks edn, Baltimore, MD, Johns Hopkins University Press.

Barkan, E. & Karn, A. (2006). *Taking wrongs seriously: apologies and reconciliation*, Stanford Calif, Stanford University Press.

Bavelas, J. (2004). *An analysis of formal apologies by Canadian churches to first nations.* Victoria (CAN): Center for Religion & Society, University of Victoria.

BBC (2008a). Full Text: Apology to Aborigines. *BBC online.* February 13. www.bbc.co.uk Accessed: April 10, 2010.

BBC (2008b). Australia apology to Aborigines. *BBC online.* February 13. www.bbc.co.uk Accessed: April 10, 2010.

CBS (2008). PM cites 'sad chapter' in apology for residential schools. *CBC News.* www.cbc.ca Accessed: April 10, 2010.

Celermajer, D. (2009). *The sins of the nation and the ritual of apologies*, Cambridge & New York, Cambridge University Press.

Cunningham, M. (1999). Saying Sorry: the Politics of Apology, *The Political Quarterly Publishing Co, Ltd*, p. 285.

Daye, R. (2004). *Political forgiveness: lessons from South Africa*, Maryknoll N.Y, Orbis Books.

Digeser, P.E. (2001). *Political forgiveness*, Ithaca, NY, Cornell University Press.

44 See Tavuchis 1991; Celermajer 2008; Smith 2008; Thompson 2008; Bavelas 2004; Ohlstain 1989.

Gibney, M. et al. (ed), (2008). *The Age of Apology: Facing up to the past*, Philadelphia, Pennsylvania, University of Pennsylvania Press.

Gillies, R. (2008). Canada apologies to Indians for taking kids from families. *Associated Press*. June 12. http://articles.sfgate.com Accessed: April 10, 2010.

Govier, T. & Verwoerd, W. (2002a). The Promise and Pitfalls of Apology, *Journal of Social Philosophy*, 33(1), 67–82.

Govier, T. & Verwoerd, W. (2002b). Taking Wrongs Seriously: A Qualified Defense of Public Apologies, *Saskatchewan Law Review*, 65, 139–162.

Graham, I. (2005). Guildford Four: Blair Apology Exceeds Expectations. *The Press Association Limited*, February 9.

Griswold, C.L. (2007). *Forgiveness: a philosophical exploration*, Cambridge & New York, Cambridge University Press.

Lane, D. (2005). The 30yr apology, *The Mirror*, February 10.

Lazare, A. (2004). *On apology*, Oxford & New York, Oxford University Press.

Lind, J.M. (2008). *Sorry states: apologies in international politics*, Cornell University Press, Ithaca.

Millar, F. (2005). Blair Apology Exceeds Families' Expectations, *The Irish Times*, February 10.

Minow, M. (1998). *Between vengeance and forgiveness: facing history after genocide and mass violence*, Boston, Beacon Press.

Office of the Prime Minister of Australia (2008). Stolen Generations invited to Parliament for the National Apology. Joint Media Release with Minister for Indigenous Affairs. February 10. www.pm.gov.au Accessed: April 10, 2010.

Olshtain, E. (1989). Apologies across languages. In S. Blum-Kulka, J. House & G. Kasper (eds.), *Cross-cultural pragmatics: Requests and apologies*. Norwood NJ, Ablex.

Smith, N. (2008). *I was wrong: the meanings of apologies*, Cambridge & New York, Cambridge University Press.

Tavuchis, N. (1991). *Mea culpa: a sociology of apology and reconciliation*, Stanford Calif, Stanford University Press.

Thompson, J. (2008). Apology, justice, and respect: A critical defense of political apology. In M. Gibney, R.E. Howard-Hassman, M. Coicaud & N. Steiner (eds.), *The age of apology: Facing up to the past*. Philadelphia: University of Pennsylvania Press, 31–44.

PUBLIC RECONCILIATION AT THE SOUTH AFRICAN TRC: THE IMPACT OF THE VICTIM HEARINGS

Annelies Verdoolaege

1. THE SOUTH AFRICAN TRUTH AND RECONCILIATION COMMISSION

The South African Truth and Reconciliation Commission was called into existence in July 1995. The Preamble of the Promotion of National Unity and Reconciliation Act No 34 of 1995 (the TRC Act) stated that the objectives of the TRC were to promote national unity and reconciliation, amongst others by establishing as complete a picture as possible of the gross violations of human rights which were committed under apartheid, by facilitating the granting of amnesty to apartheid perpetrators under certain conditions, and by providing recommendations to prevent future violations of human rights.[1] In order to achieve these ambitious tasks, three committees were put into place: the Committee on Human Rights Violations (HRVC), the Amnesty Committee and the Committee on Reparation and Rehabilitation.

The HRV Committee – which is the focus of this article – was in charge of collecting written victim statements and of organising the Human Rights Violations hearings, where a representative sample of victims was allowed to testify in public. The HRVC gathered close to 22,000 statements, covering 37,000 violations; this is more than any other previous truth commission had achieved.[2] These statements were recorded by trained statement takers who conducted interviews with victims of apartheid all over the country. Between April 1996 and June 1997 a little under 2000 of these victims told their stories before the HRV Committee. Over these 15 months 83 hearings took place in public places such as town halls, schools, churches and civic centres.[3] The emphasis of the HRV hearings was on "the validation of the individual subjective experiences of people who had previously been silenced or voiceless".[4] Supporters of the TRC

1 TRC Report 1998: 54.
2 Graybill 2002: 8.
3 TRC Report 1998: 278.
4 TRC Report 1998: 111.

claimed that to tell their stories of suffering and misery was a healing and cathartic experience for most of the victims. The mere fact that these survivors were allowed to talk about the past meant a lot to them; it showed that their experiences were officially acknowledged and this made them feel respected as human beings.[5]

Because of the impact it had on the victims and also because the media brought this Committee to the attention of the national and international public, the Human Rights Violations Committee has often been considered as one of the most successful components of the TRC.

2. RECONCILIATION DISCOURSE AND THE ARCHIVE

The Human Rights Violations hearings provided a forum for thousands of apartheid victims to talk about the atrocities they had experienced under the apartheid regime – torture, rape, arson, the murder or abduction of beloved ones. Based on a thorough reading of all of the Human Rights Violations testimonies, as available on the Official TRC Website and a discursive analysis of 30 of them, my research concluded that at these HRV hearings a specific kind of reconciliation discourse was constructed. This reconciliation discourse was created through interaction between the testifiers, the HRV commissioners and the audience, and it contained various specific features. The notion of reconciliation was a fundamental aspect of this discourse.[6] One of the central propositions of my research is that the South African Truth and Reconciliation Commission should be regarded as a mechanism to produce power through discourse. This power should be regarded as constructive, hence exerting a positive impact on South African society, as we will see at the end of this article.

What I will illustrate here is the manner in which the concept of reconciliation was interpreted in a number of multidimensional ways before the HRV Committee. The fact that reconciliation was *allowed* to be regarded as a multilayered concept, with a wide variety of different definitions, is one of the reasons for the HRV discourse being turned into such a powerful tool with regard to post-apartheid nation-building. By giving an overview of the domains covered by the concept of reconciliation, we will get an insight into the *Foucaultian archive* of the Human Rights Violations hearings. The concept of the archive takes a central place in Foucault's 'Archéologie du Savoir' (1969) – translated as 'The Archaeology of Knowledge' (2002). One of the main objectives of the TRC was to reconstruct the apartheid experience, and to record and treasure this experience, to serve as a reminder of the past for future generations.

5 See Picker 2003: 20.
6 For a detailed analysis I refer to Verdoolaege, 2008.

In this way, indeed, the TRC can be considered as a public archive, "marking the institutional passage from the private to the public", as referred to by Derrida.[7] However, in 'The Archaeology of Knowledge' Foucault explains that when talking about the archive, he does *not* refer to the material archive:

> "By this term I do not mean the sum of all the texts that a culture has kept upon its person as documents attesting to its past (…); nor do I mean the institutions, which, in a given society, make it possible to record and preserve those discourses that one wishes to remember and keep in circulation."[8]

Foucault then gives a long list of definitions of what he does mean by the term archive, among which the following are especially relevant to my theoretical approach:

> "The archive is first the law of what can be said, the system that governs the appearance of statements as unique events. But the archive is also that which determines that all these things said do not accumulate endlessly in an amorphous mass (…). [I]t is that which, at the very root of the statement-event, and in that which embodies it, defines at the outset *the system of enunciability.* [I]t is that which defines the mode of occurrence of the statement-thing; it is *the system of its functioning* (…) [I]t is that which differentiates discourses in their multiple existence and specifies them in their own duration (…) [I]t reveals the rules of a practice that enables statements both to survive and to undergo regular modification. It is *the general system of the formation and transformation of statements.*"[9]

The archive can only be established by contextualising the statement: "we must grasp the statement in the exact specificity of its occurrence; determine its conditions of existence, fix at least its limits, establish correlations with other statements that may be connected with it, and show what other forms of statements it excludes".[10] According to Foucault, it is obvious that the archive of a society, culture or civilisation cannot be described exhaustively, nor can it be described in its totality. For the never completed, never completely achieved uncovering of the archive, Foucault uses the term *archaeology.* When a researcher understands how the archive has been established and why one statement appears instead of another, he or she will get an insight into the regimes of power that are operating behind the use of a certain discourse. Foucault's archaeology refers to the deconstruction of these societal power relations. My motivation for using Foucault's framework is exactly the insights it yields in the interaction between repertoires of statements on the one hand and configurations of power

---

7 Derrida 1996: 30; 2002: 49.

8 Foucault 2002: 145.

9 Foucault 2002: 145–146, italics in original.

10 Foucault 2002: 30–31.

in society on the other. The fact that certain statements were preferred in the context of the TRC revealed particular patterns of power relations at the actual HRV hearings: in the interactionally constructed HRV discourse, the TRC commissioners often took the initiative in shaping the conversation, guided by specific motivations. The testifiers and the audience of the HRV hearings added other features to this discourse, also because they wanted to realize specific aspirations. In this article, though, I will not talk about the power relations that were established or illustrated at the HRV hearings themselves. I will rather discuss another level of power exertion, namely the impact of the specifically constructed reconciliation discourse on post-apartheid South Africa.

I will only deal with a particular component of the Foucaultian archive, as I will illustrate how, at the victim hearings, testifiers were allowed to talk about/frame/conceptualize the term reconciliation. Other components of the archive, such as investigating why the HRV committee members only asked particular questions, why the victims only talked about certain aspects of their past experience, or why certain expressions were excluded from the HRV discourse, will not be dealt with here. By uncovering this aspect of the HRV archive we will get an insight into certain power relations of the TRC vis à vis South African society.

3. RECONCILIATION AS A MULTIDIMENSIONAL TERM AT THE HRV HEARINGS

In this section I will demonstrate how the testifying HRV victims all gave a very personal interpretation of the concept of reconciliation. There seemed to exist a wide range of acceptable conceptualizations, going from testifiers who openly supported the idea of reconciliation in South Africa, to testifiers who were much more critical. I will first refer to six *ideal* testifiers; testifiers who seemed to be personifications of the most-preferred HRV reconciliation discourse. Their utterances tended to be highly valued by the HRV commissioners, and they seemed to comply largely with the preferred victim profile as constructed by the TRC. What all of these testifiers had in common was that they were in favour of reconciliation. Nevertheless, there clearly was individual variation regarding the ways in which reconciliation was interpreted. Thereafter, I will pay attention to a few victims who did not straightforwardly adhere to reconciliation, so who interpreted the concept in yet a different way. Finally, the link between reconciliation and forgiveness will be explored in more detail, as this was one particular understanding of reconciliation before the HRV Committee.

GREGORY BECK

The first *ideal* testifier I will discuss is Mr. Gregory Beck, who testified in Johannesburg in April 1996. He was a policeman and while on patrol in Soweto he had been shot by members of the United Democratic Front, one of the anti-apartheid organisations. When asked about his relationship to other people – specifically to the perpetrators who attacked him – by commissioner Magwaza, Mr. Beck speaks out in favour of forgiveness quite spontaneously:

> *DR MAGWAZA*: Mr Beck it is obvious that your life changed after the attack, I would like to ask in what way did your life change in your relationship with other people or relationship with liberations movements? How did your life change in relation to your work? And how did your life change generally because something did change?[11]

> *MR BECK*: Yes more than likely. If all these things didn't come to the fore of what happened, then maybe I would still bear a grudge. *The reason why my life changed is that I've now learnt from all the stories I've learned from and the example that our State President has brought us for forgiving after he went through all these atrocities as well, and he can forgive, and I became more tolerant now and more understanding, which before I wasn't. I can understand now from both sides*, and people's problems daily in my job as well.

Throughout his testimony, Mr. Beck overtly tries to comply with this image of a citizen of the new South Africa. He constantly uses terms such as "us", "ours", "every South African", "our State President", indicating his inclusive interpretation of the South African nation. People who do not want to abide with the new constellation should be excluded. Mr. Beck clearly states that all South Africans have suffered, they all had to pay in order to be liberated – and they all should take President Mandela as an example. This testifier seems to be committed to living together peacefully with all citizens who embrace the transformation to democracy:

> *MR BECK:* Now it becomes more clear to me what was really going on and the balance between the State at that time and the liberation movements, and I can see the viewpoint of the liberation movement as well, which they hold, or which they held to bring about what we are experiencing *in this new South Africa of ours*, and that cost *us all* to be liberated.

> (...)

[11] All these fragments are literally taken from the Official TRC Website (www.justice.gov.za/trc/). The italics are my own.

> *MR BECK:* Well I know that the Commissioner of Police is trying his utmost to instill *into every policeman the new idea of the new South Africa, to be community orientated,* and to build up a good and firm and better image towards every South African, and I feel that a policeman in today's time, after hearing all these stories of the various atrocities, is still not prepared to abide with *the new South Africa, and with the new transparency that we have,* and democracy, then he must be kicked out of the police service.
>
> (...)
>
> *MR BECK:* The reason why my life changed is that I've now learnt from all the stories I've learned from and the example that *our State President has brought us* for forgiving after he went through all these atrocities as well.

These extracts tell us that, in the case of Gregory Beck, reconciliation was mainly framed by referring to *national unity.* Mr. Beck was the prototypical example of an individual who had undergone a complete transformation, from supporting the apartheid state as a policeman in earlier days to appreciating the anti-apartheid struggle and the new dispensation in the present. Mr. Beck strongly identified with the new South Africa and this identification was then the point of departure to emphasize his commitment to reconciliation. Taking "our State President" as an example, he explicitly mentioned that he had been turned into a forgiving, tolerant and understanding citizen. We clearly get an interpretation of reconciliation that was highly valued by the TRC commissioners, since it was based on an internal transformation process and a strong commitment to national unity. This interpretation of reconciliation fits in what Wilson calls the *mandarin-intellectual narrative.*[12] This narrative rejected an individually-oriented notion of reconciliation and focused on a more abstract understanding of reconciliation. Within this approach, reconciliation was situated on the level of the nation; South Africans were urged to reconcile with their past rather than with each other.

PAUL WILLIAMS

Mr. Paul Williams testified in Heideveld, also in April 1996. He got injured when members of the liberation movement APLA (Azanian People's Liberation Army) attacked the St-James church in Cape Town in 1993. Mr. Williams explicitly tells the Commission that he is prepared to reach out to the perpetrators. There is no bitterness in his heart and he seems to have totally forgiven them:

---

12 Wilson 2001: 106.

MR NTSEBEZA: Now in view of that what – what would you like the Commission to establish?

MR WILLIAMS: Ja okay – well from my – from my level as human being my personal level, I feel I have forgiven them. *And when I say forgiven them I bear no grudges against them. There's absolutely no bitterness within my heart towards them. If I come face to face with them I'll be prepared to hug them out of Godly love.* (...)

Immediately thereafter, Mr. Ntsebeza inquires about the testifier's opinion regarding the amnesty process. Again, Mr. Williams stresses that he wants to reconcile with the perpetrators, although this time he refers to the religious context as well.

MR NTSEBEZA: And finally I would like to ask a question I've asked to lot of people who have been at the receiving end. If Maqoma for instance who is serving a period of imprisonment for this attack – were to apply for Amnesty and in the view of the Amnesty Committee it could be found after all the various tests have been applied to his case that he deserves to be granted Amnesty *and he were to walk the streets as a free person as a consequence of that process. What would your reaction be?*

MR WILLIAMS: Like I said advocate, it is beyond my control that him being granted Amnesty, but should he go free and walk on the streets, *my duty as committed Christian should be I think to reach out to him. And that is what I would like to do.*

We clearly see that Paul Williams predominantly framed reconciliation *religiously*. It was mainly as a committed Christian that he wanted to reach out to his perpetrators. He did not feel any bitterness in his heart and he claimed to have completely forgiven them "out of Godly love". It was the bible that had taught him to love his enemies and it was also based on his belief that he supported the TRC amnesty process. Here we are dealing with an approach to reconciliation in which the personal self plays only a minor role: Mr. Williams was prepared to reconcile with his attackers, but based solely on his religious conviction. In this testimony reconciliation was conceptualised on a meta-level, since it was believed to find its source not in human encounters, but in supra-natural forces.

METRO BAMBISO

Mr. Metro Bambiso testified in Grahamstown, in April 1997, about his detention and torture by the police. Mr. Bambiso was not only treated as a victim by the HRV commissioners; he was also explicitly identified as a perpetrator. In fact, at the beginning of his testimony he spontaneously related how he and his comrades decided to necklace[13] an informer. Later on, Mr. Bambiso stated that he was prepared to reconcile with the people who had tortured him – he wanted to accept the apologies of his perpetrators and he was not revengeful. In addition, he also seemed to be prepared to reconcile with his victims, since he explicitly said that there was peace between them. In one and the same person we thus have a testifier who represented the group of reconciliation-oriented victims as well as the group of reconciliation-oriented perpetrators. Also Mr. Bambiso referred to President Mandela as a role model to follow when it comes to peace and reconciliation in South Africa. He seemed to highly respect the President and he agreed with the necessity to establish a united nation:

> *MR BAMBISO*: My request to the Commission is that I would like the Commission to bring the perpetrators to the community in Bedford to apologize to them. The reason for this is that I want to respect the President of this country, because he said that we have to be united in this country. *I do not want to revenge on what happened to me. What the President has already said, I agree with reconciliation.*
>
> (...)
>
> *MR BAMBISO*: Firstly, the reason why I referred to reconciliation is that I know that if victims or people who were oppressed by the white people, *if we want to revenge our country will not develop.* It will not be the country that we would like South Africa to be, because if I can take a gun and go to town to revenge what happened to me, *there will not be reconciliation, because our President is preaching peace in our country. I am supporting peace in this country.* That is the reason why I stated these. I do not whether the Commission understands me clearly.
>
> (...)
>
> *CHAIRPERSON MANTHATA*: What is the situation between yourself and the families of the victims? *Is there peace between you*?
>
> *MR BAMBISO*: *Yes, there is peace between us.*
>
> (...)
>
> *CHAIRPERSON MANTHATA*: As you referred to the plans that are to be made in order to reconcile and develop this country, what advice would you say?
>
> *MR BAMBISO*: What I would like to say is *that people are to be united and work together to build this country.*

---

13 Necklacing became a common method of lethal lynching during disturbances in South Africa in the 1980s and 1990s, often against a suspected collaborator with the apartheid system.

The testimony of Metro Bambiso formed the basis for yet another way of framing reconciliation. As a victim of state security violence, Mr. Bambiso wanted to reconcile with the perpetrators; he was prepared to accept their apologies and to reconcile with them. Like Mr. Beck, Mr. Bambiso expressed community awareness, which gave his individual reconciliation a national dimension. In this case, though, reconciliation was even further developed, since Mr. Bambiso also played the role of a repenting perpetrator. He was the personification of both a reconciliation-oriented victim and a remorseful perpetrator. Hence, he was a prime example of reconciliation in the new South Africa – where every one, according to Archbishop Tutu for instance, was a victim as well as a perpetrator.

PHEBEL ROBINSON

Ms. Phebel Robinson testified in Winelands, in October 1996; her husband had been detained and tortured by the police and he died in prison. This lady seemed to be very proud of her husband's solidarity towards the community and in the course of her testimony she referred to this community spirit several times:

> *MS ROBINSON:* My husband wasn't scared, he was not afraid of anyone and he fought for human rights. *He was a man for his community. He supported the poor, and the people that were battling.* So many times I said to him: "You've got no time for your own house and your own family, we've got just as many problems but you are never here when I need you." And he said: "But my wife you know where I am going to and you know my cause is a contribution to the struggle." So once again I say that *he was not afraid of anybody and he stood for what he believed in and for his community. There are many people here that can bear testimony to that – to the fact that he stood for his community.*
>
> (...)
>
> *MS ROBINSON:* (...) But I do not have any children of my own. *As somebody said to me in other words I am raising the community's children and I said yes, that is what my husband left me to do.*

When considering this testimony, there are significant resemblances to the one of Mr. Beck. Ms. Robinson expressed a strong sense of *community spirit*, with regard to her late husband as well as with regard to her present-day personal position. This kind of solidarity with members of the community can be seen as an aspect of national awareness – it indicated that one is prepared to live peacefully together with fellow citizens, regardless of their positions under apartheid or their social or ethnic backgrounds. Also like Mr. Beck, Ms. Robinson clearly interpreted reconciliation in a more abstract, non-individual sense, approaching it from a national/communal rather than from an individual angle. The fact that both of these victims belonged to the Coloured community, a group of people that sometimes struggled with identifying with the new South Africa, might be indicative. It is a population group that was disadvantaged under apartheid, but whose members sometimes allied with the National Party – the party that installed apartheid, but that expressed itself in Afrikaans, the mother tongue of the majority of Coloured people. In addition, part of the Coloured community feels disadvantaged under the new dispensation.[14] Therefore, proclaiming their affinity with post-apartheid South Africa and its symbols like Nelson Mandela, and stressing their solidarity with fellow community members was particularly relevant in the case of these testifiers.

MZOTHULI MAPHUMULO

Mr. Mzothuli Maphumulo testified in Newcastle, in September 1996; three of his children were killed by members of the ANC (African National Congress). Mr. Maphumulo identified as an IFP (Inkatha Freedom Party) member, although he also seemed to be open-minded towards members of the ANC. In fact, he presented himself as a mediator between these warring parties:

> *MR MAPHUMULO:* No, I was helping the ANC instead, because I would be taken by members of the ANC and they would say I should go and talk to the youth of the ANC, maybe they would understand me because I was an elderly person. *And at times I would tell them that I should not be treated as if I was a member of IFP as well as the ANC. I was a member of the IFP, but I would go and sort their problems out for them.*

In the testimony of Mr. Maphumulo reconciliation was lifted to the *political level*. Although a member of the IFP, and a victim of ANC violence, Mr. Maphumulo presented himself as a mediator between these political factions. Importantly, his tolerance and understanding towards the different political parties not only referred to the past, it also extended to the present and the future. This testifier was open-minded and prepared to cooperate constructively to the building of a reconciled society. In the course of his testimony reconciliation was in the first place given a personal interpretation. Indeed, Mr. Maphumulo had lost three sons as a result of political violence, which turned his reconciliation-oriented attitude into a great sacrifice. The commissioners appreciated this attitude enormously and considered the ability to reconcile with the perpetrators after such a terrible tragedy as a feature of unsurpassed personal merit. In addition to this personal touch, reconciliation was also given a political dimension, transcending the individual incident, and being made relevant to South African society at large.

14 Frost 1998: 106–107.

Reconciling different political factions was indeed crucial immediately after the transition to democracy – and also later on it remained a major political issue.

STEPHANIE KEMP

Mrs. Stephanie Kemp is the last ideal testifier I would like to discuss. She testified in Durban, in October 1996 and she had been detained and tortured in prison. This lady had had a white Afrikaner upbringing, which means that she belonged to the higher social classes. She became an active member of the South African Communist Party and after her detention she went into exile to London. She was absolutely committed to reconciliation in South Africa, as is clear from the following extract:

> *MRS KEMP: Without question reconciliation is necessary for the survival of our country.* And I think if it wasn't for our president, it would have perhaps been harder for me and many people like me, to even contemplate the possibility of reconciliation.

What is very striking in the testimony of Mrs. Kemp is that we learn how she has been torn apart by an identity struggle – as an Afrikaner anti-apartheid activist:

> *MRS KEMP:* By the early 1960s when I was at the University of Cape Town, studying physiotherapy I had come to the painful realization that the poverty, that Sharpeville and detention without trial were ways in which my own people were trying to claw their way into white privilege in our country. *I never spoke Afrikaans again* until my return from exile in 1990.
>
> (...)
>
> *MRS KEMP: But I was born an Afrikaner*, and from childhood we were fed, force fed if I might say on the glory of our people in the Anglo Boer War.
>
> (...)
>
> *MRS KEMP:* For me the horror of the apartheid years is compounded by the loss to me through *its prostitution of my language and my culture*. The direction that Afrikaner nationalism took into obliterating all in its wake now, no matter how murderously, I lay at the feet of the Broederbond, the Dutch Reformed Church and the National Party.
>
> (...)

MRS KEMP: I think I feel particularly bitter because once I came back into the country I found that it did matter to me that I wanted my culture back. I did feel – *I do feel very bitter and angry that these people took my language, they took my being,* and they turned it into this machine.

Mrs. Kemp's approach to reconciliation also fitted in the mandarin-intellectual narrative, since she explicitly expressed her support for national reconciliation. However, in this case reconciliation was given an extra dimension that was not so much a political rather than an *ethno-cultural* one. Mrs. Kemp seemed to struggle with her white/Afrikaner identity, since she actually presented a symbiosis between an anti-apartheid activist and a beneficiary of the apartheid system. In her testimony the opposition between white/Afrikaner and victim of the apartheid regime/Communist was transcended. Clearly, it was reconciliation between bearers of the Afrikaner culture and speakers of Afrikaans on the one hand, and ANC activists and apartheid exiles (so people who tended to be opposed to both the Afrikaner culture and Afrikaans) on the other hand that was at stake. Based on Mrs. Kemp's testimony reconciliation was given a national dimension, whereby reconciliation should take place in the first place between Afrikaners and non-Afrikaners – not, as was the case with Mr. Maphumulo for instance, between members of the IFP and the ANC.

NON-IDEAL TESTIFIERS

By paying attention to the way reconciliation was framed by these ideal testifiers, we should not forget that, sometimes, reconciliation was also conceptualised in a less preferred manner before the HRV Committee. Testifiers were allowed to express their resistance against reconciliation, for instance by only *conditionally* accepting reconciliation. This happened in the testimony of Mr. John Buthelezi, who testified in Duduza in February 1997 and who related a story about detention, torture and betrayal. Mr. Buthelezi explicitly mentioned that he would only reconcile after he had met the traitors or informers:

MR BUTHELEZI: I will explicitly emphasize the fact that *I will never reconcile until I mention those who wanted to attack me and kill me.*

MR LEWIN: Could we have quiet please.

MR BUTHELEZI: *I will only reconcile if I will be given opportunity to see those people who called me informers,*

(...)

> *MR BUTHELEZI*: (…) I want to tell you that I will only reconcile when only I could be given opportunity to see those people who were painting others black and yet they were the evil ones, the traitors and the informers. *That is when I will reconcile.*
>
> *MR MANTHATA*: *Order please. Order, order please. We are asking you could you please be quiet.* Go on.

The audience is very noisy when listening to Mr. Buthelezi's testimony, probably because he implies that the informers belong to the community and that they are even present in the hall. The leading commissioners try to calm down the audience, in order for the testifier to complete his story. What is striking, is that, in spite of his resistance against reconciliation, Mr. Buthelezi is allowed to express his feelings. This tells us that a negative conceptualization of reconciliation was also a possibility before the HRV Committee.

A similar example comes from Mr. Patrick Morake, a young man who was attacked by a group of right-wing Afrikaners, an attack whereby his car was destroyed. He testified in Welkom, in October 1996. This testifier did not openly speak out against reconciliation like Mr. Buthelezi. Nevertheless, he did express clear resentment vis à vis white people:

> *COMMISSIONER GCABASHE*: How do you feel ever since this has happened?
>
> *MR. MORAKE*: This occurrence changed my life so drastically. *I feel I have this deep hatred for a white person.* When I see a white person, especially at night I have these negative thoughts and even at work when I white person speaks to me I just look at him. *I totally distrust them because during the day they are people and in the evening they are killers.* Even when I'm driving a car and passing through Brandfort these thoughts come back to me so vividly as if it only happened yesterday. I just don't know how to explain this. Each time I think of this occurrence and I think of this attack… (incomplete)
>
> (…)
>
> *COMMISSIONER GCABASHE:* Now, when you say, ever since this incident took place and you have this problematic relationship with white people, *did you ever try to get any treatment or some counselling with regard to that?*
>
> *MR. MORAKE:* No, I've never thought of getting any treatment because *I feel that where they are, they are the ones who should be getting the treatment.* I think where they are they are the ones who are supposed to receive the treatment because I think they were the ones who are sick.

In this fragment, Mr. Morake argues that he feels this deep hatred for white persons; he distrusts them completely, since "they are people during the day, but killers at night". It is likely that utterances such as these were not appreciated by the HRV commissioners. Nevertheless, though, the commissioner showed understanding by proposing a treatment for his traumatic state of mind.

The last testifier I would like to refer to is Nelson Jantjie who testified in Karoo, in October 1996. He talked about his sister who was shot by the police and about his own imprisonment. The terms reconciliation or forgiveness were not mentioned in this testimony. The testifier was clearly very angry, but he did not openly refuse to reconcile. In this case reconciliation seemed to be regarded as a possibility by the HRV commissioners. Commissioner Seroke tried to temper his anger by emphasizing the necessity for peaceful coexistence; she even argued that she understood Mr. Jantjie's anger:

> *MR JANTJIE: I am angry, I am not working* – I have been tortured by police, I suffer, I am of ill health, I am unemployed, I suffer, my kidneys are not all right.
>
> *MS SEROKE:* We understand – we understand.
>
> *MR JANTJIE:* These people – *the perpetrators they are alive, what are you doing about them* – my life is ruined, what are you doing about them? They were not even jailed, I could not even go to my sister's funeral, I was in detention.(...)
>
> *MS SEROKE:* Mr Nelson we understand your situation.
>
> *MR JANTJIE*: I am in pain, this police that tortured me, they are working, I am unemployed, these people walk pass me everyday, the others are in De Aar – they still under employment, I cannot work for myself because of them. I don't gain anything from that – my children they all over the streets, they are criminals, they do not go to school.
>
> *MS SEROKE:* We understand your pain, *but we ask that you try to control yourself.* So that even when we ask our investigation team to find – to find out what happened, *we as the Truth Commission would like to reach a place where there can be peace and forgiveness.*

The underlying message here appeared to be that resentful testifiers could also be moved towards reconciliation. Mr. Jantjie's expressions of hatred were not really addressed, although the commissioner kept stressing that she understood his situation. The victim was allowed to be angry, but according to the reaction of the commissioners all hope should not be abandoned when it comes to promoting reconciliation.

When considering these three 'non-ideal' testifiers, we notice that before the HRV Committee essentially every expression and motivation of reconciliation was accepted. Testifiers were allowed to express hatred and resentment, as long as these sentiments could be rectified, for instance by ignoring them and stressing peace and forgiveness instead; they were also allowed to only conditionally accept reconciliation – all of which turning reconciliation into a multilayered and inclusive concept, a concept most South Africans could relate to.

4. INTERPRETING RECONCILIATION BEFORE THE TRC – TOO MUCH FORGIVENESS?

One of the ways in which reconciliation was interpreted before the HRV Committee was according to what Wilson calls the *religious-redemptive narrative*.[15] The religious-redemptive narrative pursued a notion of reconciliation as a common good, defined by confession, forgiveness and redemption, and the exclusion of vengeance. This kind of reconciliation discourse did not so much seek the reconciliation of the nation, but the reconciliation between individuals within the nation. One of the main critiques formulated vis à vis the TRC was that this religiously oriented interpretation of reconciliation was too prominently present at the HRV hearings. Colvin for instance, claims that the dramatic figure of Desmond Tutu, dressed in his purple robe, urging not only victims, but all South Africans, to put the ethic of forgiveness into practice, had been an enduring image of the TRC.[16] Some critics argue that the Christian doctrine of forgiveness seemed to be continually invoked, together with other religious values such as the importance of the community and the sanctity of the truth (Corry & Terre Blanche 2000: 9). Also Claire Moon, in her work 'Narrating Political Reconciliation', tells us that "the language of forgiveness dominated the public hearings of the TRC".[17] Moreover, she states that the TRC discourse was "compounded by the co-presence of Christian discourses on forgiveness".[18] Renner (2012) claims that before 1993, reconciliation in South Africa tended to be largely related to political negotiations and power sharing. It was only after 1994 that reconciliation became firmly associated with the TRC and with "practices of truth-telling, healing and forgiveness".

Although a number of authors have been trying to take forgiveness out of its traditional exclusive association with personal religion and morality, such as Shriver[19] and Derrida,[20] in the case of the TRC forgiveness tends to be largely located in the religious domain, indeed. One of the reasons for this was that Chairman Desmond Tutu in particular used to frame the HRV testimonies in theological terms – although this was also a recurring feature amongst other committee members with a religious background, such as Alex Boraine, Piet

15 Wilson 2001: 104–109.
16 Colvin 2003: 9.
17 Moon 2008: 122.
18 Moon 2007: 163.
19 Shriver 1997.
20 Derrida 2001.

Meiring and Reverend Finca. In addition, also the hall where the hearings took place was usually transformed into a proto-religious setting: the tables were covered in long white cloths, flowers were displayed, and a candle was lit at the beginning of the hearings.[21]

I will not underestimate the power of the Christian doctrine before the HRV hearings, and indeed, when going over the victim testimonies, the terms reconciliation and (personal) forgiveness were used interchangeably by a number of committee members and testifiers. However, the gist of my argument is that the HRV hearings allowed for multiple interpretations of the reconciliation concept in the first place. Reconciliation sometimes fitted into Wilson's *religious-redemptive narrative* – as is the case with Mr. Paul Williams –, but also cultural, political and nationalist conceptualisations were common. Linking reconciliation with the Christian notion of forgiveness was only one way in which the concept of reconciliation was given shape. Besides, as we understand from the testimony of Mr. Gregory Beck, the word *forgiveness* was also used when the testifier's interpretation of reconciliation fitted into the nation-building narrative.

Associating reconciliation with forgiveness, healing and confession is an aspect of the Judaeo-Christian tradition, to which a large part of the South African population belongs. This is possibly why, apart from a few scholars, these religious interpretations of reconciliation by the HRV commissioners were not extensively criticized. Another reason for this uncritical approach could be that some African traditional values often associated with the TRC also contained strong elements of communal healing and restoration. I am particularly referring here to the concept of *ubuntu,* an African philosophical concept that is generally translated as *humaneness* – literally 'people are people through other people'.[22] *Ubuntu* has often been described as one of the basic ideas behind the truth and reconciliation commission, since it involves that when hurting someone else you also hurt yourself. Only by listening to their victims, and by trying to empathize with them, perpetrators can try to liberate themselves. In the course of the HRV hearings, also the term *ubuntu* was regularly referred to, especially by Bishop Tutu. Most South Africans were sympathetic towards this concept as it was presented as a highly exclusive and typical African idea. This discourse of *ubuntu* complemented the Christian discourse of forgiveness, and we could even say that both of the discourses reinforced each other.

As I will illustrate in the next section, it is this multilayeredness of the term reconciliation that caused the TRC to exert a great deal of power on South African society.

---

21 Bozzoli 1998: 170.

22 TRC Final Report 1998, 1/5: 124–127.

5. RECONCILIATION AND SOCIETY

By referring to various HRV testifiers I have tried to uncover a part of the archive of the Human Rights Violations hearings. It seems to be clear that a lot of space was left for the testifiers to interpret reconciliation in a way that suited their own personal experiences, ranging from victims who unconditionally wanted to reconcile with their perpetrators, to victims who were angry and frustrated, but who were still received with a great deal of understanding by the HRV commissioners. I would argue that it is the existence of multiple versions of the reconciliation-concept that caused the reconciliation discourse to have a fundamental impact on South African society. Because the term was so multidimensional and inclusive, it was acceptable to a wide variety of South Africans. Because of its multilayeredness many people could identify with this concept, and because of its vagueness, the debate on reconciliation was sustained in South Africa.

It is remarkable to see how the term reconciliation dominated societal discourse during the proceedings of the TRC and in the years following the Commission's work. I would like to distinguish two separate ways in which reconciliation discourse impacted on society in that period.

First of all there is the concrete use of the term reconciliation, alongside terms like 'rainbow nation', 'transformation' and 'ubuntu'. For more than two entire years – from April 1996 till July 1998 – South African society was permeated by the proceedings of the HRV Committee. The national as well as the international media devoted a lot of attention to the hearings of the HRVC.[23] As also claimed by Goodman,[24] "it was especially the individual public hearings, along with extensive media coverage, that caused the notion of reconciliation to filter through to South African society". Not only did the media cover the proceedings of the TRC to its full extent, also special programmes and documentaries were broadcast, such as *Special Report* and *Long Night's Journey Into Day*; in all of these programmes the concept of reconciliation took a prominent position. Looking into the domain of culture, also post-apartheid theatre was preoccupied with the theme of reconciliation. A number of plays dealt explicitly with the TRC – the best known probably being 'Ubu and the Truth Commission', by Jane Taylor, but also the general themes of forgiveness and reconciliation were discussed elaborately. Apparently, in that post-1994 period, even former practitioners of protest theatre turned to the theatre of reconciliation.[25] On an academic level as well, the discourse of reconciliation definitely left its traces. Numerous courses, debates, conferences and discussion groups have been set up, all of which concentrating on the issue of reconciliation in South Africa. Also

---

23 Wilson 2001: 21.

24 Goodman 2003: 80.

25 Mda, 2002: 281.

the number of academic publications on reconciliation has skyrocketed in post-1994 South Africa: Brian Frost's 'Struggling to Forgive, Nelson Mandela and South Africa's Search for Reconciliation' (1998), Mark Hay's 'Ukubuyisana. Reconciliation in South Africa' (1998), John de Gruchy's 'Reconciliation: restoring Justice' (2002), Chapman & van der Merwe's 'Truth and reconciliation in South Africa: did the TRC deliver?' (2008) and du Bois & du Bois-Pedain 'Justice and Reconciliation in post-apartheid South Africa' (2008) are but a few examples. On an institutional level, the TRC formed only part of the institutions of 'redress' developed by the new government. Already during the Mandela era, but mainly afterwards, long-lasting initiatives were taken on this institutional level. Let me just mention some of the initiatives taken in post-1994 or post-TRC South Africa[26]: the activities of the Centre for the Study of Violence and Reconciliation (CSVR) – which was established in 1989 – were extended, amongst others by launching the Khulumani Support Group in 1995 and by setting up a 'Register of Reconciliation' in 1997; the Institute for the Healing of Memories was established in August 1998; and the Institute for Justice and Reconciliation was launched in May 2000. Small-scale initiatives were taken, such as the Lyndi Fourie Foundation and also universities participated in this drive towards reconciliation – like the University of Cape Town with its Transitional Justice Project and its Centre for Conflict Resolution. Initiatives were also taken to introduce reconciliation at the grassroots level of South African society. In 'Learning to Live Together',[27] Verwoerd gives a few examples of individuals who came together through the TRC, and who continued their journey of personal reconciliation also after the TRC had finished. Apartheid victims or their relatives helped to promote healing among other traumatised victims, while apartheid perpetrators were committed to help reconstructing the communities where they made havoc. In addition to the personal initiatives, this publication also illustrates practices of social reconciliation. All over South Africa community leaders were trying to enhance reconciliation, for instance by creating a platform for interracial cooperation and dialogue.[28] In organisations and companies, reconciliation was built through training and participation, and at schools and among student leaders reconciliation was brought into practice as well, often with the help of committed volunteers. Also Boraine argues that "there are numerous examples in South Africa where the commitment to reconciliation, religious or secular, has transformed lives and has brought about a change of behaviour and a genuine attempt to right the wrongs within society".[29] "Despite our country's history of conflict and prejudice", he continues, "there are countless examples of black and white finding each other and working

26 www.csvr.org.za.

27 du Toit 2003.

28 du Toit 2003: 280.

29 Boraine 2000: 363.

together". Also internationally, reconciliation became the identifying label of South Africa – only look at the fact that South Africa is regularly framed as a 'rainbow country' or a 'multicultural' nation, characterised by 'diversity' and peaceful coexistence.[30]

Secondly, and to my opinion more fundamental, is the fact that the HRV reconciliation discourse opened up the *debate* on reconciliation in South Africa. After the transition to democracy in 1994 a new discourse had to be established to talk about South African society. As claimed by Gobodo-Madikizela, "it is always necessary to forge a vocabulary of peace in the aftermath of mass tragedy".[31] People had to start thinking about one another differently, which also involved talking about and to one another by means of a language adapted to the new dispensation. According to my interpretation, it is in this search for a new socio-political discourse that the TRC acted as a catalyst, with the HRV reconciliation discourse forming the foundation of this wider societal discourse. Also Doxtader & Villa-Vicencio argued that, after the TRC, reconciliation "fostered important debates".[32] The significance of these debates being that South Africans were provoked to ask questions about the possibilities to deal with the apartheid past through the concept of reconciliation. People started to reflect on reconciliation and to look at the feasibility of reconciliation in their personal lives. Norval is also convinced that some of the lasting contributions of the TRC are of a discursive nature, stating that the TRC has "provoked open and democratic debate [...] as well as reflection on the character of justice, truth and the role of memory and reconciliation in a fledgling democracy".[33] Indeed, I would claim that it is partly as a result of the HRV reconciliation discourse that reconciliation became a point of discussion in South Africa. The concept became part of South African public life, which might have influenced people's perspective on society.

Therefore, we can take this impact of the HRV reconciliation discourse one step further, and argue that the TRC even contributed to the continuation of an *atmosphere of reconciliation* among South Africans after 1994. This is also put forward by Gibson after having carried out his research on current day attitudes towards reconciliation in South Africa.[34] He maintained that "[those South Africans] who are more accepting of the TRC's version of the truth are more likely to be reconciled" and "accepting the TRC's truth certainly did not contribute to 'irreconciliation'".[35] To me, the impact of the TRC discourse might not have been manifest; it is not a tangible result we can clearly pinpoint. Instead, it can be described as an underlying current, a *tendency to reconciliation* many South Africans might not be openly aware of. This corresponds to the ideas

30 Rassool 2000: 1.
31 Gobodo-Madikizela 2003: 56.
32 Doxtader and Villa-Vicencio 2003: XIV-XVI.
33 Norval 2009: 312.
34 Gibson 2004.
35 Gibson 2004: 334–335.

expressed by Antjie Krog in the epilogue to the 1999-edition of her book 'Country of My Skull'. In this postscript she wonders whether the TRC process has indeed achieved reconciliation in South Africa. What is *not* visible, she claims, is "reconciliation as a mysterious Judaeo-Christian process". Instead, what we see daily is "reconciliation as one of the most basic skills applied in order to survive conflict". Therefore, Krog also seems to be convinced that it is first and foremost in the daily lives of South Africans that we find this intangible spirit of reconciliation.

The impact of the TRC on post-apartheid society can indeed be illustrated by means of a number of concrete practices, as I showed earlier on in this section. One can argue, though, that these practices (books, courses, conferences) can largely be situated on the level of academic and intellectual discourse – although there have been many examples of practices of social reconciliation where communities have started to actually listen to each other and to get together.[36] The more fundamental and also wider impact of reconciliation discourse on society is more of an abstract nature: people started to reflect on reconciliation and to consider the validity of a particular interpretation of reconciliation in their own lives.

It is important to note, however, that the impact of the TRC reconciliation discourse mainly seemed to be notable in the years immediately following the Commission's proceedings. According to the South African Reconciliation Barometer 2008 there was a decline relating to optimism about the co-existence between people of different races. In explaining these findings regarding race relations, the Barometer referred to some incidents that had an impact on public opinion, such as the racist video at the University of the Free State in March 2008 and the xenophobic attacks in May 2008. Additionally, a few years ago there seemed to be a decrease in economic and physical security in South Africa, and, as the Reconciliation Barometer concluded, "... severe economic insecurity has the potential to aggravate what remains a very raw wound in our society".[37] Nevertheless, the results of the SA Reconciliation Barometer 2010 highlight a number of positive inroads again: "Importantly, a majority of South Africans still believe that a unified country is a desirable goal, and despite some reservations about whether or not this can occur in practice, this represents a crucial foundation for reconciliation". Also, despite the time that had passed since the conclusion of the TRC "most South Africans still feel that forgiveness for the crimes of the past is possible, and agree on the importance of moving forward collectively".[38] This indicates that even 17 years after the end of apartheid the concept of reconciliation – even with the link to forgiveness – is

---

36 du Toit 2003.

37 www.ijr.org.za/politicalanalysis/reconcbar/sarb-media-report-final.pdf..

38 http://sabarometerblog.files.wordpress.com/2011/03/sa-reconciliation-barometer-10th-round-report-web-final.pdf.

still present in societal discourse. It also shows that reconciliation still needs to be worked on. A stable and democratic situation in South African cannot be taken for granted; keeping the debate on reconciliation going and restoring trust in the state institutions are two ways in which the new presidency might be able to realize reconciliation at a profound level.[39]

6. CONCLUSION

It is quite likely that the HRV Committee's reconciliation discourse has shaped the way South Africans think, feel and act. As Gerwel puts it, the initial idea of the TRC was to deal with the past as quickly and efficiently as possible, so that South Africans could put the past behind them.[40] However, the TRC became so dominant in everyday life that it began to take a life on its own.

I have tried to illustrate that at the HRV hearings, the term reconciliation was constructed in a very vague and multidimensional manner. One of the effects was that most South Africans could relate to the polysemic and highly inclusive notion of reconciliation. They could identify with one unifying concept and this turned them into proud citizens of the new South Africa. I would argue that the vagueness of the term reconciliation was a deliberate choice from the side of the TRC. It was an inevitable choice: defining reconciliation unambiguously and restricting reconciliation discourse in such a way that it would only allow for a number of limited interpretations, would never have had the same impact on South African society. If this had been the case, the debate on reconciliation would not have become so dominant in South Africa and never would so many people – both nationally and internationally – have started to reflect on the value of restorative justice and peaceful conflict resolution. Deconstructing an aspect of the Foucaultian archive of the victim hearings, by illustrating how multifaceted the HRV reconciliation discourse was, made us understand how powerful a tool this discourse has been in post-TRC South Africa. I hope to have shown that this power should definitely be seen as a constructive and advantageous force in terms of South Africa's future.

REFERENCES

Boraine, A. (2000). *A Country Unmasked. Inside South Africa's Truth and Reconciliation Commission*. Cape Town: Oxford University Press.

Borer, T.A. (2001). Reconciliation in South Africa. Defining Success. *Kroc Institute Occasional Paper, March 2001.*

39 Hofmeyr 2009: 7.

40 Gerwel 2000: 123.

Bozzoli, B. (1998). Public Ritual and Private Transition: The Truth Commission in Alexandra Township, South Africa 1996. *African Studies* 57 (2), 167–195.

Centre for the Study of Violence and Reconciliation Website (2011). www.csvr.org.za.

Chapman, A.R. and van der Merwe, H. (2008). *Truth and reconciliation in South Africa: did the TRC deliver?.* Philadelphia: University of Pennsylvania Press.

Colvin, C.J. (2003). Limiting Memory: the Roots of Storytelling in Post-Apartheid, Post-TRC South Africa. In *Telling Wounds. Narrative, Trauma & Memory. Working through the SA armed conflicts of the 20th century. Proceedings of the conference,* C. van der Merwe and R. Wolfswinkel (eds.). Stellenbosch: Van Schaik Content Solutions, 234–244.

Corry, W. and Terre Blanche, M. (2000). Where does the blood come from?: True stories and real selves at the TRC hearings. *Psychology in Society* 26: 6–17.

Derrida, J. (1996). *Archive fever. A Freudian impression.* Chicago: The University of Chicago Press.

Derrida, J. (2001). *On Cosmopolitanism and Forgiveness.* London: Routledge.

Derrida, J. (2002). Archive Fever in South Africa. In *Refiguring the Archive,* C. Hamilton et al (eds.), Cape Town: David Philip Publishers, 38–80.

Doxtader E. and Villa-Vicencio, Ch. (2003). Introduction: Profiling Violence and the Potential for Reconciliation. In *Through Fire with Water. The roots of division and the potential for reconciliation in Africa*, E. Doxtader and Ch. Villa-Vicencio (eds.). Claremont: David Philip Publishers, XIII-XXII.

Du Toit, F. (2003). *Learning to live together. Practices of social reconciliation.* Cape Town: Institute of Justice and Reconciliation.

Foucault, M. (1969). *L'archéologie du savoir.* Paris: Bibliothèque des Sciences Humaines.

Foucault, M. (2002). *The Archaeology of Knowledge.* London & New York: Routledge.

Frost, B. (1998). *Struggling to Forgive, Nelson Mandela and South Africa's Search for Reconciliation.* London: Harper Collins Publishers.

Gerwel, J. (2000). National reconciliation: holy grail or secular pact? In *Looking Back, Reaching Forward, Reflections on the Truth and Reconciliation Commission of South Africa,* Ch. Villa-Vicencio and W. Verwoerd (eds.). Cape Town: University of Cape Town Press, 277–286.

Gibson, J.L. (2004). *Overcoming Apartheid. Can Truth Reconcile a Divided Nation?* New York: Russell Sage Foundation.

Gobodo-Madikizela, P. (2003). Alternatives to Revenge: Building a Vocabulary of Reconciliation Through Political Pardon. In *The Provocations of Amnesty: Memory, Justice and Impunity,* Ch. Villa-Vicencio and E. Doxtader (eds). Claremont: David Philip Publishers.), 51–60.

Gobodo-Madikizela, P. (2008). Radical forgiveness: transforming traumatic memory beyond Hannah Arendt. In *Justice and Reconciliation in Post-Apartheid South Africa,* F. De Bois and A. Du Bois-Pedain (eds.). Cambridge: Cambridge University Press, 37–61.

Goodman, T. (2003). Setting the Stage. A Cultural Approach to the South African Truth and Reconciliation Commission. *Yale Journal of Sociology* 3, 77–92.

Graybill, L.S. (2002). *Truth and Reconciliation in South Africa. Miracle or Model?* Boulder: Lynne Rienner Publishers, Inc.

International Center for Transitional Justice Website (2011). www.ictj.org/.

Hofmeyr, J. (2009). Reconciliation and the Zuma presidency. *South African Reconciliation Barometer Newsletter* 7/1: 7. 2009. Cape Town: Institute for Justice and Reconciliation.

Khulumani Support Group Website (2011). www.khulumani.net/home.

Krog, A. (1998). *Country of My Skull: Guilt, Sorrow, and the Limits of Forgiveness in the New South Africa*. Parklands: Random House South Africa.

Mda, Z. (2002). South African theatre in an era of reconciliation. In *The Performance Arts in Africa. A reader*, F. Harding (ed.), London: Routledge, 279–289.

Moon, C. (2007). States of Acknowledgement: the politics of memory, apology and therapy." In *Crime, Social Control and Human Rights: from moral panics to states of denial. Essays in honour of Stan Cohen*, D. Downes et al (eds.). Cullompton, Devon: Willan Publishing.

Moon, C. (2008). *Narrating Political Reconciliation. South Africa's Truth and Reconciliation Commission*. Lanham: Lexington Books.

Norval, A.J. (2009). No reconciliation without redress: articulating political demands in post-transitional South Africa. *Critical Discourse Studies* 6(4), 311–321.

Official TRC Website (2011). www.justice.gov.za/trc/.

Parlevliet, M. (1998). Considering Truth. Dealing with a Legacy of Gross Human Rights Violations. *Netherlands Quarterly of Human Rights* 16(2), 141–174.

Picker, R. (2003). Victim's Perspectives about the Hearings. *Paper Online:* www.csvr.org.za/papers/pappick.htm.

Rassool, C. (2000). The Rise of Heritage and the Reconstitution of History in South Africa, *Kronos: Journal for Cape History* 26, 1–21.

Renner, J. (forthcoming in 2012). *Discourse, Normative Change, and the Quest for Reconciliation in Global Politics*. Manchester: Manchester University Press.

South African Reconciliation Barometer (2008). www.ijr.org.za/politicalanalysis/reconcbar/sarb-media-report-final.pdf.

Shriver, Jr. D.W. (1997). *An Ethic For Enemies. Forgiveness in Politics*. New York: Oxford University Press.

TRC Act Online (1995). www.doj.gov.za/trc/trc_frameset.htm.

Truth and Reconciliation Commission of South Africa Final Report (1998). *Volumes 1–5*. Cape Town: Juta & Co Ltd.

Verdoolaege, A. (2008). *Reconciliation Discourse. The Case of the Truth and Reconciliation Commission*. Amsterdam: John Benjamins Publishing Company.

Villa-Vicencio, Ch. and Verwoerd, W. (2000). Constructing a Report: Writing Up the 'Truth'. In *Truth versus justice: the morality of truth commissions*, R.I. Rotberg and D. Thompson (eds.), Princeton: Princeton University Press, 279–294.

Wilson, R.A. (2001). *The politics of Truth and Reconciliation in South Africa. Legitimising the Post-Apartheid State*. Cambridge: Cambridge University Press.

SHOULD CHRISTIAN CONTRIBUTIONS TO TRANSITIONAL JUSTICE FOCUS ON RECONCILIATION?

Learning from El Salvador

Stephen J. Pope

1. INTRODUCTION

November 2009 saw the commemoration of the twentieth anniversary of the notorious massacre of six Jesuits, their housekeeper, Elba Ramos, and her daughter, Celia, at the University of Central America.[1] March of 2000 commemorated the thirtieth anniversary of the assassination of Archbishop Oscar Romero[2] and the following December marked the kidnapping, rape, and murder of the four American churchwomen – Maura Clarke, Ita Ford, Dorothy Kazel and Jean Donovan.[3] Such commemorations are important for the world, but they are especially important in El Salvador because of the way in which memories of injustice have been systematically denied and repressed. All of these figures were deeply committed to peace in El Salvador, but they insisted that the way to attain authentic peace is through justice. Their lives were rooted in a Catholic Christian faith and enlivened by the Second Vatican Council, according to which the church is most herself when she walks in solidarity with the poor and advocates policies to end structural injustice.

Thirty years after Romero's martyrdom, we are now in the age of "transitional justice" in which the language of reconciliation has come to play an increasingly important role in our moral lexicon. This is particularly true of Christian ethics, especially after the public successes of the South African Truth and Reconciliation Commission and its charismatic chair, Archbishop Desmond Tutu.[4] The international acclaim of the TRC (not always articulated as loudly in South

1 See Doggett 1993, Whitfield1994, and Sobrino et al. 1990.
2 See Brockman 1989 and Romero 1985.
3 See Noone 1995.
4 See Tutu 1999.

Africa itself) sometimes tempts us to forget that the language of reconciliation was employed in El Salvador, as well as in Chile and Argentina, well before the South African experiment was conceived. Yet human rights activists in Latin America often suspect that appeals to reconciliation amount to a subtle attempt to evade accountability. Nowhere is this more the case than in El Salvador, whose history from colonialism to the present has been pervaded by impunity.[5]

The church promotes mercy, forgiveness, and reconciliation as primary expressions of the virtue of charity, the grace inspired love of God and neighbor. Christian contributions to transitional justice around the world have often focused on reconciliation. As political scientist Daniel Philpott points out: "Religiously based approaches to transitional justice often endorse human rights as a goal. But neither human rights nor punishment for human rights violators is their common orienting conception. The idea around which religious voices most converge, rather, is reconciliation."[6]

Philpott's claim is descriptive, but it supports the normative proposal that the church ought to make reconciliation its central focus. Yet we have to ask: how can the church make reconciliation its central focus without tacitly supporting impunity? This chapter draws from the Salvadoran experience, if, for reasons of space, in merely illustrative and suggestive ways, to distinguish appropriate from inappropriate moral appeals to reconciliation. Its central claim is that morally appropriate appeals to reconciliation in Christian ethics ought also to be centered on the pursuit of justice, which it can never regard justice as dispensable. This is not deny the primacy of charity for Christian ethics, but it is to propose that the church, to be true to her mission, ought to interpret justice for victims as the central way of being faithful to charity.

This article proceeds in four steps: first, it provides a thumbnail sketch of the Salvadoran context; second, it examines the status of reconciliation and justice in the Salvadoran church; third, it offer a brief account of justice as the path reconciliation; and finally, it discusses the relation between liberal justice and Christian reconciliation.

2. HISTORICAL CONTEXT

The Salvadoran civil war raged from1980–1992 and led to the killing of approximately 75,000 people out of a population of 5 million, including 8,000 victims of forced disappearances. The human rights organization Americas

5 See Montgomery 1995, Binford 2004, and Wood 2003.

6 Philpott 2007, p. 12. See also, Philpott 2006. Philpott is not saying anything like "justice is a bad idea for Christians," as Stanley Hauerwas does in *After Christendom*? (Hauerwas 1991: 45), The latter is addressed by Stout 2004.

Watch called the 1980s in El Salvador the "decade of terror."[7] As the war began, death squads and assassins operated freely in the cities, and as the war progressed the military conducted rural counter-insurgency warfare in ways that included thousands of extra-judicial killings and hundreds of massacres.

In April 1990 the UN Secretary-General called together representatives from the FMLN (the Farabundo Martí para Liberación Nacional) and the Salvadoran government in Geneva to satisfy an earlier agreement to pursue regional peace. After extended negotiations an agreement was made and a cease-fire declared in September 1991. Signed in January 1992, the Chapultepec Peace Accords intended not only to end armed hostilities but also to address the underlying causes of the conflict, to establish a process of democratization, and to promote reconciliation among Salvadorans.

The Peace Accords provided for the reduction and professionalization of the Salvadoran armed forces, including their withdrawal from internal security, political, and economic affairs. By 1993, the armed forces had been reduced to 15,000 from a war time high of 63,000. A post-war purge of military officers associated with corruption and human rights abuses was completed on the recommendation of a UN sponsored Ad Hoc Commission on Human Rights. More than 35,000 former guerrillas and soldiers were given land and most were also granted agricultural credits,[8] but victims (neither direct nor indirect) were not given reparations.

The Peace Accords mandated the formation of a truth commission to investigate the most significant acts of violence that occurred during the war. It was to "create confidence in the positive changes which the peace process is promoting and to assist the transition to national reconciliation."[9] The truth commission documented over 22,000 complaints, of which 60% concerned extrajudicial killings, 25% forced disappearances, and 20% torture. The appointment of three distinguished non-Salvadorans was intended to signal their political independence and so build credibility for their judgment, but it also raised questions about their ability to build local constituencies for their proposals. Testimonies were taken privately to protect witnesses, but this very confidentiality limited the ability of the truth commission to stimulate public deliberation about national identity. In these ways it was quite different from the TRC.

The truth commission report, entitled *From Madness to Hope: The 12 Year War in El Salvador*, was issued in 1993.[10] It determined that 85% of the killings and other crimes were caused by "agents of the state" and 5% by the guerrillas. The report's controversial identification of specific individuals responsible for

7 Americas Watch 1991.
8 See Grenier 1999.
9 Www.usip.org/files/file/ElSalvador-Report.pdf.
10 Ibid.

ordering human rights abuses, e.g., the naming of Minister of Defense General René Emilio Ponce as authorizing the UCA killings, did not help with the government's reception of the document or its recommendations. Most glaring was its failure to acknowledge the extensive use of gender based violence, and particularly rape, as weapons of repression and war.[11]

The commission recommended, among other things, that the state remove violators of human rights from the military or public offices, take steps to place the armed forces under greater civilian control, extensively reform the Salvadoran judiciary, and develop a system of reparations for victims. The latter were to include a special fund for payment of reparations, a national monument to the victims, a national holiday to commemorate the victims, and a public forum to discuss the report's findings.

The then-president of the republic, Alfredo Cristiani, repudiated the report for failing to promote national reconciliation. He insisted that Salvadorans needed to forgive and forget the past rather than open up old wounds. "What must be done now," he said to the nation, "is to see what has to be done to erase, eliminate, and forget everything in the past."[12] Cristiani led the national legislature quickly to push through the "General Amnesty Law for the Consolidation of Peace" that protected all former combatants from both civil and criminal liability for political crimes committed during the war.

The leadership of both the right wing ARENA party and the leftist FMLN supported the amnesty because it protected their own agents from future prosecution. The amnesty led to the release of both the soldiers convicted in the November 1989 UCA massacre and the FMLN ex-combatants held for the June 1985 assassination of four off-duty Marines (and nine other people) at a café in San Salvador.[13] The truth commission report intended to bring accountability to El Salvador, but the government's reaction reinforced the culture of impunity. Given this situation, it is understandable why in El Salvador, as human rights scholar Margaret Popkin points out, "few perpetrators of heinous crimes have asked for pardon, and few survivors have had the opportunity to decide whether they are able to forgive those responsible for the fate of their loved ones, since the perpetrators have not been identified."[14] El Salvador was thus left with conditions favoring neither accountability nor forgiveness.

The recommendations of the truth commission that were not already part of the Peace Accords were largely ignored. According to Salvadoran economist Alexander Segovia, the recommendations were not accepted for three reasons: first, the report was not the product of a negotiation process involving the major

11 See Tombs 2006: 64–67. See also Dewirst 1998, at Center for the Study of Violence and Reconciliation, www.csvr.org.za/index.php?option=com_content&task=view&id=562, accessed January 14, 2010.

12 Presidential Address to the Nation (March 18, 1993), cited in Popkin 2000: 150.

13 See *From Madness to Hope*, IV.E.

14 Ibid.

concerned parties and therefore did not enlist forces that would find compliance attractive; second, the Salvadoran government lacked the political will to accept the recommendations and so was unwilling to allocate any resources to their implementation (it is especially significant that the Salvadoran government did not undergo a regime change prior to the constitution of the truth commission, as was the case in Chile, Argentina, and South Africa); and third, the recommendations pertaining to reparations were hampered by design flaws regarding the source and distribution of the funding.[15]

Cristiani himself reported to the United Nations that he would comply with the truth commission's recommendations to the extent that they were in harmony with (i.e., already mandated by) the Peace Accords and would "contribute to the reconciliation of the Salvadoran society".[16] Government non-compliance, especially regarding reparations, was facilitated by the general passivity of civil society and NGOs.[17] The leaders of the FMLN did not engage in advocacy for the victims in this regard, Segovia reports, because some believed individual reparations would be financially unfeasible, others judged that public funds could be put to better use on other projects, and yet others were preoccupied with political in-fighting.[18]

Despite the stated desire in many quarters for reconciliation, El Salvador remains a highly polarized society. Economically, it is marked by gross inequality in wealth and income, education, and health. The highest ten percent of the population makes 40% of the country's annual income while the lowest twenty percent makes 7.5% of the national income.[19] Less than half of Salvadorans graduate from the sixth grade, only one third complete ninth grade, and only one-fifth graduate from high school. These percentages reflect the national average; conditions are worse in the countryside. Lack of economic opportunity and widespread deprivation fuel very high levels of drug and alcohol abuse, domestic violence, urban crime, and mass migration to the north (1 out of every 5 Salvadorans currently resides in the United States[20]). Gangs have become a major but not the only source of lethal violence in El Salvador.[21] With 71 people per 100,000 killed in 2009, El Salvador has the highest homicide rate in Latin America, five times that of Mexico and ten times that of the United States.[22]

---

15 Cited in Segovia 2006: 159.

16 Cited in ibid.

17 Ibid.

18 Ibid.: 159–60.

19 See "El Salvador- Poverty and Wealth," *Encyclopedia of the Nations*, www.nationsencyclopedia.com/economies/Americas/El-Salvador-POVERTY-AND-WEALTH.html, accessed January 3, 2010. U.S. Agency for International Development (USAID), El Salvador's per capita income is the "fifth lowest in the Western Hemisphere (when adjusted to reflect the cost of living)."

20 See the El Salvador country report provided by the Migration Information Service at www.migrationinformation.org/USFocus/display.cfm?id=765. Accessed January 7, 2010.

21 See Arana 2006.

22 See Wilkinson 2009.

Politically, El Salvador tends to be divided between political extremes with little room for centrist political affiliation.[23] According to a recent German study,

> The deep polarization and distrust between the two major parties, ARENA and FMLN, reflects a deep division within society along the ingrained socioeconomic cleavage of rich and poor, and has quite substantially hindered the development of a more democratic political culture. Seventeen years after the official end of the Salvadoran civil war, this polarization remains strong, as the results of the legislative elections in January 2009 show: In a close contest, FMLN and ARENA won the largest number of seats, respectively with 35 and 32 out of a total of 84.[24]

The influence of this political polarization on the Salvadoran legal system leaves victims of the civil war unable to attain justice through regular legal channels. Those seeking justice have had to go outside El Salvador, for instance, to the Inter-American Court,[25] the Spanish court,[26] or the United States judicial system.[27]

---

23 See Barnes 1998.

24 "BTI Country Report: El Salvador," "Shaping Change – Strategies of Development and Transformation," at www.bertelsmann-transformation-index.de/en/, accessed January 23, 2010.

25 In the Romero case, on January 4, 2000, the Inter-American Court of Human Rights condemned the "strategic and concerted actions that kept the Supreme Court of Justice, the Office of the Public Prosecutor of the Republic and the Courts from acting impartially and seeking a fair trial with due process guarantees." The court made three recommendations: judicial investigation to bring the perpetrators and intellectual authors to justice, payment of reparations to the indirect victims; and conformity of Salvadoran law to the American Convention and to nullify the 1993 General Amnesty Law. See www.oas.org/en/topics/human_rights.asp, accessed January 7, 2010. It should also be noted that in 2000, the Inter-American Commission of Human Rights ruled that El Salvador's failure to investigate and prosecute those responsible for the assassination of Romero constituted a violation of human rights. FMLN President Mauricio Funes recently made an unprecedented act of public atonement on the twentieth anniversary of the UCA massacre and he has promised to investigate the assassination of Archbishop Romero, identify the guilty parties, and make appropriate reparations payments. He has not agreed to work to overcome the notorious 1993 amnesty law.

26 See Wilkinson and Renderos 2009.

27 Former Col. Nicolas Carranza, the Salvadoran Vice-Minister of Defense (1979–80) and then head of the Treasury Police, was judged by a US court in Memphis in 2003 to be guilty of torture, extrajudicial killing and crimes against humanity. A Miami court in 2002 convicted former Salvadoran Ministers of Defense General José Guillermo Garcia (1979–80) and Eugenio Vides Casanova of torture and other human rights abuses and ordered them to pay 54.6 million in damages. See CNN, 2005, at www.cnn.com/2005/LAW/11/19/torture.trial.ap/, accessed January 1, 2009; Preston 2005; Hearn 2009.

3. THE CHURCH

The Christian community in El Salvador, Catholic and Protestant, is also highly polarized. Salvadorans tend to be deeply religious, and the vast majority describe religion as an important part of their lives. 55% of Salvadorans are Roman Catholic and 29% are Protestant, roughly three fourths of whom are Pentecostal evangelicals.

The Salvadoran Catholic church has traditionally been given privileges by the government, particularly in education, and in exchange provided moral and religious support for the government and ruling elites. In the wake of Vatican II, however, many priests, particularly in rural areas, began to promote democratic values and human rights. Most Catholic bishops in El Salvador in the 1970s and 1980s resisted this tendency, but a few who embraced the "preferential option for poor." They became convinced that true peace could only be achieved by holding the government accountable for its human rights abuses.

The major expression of the option for the poor was the grassroots mobilization of base Christian communities.[28] The investigatory and advocacy activities of the Legal Aid Office (*Tutela Legal*) of the Archdiocese of San Salvador were an important expression of this commitment; the Human Rights Institute of the University of Central America (IDHUCA) continues this kind of work today. The church was increasingly persecuted and, in fact, became a "church of martyrs," as Jon Sobrino puts it, that included 20 parish priests, seven Jesuits, and countless catechists and other laypeople.[29]

After the war, Archbishop Arturo Rivera y Damas (1983–94) attempted a policy of promoting national reconciliation while opposing impunity.[30] Religious leaders from a variety of churches were deeply involved in supervising the implementation of the Peace Accords and in holding both sides accountable to their commitments. The prophetic voice of the church was spoken, according to political scientist Andrew Stein, when Catholic officials pressed for judicial reform and[31] criticized those irresponsible media elites whose style of journalism continued the demonization of adversaries and ideological polarization of the war years. At a time when many political leaders (most especially ARENA leaders) tried to downplay and forget the past, Catholic officials constantly reminded the public and governing elites of what was done so as to create values, practices and institutions different from those that had led to the outbreak of the civil war.[32]

---

28 Azevedo (1993). See also Klaiber 1998, Galdámez 1986, Lee 2000.
29 See Sobrino 2003, Peterson 1997, and Cardenal 1990.
30 See Brett 2008.
31 Seider and Costello 1996.
32 Stein 1998 at *asa.international.pitt.edu/LASA98/Stein.pdf, accessed January 3, 2010.*

In April of 1995, Fernando Saenz Lacalle was appointed archbishop of San Salvador. His own deeply conservative religious convictions led him to retreat from his predecessors' official Catholic defenses of human rights, lobbying for socio-economic structural reforms, and mobilization of grassroots organizations.[33] Saenz Lacalle promoted a highly clerical (rather than lay centered) focus in church life that generated a more "vertical" and purportedly a-political interpretation of sacraments, religious devotions, morality, and spirituality. Instead of going out to work with the poor in their own setting, one commentator put it, pastors in the more clerical mold of religious leadership believed it was their role to wait for the poor to come to them.[34]

Thus while Pope John XXIII had earlier spoken of the church in the developing world as the "church of all, and especially the church of the poor,"[35] observers discern in this period a growing alienation throughout Latin America of the "church of the base" from the hierarchy.[36] This situation reflects the Vatican's campaign against liberation theology since the mid-1980s.[37] Vatican appointments under John Paul II ensured that by the time Saenz Lacalle was appointed archbishop, there were no longer any bishops, "willing and able to continue the policies initiated by Rivera y Damas."[38]

The visit of John Paul II to El Salvador in 1996, paid for by the government and wealthy Salvadorans, was interpreted by many to be a "sign of reconciliation between church and state" and as a "symbolic gesture indicating that the church and state had to return to the previous status quo."[39] As reconciliation was increasingly advanced within Catholic teaching, one could legitimately wonder if forgiveness did not subtly begin to supplant justice.[40]

---

33 See Johnson 2000 at www.thetablet.co.uk/article/6873, accessed January 7, 2010.

34 See Williams 1998: 186.

35 John XXIII 1962. Cited in Gutierrez 1993: 244.

36 See De la Serna 2005.

37 See Catholic News Agency 2009, at www.catholicnewsagency.com/news/benedict_xvi_cautions_against_dangers_of_marxist_liberation_theology/, accessed January 7, 2010. See Congregation for the Doctrine of the Faith 1986, available at www.vatican.va/roman_curia/congregations/cfaith/documents/rc_con_cfaith_doc_19860322_freedom-liberation_en.html, accessed January 14, 2010.

38 Betances 2007: 95.

39 Ibid.

40 For example, Cardinal Alfonso López Trujillo, Prefect of the Pontifical Council for the Family and sharp critic of liberation theology, commented on the 20th anniversary of the Puebla Conference on the meaning of authentic liberation: "It is a liberation with broader evangelical tasks, worlds apart from those that spread a reduced vision: an integral and profound liberation like that proclaimed by Jesus, consisting in forgiveness and reconciliation; a liberation that is not reduced to the simple economic, political or cultural dimension; a liberation that steers clear of curtailment or ambiguity and is not based on ideologies; a liberation faithful to God's Word and the Church's Tradition." Reconciliation is not related to justice in this document. See www.vatican.va/roman_curia/pontifical_councils/family/documents/rc_pc_fam, accessed January 13, 2010.

This chapter focuses mainly on the Catholic church, but Pentecostalism has also come to play major role in Salvadoran Christianity today.[41] Pentecostals have come to dominate the Protestant churches in El Salvador in part because of backing from wealthy Americans willing to dedicate ample financial resources to promote this form of Christianity through the popular media and mass meetings. Salvadoran Pentecostals tend to embrace an apocalyptic eschatology that makes them suspicious of merely secular, state-driven solutions to human suffering and averse to church involvement in any kind of political activity, including those intending to bring structural change to the root causes of social injustice.[42] The church should be a place of refuge, they teach, neither political activism nor social protests.

Pentecostal membership exploded during the civil war for a variety of reasons. Unlike Catholics, Pentecostal recruits were not asked to be socially engaged and so were not subjected to systematic persecution by the state. Pentecostal communities are typically smaller, more personal, and more engaged in the lives of congregants than Catholic parishes. Pentecostal membership encourages an improvement in lifestyle that is beneficial personally (e.g., by teaching abstinence from alcohol), domestically (e.g., by insisting on marriage fidelity and family responsibility), and even financially (e.g., by encouraging frugality and self-discipline).

Correcting some stereotypes, historian Philips Williams points out that Salvadoran Pentecostals neither see the status quo as morally legitimate, nor deny the reality of widespread innocent suffering, nor support the ARENA party in large numbers. Yet they do tend to believe that since God alone gives salvation, political activity will not make any appreciable difference to world history. As Williams puts it, Pentecostal converts, "continue to live 'in' the world but distinguish themselves by adopting a radically different lifestyle. Preaching against sin, they venture out into the world, denouncing worldly things and calling on people to transform their lives as they have."[43]

Some time ago, sociologist David Martin pointed out that Pentecostalism in Latin America helps "to implant new disciplines, re-order priorities, counter

---

41 This section of the article ventures some generalizations about Salvadoran Pentecostalism. As Frank D. Macchia points out, there is a great diversity within the worldwide Pentecostal movement that includes diverse views of Christian eschatology. This diversity having been noted, according to Macchia, the otherworldly salvation preached by Pentecostal eschatology generally focuses on only collective change but on "winning people to Christ in preparation for eternity." See his "Pentecostal and Charismatic Theology," in Walls 2008: 287.

42 It should be mentioned that the Lutheran Synod of El Salvador, particularly under the leadership of Bishop Medardo Gómez-Soto, has been strongly opposed to the amnesty. See Gomez 1990.

43 Williams 1998: 194. Hannah W. Stewart-Gambling and Everett Wilson hold that many Pentecostals reject politics because they involve striking deals with powerful elites who are largely Catholic. They also point out that many Pentecostals are involved in "substantial local community and even national social service involvement, which can easily have political implications." Ibid.: 233.

corruption and destructive machismo, and reverse the indifferent and injurious hierarchies of the outside world. Within the enclosed haven of faith a fraternity can be instituted under firm leadership, which provides for release, for mutuality and warmth, and for the practice of new roles."[44] Victims of human rights abuses learning to dwell in this "haven" are encouraged to forgive their perpetrators from the heart – whether they know who their perpetrators are or not – and consent to the fact that God alone will be the "judge of the living and dead." Salvadoran Pentecostals do not see the point of devoting time and energy to the pursuit of retributive justice. They have little motivation to support collective action to promote public accountability for individual perpetrators or to end the "culture of impunity".

4. JUSTICE AS THE PATH TO RECONCILIATION

Salvadoran Pentecostals, conservative Catholics, and the political elites of left and right hold strongly divergent positions on many questions, but they agree on giving priority to reconciliation rather than justice. Yet one has to ask: what is meaning of "reconciliation" in this context? This term, as has been pointed out, is "much used" but "seldom defined".[45] Those who assume it can be detached from justice tend to identify reconciliation with political coexistence based upon reciprocal recognition of common political rights that renounces lethal violence as a means of resolving political disputes. Bare political coexistence is of course radically different from the deep religious reconciliation that will take place in the Kingdom of God.

Salvadoran Pentecostals and conservative Catholics have strikingly different eschatologies, theologies of the "last things". The latter do not, for example, tend to view the world as radically hostile to faith or even as satanic. Yet both communities share the belief that the Kingdom of God is radically separate from this-worldly attempts to secure justice. Though they recognize that justice is better than injustice, both insist that Christians ought to promote forgiveness and political reconciliation even in the midst of perpetrator denial or self-justification.

Such a position can easily slide into the even stronger claim that reconciliation makes justice unnecessary and even irrelevant. God's action, not political manoeuvring, will establish true reconciliation. In this context, forgiveness – a sign of the virtue of charity (emphasized by Catholics) and of the working of the Holy Spirit (emphasized by Pentecostals) – provides a strong reinforcement for impunity. It is invoked to support the view that Christians ought to value political coexistence because gives the stability, order, and peace within which

44 Martin 1990: 284.
45 Van Antwerpen 2008, p. 46.

individuals can try to live the gospel. It regards the attempt to pursue justice is a threat to these goods when it disrupts social harmony;[46] indeed, it can regard justice as the enemy of reconciliation. This was especially the case in El Salvador during the repression, when any appeal to "justice" was regarded as inherently "political", but it continues to be seen in El Salvador today.

There are obvious differences between political coexistence and the fullness of eschatological reconciliation,[47] yet there are biblical and theological reasons for challenging the assumption that justice in the present dispensation has little or nothing to do with eschatological reconciliation. There are strong biblical reasons for regarding the Kingdom of God as the divine fulfillment of human history "on earth as it is in heaven".

The in-breaking of the Kingdom refers to the working of the divine will in real if fragile and flawed human communities here and now, a movement that makes the Kingdom "already" but "not yet".[48] As Biblical scholar N. T. Wright puts it, the meaning and message of Jesus was not about "rescuing individual souls from the world but about saving humans so that they could become part of his project of saving the world."[49] The hope of the Gospels is the same hope expressed in Ephesians 1, Romans 8, and Revelation 21, Wright maintains, "for the renewal and final coming together of heaven and earth, the consummation precisely of God's project to be savingly present in an ultimate public world."

Christians are thus called to live in light of a Kingdom that is both "already" and "not yet." Those who see no relation between the present and the future achievement of reconciliation ignore the "already". Those who ignore the "not yet" are prone to identify them. Respecting the dialectical tension between "already" and "not yet" allows us to see both connections and differences between justice here and the Kingdom of God. The dialectical tension energizes those who affirm what theologian Peter Phan calls "Christian political spirituality" that is "oriented to the Kingdom of God, lived out not away from but within history and the world, animated by the preferential option for the poor and a willing acceptance of persecution and even martyrdom, and actualized within the unity of contemplation and liberation."[50]

46 According to David Laitin, "Dualism in Christianity is certainly does not arise with Pentecostalism. In fact, the distinction between God's way and the way of the world is part of a long tradition that includes Augustine's sharp disjuncture between the city of God and the city of man and the Lutheran notion of two kingdoms. While Salvadoran Pentecostals might have never read Augustine or even Luther, they stand within this tradition. Drawing from Weber, we might say that high theology is translated into a "practical religion" that informs personal ethos at a particular time." Laitin 1978: 563–92. Laitin's characterization of Augustine and Luther is not uncontroversial.

47 See Walls 2000.

48 See Jeremias 2002 and Jeremias 1997.

49 Wright 2008, at www.christiancentury.org/article.lasso?id=4862, accessed January 15, 2010.

50 Phan 2007: 27.

Desiring to cooperate with grace in order to pursue the divine *telos* of human history generates an existential concern for an integral human development based on justice. As the Pastoral Constitution on the Church in the Modern World put it, through their work in the world, people have been "contributing by their personal industry to the realization in history of the divine plan".[51] Though "we must be careful to distinguish earthly progress clearly from the increase of the kingdom of Christ, such progress is of vital concern to the kingdom of God, insofar as it can contribute to the better ordering of human society."[52] This position – one that deeply influenced Archbishop Romero and the Jesuits of the UCA – regards impunity as radically opposed to the Kingdom in the way that it both denigrates victims and facilitates future injustice. In the midst of intense repression, Romero expressed hope that the church and government could be reconciled but under conditions of justice that would have minimally to include, "an explanation of what has happened to the many citizens who have disappeared, an end to arbitrary arrests and torture."[53]

A balanced and partially realized Christian eschatology--one living in the tension between the "already" and "not yet"--can regard the slow process of creating conditions that encourage a growing sense of social cooperation, shared identity, and social trust as contributing, if only in modest and partial ways, to the realization of God's will on earth. This is not, of course, to say that social reformers are "constructing" the Kingdom of God as if it were yet another human institution. As John Fuellenbach notes, "we cannot create or build the kingdom of God. It is God's work and gracious gift, but our actions make a difference … We are God's cooperators, but the kingdom remains God's until its final coming."[54]

We co-operate with God's will by restructuring relationships so that they are characterized by peace based on justice. What this means concretely can be seen in the approach to reconciliation and justice advocated by the leadership of the Central American Province of the Society of Jesus.[55] The Jesuit rector of the UCA, José María Tojeira, S.J., is rightly concerned that the appeal to forgiveness has been used as a way of encouraging passivity: "Since there are clear responsibilities in the commission of a crime," he points out, "no one can say

51 Paul VI 1965. See also Paul VI 1975: no. 13. John Paul II continued this message when he wrote: building the kingdom means working for liberation from evil in all its forms … The Kingdom of God is the manifestation and realization of God's plan of salvation in all its fullness." In John Paul II 1990, available at www.vatican.va/holy_father/john_paul_ii/encyclicals/documents/hf_jp-ii_enc_07121990_redemptoris-missio_en.html, accessed January 16, 2010.

52 Paul VI 1965: no. 39.

53 Romero 1985: 83. Romero lamented that the "national crisis" was in part based on the fact that "so many fearful crimes go unpunished, a good number of them carried out either openly or, it is popularly reported, in civilian disguise by the security forces." Ibid.: 123.

54 In Fuellenbach 1995: 34.

55 See Pope 2003.

that doing justice should be left to God, an affirmation trying to eliminate human justice."[56]

The judicial process is the normal means for securing public accountability and victim vindication. A judge from a Salvadoran lower court ruled in 2000 that the amnesty law cannot be used to protect public officials who ordered the UCA massacre because the Salvadoran constitution does not allow self-amnesty. Nevertheless, the judge also ruled that the crimes can no longer be prosecuted because they fall outside the ten year statute of limitations. This decision to close the case on the basis of the stature of limitations was upheld on appeal in 2001.[57] The key legal issue concerns whether the amnesty is still binding and whether the statute of limitations can protect perpetrators of crimes against humanity.

While not all cases of human rights violations can be resolved through judicial processes, it is important, when possible, to "proceed with clarity and determination in those cases where there is reasonable evidence of responsibility."[58] Tojeira maintains that prosecuting criminals helps to strengthen the rule of law, build up the common good, affirm the dignity of the direct and indirect victims, and promote the rehabilitation of offenders.[59]

Tojeira and the Jesuit community have for some time supported post-conviction pardons for the intellectual authors of the UCA massacre.[60] What theologian Nigel Biggar claims about transitional justice in South Africa and Northern Ireland also applies to El Salvador: "justice is primarily not about the punishment of the perpetrator, but about the vindication of the victims, both direct and indirect."[61] There is no contradiction between extending personal forgiveness to perpetrators and pursuing public justice in the courts in a way that can both "correct the victimizers" and "restore dignity to the victims". Public accountability through trials not only vindicates victims – it can also help them forgive, particularly if perpetrators are repentant. Moreover, Sobrino notes, authentic forgiveness works for the healing of the community through

56 See posting at the University of Central America website from April 26, 2000 entitled, "The Central American University 'Jose Simeón Canas' (UCA) refutes the resolution made by the Attorney General of the Republic in regards to the Jesuits' case," at www.uca.edu.sv/nuevo/fgrenglish.html, accessed January 2, 2010.

57 See U.S. Department of State, Report on Religious Freedom, El Salvador, 2001, at www.state.gov/g/drl/rls/irf/2001/5639.htm, accessed January 18, 2010.

58 Ibid, "Central American University."

59 The Jesuits have said they will not support the Spanish prosecution of the intellectual authors of the UCA massacre because they believe that justice is best accomplished in El Salvador. They want the government of El Salvador to take responsibility and publicly to recognize the intellectual authors of the crime. Tojeira explained that the Jesuits "will not participate in those judicial activities that go beyond the framework of the Salvadoran legal system or international obligations deriving from pacts or treaties signed by El Salvador." In Humphrey 1998, at http://ncronline.org/node/2587, accessed January 3, 2010.

60 See Christian 1991, at www.nytimes.com/1991/10/06/world/jesuits-won-t-reject-amnesty-in-salvador-killings.html?pagewanted=1, accessed January 16, 2010.

61 Biggar 2003: 7.

encouraging both the conversion of individual sinners and the transformation of the social structures from which oppressors have benefited.[62]

Restructuring relationships is best pursued by promoting justice not only by means of publicly vindicating victims but also by working for the structural reform of political-legal and socio-economic institutions. The true test of social reconciliation must be how well victims of violent repression have been reincorporated into their local communities and into the wider Salvadoran society. Reincorporation cannot be accomplished simply by religious leaders exhorting people to forgive and be reconciled, but also through capacity building and the empowerment of the victims. Justice in El Salvador must thus include social recognition of the dignity of victims and their communities through the provision of educational and employment opportunities, mental health resources, and compensation for human rights abuses.[63] Reparations are a necessary component of reconciliation based on justice, and certainly do more for victims than does the punishment of their tormentors. Trials, truth commissions, and appeals to forgiveness typically focus on individual perpetrators and victims in ways that can obscure the need for society as a whole to take responsibility for broad structural and institutional reforms. Victims' groups and other NGOs cannot be the sole advocates for justice to victims, especially in places like El Salvador where such groups tend to be relatively weak.

5. LIBERAL DEMOCRACY AND CHRISTIAN RECONCILIATION

Objections to the claim that the church ought to promote reconciliation through justice come from two directions: liberal critics of reconciliation and religious critics of liberalism. First, liberal critics of reconciliation such as Amy Gutman and Dennis Thompson[64] maintain that the language of reconciliation is religiously and morally overbearing and parochial. While some human rights activists are happy to use a secularized interpretation of reconciliation, they would prefer dropping the notion altogether. The language of rights is sufficient, they think, to give moral legitimacy and direction for the consolidation of democracy in pluralistic societies.

One can respond to this criticism by arguing that some forms of liberalism recognize that pluralistic democracies can be based on a moral consensus about fundamental human values. These values can include the humanly intelligible goals of social and political reconciliation without having also to embrace a religiously substantive account of reconciliation. Even those who eschew any

62 See Sobrino 1986.
63 See Lira 2006.
64 Gutman and Thompson 2004: ch. 6.

transcendent source of human transformation often recognize, for example, the moral depth of reconciliation attained through the sincere extension of forgiveness to a contrite perpetrator.[65]

Daniel Philpott maintains that reconciliation can be employed within a chastened approach to liberal democracy that would be willing to "renounce any strong requirements for 'public reason' and be open to importing into the political order concepts whose roots lay in theology or other comprehensive conceptions."[66] Just as contemporary moral culture includes respect for human rights, so it can be expanded, on the basis of an account of what allows communities to flourish, to endorse reconciliation with justice. The church can participate in public discourse in a way that expands the wider society's understanding of both reconciliation and justice. In Catholic terms, "natural law" discourse about these moral standards can inform public dialogue.

A second criticism, coming from the opposite direction, holds that the church should not allow herself to be compromised by endorsing the liberal version of justice that characterizes the contemporary nation-state. This view holds that the church's endorsement of the kind of thin political reconciliation pursued by truth commissions put her at risk of political manipulation and of confusing Christians about the divine basis of eschatological reconciliation. Instead of underwriting a secular pseudo-reconciliation, the church ought to place her energies in learning how to be a reconciled community – something the church is not today, especially in El Salvador – so that she can stand as a witness to the gospel and as a sign of contradiction to the pseudo-peace offered by the nation-state.

In response one can say that it is simplistic to dismiss "the" liberal version of justice. There are multiple and competing views of justice in liberalism and the church can and must be selective regarding which versions of justice she will endorse. Despite its problems, El Salvador has become a relatively more just society by attempting to incorporate important features of liberal democracy, including separation of powers, respect for human rights, and religious pluralism. Pseudo-reconciliation is of course a danger in both church and society. It is possible, moreover, to maintain that the church's first priority ought to be to work to become a more reconciled community while also advocating public measures promoting social and political reconciliation. Far from competing, the former in fact reinforces the latter.

---

65 See, for example, the case of South African Ginn Fourie's forgiveness of Letlapa Mphahlete described at The Forgiveness Project, www.theforgivenessproject.com/stories/fourie-letlapa, accessed January 7, 2010. On social scientific, non-religious approaches to forgiveness, see Worthington 2005.

66 Philpott 2006: 41.

6. CONCLUSION

We can conclude by noting some important dimensions of the claim that justice is a critically necessary component of the path to reconciliation. The Christian call to attend to the "least" of our brothers and sisters implies that the church has a special role in not allowing society at large and political elites in particular to forget about victims or unfairly to subordinate their well-being to that of more privileged classes. This means, negatively, that we must beware of ways in which "cheap forgiveness" can be high-jacked by powers that want, as Alfredo Cristiani put it, "to erase, eliminate and forget everything in the past".[67] At the very least, Christian ethics ought to resist being co-opted by those who seek to protect perpetrators' anonymity, immunity, and purported moral legitimacy.

Retaining the centrality of justice within the commitment to reconciliation also means, positively, that the church will play a limited but real role in promoting reconciliation to the extent that she embraces her mission of being, as Archbishop Oscar Romero put it, a "voice for the voiceless". More importantly, though, the church would do even better to learn how to function as a community in which victims can speak with their own voices and in ways that are heard and respected within both church and society. For either to happen, the church must not allow the ideal of unity, social harmony, and communion to tempt her to ignore injustice, avoid conflict, and fear "taking sides" in when morally necessary. The church is to be a sign of unity, but, as Romero put it, "we cannot, as the price of this unity, abandon our mission."[68] The church's recognition of the centrality of solidarity implies that reconciliation ought to be pursued only in and through means that acknowledge the dignity of victims, their right to public vindication, and society's responsibility to provide resources that can assist in their healing. Under these conditions, Philpott is right to claim that reconciliation is the goal around which religious voices ought to converge.

We can conclude with a positive note. El Salvador continues to be polarized but there are hopeful signs. Young people are increasingly becoming personally involved in international solidarity as pilgrims, volunteers, and advocates.[69] The new Archbishop of San Salvador, Msgr. Luis Escobar Alas, has pledged to continue the legacy of Oscar Romero's commitment to justice for the poor. The church has recently led the country's opposition to gold mining, a practice that has already devastated the environment of many locations in central America and had an especially negative impact on the poor.

The current president, Mauricio Funes of the FMLN, has publically recognized the UCA massacre as a crime that needs to be investigated. He has

---

67 Presidential Address to the Nation (March 18, 1993), cited in Popkin 2000: 150.

68 Romero 1985: 81.

69 See Brackley 2009 at www.romerotrust.org.uk/crossres.pdf, *accessed January 18, 2010.*

apologized for the government's abuse of human rights during the war,[70] acknowledges the futility of attempting to achieve reconciliation without justice, and announced that he intends to cooperate with the Interamerican Court for Human Right's 2000 recommendation to prosecute the perpetrators of the Romero murder and to make reparations to surviving victims. He has also publically acknowledged that the government of El Salvador was guilty of protecting, collaborating with, or even participating in the work of the death squad that murdered the archbishop.[71] Most impressive of all, there are many grassroots organizations that continue to accompany the struggling people of El Salvador who will not give up on the quest for justice and human dignity. When the voices of these people converge on reconciliation, we will know that thc culture of impunity has been defeated.[72]

REFERENCES

Americas Watch (1991). *El Salvador's Decade of Terror: Human Rights since the Assassination of Archbishop Romero.* New York, NY: Yale University Press.

Arana, Ana (2005). How the Street Gangs Took Central America. *Foreign Affairs* 84, 98–110.

Azevedo, Marcello de C. (1993). Basic Ecclesial Communities. In *Mysterium Liberationis: Fundamental Concepts of Liberation Theology*, edited by Ignacio Ellacuría and Jon Sobrino,. Maryknoll, NY: Orbis Books, 636–653.

Barnes, William A (1998). Incomplete Democracy in Central America: Polarization and Voter Turnout in Nicaragua and El Salvador. *Journal of Interamerican Studies* 40(3), 63–101.

Betances, Emilio (2007). *The Catholic Church and Power Politics in Latin America: The Dominican Case in Comparative Perspective.* Lanham, MD: Rowman & Littlefield.

Biggar, Nigel, ed. (2003). *Burying the Past: Making Peace and Doing Justice after Civil Conflict.* Washington, D.C.: Georgetown University Press.

Binford, Leigh, ed. (2004). *Landscapes of Struggle: Politics, Society, and Community in El Salvador.* Pittsburgh, PA: University of Pittsburgh Press.

Brackley, Dean (2009). Crosses and Resurrections; Good News from Central America. 2009 Romero Lecture, Edinburgh. www.romerotrust.org.uk/crossres.pdf (accessed January 18, 2010).

Brett, Edward T. (2008). Archbishop Arturo Rivera y Damas and the Struggle for Social Justice. *The Catholic Historical Review* 94, 717–739.

Brockman, James R (1989). *Romero: A Life.* Maryknoll, NY: Orbis Books.

---

70 Emilio San Pedro, "El Salvador President Mauricio Funes in Abuse Apology," BBC, January 17, 2010, at http://news.bbc.co.uk/2/hi/americas/8463929.stm, accessed January 18, 2010.

71 See BBC, "Official El Salvador Apology for Oscar Romero's Murder," March 25, 2010, at http://news.bbc.co.uk/2/hi/8586560.stm, accessed April 25, 2011.

72 Thanks to Barbara Pope, Thomas Kelly, J. Donald Monan, S.J., for helpful feedback on this paper.

BTI Country Report: El Salvador. Shaping Change – Strategies of Development and Transformation." Bertelsmann Stiftung. www.bertelsmann-transformation-index.de/en/ (accessed January 23, 2010).

Cardenal, Rodolfo (1990). The Martyrdom of the Salvadorean Church. In *Church and Politics in Latin America*, edited by Dermot Keogh, London, England: Macmillan, 225–246.

Catholic News Agency (2009). Benedict XVI Cautions against Dangers of Marxist Liberation Theology. December 7. www.catholicnewsagency.com/news/benedict_xvi_cautions_against_dangers_of_marxist_liberation_theology (accessed January 7, 2010).

Christian, Shirley (1991). Jesuits Won't Reject Amnesty in Salvador Killings. *New York Times*, October 6. www.nytimes.com/1991/10/06/world/jesuits-won-t-reject-amnesty-in-salvador-killings.html?pagewanted=1 (accessed January 16, 2010).

Congregation for the Doctrine of the Faith (1986). Instruction on Christian Freedom and Liberation. Vatican website, March 22, 1986. www.vatican.va/roman_curia/congregations/cfaith/documents/rc_con_cfaith_doc_19860322_freedom-liberation_en.html (accessed January 14, 2010).

CNN (2005). Former Salvadoran Official Held Liable for Torture Jury Awards $6 Million to Four Victims. November 19, 2005. www.cnn.com/2005/LAW/11/19/torture.trial.ap (accessed January 1, 2009).

De la Serna, Eduardo (2005). The Crisis of Christianity in Latin America. In *Christianity in Crisis?*, edited by Jon Sobrino and Felix Wilfred. London, England: SCM Press, 84–88.

Dewirst, Polly (2010). Frozen Emotions: Women's Experience of Violence and Trauma in El Salvador, Kenya and Rwanda. *Development Update 2.2*, (January 14, 2010), www.dsvr.org.za/index.php?option=com_content&task=view&id=562.

Doggett, Martha (1993). *Death Foretold: The Jesuit Murders in El Salvador.* Washington D.C.: Georgetown University Press.

Encyclopedia of the Nations s.v. El Salvador – Poverty and Wealth, (January 3, 2010), www.nationsencyclopedia.com/economies/Americas/El-Salvador-POVERTY-AND-WEALTH.html.

Fuellenbach, John (1995). *The Kingdom of God: The Message of Jesus Today.* Maryknoll, NY: Orbis Books.

Galdámez, Pablo (1986). *Faith of a People: The Story of a Christian Community in El Salvador, 1970–1980.* Maryknoll. NY: Orbis Books.

Gomez, Medardo Ernesto (1990). *Fire against Fire: Christian Ministry Face-to-Face with Persecution.* Minneapolis, MN: Fortress.

Grenier, Yvon (1990). *The Emergence of Insurgency in El Salvador: Ideology and Political Will.* Pittsburgh, PA: University of Pittsburgh Press.

Gutierrez, Gustavo (1993). Option for the Poor. In *Mysterium Liberationis*, edited by Ignacio Ellacuría and Jon Sobrino, Maryknoll, NY: Orbis Books, 244.

Gutman, Amy and Dennis Thompson (2004). *Why Deliberative Democracy?* Princeton, NJ: Princeton University Press.

Hauerwas, Stanley (1991). *After Christendom?*. Nashville, TN: Abingdon.

Hearn, Rebekah (2009). Memphian Carrana Found Guilty of Human Rights Abuses. *The Memphis Daily News*, March 19, 2009.

Humphrey, Michael (2008). Salvador Archbishop: Don't Reopen Murder Cases. *National Catholic Reporter*, November 18, 2008. http://ncronline.org/node/2587 (accessed January 3, 2010).

Jeremias, Joachim (2002). *Jesus and the Message of the New Testament*. Minneapolis, MN: Fortress.

Jeremias, Joachim (1977). *New Testament Theology: The Proclamation of Jesus*. New York, NY: Charles Scribners' Sons.

John Paul II (1990). *Redemptoris Missio*. Vatican website. December 7, 1990. www.vatican.va/holy_father/john_paul_ii/encyclicals/documents/hf_jp-ii_enc_07121990_redemptoris-missio_en.html (accessed January 16, 2010).

Johnson, Marianne (2000). The Hand of Opus Dei in El Salvador. *The Tablet*, November 18, 2000. www.thetablet.co.uk/article/6873 (accessed January 7, 2010).

Jones, L. Gregory, ed. (2000). *Theology and Eschatology at the Turn of the Millennium*. Malden, MA: Blackwell.

Klaiber, Jeffrey (1998). *The Church, Dictatorships, and Democracy in Latin America*. Maryknoll, NY: Orbis Books.

Laitin, David (1978). Religion, Political Culture, and the Weberian Tradition. *World Politics* 30(4), 563–592.

Latin American Herald Tribune (2009). Massacre of Jesuits in El Salvador 'Premeditated'. *Latin American Herald Tribune*, November 30, 2009.

Lee, Bernard J. (2000). *The Catholic Experience of Small Christian Communities*. Mahwah, NJ: Paulist.

Lira, Eizabeth (2006). The Reparations Policy for Human Rights Violations in Chile. In *Handbook of Reparations*, edited by Pablo de Greiff. New York, NY: Oxford University Press, 55–102.

Macchia, Frank D (2008). Pentecostal and Charismatic Theology. In *The Oxford Handbook of Eschatology*, edited by Jerry L. Walls. New York, NY: Oxford University Press, 280–294.

Martin, David (1990). *Tongues of Fire: The Explosion of Protestantism in Latin America*. Oxford: Basil Blackwell.

Montgomery, Tommie Sue, (1995). *Revolution in El Salvador: Origins and Evolution*. second ed. Boulder, CO: Westview Press.

Noone, Judith M (1995). *The Same Fate as the Poor*. Maryknoll, NY: Orbis Books.

Organization of American States. "Human Rights." OAS. www.oas.org/en/topics/human_rights.asp (accessed January 7, 2010).

Paul VI (1965). *Gaudium et Spes*. Second Vatican Council, December 7, 1965.

Paul VI. (1975). *Evangelii Nuntiandi*. Apostolic exhortation, December 8, 1975.

Peterson, Anna L (1997). *Martyrdom and the Politics of Religion: Progressive Catholicism in El Salvador's Civil War*. Albany, NY: SUNY.

Phan, Peter (2007). Christian Social Spirituality: A Global Perspective. In *Catholic Social Justice: Theological and Practical Explorations*, edited by Philomena Cullen, Barnard Hoose, and Gerard Mannion, New York, NY: Continuum, 27.

Philpott, Daniel (2007). Religion, Reconciliation, and Retributive Justice: The State of the Field. *SSRC Working Papers*, (October 12, 2007), www.global.ucsb.edu/orfaleacenter/luce/luce08/documents/Philpott_SSRC-working-paper.pdf.

Philpott, Daniel (2006). *The Politics of Past Evil: Religion, Reconciliation, and the Dilemmas of Transitional Justice*. Notre Dame, IN: University of Notre Dame Press.

Planchart, Reinaldo Figueredo and Thomas Buergenthal (1993). From Madness to Hope: the 12-year war in El Salvador: Report of the Commission on the Truth for El Salvador. *United States Institute of Peace*, www.usip.org/files/file/ElSalvador-Report.pdf.

Pope, Stephen J (2003). The Convergence of Forgiveness and Justice: Lessons from El Salvador. *Theological Studies* 64: 812–835.

Popkin, Margaret (2000). *Peace without Justice: Obstacles to Building the Rule of Law in El Salvador.* University Park, PA: Pennsylvania State University Press.

Preston, Julia (2005). Ex-Salvadoran Colonel is Ordered to Pay for Crimes Against Humanity. *New York Times*, November 19.

Romero, Oscar Arnulfo (1985). *Voices of the Voiceless: The Four Pastoral Letters and Other Statements*. Maryknoll, NY: Orbis Books.

San Pedro, Emilio (2010). El Salvador President Mauricio Funes in Abuse Apology. *BBC*, January 17. http://news.bbc.co.uk/2/hi/americas/8463929.stm (accessed January 18, 2010).

Seider, Rachel and Patrick Costello (1996). "Judicial Reform in Central America: Prospects for the Rule of Law." In *Central America: Fragile Transition*, edited by Rachel Seider, London, England: Harper Collins/ILAS, 170–171, 182–192.

Segovia, Alexander (2006). The Reparations Proposals of the Truth Commissions in El Salvador and Haiti: A History of Non-Compliance. In *The Handbook of Reparations*, edited by Pablo de Grieff. New York, NY: Oxford University Press.

Sobrino, Jon. (1986). Latin America: Place of Sin and Place of Forgiveness. In *Forgiveness*, edited by Casiano Floristán, Christian Duquoc, and Marcus Lefébure, Edinburgh: T&T Cark, 45–56.

Sobrino, Jon. (2003), *Witnesses to the Kingdom: The Martyrs of El Salvador and the Crucified Peoples*. Maryknoll, NY: Orbis Books.

Sobrino, Jon, and Ignacio Ellacuría (1990). *Companions of Jesus: The Jesuit Martyrs of El Salvador.* Maryknoll, NY: Orbis Books.

Stout, Jeffrey (2004). *Democracy and Tradition*. Princeton, NJ: Princeton University Press.

Strocka, Cordula (2006). Youth Gangs in Latin America. *SAIS Review* 26.2 (2006), 133–146.

Terrazas, Aaron. Salvadoran Immigrants in the United States. Migration Policy Institute. www.migrationinformation.org/USFocus/display.cfm?id=765 (accessed January 7, 2010).

Tombs, David (2006). Unspeakable Violence: The UN Truth Commissions on El Salvador and Guatemala. In *Reconciliation, Nations, and Churches in Latin America*, edited by Iain Maclean. Aldershot, England: Ashgate, 2006, 64–67.

Tutu, Desmond Mpilo (1999). *No Future Without Forgiveness*. New York, NY: Doubleday.

University of Central America (2000). The Central American University 'Jose Simeón Canas' (UCA) refutes the solution made by the Attorney General of the Republic in regards to the Jesuits' case. April 26, 2000. www.uca.edu.sv/nuevo/fgrenglish.html (accessed January 2, 2010).

U.S. Department of State (2001). *Report on Religious Freedom El Salvador 2001*, from Bureau of Democracy, Human Rights, and Labor. www.state.gov/g/drl/rls/irf/2001/5639.htm (accessed January 18, 2010).

Van Antwerpen, Jonathan (2008). Reconciliation Reconceived. In *The Politics of Reconciliation in Multicultural Societies*, edited by Will Kymlicka and Bashior Bashir. New York, NY: Oxford University Press, 2008.

Walls, Jerry L. ed. (2008). *The Oxford Handbook of Eschatology.* New York, NY: Oxford University Press.

Whitfield, Teresa (1994). *Paying the Price: Ignacio Ellacuría and the Murdered Jesuits of El Salvador.* Philadelphia, PA: Temple University Press.

Wilkinson, Tracy and Alex Renderos (2008). In El Salvador, a New Push for Justice in Priests' Slayings. *Los Angeles Times*, November 13.

Wilkinson, Tracy (2009). El Salvador Grapples with Rising Bloodshed. *Los Angeles Times*, May 13.

Williams, Philip J. (1998). The Sound of Tambourines: The Politics of Pentecostal Growth in El Salvador. In *Power, Politics, and Pentecostals in Latin America*, edited by Edward L. Cleary and Hannah W. Stewart. Westview Press, 1998.

Wood, Elisabeth Jean (20030. *Insurgent Collective Action and Civil War in El Salvador.* New York, NY: Cambridge University Press.

Worthington, Everett L., ed. (2005). *Handbook of Forgiveness.* New York, NY: Taylor & Francis.

Wright, N.T. (2008). Kingdom Come: The Public Meaning of the Gospels. *Christian Century*, June 17. www.christiancentury.org/article.lasso?id=4862 (accessed January 15, 2010).

PUBLIC FORGIVENESS AT THE BOUNDARY OF THE SECULAR AND THE RELIGIOUS

How do we read the terrain?

Robert SCHREITER

1. INTRODUCTION

One of the persistent challenges in post-conflict peace-building is negotiating the multiple frameworks out of which actors are working as they try to reconstruct societies together. Sometimes the differences are proper to the people who have been engaged in the conflict; indeed, differences in cognitive frameworks can be one of the causes of conflict itself. But alongside the participants in the conflict are those outside actors who enter the post-conflict zone to help build peace: international peacekeeping forces, NGOs, humanitarian organizations, expatriates, and other international institutions. Finding a way to translate principles and policies from one framework into another is now recognized as a major task that needs to be undertaken if peace-building is to be a successful and sustainable operation.

This chapter focuses on one such zone for translation; namely, the space where secular and religious frameworks meet in the post-conflict peace-building process. On the one hand, it has been widely recognized that such key concepts as forgiveness and reconciliation have – at least for the West – significant religious roots. But on the other hand the principles, policies and actions that flow from these concepts are not entirely congruous or even compatible with one another. There has developed a spectrum of positions regarding how – or even whether – secular and religious approaches to peace-building can work together. Some would argue that in rebuilding after conflict religion is as much the problem as it is the solution, and therefore should be excluded from the process. On this view, religion is seen as intrusive, coercive, and indifferent to certain matters of justice and of human suffering. On the other end of the spectrum, religion is seen as the most important component of peace-building. Attitudes toward Archbishop Desmond Tutu's deliberate use of Christian concepts and symbols in the sessions of the South African Truth and Reconciliation Commission are evidence of the array of opinions on the relation of the secular and the religious in peace-building.

What I will attempt to do here is explore some of the basic concepts that underlie one set of religious frameworks for peace-building, focusing on the concepts of reconciliation and forgiveness. I will try to translate these insights into a more secular discourse to show both their potential contributions and their limits. These references to potential contributions and limits will in some measure cut both ways: for religious as well as secular approaches. Communication across different cognitive frameworks requires this kind of two-way traffic. Religion has its biases and limits, but so do secular worldviews. Much of this more reflective approach to elements of political reconciliation and forgiveness is still in an early stage of conceptual development. Most of it is less than a half-century old. For that reason I believe much still needs to be learned.

The one set of religious frameworks is that of the Abrahamic faiths – Judaism, Christianity, and Islam. My principal focus will be on Christianity since, as a religious framework, it has at this point in time the most developed thought on this area.[1] It needs to be recognized that even among these faiths, there are differences amid many commonalities. If one were to look to East and South Asian traditions (the religions of India and Buddhism), or to more local ethnic traditions, the picture would be even more different.[2] To be able to include all of these religious traditions is simply beyond the scope of what can be done here.

The same case can be made for the "secular" sphere. It is widely acknowledged today that there are multiple modernities. With this multiplicity come overlapping, but not entirely coinciding, understandings of secularity. My focus here will be European concepts of secularity, although one can certainly ascertain differences even within that approach.

In the process of "translating" fundamental Christian concepts into secular discourse, I will be making reference to observations made by other authors in this book. In so doing I hope to give the presentation some cohesion and I hope a greater relevance to the questions of public forgiveness this book is addressing.

1 A leading figure in Jewish thought on this matter is Marc Gopin 2000. In Islam see especially the work of Mohammed Abu-Nimer 2003. For one set of Christian approaches, see Robert Schreiter, R. Scott Appleby, and Gerard Powers 2010.

2 Regarding Buddhism, see the history of the relationship between Nagase Taksashi and Eric Lomax, referred to by two other authors in this book. Van Roermund makes the helpful observation that a political theology underlies the position of the Abrahamic faiths, whereas one might construe Buddhism and especially ethnic traditions to have an "oiko-logy" at their base. I believe this to be the case.

2. RELIGIOUS VIEWS OF RECONCILIATION

In Christian faith, reconciliation is the more comprehensive conception within which forgiveness is to be understood. The direct references to reconciliation in the New Testament are few, but carry within them the narrative of God's purposes for the world. The key founding text is Romans 5:1–11, wherein Paul talks about how the world has been justified (that is, made right or put into right relation) to God by God's own action. God is the creator of the world, but humanity has turned away from God. But even in that turning away God did not cease to love humankind. Through the agency of his Son God has reconciled the world to God's very self. This reconciliation is effected by the forgiveness of sins. This process has been begun in the death and resurrection of his Son, Jesus Christ, and will only be completed at the end of time (cf. Eph 1:10) when all of creation will be gathered together in Christ.

In other passages, notably 2 Corinthians 5:17–20, Paul repeats this message but extends it further to say that this reconciling work has now been entrusted to those who follow Christ as a ministry of reconciliation. Thus, the reconciling work of God in Christ is to be continued in the world by the disciples of Jesus. They are "ambassadors for Christ's sake." (2 Cor 5: 20).

Out of this larger framework of the Christian understanding of reconciliation, I would like to bring forward three aspects that engage secular analogues in understanding the larger process of political reconciliation. They are: (1) the ec-centric or exocentric character of reconciliation and the logic that governs its discourse; (2) the ambivalent powers of narrative; and (3) negotiating constructs of suffering.

2.1. THE EXOCENTRIC CHARACTER OF RECONCILIATION

What does this narrative of creation – fall – redemption – reconciliation tell us about the Christian understanding of reconciliation processes? First of all, it gives the work of reconciliation a de-centered or exocentric character. Reconciliation cannot be adequately understood as solely a matter between two aggrieved parties. There are elements or actors at play that reach outside the immediate sphere of the two parties that must be taken into consideration. From the Christian perspective this outside or exocentric element has a transcendent character; there is a sense that every action worked by human beings against other human beings has repercussions far beyond the deed itself or the relationship between the actors: it reverberates into the very fabric of all creation and to the Creator. As such, God becomes an intrinsic actor in the repair of every form of human breach. Far more than that: it is only God who can encompass the implications of every human act in a way that can lead to repair of that breach. Reconciliation, therefore, has an intrinsically eccentric character since it is never just about the actions between discrete human beings or communities; it has to be understood in terms of its ontological or cosmic dimensions as well.

The capacity to reconcile, then, cannot be understood solely as a moral project, although the engagement of all the dimensions of our humanity is involved. Christians understand reconciliation as a gift from God, a gift freely given to a humanity that of itself cannot repair the breaches or heal the wounds that it has inflicted upon itself.

This quality of gift governs the logic of reconciliation. "Gift" is to be understood here not in the modern or postmodern sense of something given to another out of one's excess wealth, but as an exchange that is intended to set up a relationship. This particular relationship is not contingent upon a set of conditions or the moral achievements of humanity, but is unconditional in character. Here is where the "excess" resides. The unconditional character is offered not so much in light or moral responsibility as it is in light of an ontological teleology: human beings are made in the image and likeness of God (cf. Gen 1:26–27), thus having endless potential for good. Because of humans' fallen nature, however, they also have potential for evil.

Reconciliation in the instances in which it occurs is grounded both in a protology – of God as sovereign Creator – and an eschatology – of a completion of creation and a gathering together of all things together in God through the work of Jesus Christ. The experience of reconciliation is the experience of "new creation" (cf. 2 Cor 5:17): "if anyone is in Christ, there is a new creation." By that is meant that reconciliation is not simply a repair of breaches or healing of wounds as though they never happened. Rather, something new comes about that is in continuity with elements of the past but at the same time goes beyond them. The work of reconciliation occurs in what might be called "alternative social formations" or new social spaces that are created so that something different from the past might occur.

If gift is at the heart of the logic of reconciliation, then its action is marked by symbolic and ritual behavior. The deep ontological character of reconciliation cannot be described or explained adequately by instrumentalist thinking and behavior. Symbol is used here in the sense of something that participates in the reality it points to and represents; ritual is understood as those recurrent and recursive patterns of making and maintaining meaning.

All of this may appear at first glance to be quite distant from the practicalities of post-conflict peace-building in its political, juridical, or programmatic character. It bespeaks perhaps too an anthropology that is not at home in a secular sphere. It breathes through the "porous self" between the seen and the unseen world that Charles Taylor talks about in his work on a secular age.[3] It may seem to compromise human autonomy and a discourse of human rights. It

3 Taylor 2007: 37–41.

can be used to allay the pursuit of justice. It may appear to be crouching beneath the canopy of an ambivalent if not outrightly oppressive master narrative. But to see it only in such a light misses the purpose, or perhaps the level on which this discourse of reconciliation is trying to operate. Two recurrent experiences in post-conflict reconstruction appear to corroborate a vision of an exocentric reconciliation such as this one.

First of all, there is sheer enormity and complexity of the project of reconstruction, especially after protracted conflict. It is not simply a matter of resolving the issues that triggered the conflict, since those issues have since metastasized into rhizomes of complexity. Those issues have often also been nurtured by a host of other causes, twists and turns of manipulative use of power, grudges and remembered grievances. Poverty and social oppression, for example, feed into many of the conflicts of the world. As a result disentangling the threads that have become knotted together in the fabric of conflict is a formidable one. Conflicts, and post-conflict resolutions, often get "stuck". Margaret Smith's description of the peace process in Northern Ireland is a good example of this. Those who work in conflict transformation have come to stress the non-linearity of post-conflict work and the need for what John Paul Lederach has called a "moral imagination" that allows one to see the conflict on terms other than those pronounced by the conflicted parties involved.[4] For him the moral imagination means a capacity to see paradox where others see polarities; to imagine a future where there is a place for both me and my enemies; a place where creativity and risk can be engaged. One needs, in other words, a larger vision out of which new possibilities can emerge beyond the more narrow set of rules that arises out of protracted conflict. One needs a view of the potential and the limits of human beings and the communities they create. One needs some kind of overarching narrative out of which one operates – something Margaret Smith refers to as a "superordinate sense of identity."

Second, the tropes of a discourse of reconciliation do not entirely reduce themselves to the precision of logic or the careful exactitudes of law. They communicate more with the aporia out of which both logic and law must sometimes operate and try to negotiate. (Here Veraart, citing Böckenförde, notes that the liberal state rests on premises that it cannot guarantee.) How do we make punishment commensurate with the crime committed? Why do we insist on actions of reparation that do not bring back the dead? Here the language of ritual, sacrifice, expiation, and atonement – all of which (except perhaps ritual) are problematic to Western minds – comes into play. All of these bespeak protocols that have played themselves out in a host of cultures through history, but remain obscure or even obscurantist today for secular people. They try to bridge our immediate, perceptible situation with those transcendent realities

4 Lederach 2005.

that come into play when we deal with irretrievable loss, crushing contradiction, and unbounded suffering.

So can some boundary be drawn between the religious and the secular in contemporary peace-building? In keeping with the sentiment that we are working here with paradox rather than polarities, we see the boundary not as a clean and clear demarcation, but "overlapping, entangled, and mutually reinforcing",[5] a shared struggle to understand reconciliation. In other words, the boundary is not sharply defined. Appeals on the part of secular parties to principles such as universal human rights represent an exocentric approach to reconciliation as well. Consequently, the moral approach, seen philosophically, politically, or judicially, can have considerable depth. A religious approach might be particularly helpful in supplying that transcendent or ontological dimension upon which a moral approach can rest.

2.2. THE AMBIVALENCES OF NARRATIVE

Narratives play a central role in reconciliation processes. Narratives carry identities and help define the identities of the actors in the process. They also carry accounts of the conflict itself: how it began, how it progressed, and how we have been brought to the point where we find ourselves now. Narrative is the forum where memory and forgetting – key elements in the forgiveness process – are lodged.

The role of narrative is acknowledged at a number of points in the reconciliation process. It is important in truth recovery processes if such are initiated. Victims' or survivors' recounting of what has happened to them can have, as Margaret Smith has pointed out, a cathartic value, inasmuch as silence is broken about past events and truth is acknowledged. Narratives can also counter other, "official narratives", as victims and survivors tell their stories to put the lie to oppressors' versions of what has happened. But perhaps most importantly, the transformation of group narratives, in what has been called in light of the experience of the South African TRC "dialogical" truth, into a more encompassing narrative that respects and includes the narratives of both or all contested parties. It is essential for creating a new, common, and single narrative that makes for a peaceable future.

Narratives of victimhood can be initially empowering to victims, but can also lock them into an identity that does not provide release from suffering. They can make further change impossible. Especially when such narratives are transmitted to the next and subsequent generations, they can become toxic for those who carry these narratives. So there is an ambivalence about the power of narrative since it can be both constructive and destructive. The same narrative

5 Stephen Pope in his chapter in this volume, quoting Jonathan Van Antwerpen.

can, at different times, carry each of these qualities and, for some parties, carry them both at the same time.

The Christian narrative of reconciliation moves through creation – fall – redemption – and consummation. In so doing, it offers an anthropological model of creation being essentially good (thus redeemable at future points), fallen into different levels of wrongdoing, but then rescued from alienation and then transformed (not simply returning to the prior state) and eventually reunited with its Creator. Told from the perspective of the transcendent or superordinate perspective, it also offers a map or trajectory for wrongdoers and even for victims. Particularly in dealing with the mysterious moment of redemption and transformation, it attempts to chart a path whereby the past is acknowledged and recognized, but wherein the past does not continue to define the present and the future. What the German theologian Johann Baptist Metz has called the "dangerous memory" of Jesus Christ throws a perspective on even the most abject suffering so as not to allow that suffering to define utterly the victim.[6] The victim can be rescued and transformed – as can the wrongdoer. In a secular perspective, this can generate the energy and sustain the hope that provide the conditions of possibility for political reconciliation. As should be evident, a Christian or religious narrative does not necessarily stand over against a possible secular narrative. Indeed, they often share commonalities (such as a commitment to the dignity of the human person). Differences may come, rather, in how encompassing the narrative is intended to be as it connects with the basic commitments of the parties concerned.

2.3. NEGOTIATING CONSTRUCTS OF SUFFERING

This might be seen as a subset within the power of narrative. Suffering in itself is not ennobling; left to its own deserts, suffering is destructive of human beings. It is the relationship to that suffering, in acts of resistance and resilience, that can overcome the toxicity of suffering. Such constructs can provide a trajectory that leads to transformation.

Narratives of victimhood that leave victims as victims may be important in early stages in order to acknowledge the injury that victims have undergone. But over time, if there is no narrative out of the cycle of suffering, it breeds only a festering resentment once the heuristic power of anger has been exhausted. If narratives of victimhood end in defeat, they are doubly destructive since they sap the dignity of the victim and hinder future moral agency.

Perhaps the most important construct that Christianity offers for overcoming suffering is placing one's own narrative of suffering in the narrative of the suffering, death, and resurrection of Jesus. Jesus was innocent and did not

6 Metz 1970.

deserve to suffer. However, he took on suffering to be in solidarity with those who suffer. God did not abandon him, but raised him up to new, transformative life.

Adopting this narrative of Jesus is an act of resilience. Resilience is developed and maintained by referring to a foundational story that helps protect the dignity and the humanity of those who suffer. It takes the current narrative of suffering and relocates it in a foundational narrative. In so doing, a new perspective can be gained on one's own suffering.

Another construct for suffering that Christian reconciliation offers is ultimate justice. At the end of time justice will be done to all those who received imperfect or even no justice in this world. All things will be brought together in Christ, and "God will be all in all" (1 Cor 15:28). This is the final act in the narrative that serves as the ontological foundation for the Christian understanding of reconciliation.

It would be fair to say that narratives, from a structural point of view, do not differ significantly in religious or secular usages. The content – actors, episodes, and resolution – will be different inasmuch as their frameworks allow and disallow certain content. One place where differences between a religious and a secular point of view may arise in a preference for analytic approaches that rely on *Realpolitik*, in which balancing of powers takes precedence over the constructions of narrative. Religious approaches, in general, are likely to adhere more closely to narrative.

3. FORGIVENESS

Christian forgiveness shares in the same religious narrative and framework as does reconciliation. In this understanding, forgiveness is both a process and a moment in the larger sphere of reconciliation. God is the author of forgiveness and the only one capable of comprehending what needs to be forgiven and the consequences of forgiveness. God's forgiveness is unbounded inasmuch as it grows out of God's unconditional love, his mercy or *hesed*. We as God's creatures are called to participate in that work of forgiveness, since we have been recipients of that love. Here I would like to single out three dimensions of public forgiveness that have been much discussed and trace as best I can the boundaries between religious and secular forgiveness here. These are: (1) Are there unforgivable deeds? (2) Can groups forgive? (3) Does forgiveness require apology and repentance?

3.1. ARE THERE UNFORGIVABLE DEEDS?

The violence of the twentieth century, and especially the Holocaust, has raised the question of whether there are certain acts or deeds that are unforgivable. When we are in the presence of what Hannah Arendt has called "radical evil"[7] or deeds that are deemed "unspeakable" inasmuch as they overwhelm our capacity for articulation, can these be forgiven? And even if they can, should they be forgiven?

This has been a matter of considerable debate – again especially around the Holocaust with its prototypical icon, Auschwitz, as a place of calculated, sustained acts of evil. Any suggestion of forgiveness in such settings would mean mitigation or condonation in some measure of what happened there.

In the Christian vision there is but one sin that cannot be forgiven, what is called "the sin against the Holy Spirit" (Matthew 12:31–32). The idea that all other sins can be forgiven grows out of the belief that to limit God's power to forgive is to limit God's sovereignty over what God has created. It is to make God less than God, and in the process to diminish his unconditional love and offer of forgiveness. In the Gospels, Jesus proclaims that the only sin that cannot be forgiven is the sin against the Holy Spirit. Jesus does not go on to explain just what that sin might be. Commentators through history have suggested that it consists in believing that there are sins God cannot forgive. To hold such a view means that one refuses to enter into relationship with the forgiving God who makes forgiveness possible.

In this short space one cannot resolve the debate that has gone on in Jewish and Christian (and secular) circles for more than sixty years as to whether radical evil action can be forgiven. Let me just make the religious case I have been espousing here. To say that human beings are capable of evil of such a magnitude that it cannot and should not be forgiven suggests, first of all, that there is radical evil that cannot be countered by a (at least equal) radical good. Does the "bounded" secular world (to use Charles Taylor's language once again) allow only for radical evil and not for radical good? To borrow from MacLachlan's understanding of the emotional model of forgiveness, is the positing of radical evil made on emotional or cognitive grounds? Second, what kind of anthropology does such a positing of radical evil require? Such evil action beyond the pale, so to speak, inadvertently can free us from any responsibility for it. It is the work of monsters, not human beings like us. Arendt spoke of radical evil, but also of its banality as embodied in figures such as Adolf Eichmann. Research in psychology suggests that radical evil is often perpetrated by very ordinary people. According

7 The term was first used in correspondence with Karl Jaspers 1993: 166. It was later developed especially in light of what Arendt called the "banality of evil" as exhibited in Adolf Eichmann.

to some estimates, only about seven percent of those involved in radical evil such as genocide are deeply pathological.[8]

As was already noted, the religious anthropology of the Christian understanding of reconciliation sees human beings as fallible, yet capable of conversion and redemption. They are capable of great wrongdoing but also capable of great good. To consign some human beings as creatures beyond hope and redemption would open the door, in a perverse way, to a logic of extermination that is a crooked-mirror image of the radical evil that we propose to punish or eliminate: some human beings do not deserve a place in the human family and cannot undergo the change that might make admission into that circle possible.

To say that certain deeds are unforgivable may be a vehicle for expressing our outrage and our sense of violation. But it may also be a way of distancing ourselves from possibilities within ourselves that we cannot countenance.

3.2. CAN GROUPS FORGIVE?

A number of authors in this book have reviewed the literature and explored the question about group forgiveness, something that lies at the basis of the possibility of public forgiveness. They note that some have argued that forgiveness only makes sense at the level of interpersonal forgiveness. To speak of public forgiveness is to move what is a private matter into the public sphere in an improper way. Moreover, to say that a group forgives when individuals within the group have not come to forgiveness (for example, they may still harbor feelings of resentment or a desire for revenge) is to victimize victims once again. On this view, public forgiveness is a kind of category mistake.

The religious view of reconciliation and forgiveness sketched out here would suggest that humankind has been forgiven by God as the condition of possibility for the forgiveness of individuals. If one holds to an individualist view of society, that the group is no more than the sum of its individual members, then a group granting forgiveness makes no sense. But most societies today are still collectivist in nature to some degree, and what any individual does may redound to the whole group. Thus an individual may bring shame upon the entire group. By the same token, when leader of the aggrieved pronounces (in a performative act) that the wrongdoing is to be forgotten, no one in the group is allowed to retaliate. One sees the possibility of group forgiveness in a contrary action. In these same collectivist settings one finds a reluctance to talk about public forgiveness for another reason: to need to forgive is considered a sign of weakness or incapacity to maintain face. Such an attitude of refusal implies that there is agency in the group as group.

8 Waller 2007.

In a word, a secular bias for an individualist and privatized anthropology may be showing here. Ideas of forgiveness may get too tied up with what MacLachlan has called the emotional model. As she might put it, emotions are a necessary but not sufficient condition for comprehending forgiveness. The more ontological model of Pauline justification may serve as a better basis for understanding social or public forgiveness. As set forth in Romans 5:1–11, God has justified or rectified the whole world. Justification is about re-establishing right relationship between God and humankind. In the Hebrew Scriptures, right relationship is one of the fundamental definitions of justice.

Here the questions of an ethic of reconciliation that Daniel Philpott has been elaborating come to mind. Forgiveness is about relationships – not just between individuals but also the relationships between concepts such as justice in its many varieties (retributive, restorative), reparation, apology, and the construction of a different kind of future. It may be, as Arendt put it, the renewal of trust required to sustain a political space (Trudy Govier's idea of "invitational forgiveness" comes to mind here)[9], or as MacLachlan has put it, "political forgiveness releases us just enough to be able to more forward together."

Some may take this as equivocating on the meaning of forgiveness to the point that forgiveness means everything and therefore means nothing. Forgiveness is about foregoing resentment. It is about remembering the past in a different way. It is about being able to differentiate between the doer and the deed. But at its deepest level it is about a renewal of trust and a commitment to forge a different kind of future. Arendt's idea of the important relationship of forgiving and promising that Catherine Guisan has articulated elsewhere in this book comes into play here. There is a promissory dimension to forgiveness. It is not simply about the past. It also points to a future.

3.3. DOES FORGIVENESS REQUIRE APOLOGY AND REPENTANCE?

In most constructions of forgiveness – and especially public forgiveness – apology by the wrongdoer and acceptance of that apology by the victim is seen to be fundamental to forgiveness and reconciliation. When Willy Brandt as Chancellor of West Germany dropped to his knees at Auschwitz, this was taken to be a profound sense of apology. The millions of marks that West Germany paid to the state of Israel was intended to work as a visible act of repentance, even though the state of Israel did not yet exist during the Nazi holocaust. Apology and repentance by the wrongdoer is taken as a condition of possibility for a reconciled future.

9 Govier & Hirano 2008:429–444.

As attractive as this model may be, we have also to deal with the fact that such apology and repentance often does not take place. Despite continuing efforts for more than a decade, Japan refuses to apologize to South Korea for the "comfort women", who were forced to provide sexual services to members of the Japanese army. General Augusto Pinochet, to his dying day, maintained that he had been the savior of Chile, despite killing more than three thousand people in the aftermath of his coup against the Allende government.

Is forgiveness ruled out if there is no apology and repentance? I will not deal here with the problem of when a sincere apology is offered, but not accepted by the victims. That issue has more to do with the nature of apology than the larger picture of forgiveness being addressed here.

As already noted, forgiveness is situated within the larger framework of reconciliation for Christians. One of the fundamental insights for the Christian approach is that God begins the process by healing the victim. This idea is built upon two foundational points. First, we see in the teaching of the great prophets of Israel and in the ministry of Jesus that God sides particularly with those who have been marginalized and who suffer: the poor, the widow, the orphan, and the stranger. This is enshrined in Catholic Social Teaching as the "preferential option for the poor". Given this position, it would be natural to assume that God looks out for victims in a special way.

The healing that God can bring out for victims is a restoration of their humanity. Given the Christian anthropological view that human beings are created in the image and likeness of God, restoring humanity means first of all restoring the agency of the victim – the victim's capacity to act. Victimhood can be understood as being acted upon, and being powerless to respond. The restoration of agency is the beginning point of healing. The capacity to forgive represents an important culmination of that capacity to act.

Can there be forgiveness if there is no sign of remorse from wrongdoers? This leads to a second foundational point. If the victim's release from the grip of the past is dependent upon the wrongdoer's remorse, then the victim can be held hostage to the wrongdoing of the past forever. And if this is so, then the victim's agency is also forever compromised. This cannot be squared with the Christian understanding of God's power, God's mercy, and God's capacity to forgive. We know, in fact, that people do sometimes forgive even when there is no repentance. This is clearly an act of agency on their part. We see this also in situations where the wrongdoers cannot repent, since they are now dead. Forgiveness itself manifests additional dimensions in cases where forgiveness without repentance occurs. It can create the social space that allows wrongdoers to repent. Govier has explained this as what she calls "invitational forgiveness" wherein that social space provides a forum for forgiveness. Such forgiveness goes beyond dealing with the past; it is an active step toward creating a different future.

One must also note that forgiveness does not necessarily mean that repentance or atonement will not have to be done. This is the case in many acts of personal forgiveness but it is also especially necessary in acts of public forgiveness. Forgiving requires a complex mixture of remembering and forgetting. To remember only leads to getting stuck in the past; to forget only demeans the suffering of victims and their very human dignity. Especially if one looks at the role of retributive justice in society (where the state is to have monopoly on violence, or the meting out of justice is seen as a rebalancing of society), then punishment is still in order even if the wrongdoer has been forgiven by the victim.

As was the case with other dimensions of reconciliation treated above, forgiveness in the Christian sense again exhibits the exocentric dimension of reconciliation. In so doing, it does not play down the importance of human agency, but rather recognizes the frailty and finitude of human life. As Charles Griswold has put it, forgiveness depends upon an anthropology that sees human beings as limited and capable of making mistakes.[10] Forgiveness makes such mistakes in some measure correctible.

4. CONCLUSION

So how shall we read the terrain at the boundary of the secular and the religious when it comes to public forgiveness and possible reconciliation? To extend Böckenförde's insight a bit, any framework must posit some points upon which it will stand. For Christianity the basic point is its understanding of God as the creator and sustainer of all that is. This opens up an exocentric view of the processes of forgiveness and reconciliation. A secular reading might start by positing human rights as the point upon which all else stands. Human rights as a basis need not include an exocentric element – although there are Christian understandings of human rights as well. What is clear in any case is that the framework or worldview out of which actors in conflict work surely influences their actions. These actions have strengths and limitations in each instance, some of which I have tried to point out here. Too much emphasis on the exocentric quality of forgiveness and reconciliation can lead to a passive stance against injustice and the healing that leads to forgiveness. Too much emphasis on the bounded character (again, to use Taylor's term) can lead to situations where nothing can change. A deeper critique of all these points – reconciliation, suffering, forgiveness – still needs to be done and goes beyond the scope of what has been said here. Simply to contrast a religious and a secular perspective can lead to trying to establish an unusual oppositional symmetry. The emerging discussion of the "post-secular" society, wherein neither religion nor secularity

10 Charles Griswold 2008:211.

utterly dominates the other, may be the best way forward. To be sure, the boundaries and relative influence of each vary from place to place. In looking at the terrain here I have not pretended to try to map out all those boundaries. Rather, this should be understood as a plea for religious and secular actors in post-conflict situations to know enough about the outlooks of the other to be able to work together to bring about forgiveness and reconciliation.

REFERENCES

Abu-Nimer, M. (2003). *Non-violence and peace building in Islam*. Gainesville: University of Florida Press.

Arendt, H. & Jaspers, K. (1993). *Correspondence: 1926–1959*. New York: Harcourt and Brace.

Gopin, M. (2000). *From Eden to Armageddon: The future of world religions, violence and peacemaking*. New York: Oxford University Press.

Govier, T. & Hirano, C. (2008). A conception of invitational forgiveness. *Journal of Social Philosophy* 39, 429–444.

Griswold, C. (2008). *Forgiveness: A philosophical exploration*. Cambridge: Cambridge University Press.

Lederach, J.P. (2005). *The moral imagination: The art and soul of peacebuilding*. New York: Oxford University Press.

Metz, J.B. (1970). *Befreiendes Gedächtnis Jesu Christi*. Gütersloh: Matthias Grünewald Verlag.

Schreiter, R. & Appleby, R.S. & Powers, G. (eds.) (2010). *Peacebuilding: Catholic theology, ethics, praxis*. Maryknoll, NY: Orbis Books.

Taylor, C. (2007). *A secular age*. Cambridge, MA: Harvard University Press.

Waller, J. (2007). *Becoming evil: How ordinary people commit mass killings and genocide*. New York: Oxford University Press.

www.ingramcontent.com/pod-product-compliance
Ingram Content Group UK Ltd.
Pitfield, Milton Keynes, MK11 3LW, UK
UKHW051043120926
8556IPUK00031B/859